Chinese (Taiwan) Yearbook of International Law and Affairs

Edited by

Ying-jeou Ma

VOLUME 31 (2013)

The Chinese (Taiwan) Society of International Law —
The Chinese (Taiwan) Branch of the International Law Association

BRILL
NIJHOFF

LEIDEN | BOSTON

All correspondences concerning the Yearbook should be sent to:

Professor Chun-i Chen
P.O. Box 1-171 Mucha, Taipei 116, Taiwan, ROC
Tel: 886-2-29388218
E-mail: yearbook@nccu.edu.tw

ISSN 0731-0854
ISBN 978-90-04-30609-7 (hardback)
ISBN 978-90-04-30650-9 (e-book)

This book is printed on acid-free paper

Contents

Preface

We are delighted to present Volume 31 of the *Chinese* (*Taiwan*) *Yearbook of International Law and Affairs*, which includes articles and international law materials relating to the Asia-Pacific and, specifically, the Republic of China (ROC) on Taiwan in 2013.

This volume begins with six articles. In the first article, Professor Roda Mushkat of Johns Hopkins University analyzes the implementation of the Sino-British Joint Declaration on the Question of Hong Kong from legal and policy perspectives. Professor Erik Franckx and Mr. Marco Benatar of Vrije Universiteit Brussel authored the second article, in which they analyze the duty of cooperation under the United Nations Convention on the Law of the Sea (UNCLOS) for countries bordering (semi-)enclosed seas. Furthermore, by comparing regional anti-terrorism conventions in Asia, Professor Irena Ilieva of the Bulgarian Academy of Sciences stresses their implications for the protection of human rights.

In the fourth article, Professor Björn Ahl of the University of Cologne explores the delimitation of treaty-making powers between Mainland China and Hong Kong under their constitutional framework. Dr. Jure Vidmar of the University of Oxford, in the next article, surveys the modern practice of recognition of states and governments with a focus on case studies of Kosovo, Libya, and Taiwan. In the final article, Dr. Tomoko Yamashita of Kyoto University examines war compensation cases brought by Chinese and Korean victims in Japanese courts. The article focuses on whether *jus cogens* norms can invalidate procedural obstacles such as the waiver of claims under treaties and state immunity.

In the Special Report section, Professor Michael Sheng-ti Gau (高聖惕) of National Taiwan Ocean University provides an overview of the ongoing arbitration that the Philippines initiated against Mainland China, which has so far refused to respond, under the UNCLOS in 2013. The maps included in this report also demonstrate respective claims of Taipei, Beijing and Manila in the South China Sea.

The Contemporary Practice and Judicial Decisions section contains materials on the ROC's state practice in international law. These documents explain Taiwan's participation in the International Civil Aviation Organization (ICAO) after a departure of 42 years since the ROC lost its representation in the United Nations in 1971, its position on East and South China Seas, and responses to Mainland China's declaration of an Air Defense Identification Zone (ADIZ). Notably, the section collects statements on the development of the *Guang Da*

Xing No. 28 fishing boat incident. In May 2013, the Philippines Coast Guard shot dead a Taiwanese fisherman with automatic weapons in the overlapping exclusive economic zones of the two countries. The ROC's approach to dealing with this incident reinforced its commitments to the peaceful settlement of international disputes based on international law. The subsequent Treaties/Agreements section selects various instruments that the ROC concluded, including the Economic Cooperation Agreement with New Zealand and the Economic Partnership Agreement with Singapore.

Volume 31 represents a milestone of the *Yearbook* since its publication in 1981. The volume is published by Brill which, formerly known as Nijhoff, has a long and world-wide reputation for publishing leading law journals. I hope our cooperation will allow a wider range of readers to understand legal and political issues on the Asia-Pacific region and Taiwan. I also warmly welcome prominent international law scholars who recently joined our editorial board, including Judge Helmut Tuerk of Austria, Professors Seung Hwan Choi of Kyung Hee University, Władysław Czapliński of Polish Academy of Sciences, Jacques deLisle of University of Pennsylvania, Erik Franckx of Vrije Universiteit Brussel, Julian Ku of Hofstra University and Stefan Talmon of University of Bonn.

Finally, I would like to extend my gratitude to Professors Chun-i Chen (陳純一), Pasha Hsieh (謝笠天), Winnie Ma (馬若梅), Judges Chun-Liang Lai (賴淳良) and I-Hon Hsiao (蕭一弘), Ms. Chun-li Ouyang (歐陽純麗) and Dr. Pei-Lun Tsai (蔡沛倫) for their efforts in putting together this volume. The assistance of Lee & Li Attorneys-at-Law in translating Chinese documents into English is also gratefully acknowledged.

Ying-jeou Ma (馬英九), *S.J.D.*
Editor-in-Chief
April 2015

The Intricacies of Implementing International Law: A Juxtaposition of Theories with the Actualities of the Sino-British Joint Declaration Regarding the Future of Hong Kong

Roda Mushkat

Table of Contents

I Introduction

International law is both theory rich and theory poor. The abundance is attributable to the proliferation of schools of thought—some normative, some positivist, some purely abstract, some policy oriented, some geared toward system maintenance, and some poignantly critical—their diversity, their multiple origins, and their range of concerns. The sense of insufficiency stems from the often less-than-satisfactory fit between theory and reality and severe

* Professor of International Law, Hopkins-Nanjing Center, Paul H. Nitze School of Advanced International Studies (SAIS), Johns Hopkins University and Honorary Professor, Faculty of Law, University of Hong Kong. I wish to thank Miron Mushkat for helping me navigate through social science territory, but I am solely responsible for the views expressed herein.

 | DOI 10.1163/9789004306509_002

fragmentation in the absence of constructive bridge-building or serious efforts to achieve at least a partial synthesis. There are thus gaps in the theoretical façade, whose development is impeded by excessive, zero-sum-style intellectual competition in areas where pursuing complementarity might prove potentially beneficial.

This duality, the wealth of ideas and the incompleteness and looseness of the conceptual architecture, manifests itself in the positivist segment of the theoretical space. That is the analytical domain where international legal researchers continue to systematically seek credible answers to the question "how nations behave," authoritatively and compellingly addressed, albeit inevitably without providing closure and a clear roadmap to follow, by a leading scholar in the field nearly half a century ago.[1] For the most part, they have employed the logic of expected consequences, assuming that actors in the global arena, when confronting choices, generate an array of alternatives, assess them in terms of their perceived net favorable effects, and select the one that best meets this criterion.[2]

In its pure and stylized, and a somewhat more elaborate and precise, form such an essentially rationalist framework thus consists of four components: alternatives (a set of feasible courses of action), expectations (the consequences associated with each alternative and the probabilities attached to them), preferences (the values ascribed by the decision maker to the expected consequences), and a decision rule (stipulating how the choice is to be made among the alternatives on the basis of the values accorded to their consequences; the notion of a cost-utility, or disutility-utility balance/equation most tellingly encapsulates this proposition).[3]

This is not an entirely homogeneous theoretical space. There are crucial differences between researchers who believe that players in an intensely competitive global milieu are primarily driven by power and its correlates (realists and their descendants)[4] and those who posit that international cooperation is

1 *See generally* Louis Henkin, *How Nations Behave: Law and Foreign Policy* (1968).

2 *See* James G. March, *A Primer on Decision Making: How Decisions Happen* 2–3 (1994).

3 *See id.* at 2–3.

4 *See* Kal Raustiala, "Compliance and Effectiveness in International Regulatory Cooperation", 32 *Case W. Res. J. Int'l L.* 387, 400–05 (2000); Oona A. Hathaway, "Do Human Rights Treaties Make a Difference?", 111 *Yale L.J.* 1935, 1944–47 (2002); Kal Raustiala & Anne-Marie Slaughter, "International Law, International Relations, and Compliance", *in Handbook of International Relations* 539–40, (Walter Carlsneas & Beth A. Simmons eds., 2002); Willam C. Bradford, "In the Minds of Men: A Theory of Compliance with the Laws of War", 36 *Arizona State L.J.* 1243, 1251–61, 1264–66 (2004).

a source of value and generally recognized as such (institutionalists).[5] A fundamental distinction may also be drawn between these two intellectual camps, largely united in their view that it is mostly reasonable to consider the State as a unitary actor, and those who disaggregate it and highlight the role played by domestic forces in shaping attitudes and policies toward international law (liberals).[6]

However, there is thought to be sufficient common ground to treat the three groups as a single (rationalist) category.[7] According to this perspective, the vital conceptual difference that needs to be emphasized is that between scholars who belong to this broad analytical cluster and those who are influenced by the logic of appropriateness.[8] This form of reasoning lays stress on the relevance of normative, as distinct from utilitarian, values that transcend the seemingly narrow ethical parameters associated with rationalism.[9] In the international legal context, it underscores the intrinsic value of collective ideas, common rules, cross-border cooperation, mutual obligations, productive worldwide discourse, and shared knowledge.[10]

Four cautionary observations are in order. First, strictly speaking, a focus on international rule-following should not be equated with a pronounced normative orientation, and vice versa. From a philosophical standpoint, rationalism is not devoid of normative underpinnings (nor do the so-called normative theories of international law lack a positivistic dimension). Indeed, utilitarianism is a normative school of thought par excellence. It does not merely qualify as such but (e.g., unlike egoism) in fact occupies a highly respectable place in the normative theory space by virtue of being agent neutral rather than agent centered:

> [T]here is a distinction between normative theories that are agent neutral, and those which are agent centered. A theory is agent neutral if it gives to everyone the same advice or aims. According to an agent neutral theory, your (theory-given) aims are better fulfilled exactly when mine are. By

5 *See* Raustiala, *supra* note 4, at 400–05; Hathaway, *supra* note 4, at 1947–52; Raustiala & Slaughter, *supra* note 4, at 540.

6 *See* Raustiala, *supra* note 4, at 409–11; Hathaway, *supra* note 4, at 1952–55; Raustiala & Slaughter, *supra* note 4, at 547–48; Bradford, *supra* note 4, at 1255–57.

7 *See* Raustiala, *supra* note 4, at 400–05, 409–11; Hathaway, *supra* note 4, at 1944–55; Raustiala & Slaughter, *supra* note 4, at 539–40, 547–48; Bradford, *supra* note 4, at 1251–61.

8 *See* March, *supra* note 2, at 57–102.

9 *See* Raustiala, *supra* note 4, at 405–09; Hathaway, *supra* note 4, at 1955–62; Raustiala & Slaughter, *supra* note 4, at 541–45; Bradford, *supra* note 4, at 1261–64, 1268–77.

10 *See* Raustiala, *supra* note 4, at 405–11; Hathaway, *supra* note 4, at 1955–62; Raustiala & Slaughter, *supra* note 4, at 541–45; Bradford, *id.*, at 1261–64, 1266–77.

> contrast, an agent centered theory gives to us at least some prescriptions or advice or aims which include indexicals. Sometimes the things an agent centered theory advises me to do will conflict with the things the same theory advises you to do. Your theory-given ends can be achieved only at the expense of mine. The classic and paradigmatic agent centered theory is egoism. Egoism tells me to pursue my good and you to pursue yours. The classic and paradigmatic agent neutral theory is utilitarianism. It tells us to promote the greatest happiness of the greatest number. Things are going better from your perspective exactly when they are going better from my perspective, according to utilitarianism.[11]

Second, the rationalist-normative dichotomy is restrictive because it leaves little room to accommodate schools of thought that do not squarely fall into one of the two categories. Constructivist,[12] eclectic/Grotian,[13] fairness/legitimacy-focused,[14] legal positivist,[15] managerial,[16] natural law-derived,[17]

---

11 *See* James Dreier, "Structures of Normative Theories", 76 *The Monist* 22, 22 (1993).

12 *See* Bradford, *supra* note 4, at 1271–73. *See also* Friedrich V. Kratochwil, *Rules, Norms, and Decisions: On the Conditions of Practical and Legal Reasoning in International Relations and Domestic Affairs* (1989); Benedict Kingsbury, "'Indigenous Peoples' in International Law: A Constructivist Approach to the Asia Controversy", 92 *Am. J. Int'l L.* 414 (1998); Anthony C. Arend, *Legal Rules and International Society* (1999); Jutta Brunnee & Stephen Toope, "International Law and Constructivism: Elements of an Interactional Theory of International Law", 39 *Colum. J. Transnat'l L.* 19 (2000); Phillip A. Karber, "'Constructivism' as a Method in International Law", 94 *Am. Soc'y Int'l L. Proc.* 189–92 (2000); Martin V. Totaro, "Legal Positivism, Constructivism, and International Human Rights Law: The Case of Participatory Development", 48 *Va J. Int'l L.* 719 (2008); Gerry Nagtzaami, *The Making of International Environmental Treaties: Neoliberal and Constructivist Analyses of Normative Evolution* (2009); Jutta Brunnee & Stephen J. Toope, *Legitimacy and Legality in International Law: An Interactionist Approach* (2010); Adriana Sinclair, *International Relations Theory and International Law* (2010).

13 *See* A. Claire Cutler, "The 'Grotian Tradition' in International Relations", 17 *Rev. Int'l Stu.* 41 (1991); Christopher A. Stumpf, *The Grotian Theology of International Law* (2006).

14 *See* Raustiala, *supra* note 4, at 405–09; Hathaway, *supra* note 4, at 1958–60; Raustiala & Slaughter, *supra* note 4, at 541–42; Bradford, *supra* note 4, at 1269–71. *See also* Thomas M. Franck, *The Power of Legitimacy among Nations* (1990); Thomas M. Franck, *Fairness in International Law and Institutions* (1995).

15 *See* Stephen Hall, "The Persistent Specter: Natural Law, International Order, and the Limits of International Legal Positivism", 12 *Eur. J. Int'l L.* 269 (2001).

16 *See* Raustiala, *supra* note 4, at 405–09; Hathaway, *supra* note 4, at 1955–58; Raustiala & Slaughter, *supra* note 4, at 542–44; Bradford, *supra* note 4, at 1261–64. *See also* Abram Chayes & Antonia Handler Chayes, *The New Sovereignty: Compliance with International Regulatory Agreements* (1995).

17 *See* Hall, *supra* note 15.

organizational-cultural,[18] and transnational legal process-oriented[19] theoretical formulations, as well as possibly the New Haven/Yale policy perspective,[20] are consistent with the notion of international rule following. However, CCA (central case approach)-like,[21] CLS (critical legal studies)-type,[22] feminist,[23] LGBT (lesbian, gay, bisexual, and transgender/transsexual)-style,[24] a (considerably less than the others) personality-related,[25] post-structuralist,[26] and TWPS (Third World-predicament-sensitive)[27] schemes are in many respects normative but cannot be portrayed as being inspired by a strong sense of international rule following, in the traditional sense of the term.

Third, micro-economic theory, and by implication rationalist thought (even if this is not yet adequately reflected in trends in the international law space) has undergone substantial transformation in recent years. Behaviorally-oriented scholars have abandoned narrow-based neoclassical propositions depicting economic man as driven by self-interest, blessed with omniscience/perfect information, engaged in conscious deliberation, and approximated by a highly stylized ideal type (representative agent).[28] *Homo economicus* has given way to *homo communicans*/*homo rationalis communicans*, homo *egualis*,

---

18 *See* Bradford, *supra* note 4, at 1273–77.

19 *See* Raustiala, *supra* note 4, at 405–09; Hathaway, *supra* note 4, at 1960–62; Raustiala & Slaughter, *supra* note 4, at 544–54; Bradford, *supra* note 4, at 1266–67. *See also* Harold H. Koh, "Transnational Legal Process", 75 *Neb. L. Rev.* 181 (1996); Harold H. Koh, "Why Do Nations Obey International Law", 106 *Yale L.J.* 2599 (1997); Harold H. Koh, "How Is International Human Rights Law Enforced", *Ind. J.L.* 1397–417 (1999).

20 *See* W. Michael Reisman, Siegfried Weissner & Andrew R. Willard, "The New Haven School: A Brief Introduction", 32 *Yale J. Int'l L.* 575 (2007).

21 *See* Tai-heng Cheng, "The Central Case Approach to Human Rights: Its Universal Application and the Singapore Example", 13 *Pac. Rim L. & Pol'y J.* 257 (2004).

22 *See* Phillip R. Trimble, "International Law, World Order, and Critical Legal Studies", 42 *Stan. L. Rev.* 811 (1990).

23 *See* Aaron X. Fellmeth, "Feminism and International Law: Theory, Methodology, and Substantive Reform", 22 *Hum. Rts. Q.* 658 (2000).

24 *See* Douglas Sanders, "Human Rights and Sexual Orientation in International Law", 25 *Int'l J. Pub. Admin.* 3 (2002).

25 *See* Bradford, *supra* note 4, at 1289–1436.

26 *See* David Kennedy, *International Legal Structures* (1987).

27 *See* Robert Johnson, "The Model Law on HIV in Southern Africa: Third World Approaches to International Law Insights into a Human Rights-Based Approach", 9 *Afr. Hum. Rts. L.J.* 129 (2009); Mohsen Al Attar & Rosalie Miller, "Toward an Emancipatory International Law: The Bolivarian Reconstruction", 31 *Third World Q.* 347 (2010).

28 *See* Roda Mushkat, "International Legal Compliance as a Rational Act: Theoretical Extensions and Chinese Realities", 20 *Transnat'l L. & Contemp. Problems* 633, 643–44 (2012).

homo parochius, and *homo reciprocans*—all of whom have complex preference functions.[29] The notion of bounded rationality—given expression in studies acknowledging that agents may merely satisfice, muddle through, and lapse into organized anarchy (in accordance with the garbage can model of decision making) rather than maximize utility—has also been firmly incorporated into the economic mainstream.[30]

By the same token, micro- or welfare economists are no longer exclusively concerned with outcomes/consequences.[31] They have come to recognize, belatedly perhaps, that procedures, or broadly speaking processes, may serve as well as a significant source of human fulfillment or happiness.[32] This realization is encapsulated in the notion of procedural or process utility, which is now commonly invoked in the welfare economics literature.[33] Again, the conceptual reorientation that is taking place in this field is not yet duly reflected in international legal research, but the gap should not obscure the fact that relevant economic thought is assuming a more multidimensional form.

The corollary is that the boundaries between rationalist and normative theories are becoming increasingly blurred. If economic-style accounts potentially offer scope for actors in the global arena to pursue goals such as achieving equity (substantive and procedural; *homo egualis*), ensuring reciprocity (*homo reciprocans*), expressing identity (*homo parochius*), securing opportunities for meaningful exchanges with other players (*homo communicans/homo rationalis communicans*), and seeking voice, unambiguously pinpointing the dividing line between these two supposedly diametrically opposed approaches may prove to be an elusive and not entirely productive undertaking.

Demarcating analytical boundaries poses a growing challenge in other academic domains characterized by intellectual fluidity. At the meta-level, the time-honored distinction between nomothetic (general and selective) and

29 *See id.* at 640–43. *See also* Herbert Gintis, *Game Theory Evolving: A Problem-Centered Introduction to Modeling Strategic Interaction* 252–56 (2000); Anne van Aaken, "Deliberative Institutional Economics, or Does Homo Oeconomicus Argue? A Proposal for Combining New Institutional Economics with Discourse Theory", in *Deliberation and Decision: Economics, Constitutional Theory, and Deliberative Democracy* 3, 19–21 (Anne van Aaken, Christian List & Christophe Luetge eds., 2004).

30 *See* Mushkat, *supra* note 28, at 644–52. *See also* Lucy F. Ackert & Richard Deaves, *Behavioral Finance: Psychology, Decision Making, and Markets* (2010); Jonathan Bendor, *Bounded Rationality and Politics* (2010); Edward Cartwright, *Behavioral Economics* (2011); Daniel Kahneman, *Thinking, Fast, and Slow* (2011).

31 *See* Mushkat, *supra* note 28, at 640.

32 *See id.* at 640.

33 *See id.* at 640.

idiographic (context-specific and detailed) theories has for all intents and purposes been relegated to the periphery in the methodologically more robust social sciences.[34] There have been some ambitious attempts to revisit the problem and systematically classify all natural and social science theories in terms of key pertinent criteria,[35] but the conceptual and practical impact of such efforts has been modest. An eclectic strategy is now typically adopted with a range of theories clearly, but not uniformly, identified (e.g., embryonic positivism, logical positivism, post-positivism, structuralism, hermeneutics, and anti-foundationalism versus positivism, constructionism, interpretivism, critical inquiry, feminism, and post-modernism)[36] and less flexible formulas are merely addressed in a perfunctory fashion. Alternatively, the quest for the hard-to-fathom analytical yardstick is abandoned but some sort of a chronologically-based classification is retained (e.g., classical paradigms such as positivism, critical rationalism, classical hermeneutics, and interpretivism versus contemporary ones such as critical theory, ethnomethodology, social realism, contemporary hermeneutics, structuration theory, and feminism).[37]

Eschewing rigid classificatory principles, and opting for contingency-like approaches, appears to be the most fruitful and practical way to impose a modicum of structure on the rich cluster of international legal theories. Here it is convenient to draw a distinction between schools of thought that primarily aim to shed light on how nations behave and those that principally are either policy oriented or pursue a critical path (disregarding classical perspectives such as the eclectic/Grotian approach, legal positivism, and natural law, which merit separate treatment). Pure types are seldom encountered in reality and each of these three categories contains elements found elsewhere. The behavioral group, the policy-focused (the enforcement[38] and New Haven/Yale schools) one, and the critical set (CCA, CLS, feminism, LGBT, post-structuralism, and TWPS) are identified as such because of the predominance, rather than dominance, of key characteristics.

34 *See* Hans Thomae, "The Nomethetic-Idiographic Issue: Some Roots and Recent Trends", 28 *Int'l J. Group Tensions* 187 (1999).

35 *See, e.g.*, Rick Szostak, "Classifying Natural and Scientific Theories", 51 *Current Soc.* 27 (2003).

36 *See* Michael Crotty, *The Foundations of Social Research: Meaning and Perspective in the Research Process* (1998); David Baronov, *Conceptual Foundations of Social Research Methods* (2004).

37 *See* Norman Blaikie, *Approaches to Social Inquiry* 109–77 (2d ed. 2007).

38 *See* Bradford, *supra* note 4, at 1254–66.

The large class of behavioral paradigms (realism/neo realism, institutionalism, liberalism, rational choice,[39] reputational model,[40] fairness/legitimacy configuration, managerialism, constructivism, transnational legal process theory, and personality-related accounts) is heavily geared toward providing explanations for State compliance with international law, or lack thereof. This issue looms large in the study of international legal behavior, and understandably so. However, compliance tends to be conceptualized in binary terms (yes versus no), which somewhat detracts from its usefulness in situations marked by a degree of ambiguity. Moreover, it is often viewed from a static standpoint (at a single point in time or over a short horizon) rather than as an ongoing process, at times featuring non-linear and even zigzag-style (shifting back and forth) movement.

The (broader) notion of implementation seems to be better grounded in the intricate realities of policy making than the (narrower) idea of compliance (see Figure 1). While the latter is more relevant for the practice of international law, the former may prove to be a superior analytical tool in certain circumstances. The two should not be regarded as competing alternatives. Compliance is an integral component of implementation, although it may be looked at in isolation. By the same token, implementation encompasses compliance, even if its other dimensions are accorded greater attention when research considerations favor a different emphasis.

Virtually all the compliance/implementation theories have been criticized on both conceptual and empirical grounds, and not exclusively by proponents of alternative formulations.[41] Their inadequacies may be attributed to the fact that, the appearance of closure notwithstanding, they constitute work-in-progress and have been sparingly tested by international legal scholars (as distinct from researchers in the field of international relations), particularly in non-Western settings. A notable example is the clearly pivotal liberal paradigm. The crucially significant competitive domestic political arena has long been relegated to the analytical periphery in international law. While there is no dearth of references to liberalism as a full-fledged school of thought with substantial bearing on international legal compliance/implementation of

39 *See id.* at 1257–61. *See also* Andrew T. Guzman, *How International Law Works: A Rational Choice Theory* (2008).

40 *See* Bradford, *supra* note 4, at 1264–66. *See also* Guzman, *supra* note 39.

41 *See* Bradford, *id.*, at 1278–89; Roda Mushkat, "Dissecting International Legal Compliance: An Unfinished Odyssey", 38 *Denv. J. Int'l L.* 161 (2009); Roda Mushkat, "Compliance with International Environmental Regimes: Chinese Lessons", 34 *Wm. & Mary Envtl. L. & Pol'y Rev.* 493 (2010).

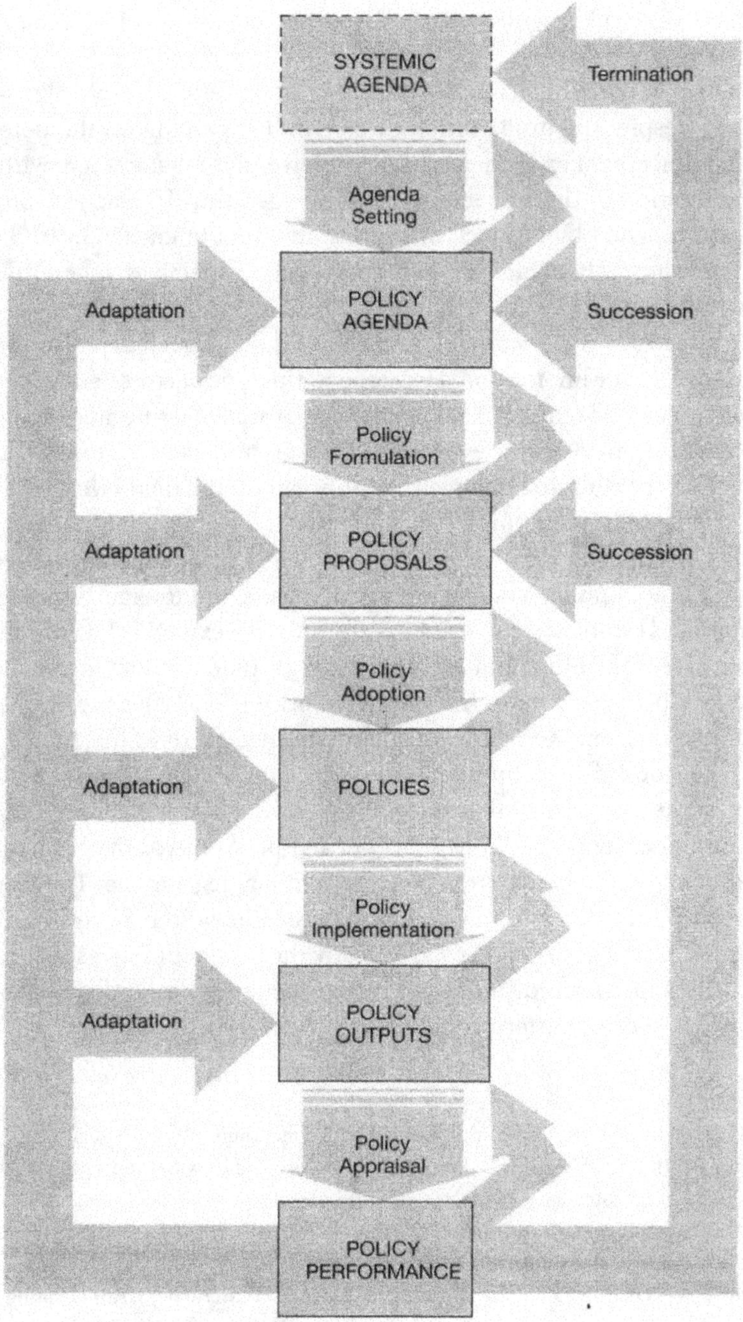

FIGURE 1 *Model of the policy making process.*
ADAPTED FROM WILLIAM N. DUNN, *PUBLIC POLICY ANALYSIS: AN INTRODUCTION* 46 (3D ED., 2004).

international law, for all intents and purposes this remains a barely explored intellectual territory.[42]

However, two additional factors account for the sense of theoretical insufficiency. First, despite the proliferation of contending paradigms, the potential scope for conceptual examination extends beyond the parameters within which the dissection of the subject has been pursued thus far. Second, progress has been impeded by the lack of serious attempts to engage in bridge-building, or productively blend different analytical perspectives. By contrast, in international relations some meaningful efforts, albeit not on a large scale, have been made to integrate competing schools of thought such as realism and constructivism.[43] In the international legal space, this type of cross-fertilization is conspicuous by its absence.[44] That is a source of weakness because monocausal explanations inevitably are less robust than multi-causal ones.

The aim of this paper is to selectively identify gaps in the theoretical edifice and to assess possibilities for employing more than one behavioral framework in grappling with the complexities of international law implementation. The literature on Chinese policy making, on the domestic and foreign (including international legal) fronts, is surveyed first in order to extract relevant ideas and pinpoint areas for fruitful inquiry. A case study is then conducted in which some pertinent behavioral patterns that have arisen following the transfer of sovereignty over Hong Kong from the United Kingdom to China, in accordance with the Sino-British Joint Declaration, are subjected to close analytical scrutiny with a view to gaining new insights into how additional, broad-based (but not comprehensive), and largely overlooked perspectives may enhance the understanding of State action in the international legal arena. The value of the exercise partly stems from the fact that generalizations regarding the implementation of international law are mostly the product of investigations focused on the experience of affluent Western democracies and this study addresses the issue in an Eastern context.

---

42 A narrowly focused exception to the rule is Joel P. Trachtman, "International Law and Domestic Political Coalitions: The Grand Theory of Compliance with International Law", 11 *Chi. J. Int'l L.* 127 (2010).

43 J. Samuel Barkin, "Realist Constructivism", 5 *Int'l Stud. Rev.* 325 (2003); J. Samuel Barkin, *Realist Constructivism: Rethinking International Relations Theory* (2010).

44 Possible exceptions include Tom Ginsburg & Richard H. McAdams, "Adjudicating in Anarchy: An Expressive Theory of International Dispute Resolution", 45 *Wm. & Mary L. Rev.* 1229 (2004); Alex Gesinger & Michael A. Stein, "A Theory of Expressive International Law", 60 *Vand. L. Rev.* 77 (2007); Andrew Woods, "Moral Judgments and International Crimes: The Disutility of Desert", 52 *Va J. Int'l L.* 633 (2012).

The juxtaposition of linearly ordered and rigidly compartmentalized intellectual perspectives originating in the West with the complex and fluid realities observed in the East is, in some respects, an instructive and sobering experience. Neatly organized and self-contained, and at times centrifugally-positioned and mutually-antagonistic, scientific-type paradigms fail to achieve a reasonable degree of correspondence with factual patterns scrutinized across a wide policy space and over time, when employed as stand-alone devices. The inevitable conclusion that emerges upon completion of this idea-centered survey and dissection of empirical material is that, proponents' narrowly-focused aspirations and assertions notwithstanding, the way forward in seeking to explain States' attitudes toward international law and their conduct in the global arena must, for the foreseeable future, entail the dismantling of fixed boundaries separating distinct models and eclectic adaptation.

II Policy Making with "Chinese Characteristics"

China has attracted ample scholarly attention both during the revolutionary, 1949–1978, and reform, post-1978, eras. Anthropologists, economists, geographers, historians, philosophers, legal researchers, political scientists, sociologists, and students of both business and public administration have endeavored to come to grips with intricate realities in what was once a hard authoritarian, rogue-like State and which currently practices, albeit not always comfortably or consistently, soft authoritarianism as a fully-integrated and prominent member of the international community. The information gathering and theory building/testing have gained momentum in the past three decades as access to data sources has progressively become less challenging and a more liberal climate has allowed a gradual broadening of the academic agenda.

In the policy domain, more intellectual resources have been channeled toward the domestic/internal side than elsewhere. This has not necessarily been always explicitly stated, but the thrust of the studies undertaken generally suggests that the authors have primarily been driven by domestic concerns. Nevertheless, a significant body of conceptually inspired work has specifically addressed the foreign/external policy dynamics. The micro (internal)-macro (external) linkages have also been carefully explored. Some, but decidedly few, of the analytical insights produced in both realms have systematically been incorporated into theoretical inquiries in the field of international law. This is illustrated in the following three sections, which seek to highlight the substantial gaps between policy-oriented scholarship and international legal research.

A Domestic Dimension

Two wide-ranging surveys have been conducted of theoretical investigations principally focused on the functioning of the internally-centered policy apparatus in post-1949 China.[45] The paradigmatic diversity captured reflects the country's evolution, aptly encapsulated in the title of a leading textbook,[46] from revolution (and isolation) to reform (and engagement). The first of the two surveys encompasses eight mostly distinct policy making models: the totalitarianism, factionalism and elite conflict, clientalism, class struggle, interest group, State/civil society dichotomy, complex bureaucracies, and culturalist constructs.[47]

The totalitarian model portrays, or rather portrayed, the Chinese political system as a structure firmly controlled by a highly cohesive and deeply-entrenched elite, heavily and successfully relying on coercive means to enforce its strategies.[48] It bears close similarity to other dictatorial or autocratic regimes, but not in all respects because it is also characterized by a forcefully articulated ideological core[49] ("[t]he leaders of the Chinese Communist Party [CCP] form a tightly knit brotherhood of experienced, competent, devoted, tough revolutionaries ... [t]hey decide policy and supervise its execution").[50]

The impression of cohesion and stability proved illusory and the totalitarian model gave way to one emphasizing factionalism and elite conflict.[51] A faction is regarded as "a maze of individual, personalized ties between a leader and his supporters."[52] The appeal of this construct has not markedly diminished, but it proved particularly compelling in the 1950s and 1960s, a period when political scientists generated ample evidence of shifting "factions working against each other."[53] However, the assumption that factionalism is confined to intra-elite machinations was eventually discarded and a more broadly based, clientalist model was put forward.[54] The latter aims "to examine not only the patron-client relationship that exists among the elites of the country, and how that

45 *See* Flemming Christiansen & Shirin M. Rai, *Chinese Politics and Society: An Introduction* 2–23 (1996); Jianrong Huang, *The Applicability of Policy-Making Theories in Post-Mao China* 17–142 (1999).

46 *See* Kenneth G. Lieberthal, *Governing China: From Revolution through Reform* (2d ed., 2004).

47 *See* Christiansen & Rai, *supra* note 45, at 2–23.

48 *See id.* at 2–3.

49 *See id.* at 2.

50 Doak A. Barnett, *Communist China: The Early Years 1949–55*, at 6 (1964).

51 *See* Christiansen & Rai, *supra* note 45, at 4–5.

52 *Id.* at 4.

53 *Id.* at 5.

54 *See id.* at 5–6.

affects policy formation but also how patron-client relationships affect the interaction between [S]tate elites and the citizens, and how that affects policy implementation."[55]

Symbolically infused shows of unity should not obscure the persistent relevance of factionalism and elite conflict in present-day China. Two groups continue to vie for influence in Chinese politics: the elitist (Shanghai) coalition and its populist (Chinese Communist Youth League/CCYL) counterpart.[56] They differ in their socio-economic background and geographic constituencies.[57] Most members of the elitist faction are "princelings", children or relatives of veteran revolutionaries or high-ranking officials.[58] They have primarily pursued their careers in the relatively affluent coastal provinces and tend to represent the interests of the entrepreneurial class.[59]

By contrast, most members of the populist faction come from less privileged families.[60] They have principally built their careers in the poorer inland provinces.[61] Many have climbed to the apex of the political pyramid through the CCYL and are consequently referred to as *tuanpai*, meaning the league faction.[62] This makes them more receptive to the plight of vulnerable social groups such as farmers, migrant workers, and the urban poor, whose voices they are inclined to echo in the corridors of power (although expressions of broad sympathy do not necessarily translate into concrete action).[63]

The class struggle construct, like its totalitarian counterpart, has receded into the background. It was the intellectual product of the late 1960s and early 1970s, a period that featured a reassessment of the rigidly hierarchical socialist model practiced in the Soviet Union, as well as the rise of the critical Left and student revolt in the Western world.[64] In China, the tension between top-down and bottom-up forms of socialism manifested itself in the two-line struggle between Chairman Mao Zedong's mass line (ideological) politics and Vice Chairman (of the CCP) Liu Shaoqi's more bureaucratic (pragmatic)

---

55 *Id.* at 6.

56 *See* Cheng Li, "The Powerful Factions among China's Rulers", Nov. 5, 2011, *available at* http://www.brookings.edu/research/articles/2012/11/05-china-leaders-li.

57 *See id.*

58 *See id.*

59 *See id.*

60 *See id.*

61 *See id.*

62 *See id.*

63 *See id.* For additional insights, see Jin Huang, *Factionalism in Chinese Politics* (2000); Victor C. Shih, *Finance and Factions in China: Elite Conflict and Inflation* (2008).

64 *See* Christiansen & Rai, *supra* note 45, at 9–10.

philosophy.[65] Pragmatism ultimately prevailed over ideological purity, but only following Mao's death.[66]

The interest group model is another antidote to the monolithic totalitarian paradigm, although both have their origins in the study of Soviet politics.[67] Its adoption has stemmed from the growing "awareness that the diversity between functional and occupational groups in socialist societies—and anywhere else—generated different outlooks, interests, and preferences."[68] An interest group is defined as an "aggregate of persons who possess certain common characteristics and share certain attitudes and values on public issues, and who adopt distinct positions on these issues and make definite claims on those in authority."[69] In the Chinese context, occupational groups such as cadres, entrepreneurs (in the collective, private, and State sectors), intellectuals, peasants, and workers, as well as people sharing highly specific functional tasks (e.g., cadres in charge of personnel management under the *nomenclatura* or party secretaries), and ethnic and religious groups have been placed in this category.[70]

Like factional activity and elite conflict,[71] interest group dynamics, particularly in circumstances where a broad and powerful de facto coalition is formed, may materially impinge on policy outcomes. A notable example is local corporationism, a phenomenon rooted in emergence during the reform era of a loose but mighty amalgam of business people and local officials-cum-entrepreneurs, reinforced by overlapping social networks (*guanxi*).[72] This politico-economic constellation of forces has single-mindedly pursued output expansion and has played a vital role in reinvigorating China's post-1978 economy.[73] At the same time, it has impeded the implementation of a more enlightened ecological agenda, designed to mitigate the enormous environmental risks the country faces.[74]

The State/civil society dichotomy highlights, albeit tentatively, the crystallization of pockets of autonomous, and politically mildly significant, at least

65 *See id.* at 10–12.

66 *See id.* at 11–12.

67 *See id.* at 12–15.

68 *Id.* at 12–13.

69 *Id.* at 13.

70 *See id.* at 13, 15.

71 *See generally* Shih, *supra* note 63.

72 *See* Roda Mushkat, "Implementing Environmental Law in Transitional Settings: The Chinese Experience", 18 *S. Cal. Interdisc. L.J.* 45, 81–82 (2008).

73 *See id.* at 81–82.

74 *See id.* at 81–82.

at the margin, initiative outside the confines of the State.[75] These pockets may not constitute a cohesive and effective aggregate, but individually they exert a modicum of bottom-up influence that possibly amounts to more than the proverbial sum of its parts.[76] The fledgling civil society is relevant in another respect, by augmenting the horizontal and vertical fragmentation of the Chinese political system, and thus enhancing the modest momentum toward greater pluralism, which has palpable implications for policy implementation.[77]

The complex bureaucracies' model also focuses on horizontal and vertical cleavages, but within the sprawling State apparatus rather than across the entire societal landscape.[78] According to this widely embraced account, the deeply fractured bureaucratic machinery (fragmented authoritarianism construct) consists of a myriad of self-contained and semi-independent work units (*danwei*) which often operate at cross-purposes.[79] To align them closely and attain a degree of coordination requires extensive and intensive bargaining.[80] Again, this has a profound effect on policy making in general and policy implementation in particular.[81]

The culturalist paradigm is predicated on the assumption that "China is a case apart, a political system which is rooted in its own past and therefore cannot be perceived on its own terms."[82] The underlying proposition is that the legacy of 4,000 years of cultural evolution, "the historical events and the structures of thought in the past determine the present."[83] This is believed to manifest itself in "a received frame of mind, an inherited psycho-sociological disposition of the people to accept or support specific forms of governance."[84] These policy configurations, in turn, "are [typically] based on a strong [S]tate ruled by an emperor and a large bureaucratic class, tolerating no independent sources of political power, and interpreting the world through an ideological-moral framework—Confucianism."[85]

75 *See* Christiansen & Rai, *supra* note 45, at 15–16.
76 *See id.* at 15–16.
77 *See id.* at 16–18.
78 *See id.* at 19–20.
79 *See id.* at 19–20.
80 *See id.* at 19–20.
81 *See id.* at 19–20.
82 *Id.* at 20.
83 *Id.* at 21.
84 *Id.* at 21.
85 *Id.* at 21.

The second comprehensive survey of domestically-oriented policy making paradigms covers similar ground but ventures further afield.[86] Elitist formulations such as the Mao (or Deng; indeed, potentially any helmsman)-in-command[87] and generational (emphasizing the political dominance of specific age cohorts, particularly the Long March generation)[88] are added to the list. So are a number of institutionalist (ideology-conflict-centered,[89] structural,[90] and normative[91]) and quasi-pluralist (politician-in-negotiation[92] and bureaucracy-in-dominance[93]) constructs. The essence of the ideology-conflict-centered and politician-in-negotiation perspectives is fundamentally consistent with some of those featured in the first survey and thus self-explanatory.

The structural paradigm and its normative counterpart, respectively, lay stress on the role played by organizational patterns, operating mechanisms (structures), principles, and rules (norms) in Chinese policy formulation and implementation.[94] The bureaucracy-in-dominance model underscores the importance, given their size and control over resources, of the CCP and State organs in this context.[95] It possesses structural attributes and shares characteristics with constructs that bring into focus institutional fragmentation (factionalism, elite conflict, clientalism, class struggle, and interest group maneuvers), whatever its sources, given that the bureaucracy is portrayed as fractured entity.[96]

The impact of culture and ideology has been accorded, whether explicitly or implicitly, less weight in research on policy making in China, which has tended to gravitate toward institutionally-grounded viewpoints. The impression given is that the linkage between cultural legacy and strategic action has loosened and that ideological fervor has largely given way to measured pragmatism.[97] The institutional dimension has also been further stretched in a pluralist direction as a result of the introduction of the network paradigm into the theoretical

86 *See* Huang, *supra* note 45, at 17–142.
87 *See id.* at 61,63, 80–84.
88 *See id.* at 60–61, 63–64.
89 *See id.* at 63–64, 85–92.
90 *See id.* at 61, 63, 92–96.
91 *See id.* at 61, 63–64, 99–100.
92 *See id.* at 63, 65–69.
93 *See id.* at 61, 63, 72–78.
94 *See id.* at 61, 63–64, 92–96, 99–100.
95 *See id.* at 61, 63, 72–78.
96 *See id.* at 72–78.
97 *See id.* at 315, 319–20, 327–28.

repertoire.[98] The underlying argument is that the current Chinese political system may partly be likened to a loosely connected web of competing (as well as complementary) power centers, none of which enjoys complete dominance.[99]

While ideological intensity has doubtless diminished in post-revolutionary China, it is premature to declare the end-of-ideology[100] (or, for that matter, to remove culture altogether from the policy equation) in the country. Institutional fragmentation is not without ideological underpinnings.[101] Nor can a clear-cut distinction be drawn between vision and ideology. The present CCP leadership appears to be broadly committed (although the strength of commitment may vary along factional lines) to a strategic blueprint known as market-preserving authoritarianism.[102]

This is a historically common institutional configuration supported by two pillars: preference for markets (albeit perhaps with a degree of concentration) as a resource allocation mechanism and political authoritarianism, which need not be hard in nature and may even assume the form of authoritarian pluralism.[103] Such a governance regime "may be defined as a system wherein political life remains under the control of a dominant party or single party apparatus."[104] Consistent with this pattern, "[s]trict limits are placed on liberty ... and military or national security organs monitor socio-political trends carefully."[105] In parallel, however, "a civil society is allowed to function apart from the [S]tate."[106] Notably, "[t]he various segments of this social body exercise a certain degree of autonomy and are thus able to reflect diverse interests."[107] Moreover, "the economy is mixed, with the market playing an increasingly important role."[108] This vision-cum-reality does not lack an ideological component.

---

98 *See generally* Ming Xia, *The People's Congresses and Governance in China: Toward a Network Mode of Governance* (2008).

99 *See generally id.*

100 *See generally* Daniel A. Bell, *The End of Ideology: On the Exhaustion of Political Ideas in the Fifties* (1988).

101 *See* Huang, *supra* note 45, at 85–92.

102 *See* Miron Mushkat & Roda Mushkat, "Economic Growth, Democracy, the Rule of Law, and China's Future", 29 *Fordham Int'l L.J.* 229, 243–44 (2005).

103 *See id.* at 243–44.

104 *Id.* at 244.

105 *Id.* at 244.

106 *Id.* at 244.

107 *Id.* at 244.

108 *Id.* at 244.

Market-preserving authoritarianism, whether of the hard or soft variety, may have additional roots, not stemming from the realm of beliefs. A potential influence not directly inspired by an ideology aiming to strike a balance between bottom-up (economic) and top-down (political) strands of thought is the self-interest, or survival instinct, of the CCP leadership. This is a public/rational choice type of an explanation,[109] which is by no means inadequately grounded in the realities of contemporary or earlier-day China, and one that may effectively be couched in terms of both self-interest[110] and survival instinct.[111]

Complexity theorists differentiate between two ways of conceptualizing complex organisms, as systems-of-action and as systems-of-entities.[112] The former approach centers on "actions, behavior, interaction, relationship, or role"[113] mostly ignoring the entities that "participate and experience them."[114] The latter focuses on "individuals, groups, associations, or aggregations of people—that is, social entities."[115] The first of the two surveys of domestically-oriented models of Chinese policy making squarely falls into this category. The second straddles both because it meaningfully extends into the domain of action.[116]

Specifically, the author explores a number of theories pertaining to how decisions are (and should be) formulated and implemented.[117] They include the rational-comprehensive construct (whereby a problem and alternative strategies to address it are thoroughly dissected),[118] bounded rationality/satisficing (whereby cognitive and resource constraints prompt greater selectively and acceptance of less-than perfect or merely satisfactory outcomes) in the

---

109 *See generally* James M. Buchanan & Gordon Tullock, *The Calculus of Consent: Logical Foundations of Constitutional Democracy* (1962).

110 *See, e.g.*, Miron Mushkat & Roda Mushkat, "The Political Economy of Sovereignty Revisited: A Re-examination of the Public Choice Model in Light of China's Accession to the World Trade Organization", 7 *Asper Rev. Int'l Bus. & Trade L.* 115 (2007).

111 *See, e.g.*, Mark Z. Li, "A Public Choice Evaluation of Modern Chinese Leaders' Political Survival", June 2012, *available at* http://markli.homestead.com/Chinese_Leaders_Political_Survival.pdf (last visited June 1, 2015).

112 *See* Neil E. Harrison & J. David Singer, "Complexity is More than Systems Theory", *in Complexity in World Politics: Concepts and Methods of a New Paradigm* 27 (Neil E. Harrison ed., 2006).

113 *Id.* at 27.

114 *Id.* at 27.

115 *Id.* at 27.

116 *See* Huang, *supra* note 45, at 104–42.

117 *See id.* at 104–42.

118 *See id.* at 104–08.

quest for a solution,[119] incrementalism/path dependence (whereby forward movement is rooted in the past, measured, and step-like),[120] mixed-scanning (whereby a middle ground is sought between comprehensive rationalism and incrementalism,[121] or decision makers undertake "a detailed examination of some [issues] with a more cursory review of the wide ... scene"),[122] optimal method (which fuses thorough rationality with extra-rational inputs),[123] contingent perspective (which eclectically embraces a range of problem solving strategies and conditions their applicability and effectiveness on fit with appropriate circumstances),[124] and garbage can pattern (characterized by ambiguity and inconsistency of goals, fluidity and instability of means, which amounts to organized anarchy).[125]

Work on domestic policy formulation and implementation in China has generally highlighted the incremental and path dependent nature of the process.[126] There have also been attempts to identify areas and periods marked by an effort to proceed in a fundamentally rational fashion, albeit perhaps falling short of the comprehensive ideal.[127] Some of these attempts have provided evidence of a variant of bounded rationality, referred to as rule-rationality due to the fact that at times decision makers do not endeavor to thoroughly (and unrealistically) dissect every possible problem they face, which would be a costly and unrealistic strategy, but devise logical rules to be followed in

119 *See id.* at 104–08.

120 *See id.* at 108–13.

121 *See id.* at 113–15.

122 *Id.* at 113.

123 *See id.* at 116–18.

124 *See id.* at 118–23.

125 *See id.* at 123–27.

126 *See generally* Susan L. Shirk, *The Political Logic of Economic Reform in China* (1993); *China's Economic Reform: The Costs and Benefits of Incrementalism* (Qimiao Fan & Peter Nolan eds., 1994); Fan Gang, "Incremental Changes and Dual-Track Transition: Understanding the Case of China", 9 *Econ Pol'y* 99 (1994); Susan L. Shirk, *How China Opened its Door: The Political Success of the PRC's Foreign Trade and Investment Reforms* (1994); *China: Two Decades of Reform and Change* (Wang Gungwu & John Wong eds., 1999); Yongnian Zheng, "Political Incrementalism: Political Lessons from China's 20 Years of Reform", 20 *Third World Q.* 1157 (1999); Alwyn Young, "The Razor's Edge: Distortions and Incremental Reform in the People's Republic of China", 115 *Q.J. Econ.* 1091 (2000); Jinglian Wu, *Understanding and Interpreting Chinese Economic Reform* (2005); Jean-Gemain Gros, "'Big Think', Disjointed Incrementalism: Chinese Economic Success and Policy Lessons for Africa, or the Case for Pan-Africanism", 11 *Afr. J. Int'l Aff.* 55 (2008).

127 *See, e.g.*, We, *supra* note 126, at 74–89.

relevant circumstances.[128] Manifestations of garbage can-style behavior have been observed as well.[129]

B *International Dimension*

Most of the participants in the quest to enhance the broad understanding of Chinese policy dynamics have been focused on the internal side of the institutional arena and have followed conceptual paths commonly associated with comparative politics and public administration (the policy component), rather than international relations. Scholars concerned with the external side have generally refrained from system-wide model-building and have sought to identify, within analytical frameworks rooted in an array of international relations theories, the specific features of decision making in the institutional segment geared toward pursuing an outward-looking agenda. However, drawing too sharp a dichotomy between internal and external perspectives is not entirely productive as the two partially overlap and the former is not without influence on the latter.

One notable point of convergence is the close attention accorded to power, believed to be the centerpiece of China's whole political façade.[130] In terms of its philosophical origins, "[t]he Confucian hierarchical structure of society is [supposed to be] based on a reciprocal exchange of righteous behavior between individuals."[131] The corollary is that, in ideal circumstances, "moral virtues should [serve as the foundation] upon which such behavior is exchanged."[132] However, in practice, "power and authority, as legitimized by a common acceptance of the codes of conduct,"[133] are regarded as the principal force shaping Chinese behavior, in the institutional domain and elsewhere.[134]

---

128 *See, e.g.*, Shirk, *The Political Logic of Economic Reform in China, supra* note 126, at 116–28; Shirk, *How China Opened its Door: The Political Success of the PRC's Foreign Trade and Investment Reforms, supra* note 126, at 19–21.

129 *See generally* Mushkat, *supra* note 72; Murray S. Tanner, *The Politics of Lawmaking in China: Institutions, Processes, and Democratic Prospects* (1999); Benjamin van Rooij, *Regulating Land and Pollution in China: Lawmaking, Compliance, and Enforcement* (2006); Benjamin van Rooij, "Bargaining about the Land Bill: Making Effective Legislation to Protect Arable Land in China", *in Lawmaking for Development: Explorations in the Theory and Practice of International Legislative Projects* 145–69 (Julia Arnacheidt, Benjamin van Rooij & Jan M. Otto eds., 2008).

130 *See* Gerald Chan, *Chinese Perspectives on International Relations: A Framework for Analysis* 28–46 (1999).

131 *Id.* at 28.

132 *Id.* at 28.

133 *Id.* at 28.

134 *See id.* at 28–30.

Mao Zedong's assertion that "political power grows out of barrel of a gun,"[135] while of greater historical than present-day relevance, is deemed to be emblematic of China's strategic positioning, at home and abroad.[136] Traditionally, in the Chinese context, other than perhaps in abstract philosophical discourse, power has come to be equated with brute force.[137] However, in recent years, in a more liberal or sophisticated intellectual climate, a broader and more subtle view of power has emerged in the form of *zonghe guoli*, or comprehensive national power (CNP),[138] a multidimensional construct including both hard and soft elements.[139]

The idea of power permeates many domestically-oriented models of the policy process in China. It also constitutes the keystone of the realist school of thought, the theoretical vehicle most emphatically and widely embraced by students of Chinese decision-making in the international sphere.[140] Although Mao's unembellished claim regarding the military basis of political power has largely been consigned to the dustbin of history, and is primarily invoked for purposes of maximizing analytical proposition's impact, the underlying logic, broadly interpreted, continues to be regarded in influential academic circles as a significant driver of China's foreign policy strategies.[141] It has thus been noted that country "may well be the high church of realpolitik in the post-Cold War world."[142]

Chinese preoccupation with the balance of power is believed to be indicative of its fundamental strategic positioning in the global arena (China's "analysts certainly think more like traditional balance-of-power theorists than do most contemporary Western leaders and policy analysts").[143] This is said to be not a recent phenomenon but one deeply ingrained in Chinese culture ("Su Qin and Zhang Yi were famous balance-of-power strategists during the Warring States period in ancient China").[144] The concept may have been briefly abandoned following the Communist Revolution, because of its bourgeois underpinnings, but it was quickly resurrected even before the country shifted in a reformist direction (e.g., Mao relied on balance-of-power tactics when managing the

135 *Id.* at 29.

136 *See id.* at 29.

137 *See id.* at 29.

138 *See id.* at 29.

139 *See id.* at 29–33.

140 *See generally* Thomas J. Christensen, "Chinese Realpolitik: Reading Beijing's World-View", 75 *Foreign Aff.* 37 (1996).

141 *See in particular id.*

142 *Id.* at 37.

143 *Id.* at 37.

144 Chan, *supra* note 130, at 33.

triangular relationships with the United States and the Soviet Union during the Cold War era).[145]

A more recent example of a situation where realists have been able to account compellingly and satisfactorily for Chinese outward-looking strategies has been the stable deterrence prevailing between the US and China in the Taiwanese context.[146] The argument advanced here is that China has displayed a sound appreciation the potential and constraints of its military capabilities and, for the most part, has acted accordingly in a consistent fashion.[147] Given the crucial nature of this case and the long time frame involved, as well as similar patterns observed in the Korean Peninsula,[148] the inference drawn by realist-type international relations scholars is that it is theoretically fruitful to assume that Chinese leaders are finely schooled in the subtleties of realpolitik and to portray them as like-minded and rational security-maximizing operators.[149]

As China's foreign policy has evolved, so has this perspective. One fundamental distinction currently favored is that between offensive and defensive realism.[150] Both approaches regard conflict as the most salient characteristic of international relations and divergences of interests between States as deep-seated.[151] However, offensive realists posit that States deliberately aim to undermine the security of others, whereas their defensive counterparts do not embrace this proposition.[152] By the same token, the former assume that conflict is a necessary rather than merely recurring feature of international politics, with inter-State cooperation confined to temporary alliances, while the

145 *See id.* at 33.

146 *See generally* Robert S. Ross, "Comparative Deterrence: The Taiwan Strait and the Korean Peninsula", *in New Directions in the Study of China's Foreign Policy* 13 (Alastair I. Johnston & Robert S. Ross eds., 2006).

147 *See generally id.*

148 *See generally id.*

149 *See generally id.*

150 *See generally* Liu Feng & Zhang Ruizhuang, "The Typologies of Realism", 1 *Chinese J. Int'l Pol.* 109 (2006); Tang Shiping, "From Offensive to Defensive Realism: A Social Evolutionary Interpretation of China's Security Strategy", *in China's Ascent: Power, Security, and the Future of International Politics* 141–62 (Robert S. Ross & Zhu Feng eds., 2008); Feng Huiyun, "Is China a Revisionist Power?", 2 *Chinese J. Int'l Pol.* 313 (2009); Yves-heng Lim, "A Tale of Two Realisms in Chinese Foreign Policy", 9 *China: A Int'l J.* 299 (2011).

151 *See generally* Liu & Zhang, *supra* note 150; Tang, *supra* note 150; Feng, *supra* note 150; Lim, *supra* note 150.

152 *See generally* Liu & Zhang, *supra* note 150; Tang, *supra* note 150; Feng, *supra* note 150; Lim, *supra* note 150.

latter take the view that some conflicts may be peacefully resolved.[153] Today's Chinese strategic posture is thought to correspond more closely to the defensive, less rigid variant of realism.[154]

Another comparatively new twist in the realist tale is a jettisoning of the notion that security (achieved through military means, as hypothesized prior to the emergence of the defensive interpretation of world order) is the principal, let alone sole, goal of the State.[155] One position articulated in a particularly elaborate manner and supported with a wide range of empirical material is that in recent years China has primarily been concerned with bolstering its international status or the accumulation of reputational capital.[156] While this does not entail a departure from either the rationalist model or the unitary actor formulation, the omission of security maximization (as well as the recourse to force) constitutes a shift beyond the strict confines of realist territory.

A broader and more elastic rationalist analytical structure implicitly eschews any clear specification of goals and means, but assumes that they are coherently organized in accordance with the logic of cost-utility.[157] The underlying idea is that Chinese strategies in the global arena are driven by nationalistic impulses, yet in a pragmatic fashion.[158] The overarching objective is to

---

153 *See generally* Liu & Zhang, *supra* note 150; Tang, *supra* note 150; Feng, *supra* note 150; Lim, *supra* note 150.

154 *See generally* Tang, *supra* note 150; Feng, *supra* note 150; Lim, *supra* note 150.

155 *See generally* Yong Deng, "Reputation and the Security Dilemma: China Reacts to the China Threat Theory", *in New Directions in the Study of China's Foreign Policy*, *supra* note 146, at 186; Yong Deng, "Better than Power: 'International Status' in Chinese Foreign Policy" *in China Rising: Power and Motivation in Chinese Foreign Policy* 51 (Yong Deng & Ming Wan eds., 2005); Yong Deng, *China's Struggle for Status: The Realignment of International Relations* (2008).

156 *See generally* Deng, "Reputation and the Security Dilemma: China Reacts to the China Threat Theory", *supra* note 155; Deng, *China's Struggle for Status: The Realignment of International Relations*, *supra* note 155.

157 *See generally* Allen S. Whiting, "Chinese Nationalism and Foreign Policy after Deng", 142 *China Q.* 295 (1995); Yongnian Zheng, *Discovering Chinese Nationalism in China: Modernization, Identity, and International Relations* (1999); Suisheng Zhao, "Chinese Nationalism and its International Orientations", 115 *Pol. Sci. Q.* 1 (2000); Peter H. Gries, *China's New Nationalism: Pride, Politics, and Diplomacy* (2004); *Chinese Foreign Policy: Pragmatism and Strategic Behavior* (Suisheng Zhao ed., 2004); Suisheng Zhao, *A Nation State by Construction: Dynamics of Modern Chinese Nationalism* (2004); Chen Zhimin, "Nationalism, Internationalism, and Chinese Foreign Policy", 14 *J. Contemp. China* 35 (2005).

158 *See generally* Whiting, *supra* note 157; Zheng, *supra* note 157; Zhao, "Chinese Nationalism and its International Orientations", *supra* note 157; Gries, *supra* note 157; Zhao, *A Nation*

maximize China's advantage (as possibly proxied by the open-ended concept of comprehensive national power), whether absolute or relative. However, the precise goals and means selected, and their combination, are a function of situation-dependent opportunities and constraints, typically subjected to a reality test or empirical validation.[159]

Another point of convergence between domestically focused and internationally centered models of the Chinese policy process, ideology, has receded into the background. Given the increasingly pragmatic thrust of post-1978 strategies, both inward- and outward-looking, ideological influences have inevitably waned, even if not vanished altogether.[160] Nationalism may of course be regarded as a form of ideological expression,[161] but in this particular case the fusion with pragmatism substantially diminishes its impact as such.[162] Traces of Marxist thought are not completely absent from policy discourse, yet a leading sinologist noted more than a decade ago that "[r]ecent IR literature in China ... reveals a gradual shift away from the traditional method of class analysis."[163]

The third point of convergence, culture, remains relevant, albeit not on a scale comparable with realism in its various shapes.[164] Indeed, historically grounded cultural accounts of Chinese international adaptation seem currently more common than those addressing the domestic side.[165] There is

---

State by Construction: Dynamics of Modern Chinese Nationalism, id.; Grieve, *supra* note 157; Chen, *supra* note 157.

159 *See generally* Whiting, *supra* note 157; Zheng, *supra* note 157; Zhao, "Chinese Nationalism and its International Orientations", *supra* note 157; Gries, *supra* note 157; Zhao, *A Nation State by Construction: Dynamics of Modern Chinese Nationalism, id.*; Grieve, *supra* note 157; Chen, *supra* note 157.

160 *See generally* Whiting, *supra* note 157; Zheng, *supra* note 157; Zhao, "Chinese Nationalism and its International Orientations", *supra* note 157; Gries, *supra* note 157; Zhao, *A Nation State by Construction: Dynamics of Modern Chinese Nationalism, id.*; Grieve, *supra* note 157.; Chen, *supra* note 157.

161 *See generally* Michael Freeden, "Is Nationalism a Distinct Ideology?", 46 *Pol. Stud.* 748 (1998); Anthony D. Smith, *Nationalism: Theory, Ideology, History* (2002); Chaim Gans, *The Limits of Nationalism* (2003).

162 *See generally* Whiting, *supra* note 157; Zhao, "Chinese Nationalism and its International Orientations", *supra* note 157; Gries, *supra* note 157; Zhao, *A Nation State by Construction: Dynamics of Modern Chinese Nationalism, id.*; Grieve, *supra* note 157; Chen, *supra* note 157.

163 Chan, *supra* note 130, at 53.

164 *See generally id.* at 55–63.

165 *See generally* Yung Wei, "A Methodological Critique of Current Studies on Chinese Political Culture", 38 *J. Pol.* 114 (1976); *Chinese Political Culture: 1989–2000* (Shiping Hua ed., 2001).

some realist-style concern, or skepticism, about the at times self-serving and uncritical invocation of culture in such contexts (e.g., it has been suggested that "officials and scholars use [cultural values] to protect China's national interest and to defend China's human rights and other records, regarding them as internal affairs").[166] Nevertheless, culture continues to be inserted into the strategic equation in a number of significant ways.[167]

To begin with, power and culture have been inextricably intertwined in Chinese history, with realpolitik long being employed "to achieve optimal [national] strategic advantage and interests."[168] This theme features prominently in the policy literature, where the strategic nature of China's culture is cogently highlighted, albeit without far-reaching claims (i.e., without necessarily ruling out additional explanations).[169] Although that apparently firmly established policy tradition is open to different theoretical interpretations, including perhaps those of the constructivist variety, it seems to correspond more closely to realist accounts of State behavior, which place "a strong emphasis on the use of force to maintain peace and order."[170]

The preoccupation with the international power structure may also have cultural origins as it may constitute "a modern expression of Confucian China's hierarchical sense of social order."[171] In this context, "the [i]dea of *mingwei* (name and status) or the rectification of name is important[, providing a framework whereby] a Chinese individual may know how to behave properly in the social order and China as a nation may know how to behave properly in the international order."[172] That conception has coincided with the culturally rooted view that "the Middle Kingdom [is positioned] at the center of the universe"[173] by virtue of its "possession of, and superior capacity in generating, the materials for both welfare and warfare."[174] Again, this may be construed from different theoretical perspectives—realist, rationalist, and constructivist (which

166 Chan, *supra* note 130, at 58.

167 *See id.* at 55–63.

168 *Id.* at 59.

169 Alastair I. Johnston, *Cultural Realism: Strategic Culture and Grand Strategy in Chinese History* (1995); Andrew Scobell, *China and Strategic Culture* (2002); Feng Huiyun, *Chinese Strategic Culture and Foreign Policy Decision-Making: Confucianism, Leadership, and War* (2007); Anthony A. Loh, "Deconstructing Cultural Realism", *in China and the New International Order* 281–92 (Wang Gungwu & Zheng Yongnian eds., 2008).

170 Chan, *supra* note 130, at 59.

171 *Id.* at 59.

172 *Id.* at 60.

173 *Id.* at 59.

174 *Id.* at 59.

stresses the interplay between culture and national/State identity)—whether in equal measure or with a mild bias (at least in practice) toward the realist and rationalist side, given the current tendency to relegate cultural manifestations of identity to the status of an "intervening [rather than a causal] variable."[175]

The singularly most fruitful constructivist explanations of Chinese responses to external stimuli have focused on the victim mentality (or, alternatively, identity), seen as the product of the Century of Humiliation that lasted from the First Opium War of 1840–42 through the proclamation of the People's Republic of China in 1949.[176] This tumultuous stretch of history was accompanied by abrupt and dramatic drop in Chinese international fortunes in that what was long "a dominant majority civilization . . . suddenly found itself in a minority position in the world. . .[, an] experience [that] became a stark tragedy, an unforeseen and certainly enormous decline and fall almost without equal in history."[177] It ushered in "an extended period of pressure, dismissal, and 'disrespect' from the West and Japan toward China's territorial integrity, legal sovereignty, and civilization value."[178]

However, the victim mentality is another theoretical variable to have largely been consigned to the dustbin of history in the international relations literature. It has mostly given way to the notion of Chinese re-awakening or re-emergence, entailing an ascent or rise to regional and global power status.[179]

---

175 *Id.* at 59. For additional insights, see Chih-yu Shih, *The Spirit of Chinese Foreign Policy: A Psychocultural View* (1990); Qingxin Wang, "Cultural Norms and the Conduct of Chinese Foreign Policy", *in China's International Relations in the 21st Century* 143–69 (Weixing Hu, Gerald Chan & Daojiong Zho eds., 2000).

176 *See generally* Allen S. Whiting, "Assertive Nationalism in Chinese Foreign Policy", 23 *Asian Surv.* 913 (1983); Peter Hayes Gries, *China's New Nationalism: Pride, Politics and Diplomacy* (2004); David Scott, *China Stands Up: The PRC and the International System* (2007); David Scott, *China and the International System, 1840–1949: Power, Presence, and Perceptions in a Century of Humiliation* (2008); Andreas B. Forsby, "An End to Harmony? The Rise of Sino-Centric China", 5 *Pol. Persp.* 5 (2011).

177 John K. Fairbank, "Introduction: The Old Order", *in* 10 *The Cambridge History of China: The Late Ch'ing: 1800–1911, Part 1*, at 3 (John K. Fairbank ed., 1978).

178 Scott, *China and the International System, 1840–1949: Power, Presence, and Perceptions in a Century of Humiliation, supra* note 176, at 2.

179 *See generally id.; China Rising: Power and Motivation in Chinese Foreign Policy, supra* note 155; *China's Ascent: Power, Security, and the Future of International Politics, supra* note 150; China Rising: Nationalism and Interdependence (David S.G. Goodman & Gerald Segal eds., 1997); *The Rise of China: An International Security Reader* (Michael E. Brown et al. eds., 2000); *China's Place in Global Geopolitics: International and Global Challenges* (Kjeld E. Brodsgaard & Bertel Heurlin eds., 2002); Nicholas R. Lardy, *Integrating China into the Global Economy* (2002); Robert G. Stutter, *China's Rise in Asia: Promises and Perils*

This lofty position is assumed to carry substantial responsibilities.[180] It is consequently argued that China is in the process of shifting, albeit not unambiguously so, from the periphery of the international system to its inner core[181] or, to put it differently, gradually shedding its identity as a revisionist State and acquiring that of a pillar of the prevailing world order.[182]

(2005); *China's "Peaceful Rise" in the 21st Century: Domestic and International Conditions* (Sujian Guo ed., 2006); David C. Kang, *China Rising: Peace, Power, and Order in East Asia* (2007); Randall P. Peerenboom, *China Modernizes: Threat to the West or Model for the Rest* (2007); C. Fred Bergsten *et al.*, *China's Rise: Challenges and Opportunities* (2008); *"Harmonious World" and China's Foreign Policy* (Sujian Guo & Jean-Marc F. Blanchard eds., 2008); John Kurlantzick, *Charm Offensive: How China's Soft Power is Transforming the World* (2008); David M. Lampton, *The Three Faces of Chinese Power: Might, Money, and Minds* (2008); Minqi Li, *The Rise of China and the Demise of the Capitalist World Economy* (2008); David Scott, *The Chinese Century? The Challenge to Global Order* (2008); Aaron L. Friedberg, *A Contest for Supremacy: China, America, and the Struggle for Mastery in Asia* (2009); Martin Jaques, *When China Rules the World: The End of the Western World and the Birth of a New Global Order* (2d ed. 2009); *Greater China in an Era of Globalization* (Sujian Guo & Baogang Guo eds., 2010); Robert S. Steinfeld, *Playing our Game: Why China's Rise Does Not Threaten the West* (2010); Brantley Womack, *China among Unequals: Asymmetric Foreign Relationships in Asia* (2010); *China's Rise in Historical Perspective* (2010); *China's Rise: Threat or Opportunity?* (Herbert S. Yee ed., 2011); Andrew Scobell & Andrew J. Nathan, *China's Search for Security* (2012); Arvind Subramanian, *Eclipse: Living in the Shadow of China's Economic Dominance* (2012); Ivan Tselichtchev, *China versus the West: The Global Power Shift of the 21st Century* (2012).

180 *See generally* Jin Canrong, "From 'China Threat' to 'China's Responsibility': Changing International Discourse on China and China's Response", in *China's Rise: Threat or Opportunity?*, *supra* note 179, at 270–79; Gilbert Rozman, "China's Quest for Great Power Identity", 43 *Orbis: A J. World Aff.* 383 (1999); Rosemary Foot, "Chinese Power and the Idea of a Responsible State", 45 *China J.* 1 (2001); Xia Liping, "China: A Responsible Great Power", 10 *J. Contemp. China* 17 (2001); *Power and Responsibility in Chinese Foreign Policy* (Yongjin Zhang & Greg Austin eds., 2001); Li Bao-jun & Xu Zheng-yuan, "China's Self-Identity Construction as a Responsible Power in the Cold War Era", 5 *Teaching & Res.* 49 (2006); Rex Li, A *Rising China and Security in East Asia: Identity Construction and Security Discourse* (2009); Shaun Breslin, "China's Emerging Global Role: Dissatisfied Responsible Great Power", 30 *Pol.* 52 (2010); Amitai Etzioni, "Is China a Responsible Stakeholder?", 87 *Int'l Aff.* 539 (2011).

181 *See generally* Yong Deng, "Escaping the Periphery: China's National Identity in World Politics", in *China's International Relations in the 21st Century*, *supra* note 175, at 175.

182 *See generally* Rozeman, *supra* note 180; Foot, *supra* note 180; Xia, *supra* note 180; Zhang & Austin (eds.), *supra* note 180; Li & Xu, *supra* note 180; Breslin, *supra* note 180; Jin, *supra* note 180.

Again, this pattern is open to different theoretical interpretations. Because a new national/State identity may be crystallizing, there may be scope for a constructivist reading, even if modest in scope, given that the accumulation of power is neither a necessary nor a sufficient condition for the exercise of international responsibility, and in light of the fact that multiple Chinese national/State identities may be pinpointed, not in harmony with each other.[183] A realist dimension is certainly present as the quest for power cannot be portrayed as a purely altruistic endeavor. However, the growing emphasis on soft power,[184] initiatives such as the good neighbor policy,[185] promotion of the vision of a peaceful rise,[186] and steadily increasing multilateral engagement[187] suggest that defensive, rather than offensive, realism currently drives foreign policy. Indeed, the basically favorable disposition toward international cooperation and general willingness to enter into collaborative schemes may tentatively be indicative of institutionalist-style (rationalist) appreciation of the benefits of joint action in the global arena and strategies reflecting this fundamental stance.[188]

---

183 *See generally* Tiejun Zhang, "Self-Identity Construction Present China", 23 *Comp. Strategy* 281 (2004).

184 *See generally* Kurlantzick, *supra* note 179; Mingjiang Li, *Soft Power: China's Emerging Strategy in International Politics* (2009); Hongyi Lai & Yiyi Lu (eds.), *China's Soft Power and International Relations* (2012).

185 *See generally* Chien-peng Chung, *China's Multilateral Cooperation in Asia and the Pacific: Institutionalizing Beijing's Good Neighbor Policy* (2010); Steven F. Jackson, *China's Good Neighbor Policy: The Evolution of Relations in Comparative Perspective* (2012).

186 *See generally* Guo (ed.), *supra* note 179; Guo & Blanchard (eds.), *supra* note 179; Jinghao Zhou, *China's Peaceful Rise in a Global Context: A Domestic Aspect of China's Road Map to Democratization* (2009).

187 *See generally* Wang Gungwu & Zheng Yongnian (eds.), *China and the New International Order* (2008); Guoguang Wu & Helen Lansdowne (eds.), *China Turns to Multilateralism: Foreign Policy and National Security* (2008); Jenny Clegg, *China's Global Strategy: Toward a Multipolar World* (2009).

188 *See generally* Gerald Chan, "China Joins Global Governance: The 10 Conundrums", in Wang & Zheng (eds.), *id.*, at 168–84; Thomas G. Moore, "Racing to Integrate or Cooperating to Compete? Liberal and Realist Interpretations of China's New Multilateralism", in Wu & Lansdowne (eds.), *id.*, at 35–50; Allen Carlson, "More than Just Saying No: China's Evolving Approach to Sovereignty and Intervention since Tiananmen", in Johnston & Ross (eds.), *supra* note 146, at 217–41; Jianjun Chen, *China's Incentives for International Cooperation: An Interactive Perspective of Chinese Foreign Policy in the Cold War Era* (1995); Hongyin Wang, "Multilateralism in Chinese Foreign Policy: The Limits of Socialization", 40 *Asian Survey* 475–91 (2000); Thomas G. Moore & Dixia Yang, "Empowered and Restrained: Chinese Foreign Policy in the Age of Interdependence", in *The Making of Chinese Foreign*

Constructivism and institutionalism are part of the specific international relations analytical repertoire, but there is an additional channel through which externally-oriented students of Chinese politics draw insights from the conceptual formulations of their internally-focused counterparts. In this particular respect, they substantially widen their theoretical horizons by advocating a micro-macro approach.[189] The essence of this research strategy consists of building broad-based models in which macro-level external constraints (e.g., structural and operational features of the international system) and macro-level internal determinants (e.g., domestic societal and institutional patterns) serve, in conjunction with micro-level influences originating in the external and internal arenas (e.g., attitudinal predispositions of decision makers abroad and at home), as the inputs (or causal variables) that generate the foreign policy outputs (the effects).[190]

The exploration of micro-macro linkages, within and beyond China's borders, has not been an open-ended journey. Strictly defined hypotheses, at times of the mathematical or quasi-mathematical variety, have been advanced and empirically assessed.[191] While the results have not been entirely successful,

---

and Security Policy in the Era of Reform, 1978–2000 191–229 (David Lampton ed., 2001); Elizabeth Economy, "The Impact of International Legal Regimes on Chinese Foreign Policy-Making: Broadening Perspectives and Policies... but Only to a Point", in *The Making of Chinese Foreign and Security Policy in the Era of Reform, 1978–2000* 230–53 (David Lampton ed., 2001); Sujian Guo & Shiping Hua (eds.), *New Dimensions of Chinese Foreign Policy* (2007); Pauline Kerr, Stuart Harris & Qin Yaking (eds.), *China's "New" Diplomacy: Tactical or Fundamental Change?* (2009); Zhiqun Zhu, *China's New Diplomacy: Rationale, Strategies, and Significance* (2010); Wang Yizhou (ed.), *Transformation of Foreign Affairs and International Relations in China, 1978–2000* (2011); Mingjiang Li, *China Joins Global Governance: Cooperation and Contentions* (2012); Robert G. Sutter, *Chinese Foreign Relations: Power and Policy since the Cold War* (2d ed., 2012).

189 *See generally* Quansheng Zhao, *Interpreting Chinese Foreign Policy: The Micro-Macro Linkage Approach* (1996).

190 *See id.*, at 18–30.

191 *See generally* Bruce B. de Mesquita, David Newman & Alvin Rabushka, *Forecasting Political Events: The Future of Hong Kong* (1985); Bruce B. de Mesquita, David Newman & Alvin Rabushka, *Red Flag over Hong Kong* (1996); Krishna P. Jayakar, "The United States-China Copyright Dispute: A Two-level Games Analysis", 2 *Communication Law and Policy* 527–61 (1997); Chien-peng Chung, *Domestic Politics, International Bargaining, and China's Territorial Disputes* (2004); Albert S. Yee, "Semantic Ambiguity and Joint Deflections in the Hainan Negotiations", 2 *China: An International Journal* 53–82 (2004); Albert S. Yee, "Domestic Support Ratios in Two-Level Bargaining: The US-China WTO Negotiations", 4 *China Review* 129–63 (2004); Hongying Wang & Matthias Kaelberer, "The Two-Level Game of China's Exchange Rate Policy", Paper presented at the annual meeting of the

particularly if examined over a long time horizon, the overall framework itself has proved useful.[192] Notably, the unitary actor assumption has been called into question as it has been established that Chinese interactions in the global arena are shaped by a multitude of actors and forces that do not necessarily operate in a uniform fashion.[193] This picture of diversity and multidirectional pressures, notably on the home front, is broadly consistent with that painted by scholars primarily concerned with the relationship between institutional fragmentation (e.g., factionalism, clientalism, and authoritarian fissures) and domestic policy outputs.

Scholars in the field of international relations have ventured, albeit selectively, into another domain where students of domestic politics have been engaged in theory building and testing: the process whereby high-level decisions are formulated and implemented in the public sector. Traditionally, most of the research undertaken from this perspective has drawn its inspiration, whether explicitly or implicitly, from the rational-comprehensive model, with that focused on the revolutionary era proving no exception to the norm.[194] The recognition of institutional complexities, both at home and abroad, has

---

International Studies Association in San Diego, Mar. 22, 2006, *available at* http://www.academic.com/meta/p98968_index.html (last visited Nov. 30, 2013); Chien-peng Chung, "Resolving China's Island Disputes: A Two-Level Game Analysis", 12 *Journal of Chinese Political Science* 49–71 (2007).

192 *See generally* Miron Mushkat & Roda Mushkat, "The Political Economy of International Legal Compliance: Pre-1997 Predictions and Post-1997 Realities in Hong Kong", 10 *University of California Davis Journal of Law and Policy* 229–46 (2004); Miron Mushkat & Roda Mushkat, "International Law and Game Theory: A Marriage of Convenience or Strange Bedfellows?", 2 *New Zealand Yearbook of International Law* 101–26 (2005); Roda Mushkat, "Chinese Border Disputes Visited: Toward a Better Interdisciplinary Synthesis", 12 *Richmond Journal of Global Law and Business* 45–91 (2012); Roda Mushkat, "Whither the Two-Level Game Model of International Legal Compliance? A Chinese Roadmap", 3 *International Journal of Public Law and Policy* 178–209 (2013).

193 *See generally* Zhao, *supra* note 189; Lampton (ed.), *supra* note 188; Sutter, *supra* note 188; Thomas W. Robinson & David Shambaugh (eds.), *Chinese Foreign Policy: Theory and Practice* (1994); Lu Ning, *The Dynamics of Foreign-Policy Decisionmaking in China* (1997); Samuel S. Kim (ed.), *China and the World: Chinese Foreign Policy Faces the New Millennium* (1998); Yufan Hao & Lin Su (eds.), *China's Foreign Policy Making: Societal Force and Chinese American Policy* (2005); Robert S. Ross, *Chinese Security Policy: Structure Power, and Politics* (2009); Hongyi Lai, *The Domestic Sources of China's Foreign Policy: Regimes, Leadership, Priorities, and Process* (2010).

194 *See* Thomas J. Christensen, Alastair I. Johnston & Robert S. Ross, "Conclusions and Future Directions", *in New Directions in the Study of China's Foreign Policy*, *supra* note 146, at 379, 379–80.

brought about a modest shift toward the incrementalism/path dependence segment of the analytical spectrum.[195] However, a more significant departure, in terms of scale, has entailed a movement from the rational-comprehensive construct toward analytical schemes reflecting the cognitive constrains facing actors in the global arena (embedded in the notion of satisficing).[196]

Notably, rule-rationality, as distinct from the act-rationality type, has compellingly and consistently been invoked to illustrate the propensity of China's leaders to pursue foreign strategies on the basis of a set of clear and coherent, but not overly elaborate and thoroughly re-evaluated (which does equate with parsimonious and static), principles.[197] Rule-rationality is a less ambitious decision-making tenet than the act-rationality variant, not requiring its adherents to painstakingly dissect situational dynamics within a rigorously specified goals-means framework.[198] The following is the vivid contemporary (albeit perhaps no longer entirely applicable) example in the Chinese context:

1. Maximize material capabilities above all. State security rests in large measure on possessing the unilateral ability to use military force against any potential adversary. The constraints on this ability should therefore be as low as technologically and economically feasible.
2. Avoid high cost commitments. This follows from the first decision rule. High costs are defined as any commitment that prevents or closes off future options to improve relative military capabilities.
3. If avoidance incurs image costs, then try to avoid high cost commitments but join low cost, high profile activities. More specifically, pursue high profile unilateral commitments and pledges, and eschew high cost multilateral commitments. This decision rule maximizes image payoffs and minimizes the chance of getting entrapped in a process over which China has less control, or in which its bargaining power is diluted by an increased number of players.

---

195 *See* Wang, *supra* note 188, at 489–90; Rex Xiao, "China: A Reform-Minded Status-Quo Power", Mar. 16, 2012, *available at* http://www.eastasiaforum.org/2012/05/16/china-a-reform-minded-status-quo-power/ (last visited June 1, 2015).

196 *See* Christensen, Johnston & Ross, *supra* note 194, at 388.

197 *See generally* Johnston, *supra* note 169; Scobell, *supra* note 169; Feng, *supra* note 169; Loh, *supra* note 169; Thomas J. Christensen, "Windows and War: Trend Analysis and Beijing's Use of Force", *in New Directions in the Study of China's Foreign Policy*, *supra* note 146, at 50; Alastair I. Johnston, "China and International Environmental Institutions: A Decision Rule Analysis", *in Energizing China: Reconciling Environmental Protection and Economic Growth* 555–59 (Michael B. McElroy, Chris P. Nielsen & Peter Lydon eds., 1998).

198 *See* Mushkat, *supra* note 28, at 644–49.

4. If the opportunities to pursue material gains are unilaterally closed off, and China has little choice but to join multilateral negotiations, then it should try to build coalitions to weaken commitments. The reason is that although fear of opprobrium may make it pay to cooperate, the total payoff may still be higher if China does not have to make any costly multilateral commitments at all. Thus China should try to create an alternative coalition of [S]tates which provides it with sufficient back[-] patting benefits to counteract the opprobrium from the avoidance of substantive commitments.
5. If unilateral opportunities to maximize relative capabilities are closed off, and coalition building unsuccessful, then China should choose the least constraining options; try to prevent the toughening of any commitments that cannot be avoided (e.g., try to dilute compliance requirements).[199]

Another often-cited contemporary example is that of the windows logic.[200] In this case, the proposition is that, when it comes to waging war, there are windows of opportunity and windows of vulnerability and those may be identified in advance by employing certain well-defined yardsticks.[201] The window analogy is deemed relevant because states of opportunity and vulnerability are not long lasting.[202] Like windows, which are frequently opened and closed, opportunities for decisive action and patterns of vulnerability emerge and recede in a dynamic fashion.[203]

While following such rules is a practice that falls short of satisfying lofty rational comprehensive standards, it may still overstate the cognitive capacities of decision makers operating in a complex and fluid environment.[204]

199 Johnston, "China and International Environmental Institutions", *supra* note 197, at 565.

200 *See* Christensen, *supra* note 197, at 53.

201 *See id.* at 53.

202 *See id.* at 53.

203 *See id.* at 53.

204 *See generally id.*; Deng, "Reputation and the Security Dilemma: China Reacts to the China Threat Theory", *supra* note 155; John W. Garver, "China's Decision for War with India in 1962", *in New Directions in the Study of China's Foreign Policy*, *supra* note 146, at 86; Michael NG-Quinn, "The Analytic Study of Chinese Foreign Policy", 27 *Int'l Stud. Q.* 203 (1983); Barbara Farnham, *Avoiding Losses/Taking Risks: Prospect Theory and International Conflict* (1994); *Decisionmaking on War and Peace: The Cognitive-Rational Debate* (Nehemia Geva & Alex Mintz eds.,1997); Rose McDermott, *Risk-Taking in International Politics: Prospect Theory in American Foreign Policy* (2001); *Integrating Cognitive and Rational Theories of Foreign Policy Analysis* (Alex Mintz ed., 2002); Steve Chan, "Judgment Heuristics and

A number of studies whose authors highlight strategic misperceptions, rather than soundness, in confronting external challenges suggest that "it is a mistake to treat the Chinese leadership as if it were always capable of rationally understanding and more or less accurately assessing power distributions, the intentions and capabilities of adversaries, and other constraints in the international system, and then acting in ways that maximize China's own security."[205]

These studies provide considerable empirical evidence supporting the contention that Chinese leaders' misguided choices have produced self-inflicted wounds in the form of potentially avoidable security threats.[206] The evidence generated convincingly shows that those choices "have been biased by some very basic pathologies of decision-making: poor estimations of trends in international balance of power and in domestic politics in China and in other [S]tates...; lack of recognition of security dilemma dynamics; ideology, historical identity, and inordinately high valuation of the symbolic importance of territory...."[207] Attention has been drawn to attribution errors, which have constituted "a key obstacle to correctly reading 'structural' signals, particularly in Maoist foreign policy...."[208] The prevalence of such errors is hardly surprising as they "are especially common among those with cognitively simplistic, binary worldviews and are typical of authoritarian personality types and of fundamentalist political movements."[209]

A possible limitation of this analytically illuminating and empirically rich work is that the decision-making pathologies identified are exclusively ascribed to cognitive factors. Organizational disarray, or at least malfunctioning, as captured by the garbage can model of policy formulation and implementation, is largely overlooked, despite the fact that it may be an equally significant

---

Prospect Theory: Practical Implications for Relations Across the Taiwan Straits", 3 *J.E. Asia Stud.* 55s (2003); Jeffrey D. Berejikian, *International Relations under Risk: Framing State Choice* (2004); Nathan A. Feezer, *Chinese Crisis Decision Making: Using a Cybernetic Approach to Interpret and Predict Beijing's Behavior under Stress* (2010); Alex Mintz & Karl DeRouen, *Understanding Foreign Policy Decision Making* (2010); Kai He, *Decision Making during Crises: Prospect Theory and China's Foreign Policy Making after the Cold War* (2012); Kai He & Huiyun Feng, *Prospect Theory and Foreign Policy Analysis in the Asia Pacific* (2012).

205 Alastair Iain Johnston, "The Correlates of Beijing Public Opinion toward the United States, 1998–2004", *in New Directions in the Study of China's Foreign Policy*, *supra* note 146, at 340, 388.

206 *Id.* at 388.

207 *Id.* at 388.

208 *Id.* at 388.

209 *Id.* at 388.

influence. The multiplicity of actors at various levels (including provincial, and not necessarily directly relevant!) of government involved in managing China's current territorial conflicts, and the lack of meaningful coordination among them, is a telling case in point.[210]

Although institutional frailties do not loom sufficiently large in cognitively-inspired research on Chinese foreign policy, it is by no means narrowly focused. Particularly interesting and noteworthy are the ongoing efforts to integrate the rational and cognitive perspectives.[211] Such efforts constitute a fundamental departure from the practice of offering mono-causal explanations, based on the assumption, whether explicit or implicit, that the many paradigms that inhabit the diverse and fragmented international relations territory are mutually exclusive and cannot be productively synthesized. This assumption is not conducive to theoretical progress.

C *Legal Dimension*

The inward- and outward-looking model-building endeavors outlined above have yielded results that are not beyond criticism. Concepts have not always been employed in a genuinely methodical fashion[212] and relationships among variables have seldom been specified with a high degree of precision.[213] By the same token, as briefly noted, certain gaps may be pinpointed in the analytical space and attempts at inter-paradigmatic integration have been few and far between. However, a non-negligible measure of cross-fertilization between the domestic and international viewpoints has been observed, ample theoretical insights have been generated, and seemingly divergent models have selectively been synthesized. Overall, substantial headway has clearly been made, meriting a favorable comparison with the limited and tentative steps taken by scholars in the field of law.

Systematic accounts of China's international legal attitudes and behavior during the revolutionary era were heavily grounded in ideological discourse,

---

210 *See* M. Taylor Fravel, "Hainan's New Maritime Regulations: A Preliminary Analysis", Dec. 2, 2012, *available at* http://taylorfravel.com/2012/12/hainans-new-maritime-regulations-a-preliminary-analysis/ (last visited June 1, 2015).

211 *See generally* Patrick James & Enyu Zhang, "Chinese Choices: A Poliheuristic Analysis of Foreign Policy Crises, 1950–1996", 1 *Foreign Pol'y Analysis* 31 (2005); Min Ye, "Poliheuristic Theory, Bargaining, and Crisis Decision Making", 3 *Foreign Pol'y Analysis* 317 (2007); Nukhet A. Sandal et al., "Poliheuristic Theory and Crisis Decision Making: A Comparative Analysis of Turkey with China", 44 *Can. J. Pol. Sci.* 27 (2011).

212 *Compare for example with* Gary Goertz, *Social Science Concepts: A User's Guide* (2006).

213 *Compare for example with* David W. Britt, *A Conceptual Introduction to Modeling: Qualitative and Quantitative Perspectives* (1997).

with scant attention accorded to additional factors (e.g., power, mostly referred in passing) whose possible influence was adequately acknowledged by social scientists even at that early juncture.[214] The starting point in comprehensively addressing the subject typically was the distinction, commonly drawn by Chinese officials and commentators, between bourgeois, or general, and socialist international law.[215] The purpose of the former principally was to govern relations among bourgeois, or capitalist, States and that of the latter those among members of the socialist fraternity.[216] The bourgeois variant was regarded as a vehicle designed to serve entrenched capitalist interests.[217]

Some modest inconsistencies were observed between this ideologically underpinned broad vision and certain specific postures adopted in concrete policy settings.[218] Notably, the emphasis on an unbridled exercise of national

---

214 *See generally* Keyuan Zou, "Chinese Approaches to International Law", *in China's International Relations in the 21st Century, supra* note 175, at 171–94; Suzanne Ogden, "Sovereignty and International Law: The Perspective of the People's Republic of China", 7 *NYU J. Int'l L. & Pol.* 1, 12 (1974); Suzanne Ogden, "An Approach of the Chinese Communists to the Study of International Law, State Sovereignty, and the International System", 70 *China Q.* 315 (1977); Byron N. Tzou, *China and International Law: The Boundary Disputes* 7–23 (1990); Jacques deLisle, "China's Approach to International Law: A Historical Perspective", 94 *Am. Soc'y of Int'l L. Proceedings* 267 (2000); Junwu Pan, *Toward a New Framework of Peaceful Settlement of China's Territorial and Boundary Disputes* 1–16, 77, 91–94 (2009).

215 *See* Ogden, "Sovereignty and International Law", *supra* note 214, at 8–15; Ogden, "An Approach of the Chinese Communists to the Study of International Law, State Sovereignty, and the International System", *supra* note 214, at 316–20; Tzou, *supra* note 214, at 8–9; deLisle, *supra* note 214, at 272–73; Zou, *supra* note 214, at 173; Pan, *supra* note 214, at 9, 77, 91–94.

216 *See* Ogden, "Sovereignty and International Law", *supra* note 214, at 8–15; Ogden, "An Approach of the Chinese Communists to the Study of International Law, State Sovereignty, and the International System", *supra* note 214, at 316–20; Tzou, *supra* note 214, at 8–9; deLisle, *supra* note 214, at 272–73; Zou, *supra* note 214, at 173; Pan, *supra* note 214, at 9, 77, 91–94.

217 *See* Ogden, "Sovereignty and International Law", *supra* note 214, at 8–15; Ogden, "An Approach of the Chinese Communists to the Study of International Law, State Sovereignty, and the International System", *supra* note 214, at 316–20; Tzou, *supra* note 214, at 8–9; deLisle, *supra* note 214, at 272–73; Zou, *supra* note 214, at 173; Pan, *supra* note 214, at 9, 77, 91–94.

218 *See* Ogden, "Sovereignty and International Law", *supra* note 214, at 10–13; Ogden, "An Approach of the Chinese Communists to the Study of International Law, State Sovereignty, and the International System", *supra* note 214, at 315; Tzou, *supra* note 214, at 10–16; deLisle, *supra* note 214, at 272–73; Zou, *supra* note 214, at 175–77; Pan, *supra* note 214, at 79–84.

sovereignty proved difficult to reconcile with the notion of class solidarity extending beyond China's borders.[219] However, this could be explained as a tactical imperative in an international environment where the bourgeois/capitalist States sought to perpetuate their dominant status by creating a layer of fully sovereign States and another layer of not fully sovereign (protected or vassal-like) ones.[220] The post-Second World War doctrine of limited sovereignty (interestingly, opportunistically resorted to by the Soviet Union) could thus be repudiated without performing an ideological volte face.[221] The fact that the concept of absolute, or unlimited, sovereignty was not unambiguously embraced rendered ideological tightrope walking less uncomfortable than would have otherwise been the case.[222]

Such intellectual maneuvering began to pose greater challenges as Chinese exposure to the outside world evolved into a more intricate enterprise.[223] A telling illustration was the inherent tension between the unwavering support for national liberation movements struggling to free themselves from the shackles of Western imperialism, often through secession culminating in the emergence of revolutionary States, and the unswerving reluctance to extend the logic to Tibet (or, for that matter, Taiwan), an entity supposedly never able of handle its external affairs and over which China long exercised full sovereignty (as distinct from suzerainty).[224] This stance was not devoid

219 *See* Ogden, "Sovereignty and International Law", *supra* note 214, at 10–13; Ogden, "An Approach of the Chinese Communists to the Study of International Law, State Sovereignty, and the International System", *supra* note 214, at 315; Tzou, *supra* note 214, at 10–13; deLisle, *supra* note 214, at 272–73; Zou, *supra* note 214, at 175–77; Pan, *supra* note 214, at 79–84.

220 *See* Ogden, "Sovereignty and International Law", *supra* note 214, at 10–13; Ogden, "An Approach of the Chinese Communists to the Study of International Law, State Sovereignty, and the International System", *supra* note 214, at 315; Tzou, *supra* note 214, 10–13; deLisle, *supra* note 214, at 272–73; Zou, *supra* note 214, at 175–77; Pan, *supra* note 214, at 79–84.

221 *See* Ogden, "Sovereignty and International Law", *supra* note 214, at 10–13; Ogden, "An Approach of the Chinese Communists to the Study of International Law, State Sovereignty, and the International System", *supra* note 214, at 315; Tzou, *supra* note 214, at 10–13; deLisle, *supra* note 214, at 272–73; Zou, *supra* note 214, at 175–77; Pan, *supra* note 214, at 79–84.

222 *See* Ogden, "Sovereignty and International Law", *supra* note 214, at 10–13; Ogden, "An Approach of the Chinese Communists to the Study of International Law, State Sovereignty, and the International System", *supra* note 214, at 315; Tzou, *supra* note 214, at 10–13; deLisle, *supra* note 214, at 272–73; Zou, *supra* note 214, at 175–77; Pan, *supra* note 214, at 79–84.

223 *See* Ogden, "Sovereignty and International Law", *supra* note 214, at 18–19; Ogden, "An Approach of the Chinese Communists to the Study of International Law, State Sovereignty, and the International System", *supra* note 214, at 319–20.

224 *See* Ogden, "Sovereignty and International Law", *supra* note 214, at 18–19; Ogden, "An Approach of the Chinese Communists to the Study of International Law, State Sovereignty, and the International System", *supra* note 214, at 319–20.

of realist elements, but those tended to be less prominently highlighted than ideological ones.[225]

As such common examples suggest, the difficulty inherent in a nearly complete reliance on ideology as the determinant of Chinese international legal behavior, and positions emphatically articulated but not consistently converted into concrete actions, stemmed from frequently witnessed gaps between theory and practice and the inevitability of having to confront not fully compatible norms. Consequently, the rejection of bourgeois international law was not as unambiguous as a heavily ideology-focused reading of pre-1978 picture would imply.[226] The shift from revolution to reform, and from isolation to integration, significantly diminished the analytical pull of the ideological factor, prompting international legal scholars to turn to culture in seeking to account for patterns of China's new, more accommodative, but apparently with distinct Chinese characteristics, approach to international law.[227]

The specific cultural framework adopted for this purpose ultimately had strong Confucian undertones.[228] The difference between *Li* (Confucianism) and *Fa* (Legalism) was thus resurrected in order to shed light on the conceptual underpinnings of the fundamental international legal re-orientation of post-1997 China, a country that embarked on multifaceted modernization in a utilitarian fashion.[229] The former construct refers to the use of moral precepts to regulate human behavior in accordance with natural law.[230] The latter was relied upon in the Chinese context as an instrument to control criminal conduct, and was viewed as a tool for imposing order rather than a vehicle for the protection of natural rights.[231]

The intrinsic superiority of *Li* over *Fa*, both in the domestic arena and in international society, was seen as being reaffirmed in reformist China although, interestingly, its hierarchical, tributary-like nature was thought to have been re-emphasized at the same time.[232] The re-emerging historical Sino-centric world order, or at least the blueprint, was accordingly depicted as one both inspired by moral virtue and non-egalitarian in character, legitimately dominated by benign China (the equivalent of an enlightened father, husband,

225 *See* Ogden, "Sovereignty and International Law", *supra* note 214, at 18–19; Ogden, "An Approach of the Chinese Communists to the Study of International Law, State Sovereignty, and the International System", *supra* note 214, at 319–20.

226 *See* Pan, *supra* note 214, at 76–94.

227 *See id.* at 76–90.

228 *See id.* at 91–94.

229 *See id.* at 71–76.

230 *See id.* at 71–76.

231 *See id.* at 71–76.

232 *See id.* at 71–76.

oldest sibling, or king, in family or other political relationships).[233] Evidence of *Li*'s revival was believed to manifest itself in various other forms, such as the time-honored preference for informal over formal modes of dispute resolution, mirroring the Confucian tradition of promoting free dialogue rather than mechanistic adjudication.[234]

Perhaps more importantly, culture was also regarded as the source of the pragmatic propensities of the new China.[235] In fact, it was inappropriate to consider them as an entirely recent phenomenon as similar patterns were present during previous historical periods, reflected for example in the responses of the Qing government to efforts by William A.P. Martin, an American missionary and Sinologist, to introduce in mid-19th century international law and its potential benefits to the country.[236] Possibly the most clear-cut expression of the old-new Chinese pragmatism was the recycled notion that "all should start from actuality," which could be interpreted as providing justification for virtually any policy stance/measure, including on the international legal front.[237]

Invoking cultural explanations is not an unfruitful pursuit if carried out selectively but, in its present, overly expansive form, it gives rise to three fundamental problems. First, the one-sided portrayal of the relationship between *Li* and *Fa*, with former decisively prevailing over the latter, rather than co-existing with it, however uncomfortably, defies logic and lacks face validity. After all, China's culture is not the product of a single philosophical tradition.[238] Confucianism alone may not adequately account for Chinese attitudes toward and use of international law.[239] Legalism is another significant strand of thought whose lasting influence cannot be overlooked.[240] And, as emphatically noted, "[t]he legalist perspective saw international relations starkly in terms of power and[S]tate interest."[241]

Second, in a similar vein, theoretical accounts exclusively based on culture may not yield sufficient insights. Phenomena such as the China's handling of its border disputes have been explored by scholars both in the field of

233 *See id.* at 73–75.

234 *See id.* at 75–76.

235 *See id.* at 76–79.

236 *See id.* at 76–77.

237 *See id.* at 79.

238 *See* deLisle, *supra* note 214, at 267–70.

239 *See id.* at 269–70.

240 *See id.* at 267–69.

241 *Id.* at 269.

international law[242] and international relations.[243] The latter have been able to paint broadly satisfactory, even if incomplete, pictures without any recourse to cultural variables.[244] The implication is not that culture should be consigned to oblivion in such contexts, but that it ought to be examined in conjunction with additional factors, preferably in greater detail and more intensively than has thus far been the case.

Third, cultural influences, although deeper and less amenable to change than ideological ones, are not cast in stone. They may ebb and flow, manifest themselves differently in different circumstances, and undergo a partial or a far-reaching transformation. Neither Confucianism nor legalism may properly be regarded as static belief systems that are not subject to decay, fine-tuning, and reconfiguration. Nor may their impact be soundly assumed to be independent of a host of (economic, political, psychological, social, technological, time-related, macro, micro, and so forth) domestic and international forces.[245]

The studies highlighting the role of ideology and culture in shaping Chinese positions vis-à-vis international law as a normative system and a governance regime carrying practical implications have largely relied on informal content analysis of relevant policy and quasi-policy statements, as well as traditional-style (unstructured but not unsystematic) ex-post scrutiny of strategically pertinent communication and conduct. Two additional paradigms have emerged in recent years, offering conceptual insights derived from hypothesis-driven

---

242 *See generally* Tzou, *supra* note 214; Pan, *supra* note 214.

243 *See generally* Chung, *Domestic Politics, International Bargaining, and China's Territorial Disputes*, *supra* note 191; Chung, "Resolving China's Island Disputes: A Two-Level Game Analysis", *supra* note 191; Alastair I. Johnston, "China's Militarized Interstate Dispute Behavior, 1949–1992", 153 *China Q.* 10 (1998); M. Taylor Fravel, "Securing Borders: China's Doctrine and Force Structure for Frontier Defense", 30 *J. Strategic Stud.* 7057 (2007); M. Taylor Fravel, *Strong Borders, Secure Nation: Cooperation and Conflict in China's Territorial Disputes* (2008); M. Taylor Fravel, "Explaining Stability in the Senkaku (Diaoyu) Dispute", *in Getting the Triangle Straight: Managing China-Japan-US Relations* 144 (Gerald Curtis, Ryosei Kokubun & Wang Jisi eds., 2010); M. Taylor Fravel, "China's Rise: Assessing China's Potential for Territorial Expansion", 12 *Int' Stud. Rev.* 505 (2010).

244 *See generally* Johnston, *supra* note 243; Chung, Domestic Politics, *International Bargaining, and China's Territorial Disputes*, *supra* note 243; Chung, "Resolving China's Island Disputes: A Two-Level Game Analysis", *supra* note 243; Fravel, "Securing Borders: China's Doctrine and Force Structure for Frontier Defense", *id.*; Fravel, *Strong Borders, Secure Nation: Cooperation and Conflict in China's Territorial Disputes, id.*; Fravel, "Explaining Stability in the Senkaku (Diaoyu) Dispute", *id.*

245 This general conclusion emerges in Ned Lebow, *A Cultural Theory of International Relations* (2009).

and elaborate empirical research, involving multiple case studies and the use of simple/descriptive (as distinct from sophisticated/inferential) statistics.[246]

One consists of TLPT, which draws on an unconventional variant of group theory—unconventional because it underplays the competitive features of interest group activity and underscores the efforts of individuals and collective entities that form advocacy coalitions, or social networks, that extend beyond national borders and serve as a vehicle for promoting economic, political, social, and technological causes/ideas.[247] Involvement in such efforts may amount to a profound learning experience that impinges on one's values, principles, and operational modes.[248] The TLPT-equivalent follows a broadly similar analytical path by positing that (China's) participation in international regimes results entails socialization in the course of which international norms are absorbed and international legal behavior, notably compliance with international law, is readjusted in a manner that renders it increasingly consistent with mainstream practices.[249]

---

246 *See generally* Ann Kent, *China, the United Nations, and Human Rights: The Limits of Compliance* (1999); Gerald Chan, *China's Compliance in Global Affairs: Trade, Arms Control, Environment, and Human Rights* (2006); Ann Kent, *The Limits of Compliance: China, International Organizations, and Global Security* (2007).

247 *See generally* Margaret E. Keck & Kathryn Sikkink, *Activists beyond Borders: Advocacy Networks in International Politics* (1998); *The Power of Human Rights: International Norms and Domestic Change* (Thomas Risse, Stephen C. Ropp & Kathryn Sikkink eds., 1999); *Restructuring World Politics: Transnational Social Movements, Networks, and Norms* (Sanjeev, Khagram, James V. Riker & Kathryn Sikkink eds., 2002).

248 *See generally* Keck & Sikkink, *supra* note 247; *The Power of Human Rights: International Norms and Domestic Change, supra* note 247; *Restructuring World Politics: Transnational Social Movements, Networks, and Norms, supra* note 247.

249 *See generally* Kent, *China, the United Nations, and Human Rights: The Limits of Compliance, supra* note 246; Kent, *The Limits of Compliance: China, International Organizations, and Global Security, supra* note 246. *See also* Margaret M. Pearson, "China in Geneva: Lessons from China's Early Years in the World Trade Organization", *in New Directions in the Study of China's Foreign Policy, supra* note 146, at 242; Samuel S. Kim, "Chinese Foreign Policy Faces Globalization Challenges", *in id.*, at 276; Ann Kent, "China's International Socialization: The Role of International Organizations", 8 *Global Governance* 343 (2002); Ann Kent, "China's Growth Treadmill: Globalization, Human Rights, and International Relations", 3 *Rev. Int'l Aff.* 524 (2004); Doug Guthrie, *China and Globalization: The Social, Economic, and Political Transformation of Chinese Society* (2008); Alastair I. Johnston, *Social States: China in International Institutions, 1980–2000* (2008); Chen Ding, "China's Participation in the International Human Rights Regime: A State Identity Perspective", 2 *Chinese J. Int'l Pol.* 399 (2009).

The second new paradigm is rooted in work by scholars in the field of international relations that is specifically geared toward the evolution of Chinese post-revolutionary identity.[250] Its proponents marshal considerable evidence in support of the constructivist proposition that, insofar as adherence to prevailing international norms is concerned, China is indeed inexorably shedding its revisionist legacy and embracing, even internalizing, mainstream values.[251] There is reason to believe that both paradigms contribute to better understanding of Chinese attitudes toward and use of international law. However, it is equally apparent that neither TLPT[252] nor the responsible stakeholder configuration[253] may provide a sufficiently robust theoretical foundation for effectively addressing the subject across space and time. Barring an unforeseen breakthrough, a multipronged and eclectic approach is needed, combining different approaches in accordance with varying situational dynamics.[254]

III Theory Meets the Sino-British Joint Declaration

In its pre-1997 incarnation, Hong Kong was the product of an asymmetrical armed conflict (the Opium Wars) that politically detached it from China and firmly incorporated it into Britain's sprawling empire.[255] Unlike other colonies, despite some formidable external challenges and internal constraints, Hong Kong has not merely prospered but has evolved into an economic powerhouse,

250 *See generally* Chan, *supra* note 246.

251 *See generally id.*

252 *See* Wang, *supra* note 188; Economy, *supra* note 188; Chan, *supra* note 188; Moore, *supra* note 188; Roda Mushkat, "Economic Development, Environmental Preservation, and International Policy Learning in China: Venturing beyond Transnational Legal Process Theory", *in Rethinking Law and Development: The Chinese Experience* 187 (Guanghua Yu ed., 2013); Roda Mushkat, "Non-Democratic State Learning of Universal Human Rights: Reconfiguring Chinese Patterns", 27 *Temp. Int'l & Comp. L.J.* 63 (2013).

253 *See generally* Deng, *supra* note 181; Zhang, *supra* note 183; Etzioni, *supra* note 180.

254 *See generally* Roda Mushkat, "Dissecting International Legal Compliance: An Unfinished Odyssey", 38 *Denv. J. Int'l L. & Pol'y* 161 (2009); Roda Mushkat, "Compliance with International Environmental Regimes: Chinese Lessons", 34 *Wm. & Mary Envtl. L. & Pol'y Rev.* 493 (2010); Roda Mushkat, "China's Compliance with International Law: What Has Been Learned and the Gaps Remaining", 20 *Pac. Rim L. & Pol'y Rev.* 41 (2011). An example of a fruitful pursuit of multipronged and eclectic research strategies is found in the field of foreign direct investment (FDI). *See* John F. Dunning, *Multinational Enterprises and the Global Economy* 79–115 (2d ed., 2008).

255 *See generally* Steve Y.S. Tsang, *A Modern History of Hong Kong* (2004).

constantly reinventing itself in the process.[256] As its re-absorption into the Chinese body politic loomed large on the horizon, it comfortably consolidated its status as a global metropolis, a sophisticated service center for the Asia-Pacific region and the world.[257]

A number of reasons have been invoked to account for these remarkable achievements, notably the impact of culture/human capital (conducive to productive endeavor) and locational advantages.[258] However, the most compelling, albeit not the sole, explanation may be found in the institutional infrastructure (an open and unfettered economic architecture, robust rule-of-law environment, and neutral and efficient civil service, and a powerful and doggedly-faithful-to-its-mission anti-graft agency) that is the legacy of British administration.[259] This is consistent with the widely held view that the quality of institutions is the principal determinant of long-term economic performance.[260]

The resumption of sovereignty by Communist China, signaled well in advance, was thus contemplated with a sense of trepidation.[261] However, it was mitigated by the fact that the departing colonial power negotiated an internationally binding bilateral agreement, the Sino-British Joint Declaration

---

256 *See generally* Alexander J. Youngson, *Economic Growth and Policy* (1982); Gavin Peebles, *Hong Kong's Economy: An Introductory Macroeconomic Analysis* (1988); Miron Mushkat, *The Economic Future of Hong* 1–16 (1990); *Managing the New Hong Kong Economy* (David Mole ed., 1996); *Economy* (David Faure & Lee Pui-tak eds., 2004); Kui-wai Li, *The Hong Kong Economy: Recovery and Restructuring* (2006).

257 *See generally* David R. Meyer, *Hong Kong as a Global Metropolis* (2000); Stephen W.K. Chiu & Tai-lok Lui, *Hong Kong: Becoming a Chinese Global City* (2009).

258 *See* Mushkat, *supra* note 256, at 5–7.

259 *See id.* at 7–11. *See also* Jacques deLisle, "Political Alchemy, the Long Transition, and the Law's Promised Empire: How July 1, 1997 Matters—and Doesn't Matter—in Hong Kong's Return to China", 18 *U. Pa. J Int'l Econ. L.* 69 (1997); Jacques deLisle & Kevin P. Lane, "Hong Kong's Endgame and the Rule of Law (I): The Struggle over Institutions and Values in the Transition to Chinese Rule", 18 *U. Pa. J. Int'l Econ. L.* 195 (1997); Jacques delisle & Kevin P. Lane, "Hong Kong's Endgame and the Rule of Law (II); The Battle over the 'People' and the Business Community in the Transition to Chinese Rule", 18 *U. Pa. J. Int'l Econ. L.* 811 (1997); John P. Burns, *Government Capacity and the Hong Kong Civil Service* (2004); Ian Scott, *The Public Sector in Hong Kong* (2010).

260 *See generally* Douglass C. North, *Institutions, Institutional Change, and Economic Performance* (1990); Edward L. Glaeser et al., "Do Institutions Cause Growth?", 9 *Journal of Economic Growth* 271–303 (2004); Daron Acemoglu, Simon Johnson & James A. Robinson, "Institutions as a Fundamental Cause of Long-Run Growth", in 1A *Handbook of Economic Growth* 385–472 (Philippe Aghion & Stephen N. Durlauf eds., 2005); Daron Acemoglu & James A. Robinson, *Why Nations Fail: The Origins of Power, Prosperity, and Poverty* (2012).

261 *See* Mushkat, *supra* note 256, at IX–XII.

(formally known as the Joint Declaration of the Government of the United Kingdom of Great Britain and Northern Ireland and the People's Republic of China on the Question of Hong Kong), with the old-new sovereign, providing for the orderly transformation of the territory into a highly autonomous, other than in matters concerning foreign affairs and national security, political unit (Hong Kong Special Administrative Region/HKSAR), with its pre-1997 institutional order remaining largely intact, perhaps even being enhanced in some respects (in accordance with the one country-two systems blueprint).[262] Moreover, the principles embodied in this instrument were faithfully, even if perhaps not in an optimal fashion (the Joint Declaration itself may be regarded as a product of satisficing, rather than superior design),[263] enshrined in a domestic constitutional vehicle, the Hong Kong Basic Law.[264]

Chinese compliance with the letter and spirit of the Joint Declaration is a matter of considerable practical and theoretical interest. The term compliance is overly narrow in this context, because of the inevitably somewhat elastic nature of that document and the absence of reasonably unambiguous monitoring mechanisms.[265] The word implementation may be better suited for these, and other similar circumstances. That is the perspective adopted here but, from whatever angle the issue is addressed, it is noteworthy that the theoretical potential of the subject has been virtually unexploited.[266] The Basic Law, which has greater practical ramifications, has been extensively researched,[267] yet again from a mostly descriptive and evaluative standpoint.[268]

262 *See generally* Roda Mushkat, *One Country, Two International Legal Personalities: The Case of Hong Kong* (1997).

263 *See generally id.*

264 *See generally* Yash Ghai, *Hong Kong's Constitutional Order: The Resumption of Chinese Sovereignty and the Basic Law* (2d ed. 1999).

265 *See generally* Mushkat, *supra* note 262.

266 The following studies contain some theoretical elements Roda Mushkat, "Hong Kong's Exercise of External Autonomy: A Multifaceted Appraisal", 55 *Int'l & Comp. L.Q.* 945–62 (2006); C.L. Lim & Roda Mushkat, "External Affairs", *in Law of the Hong Kong Constitution* 75–114 (Johannes M.M. Chan & C.L. Lim eds., 2011).

267 *See in particular Law of the Hong Kong Constitution, supra* note 266.; Ghai, *supra* note 264; *Hong Kong's Constitutional Debate: Conflict over Interpretation* (Johannes M.M. Chan, H.L. Fu & Yash Ghai eds., 2000); *Hong Kong's Constitutional Debates* (Johannes M.M. Chan & Lison Harris eds., 2005); Albert H.Y. Chen, "Constitutional Adjudication in Post-1997 Hong Kong", 15 *Pac. Rim L. & Pol'y J.* 627–82 (2006); *Interpreting Hong Kong's Basic Law: The Struggle for Coherence* (Hualing Fu, Lison Harris & Simon N.M. Young eds., 2007).

268 The following studies contain substantial theoretical elements Benny Y.T. Tai, "Basic Law, Basic Politics: The Constitutional Game of Hong Kong", 37 *Hong Kong L.J.* 503 (2007); Miron Mushkat & Roda Mushkat, "The Economic Dimension of Hong Kong's Basic Law: An Analytical Overview", 7 *N.Z. J. Pub. & Int'l Law* 273 (2009).

The question of China's steadfast, or otherwise, implementation of the Joint Declaration cannot be unequivocally answered in a comprehensive fashion not just due to the analytical difficulties it poses, but also on account of the wide range of opinions that it is likely to provoke (any of which may thus lack consensual validity). The position taken in this paper is that a distinction may be drawn between the picture on the economic side, where the proverbial glass can be said to be full, and the politico-legal side, in terms of adherence to pre-1997 Western-style/Webberian-type bureaucratic (as distinct from genuinely democratic) constellation and the rule of law, as well as the extent of autonomy granted to local institutions and pace of diffusing heavily concentrated power, where it may legitimately be portrayed as merely half full. However, the objective here is not necessarily to demonstrate the soundness of this proposition. Rather, it is to marshal whatever evidence that may be gleaned from the available material to lend support to the argument that theory building/testing in the international legal domain should be a multifaceted and eclectically conceived endeavor.

This task is pursued in two steps. First, the available theoretical explanations of Chinese strategies vis-à-vis Hong Kong, the majority of which have their origins in disciplines other than law as such (primarily international relations/political science), are surveyed in order to provide a relevant anchor for an analytically more broad-based investigation and impart a sense of continuity. Second, a number of case studies are conducted with a view to establishing that a degree of conceptual breadth, as well as flexibility, is desirable when confronting international legal realities, at least for the foreseeable future. No conclusive or overarching insights are sought regarding China's implementation of the Joint Declaration or the Basic Law.

A *Systematic Explorations of Chinese Policies toward Hong Kong in the Context of the One Country-Two Systems Framework*

As indicated, the literature on the subject is surprisingly modest, given the considerable scope it offers for theoretical illumination, but the writings produced over the years, both before 1997 (yet extending the analytical horizon beyond the end of the colonial era) and subsequently, have certain useful attributes. First, they display sufficient consistency to provide a basis for some fundamental generalizations. Second, they are not characterized by complete uniformity, a notable feature because, even without proceeding further, conceptual diversity may be invoked as a factor casting doubt on the efficacy of mono-causal and unvarying accounts of State behavior, including in situations where international law plays a part.

Consistency is largely the result of the heavy emphasis placed on actor rationality and the strong preference exhibited for State-centric theoretical formulations. Specifically, China is assumed to pursue strategies vis-à-vis Hong Kong that are underpinned by traditional-style utilitarian principles and are the culmination of thorough cost-benefit assessments (i.e., rational-comprehensive planning and execution).[269] In addition, the Chinese decision-making apparatus, the sole element in the equation apparently capable of significantly influencing policy outcomes, is for all intents and purposes treated as a homogeneous entity, not marked by a degree of heterogeneity that might carry meaningful consequences (i.e., unitary actor hypothesis).[270]

The lack of uniformity manifests itself in a certain divergence of opinion regarding the motives underlying China's seemingly methodically crafted and delivered policies. Moreover, the notion that the Chinese State positions itself with respect to Hong Kong in a cohesive fashion, without encountering any resistance from any other sources in the process, is commonly rather than universally held. The point relating to motives is that there is a subtle but nevertheless notable difference between those who, whether explicitly or implicitly, regard policy initiatives as geared toward fulfilling the national interest, however defined,[271] and those who see them, again whether explicitly or implicitly, as a reflection of the power-holders' (in this case the leadership of the Communist Party) narrow utilitarian calculus.[272]

---

269 *See generally* Lau Siu-Kai, "Pragmatic Calculations of National Interest: China's Hong Kong Policy from 1949–1997", *in Chinese Foreign Policy: Pragmatism and Strategic Behavior*, *supra* note 157, at 91–106; Ma Ngok, "The Sino-British Dispute over Hong Kong: A Game Theory Perspective", 37 *Asia Surv.* 738 (1999); Sonny S.H. Lo, *Governing Hong Kong: Legitimacy, Communication and Political Decay* (2002); Sonny S.H. Lo, "The Mainlandization and Recolonization of Hong Kong: The Triumph of Convergence over Divergence with Mainland China", *in The Hong Kong Special Administrative Region in its First Decade* 179 (Joseph Y.S. Cheng ed., 2007); Sonny S.H. Lo, "The Political Culture of Hong Kong and Mainland China: Democratization, Patrimonialism, and Pluralism in the 2007 Chief Executive Election", 29 *Asia Pac. J. Pub. Admin.* 101 (2007); Sonny S.H. Lo, *The Dynamics of Beijing-Hong Kong Relations: A Model for Taiwan?* (2008); Sonny S.H. Lo, *Competing Chinese Political Visions: Hong Kong vs. Beijing on* Democracy (2010).

270 *See generally* Ma, *supra* note 269; Lo, *Governing Hong Kong: Legitimacy, Communication and Political Decay*, *supra* note 269; Lau, *supra* note 269; Lo, "The Mainlandization and Recolonization of Hong Kong: The Triumph of Convergence over Divergence with Mainland China", *supra* note 269.

271 *See, e.g.*, Ma, *supra* note 269; Lau, *supra* note 269.

272 *See, e.g.*, Lo, *Governing Hong Kong: Legitimacy, Communication, and Political Decay*, *supra* note 269; Lo, "The Mainlandization and Recolonization of Hong Kong: The Triumph of

The national interest is seldom delineated with a high degree of precision, and understandably so, but relevant narrative suggests that China stands to greatly benefit over time from re-establishing sovereignty over Hong Kong in a credible and non-disruptive manner as it pursues re-unification and territorial control on several fronts, particularly in the Taiwanese context.[273] By the same token, although this is not a unidirectional relationship, China is estimated to be reaping substantial economic benefits from Hong Kong's semi-autonomous status and unique institutional configuration, a pattern of which its leaders are apparently fully cognizant, and that both constructively drives and prudently constrains strategies vis-à-vis capitalist and liberal Hong Kong.[274]

The Chinese national utility function, if a plausible and workable construct, may be augmented to incorporate the welfare of Hong Kong and its people. This is not an often encountered formal assertion, but such claims would not be without logical foundation, particularly in the post-1997 institutional setting, designed to achieve unity in diversity, or promote oneness of two essentially different economic and politico-legal systems (China and Hong Kong). While this line of reasoning has not featured prominently in the international law and international relations literature, the argument has preliminarily been put forward in relevant contexts[275] and there is no dearth of empirical evidence to tentatively support it.[276]

Convergence over Divergence with Mainland China", *supra* note 269; Lo, "The Political Culture of Hong Kong and Mainland China: Democratization, Patrimonialism, and Pluralism in the 2007 Chief Executive Election", *supra* note 269; Lo, *The Dynamics of Beijing-Hong Kong Relations: A Model for Taiwan?*, *supra* note 269; Lo, *Competing Chinese Political Visions: Hong Kong vs. Beijing on Democracy*, *supra* note 269.

273 *See* Mushkat, *supra* note 256, at 82.

274 *See id.* at 76–81. *See also* Li, *supra* note 256, at 357–428; Yu-wing Sung, *The China-Hong Kong Connection: The Key to China's Open-Door Policy* (1991); Y.C. Jao, "Hong Kong as a Financial Center for Greater China", in *China and the Asia-Pacific Economy* 127–44 (Joseph C.H. Chai, Y.Y. Kueh & Clement A. Tisdell eds., 1997); Yu-wing Sung, *The Emergence of Greater China: The Economic Integration of Mainland China, Taiwan, and Hong Kong* (2005); Y.C. Yao, "Hong Kong as a Financial Center of China and the World", in *China, Hong Kong, and the World* 121–51 (Lok-sang Ho & Robert Ash eds., 2006); Yu-wing Sung, "The Evolving Role of Hong Kong as China's Middleman" in *China, Hong Kong, and the World Economy*, 152–69 (Ho & Ash eds., 2006).

275 *See, e.g.*, Mushkat & Mushkat, "The Political Economy of International Legal Compliance: Pre-1997 Predictions and Post-1997 Realities in Hong Kong", *supra* note 192, at 242–43; Mushkat, *supra* note 28, at 667–68.

276 *See, e.g.*, Mary Swire, "China Emphasizes Support to Hong Kong's Development", Aug. 19, 2011, *available at* http://www.tax-news.com/news/China_Emphasizes_Support_To_Hong_Kongs_Development__51044.html (last visited June 1, 2015).

The question of the implementation of the Sino-British Declaration is addressed indirectly, rather than directly, in this context. The fact is that Hong Kong had evolved into a global metropolis during the colonial era,[277] but it has subsequently not experienced an erosion of this lofty status, enjoyed only by a handful of prominent urban centers such as London, New York, and Singapore.[278] The appropriate term to capture Hong Kong's current international positioning may be a "Chinese global city," which highlights the mainland connection and its certain socio-political implications.[279] The corollary is that Hong Kong has undergone some changes since the British government relinquished control over the territory, and consequently qualifies as a different international player from similarly successful outward-looking metropolises, but the institutional realignment has not been on a scale that might undermine its global aspirations and performance[280] (ergo the Joint Declaration can be said to have been implemented broadly in line with its letter and spirit, because otherwise post-1997 Hong Kong would have been unable to continue to flourish as an international service center).

The less favorable and thus more critical view is that Chinese strategies vis-à-vis Hong Kong are primarily driven by the interests of the Communist Party establishment,[281] succinctly encapsulated in the expression "market-preserving authoritarianism."[282] The implication is that China is pursuing in the liberally constituted capitalist enclave policies whose aim is not merely to ensure adequate overall control consistent with the one country-two systems blueprint embodied in the Sino-British Joint Declaration and the Basic Law, which conveys a vision of perforated sovereignty and institutional distinctiveness, but ones whose purpose is the mainlandization of Hong Kong.[283]

---

277 *See generally* Meyer, *supra* note 257.

278 *See generally id.*; Chiu & Lui, *supra* note 257.

279 *See generally* Chiu & Lui, *id.*

280 *See generally id.*

281 *See generally* Lo, *Governing Hong Kong: Legitimacy, Communication, and Political Decay*, *supra* note 269; Lo, "The Mainlandization and Recolonization of Hong Kong: The Triumph of Convergence over Divergence with Mainland China", *supra* note 269; Lo, "The Political Culture of Hong Kong and Mainland China: Democratization, Patrimonialism, and Pluralism in the 2007 Chief Executive Election", *supra* note 269; Lo, *The Dynamics of Beijing-Hong Kong Relations: A Model for Taiwan?*, *supra* note 269; Lo, *Competing Chinese Political Visions: Hong Kong vs. Beijing on Democracy*, *supra* note 269.

282 *See* Mushkat & Mushkat, *supra* note 102, at 243–44.

283 *See generally* Lo, *Governing Hong Kong: Legitimacy, Communication, and Political Decay*, *supra* note 269; Lo, "The Mainlandization and Recolonization of Hong Kong: The Triumph of Convergence over Divergence with Mainland China", *supra* note 269; Lo,

This entails deliberate measures to align the territory's politico-legal culture and practices with those prevailing in mainland China.[284]

Regime goals should not be automatically equated with ground-level realities because they may not be executed steadfastly and vigorously. Nevertheless, proponents of the mainlandization thesis argue, and present evidence in support of their contentions, that the strategy has proven effective and that Hong Kong is experiencing institutional and socio-psychological decay, which is the product of the gradual convergence of its politico-legal culture and practices with those seen China.[285] This is portrayed as a phenomenon that manifests itself across the entire institutional and socio-psychological spectrum, inevitably including the economic domain, rather than one merely confined to policy realms where fundamental Chinese interests, however defined, are crucially at stake.[286] To the extent that this picture is empirically valid, the principles underlying the Sino-British Joint Declaration and the Basic Law have apparently little bearing on Hong Kong's post-1997 politico-legal evolution.

"The Political Culture of Hong Kong and Mainland China: Democratization, Patrimonialism, and Pluralism in the 2007 Chief Executive Election", *supra* note 269; Lo, *The Dynamics of Beijing-Hong Kong Relations: A Model for Taiwan?, supra* note 269; Lo, *Competing Chinese Political Visions: Hong Kong vs. Beijing on Democracy, supra* note 269.

284 *See generally* Lo, *Governing Hong Kong: Legitimacy, Communication, and Political Decay, supra* note 269; Lo, "The Mainlandization and Recolonization of Hong Kong: The Triumph of Convergence over Divergence with Mainland China", *supra* note 269; Lo, "The Political Culture of Hong Kong and Mainland China: Democratization, Patrimonialism, and Pluralism in the 2007 Chief Executive Election", *supra* note 269; Lo, *The Dynamics of Beijing-Hong Kong Relations: A Model for Taiwan?, supra* note 269; Lo, *Competing Chinese Political Visions: Hong Kong vs. Beijing on Democracy, supra* note 269.

285 *See generally* Lo, *Governing Hong Kong: Legitimacy, Communication, and Political Decay, supra* note 269; Lo, "The Mainlandization and Recolonization of Hong Kong: The Triumph of Convergence over Divergence with Mainland China", *supra* note 269; Lo, "The Political Culture of Hong Kong and Mainland China: Democratization, Patrimonialism, and Pluralism in the 2007 Chief Executive Election", *supra* note 269; Lo, *The Dynamics of Beijing-Hong Kong Relations: A Model for Taiwan?, id.*; Lo, *Competing Chinese Political Visions: Hong Kong vs. Beijing on Democracy, supra* note 269.

286 *See generally* Lo, *Governing Hong Kong: Legitimacy, Communication, and Political Decay, supra* note 269; Lo, "The Mainlandization and Recolonization of Hong Kong: The Triumph of Convergence over Divergence with Mainland China", *supra* note 269; Lo, "The Political Culture of Hong Kong and Mainland China: Democratization, Patrimonialism, and Pluralism in the 2007 Chief Executive Election", *id*; Lo, *The Dynamics of Beijing-Hong Kong Relations: A Model for Taiwan?, supra* note 269; Lo, *Competing Chinese Political Visions: Hong Kong vs. Beijing on Democracy, supra* note 269.

The mainlandization idea is not altogether new. Social scientists endeavoring, in the twilight of the colonial era, to systematically chart the progress of Hong Kong following China's resumption of sovereignty drew broadly similar inferences.[287] The old and new versions have two interesting features. First, both abandon the assumption of institutional homogeneity, or the proposition that the players involved in the process of steering Hong Kong toward its post-1997 future are cohesive entities (i.e., the unitary actor hypothesis). In the old version, there were several groups—in China, Hong Kong, and in the international community—propelling the territory in different directions (continuation of colonial-era trends versus mainlandization).[288] In the new version, the Chinese side (the principal) is depicted as a single player, but the Hong Kong one is described as an amalgam of factions, some allied with the Communist regime (agents) and some opposed to it (Table 1).[289] In both versions, the forces of mainlandization eventually prevail, so the jettisoning of the unitary actor hypothesis has no practical significance.[290]

Second, politico-legal decay ultimately impinges on the economic rules of the game and performance.[291] Harming the Hong Kong goose that lays the golden egg may be a cost that the architects of mainlandization are willing

287 *See generally* de Mesquita, Newman & Rabushka, *Forecasting Political Events: The Future of Hong Kong, supra* note 191; de Mesquita, Newman & Rabushka, *Red Flag over Hong Kong, supra* note 191.

288 *See generally* de Mesquita, Newman & Rabushka, *Forecasting Political Events: The Future of Hong Kong, supra* note 191; de Mesquita, Newman & Rabushka, *Red Flag over Hong Kong, supra* note 191.

289 *See also* Tai, *supra* note 268.

290 *See generally* de Mesquita, Newman & Rabushka, *Forecasting Political Events: The Future of Hong Kong, supra* note 191; de Mesquita, Newman & Rabushka, *Red Flag over Hong Kong, supra* note 191; Lo, *Governing Hong Kong: Legitimacy, Communication, and Political Decay, supra* note 269; Lo, "The Mainlandization and Recolonization of Hong Kong: The Triumph of Convergence over Divergence with Mainland China", *supra* note 269; Lo, "The Political Culture of Hong Kong and Mainland China: Democratization, Patrimonialism, and Pluralism in the 2007 Chief Executive Election", *supra* note 269; Lo, *The Dynamics of Beijing-Hong Kong Relations: A Model for Taiwan?, supra* note 269; Lo, *Competing Chinese Political Visions: Hong Kong vs. Beijing on Democracy, supra* note 269.

291 *See generally* de Mesquita, Newman & Rabushka, *Forecasting Political Events: The Future of Hong Kong, supra* note 191; de Mesquita, Newman & Rabushka, *Red Flag over Hong Kong, supra* note 191; Lo, *Governing Hong Kong: Legitimacy, Communication, and Political Decay, supra* note 269; Lo, "The Mainlandization and Recolonization of Hong Kong: The Triumph of Convergence over Divergence with Mainland China", *supra* note 269; Lo, "The Political Culture of Hong Kong and Mainland China: Democratization, Patrimonialism, and Pluralism in the 2007 Chief Executive Election", *supra* note 269; Lo, *The Dynamics of*

TABLE 1 *Patron-client relations between Beijing and Hong Kong's political actors (Adapted from Lo,* supra *note 269, at 31.)*

Political actors	Nature of loyalties	Patron inducements to clients
Chief Executive (highest-ranking government official; client of Beijing, patron in Hong Kong)	Political loyalty to Beijing	Explicit politico-economic support, economic policies helping Hong Kong
Executive Council (ExCo; cabinet-equivalent) members (core clients)	Political loyalty to patrons Beijing and Chief Executive	Support of the Chief Executive, power, prestige, status
Principal government officials (non-clients)	Loyalty to Beijing and Chief Executive	Policy input, political influence, prestige, status
Leaders of the Democratic Alliance for Betterment of Hong Kong (pro-Beijing party; core clients)	Political Loyalty to Beijing and Chief Executive	Policy input, political influence, prestige, status, and the ability to recommend party members to Chief Executive for political appointments to advisory bodies, Central Policy Unit, and District Councils
Leaders of Liberal Party (business-based; core clients)	Political Loyalty to Beijing and Chief Executive	Policy input, political influence, prestige, status, and the ability to recommend party members to Chief Executive for political appointments to advisory bodies and District Councils
Civil servants (non-clients)	Loyalty to Chief Executive	Opportunities for career advancement, notably to join the Principal Officials Accountability System (top layer of the civil service)
Pro-democracy elite and movement	Countervailing force	Divide-and-rule tactics to split the democratic opposition, politically exclude them from participation in in ExCo, minimize their influence on the eighteen District Councils

to bear. However, if that is not the case, as seems not wholly implausible, it is reasonable to postulate that the players in question have not fully grasped the unintended consequences of the policies they are following. The corollary, in turn, presumably is that the stringent requirements of the rational-comprehensive decision-making model are not completely satisfied and that an element, even if modest, of muddling through is involved.

Two additional, theoretically relevant observations are appropriate. As indicated, there is some empirical support for the seemingly conflicting benevolent (merely in the domestic or China-wide sense of the term)/national interest-driven and the self-centered/mainlandization-inspired actor perspectives. They diverge analytically, but this does not necessarily mean that in practice one has to be embraced and the other discarded. The inherent tension notwithstanding, both may fruitfully be employed to shed light on issues in the fields of international law and international relations. Such a combination may yield superior results to mono-causal approaches.

The second conceptually noteworthy point is that whatever explanatory vehicle is adopted, it is unlikely to prove entirely effective over time. The differences between the old and new versions of the mainlandization paradigm are telling in this respect. The pre-1997 forecasters chose to emphasize factional conflict (between conservative and pro-reform cadres) on the Chinese side in relation to Hong Kong.[292] By contrast, in recent work, China is for all intents and purposes treated as a homogeneous entity, at least in this particular context.[293] The implication is that no theoretical formulation is readily applicable in all circumstances and that, unless some genuinely comprehensive and robust model emerges, addressing complex problems in an eclectic fashion is a sensible research strategy. Further such insights may be derived by examining a number of specific Chinese policy initiatives in Hong Kong that have ramifications for the implementation of the Sino-British Joint Declaration.

Beijing-Hong Kong Relations: A Model for Taiwan?, *supra* note 269; Lo, *Competing Chinese Political Visions: Hong Kong vs. Beijing on Democracy*, *supra* note 269.

292 *See generally* de Mesquita, Newman & Rabushka, *Forecasting Political Events: The Future of Hong Kong*, *supra* note 191; de Mesquita, Newman & Rabushka, *Red Flag over Hong Kong*, *supra* note 191.

293 *See generally* Lo, *Governing Hong Kong: Legitimacy, Communication, and Political Decay*, *supra* note 269; Lo, "The Mainlandization and Recolonization of Hong Kong: The Triumph of Convergence over Divergence with Mainland China", *supra* note 269; Lo, "The Political Culture of Hong Kong and Mainland China: Democratization, Patrimonialism, and Pluralism in the 2007 Chief Executive Election", *supra* note 269; Lo, *The Dynamics of Beijing-Hong Kong Relations: A Model for Taiwan?*, *supra* note 269; Lo, *Competing Chinese Political Visions: Hong Kong vs. Beijing on Democracy*, *supra* note 269.

B *Some Informative Cases*

The concept of national (or, alternatively, public) interest is fraught with considerable difficulties, as long and methodically demonstrated in the literature on public regulation.[294] Coupling it with the notion of mainlandization, or self-interest, renders it less problematic but not unassailable. The latter is in some respects akin to inflation in that pace, or the rate of change, and pervasiveness need to be specified to make it meaningful. Mainlandization, like inflation, may vary in pace (creeping, galloping, or hyper) and pervasiveness (limited or widespread). By the same token, it may face not headwinds (similar to deflationary ones that may be present in an inflationary environment, culminating in stagflation), rather than merely tailwinds. An example of the former may be the Hong Kongization or westernization of China, notably its legal system,[295] which may potentially function as a countervailing force.

As matters stand, these issues have not been thoroughly dealt with in the writings on Hong Kong's mainlandization. The picture regarding pace, pervasiveness, and possible offsetting influences is not entirely clear. Nevertheless, as pointed out, there is sufficient empirical evidence to suggest that a rationalist perspective, which somehow blends the national interest and mainlandization theses, provides the most credible framework, or at least starting point, for exploring the theoretical underpinnings of the dynamics of the implementation of the Sino-British Joint Declaration. However, it is also apparent that this analytical foundation is incomplete and that the decade and a half that has elapsed since decolonization offers additional valuable conceptual lessons.

Scholarly inquiry in the field of law is commonly perceived as a bottom-up exercise, entailing inductive progression from fact to theory, rather than a top-down undertaking, involving deductive reasoning characterized by movement from theory to fact.[296] Yet, in practice, most international legal theory building/testing in recent years has deviated from this pattern. Theoretical propositions have typically been advanced first and examples have subsequently been furnished to support them. The approach adopted here is consistent with the

294 *See Barry* M. Mitnick, *The Political Economy of Regulation: Creating, Designing, and Removing Regulatory Forms* 91–96 (1980). *See also* Miron Mushkat & Roda Mushkat, "The Political Economy of Hong Kong's 'Open Skies' Legal Regime: An Empirical and Theoretical Exploration", 10 *San Diego Int'l L.J.* 381 (2009).

295 *See generally* Peerenboom, *supra* note 179; Randall P. Peerenboom, *China's Long March toward Rule of Law* (2002); Peter T.Y. Cheung, "Who Is Influencing Whom? Exploring the Influence of Hong Kong on Politics and Governance in China", 51 *Asian Surv.* 713 (2011).

296 *See* Ian Dobinson & Francis Johns, "Qualitative Legal Research", *in Research Methods for Law* 16, 32 (Mike McConville & Winh Hong-chui eds., 2007).

traditional view. Three cases—featuring attempts to adopt national security legislation, introduce national/patriotic education, and circumscribe judicial power in Hong Kong—are analyzed without any preconceptions in order to draw further inferences regarding the implementation of international law.

1 National Security Legislation

The measures proposed, in the midst of an acute public health crisis in 2003, to dramatically enhance the internal security element of the constitutional order may have amounted to a significant departure from "the benign [institutional] practices prevailing before the transfer of sovereignty and during the initial phase of the transition to Chinese 'rule'"[297] and, by implication, from the principles embodied in the Sino-British Joint Declaration. Socio-legal scholars portrayed the national security legislation drafted by the Hong Kong government, apparently at behest of the central authorities in Beijing, with a view to be passed under Article 23 of the Basic Law, as an inherently dangerous policy mechanism incorporating into the constitutional façade "in an unpalatable form the crimes of subversion and secession, and grant[ing] the government extensive powers to ban non-mainstream groups."[298] They asserted that "[i]t has the potential, in the present climate, to pave the way for actions inconsistent with fundamental principles of human rights, and hence arguably the Basic Law as originally conceived."[299] Media commentators provided more poignant and scathing assessments:

> Taking advantage of preoccupation in Hong Kong with the SARS epidemic, the territory's pro-Beijing government has been pushing along a noxious national security bill that would leave the territory vulnerable to the sort of political repression common on the Communist mainland....
>
> The measure, known as Article 23, deals with reason, sedition, subversion, and the theft of [S]tate secrets, and includes provisions that would enable the Hong Kong government to crack down on organizations

297 Miron Mushkat & Roda Mushkat, "The Political Economy of the Constitutional Conflict in Hong Kong", 11 *Tilburg Foreign L. Rev.* 756, 757 (2003). *See also National Security and Fundamental Freedoms: Hong Kong's Article 23 under Scrutiny* (Fu Hualing, Carole J. Petersen & Simon N.M. Young eds., 2005).

298 Mushkat & Mushkat, *supra* note 297, at 757. *See also National Security and Fundamental Freedoms: Hong Kong's Article 23 under Scrutiny*, *supra* note 297.

299 Mushkat & Mushkat, *supra* note 297, at 757. *See also National Security and Fundamental Freedoms: Hong Kong's Article 23 under Scrutiny*, *supra* note 297.

> deemed to be linked to any that are banned in China, such as Falun Gong. That would seriously erode the autonomy that the former British colony was promised when it came under China's rule six years ago under the formula of "one country-two systems."
>
> Some governments ... have already protested, as have many human rights organizations, prompting predictable squawks from Beijing against meddling in its internal affairs. That can hardly be said of opponents in Hong Kong, who turned out in the tens of thousands on the 14th anniversary of the Tiananmen Square uprising, and now plan an even larger protest against Article 23 for July 1, the anniversary of the turnover of Hong Kong. The resistance draws on an expanding coalition of human rights groups, independent politicians, trade unions, journalists, academics, and students. They have correctly identified the bill as a challenge to their autonomy and fundamental freedoms, and as an attempt to impose China's arbitrary legal system on Hong Kong through the back door.
>
> China argues that Article 23 is not much different from the laws of some democratic [S]tates. That may be so, but democratic societies have checks and balances that China and other Communist [S]tates do not; in the latter, national security laws have long been a primary tool for silencing critics and subverting freedoms. The fate of Falun Gong is but one example. Another is SARS: under the new law, the dogged newspapers of Hong Kong might have been forced into the same disgraceful and dangerous silence as the national press.
>
> China's rulers also portrayed Article 23 as a critical test of national sovereignty. It is really an assault on the freedoms they promised to respect in Hong Kong for 50 years.[300]

Interestingly, and perhaps unexpectedly, given the power asymmetries, the public outcry and protest proved sufficiently effective to prompt the authorities to shelve the proposed legislation.[301] Equally noteworthy is the fact that the experience seems to have turned out to be so sobering that, during the decade or so that has elapsed since this profoundly disruptive episode, no serious efforts have been made to float the idea again, let alone to revive it in a form approximating its previous shape, in terms of scope and content. The corollary

---

300 Mushkat & Mushkat, *supra* note 297, at 757–58.

301 *See* Carole J. Petersen, "Hong Kong's Spring of Discontent: The Rise and Fall of the National Security Bill in 2003" in *National Security and Fundamental Freedoms: Hong Kong's Article 23 under Scrutiny*, *supra* note 297, 13–62, at 46–53.

is that the pro-Beijing principal-agent network in Hong Kong (Table 1) is not confident of its ability to prevail, without incurring heavy costs, on this front.

2 National/Patriotic Education

That has not been the sole, mainlandization-inspired case of its type. In 2012, in somewhat but not altogether different circumstances (no debilitating public health threats but possibly even greater political polarization between the pro-status quo/pro-authoritarian rule and pro-change/pro-democracy forces), the same institutional network, led by another Chief Executive with strong ties to the Communist Party establishment, embarked on a controversial and unpopular policy initiative to introduce or substantially deepen national education in Hong Kong.[302] The adjective "national" implies that the program extends beyond civic parameters, as conventionally understood, yet it falls short of conveying the full essence of intense "patriotic" indoctrination as long practiced on the mainland.[303]

Throughout the colonial era and even beyond, civic education in Hong Kong had been characterized by considerable depoliticization and distinctly modest focus on the nation.[304] Indeed, this had been the product of guidance emanating from top-echelons of the educational bureaucracy—notably in the form of regulations, which until 1990 prohibited the discussion of political issues in school—readily complied with by teachers many of whom refrained from addressing civic matters in any shape by effectively disregarding the narrowly specified, restrictive, and undemanding top-down directions in this respect.[305] The slightly less neutral approach adopted in 1985, following the signing of the Sino-British Joint Declaration, and immediately before and shortly after the transfer of sovereignty in 1997, has resulted in relatively limited adjustments to the curriculum and its implementation.[306]

---

302 *See generally* "Patriot Game: Teaching Hong Kongers How to be Patriotic Can Cut Both Ways", *The Economist*, Aug. 25, 2012, *available at* http://www.economist.com/node/21560908 (last visited June 1, 2015).

303 *See generally* Zhao, *A Nation-State by Construction: Dynamics of Modern Chinese Nationalism, supra* note 157, at 218–31; Gregory P. Fairbrother, *Toward Critical Patriotism: Student Resistance to Political Education in Hong Kong and China* (2003); Susan L. Shirk, *China: Fragile Superpower* 62, 164–66 (2007) Zheng Wang, "National Humiliation, History Education, and the Politics of Historical Memory: Patriotic Education Campaign in China", 52 *Int'l Stud. Q.* 783–866 (2008).

304 *See* Fairbrother, *supra* note 303, at 36–37.

305 *See id.* at 53.

306 *See id.* at 40–51.

By contrast, since the founding of the People's Republic of China, "schools, among other institutions, have been called upon to shape citizens' knowledge, attitudes, and behavior toward society, the nation, and the [S]tate through political education."[307] Such persistent attempts "to emphasize, reform, and strengthen the role of the school in the formation of students" political attitudes have been made in the name of ideological-political education (*sixiang zhengzhi jiaoyu*), moral education (*daode jiaoyu* or *deyu*), and most explicitly patriotic education (*aiguozhui jiaoyu*).[308]

The content of the mainland's brand of civic education has varied over time, but certain themes have nevertheless remained in the spotlight.[309] They have included class structure, communism, economic issues, international questions, labor conditions, morals, nation/nationalism, service to the people/masses, and world/societal history.[310] Following the post-1978 shift to reform, some topics have been relegated to the periphery, without necessarily being completely discarded (e.g., revolutionary spirit), and new ones have emerged (e.g., rule of law and scientific progress).[311] However, patriotic education has not been materially downgraded.[312]

Scholarly assessments of this sustained endeavor have generally been unfavorable. Academic observers have noted that, "[w]hen the content...was compared with nationalism in other countries, it inevitably appeared exceedingly thin."[313] For example, "[t]here was little to compare...with the substance of American nationalism and its reverence for George Washington, Abram Lincoln, the Declaration of Independence, the Constitution, the Bill of Rights, and the Pledge of Allegiance."[314] Nor was there "a counterpart to the Japanese feelings for the emperor and British pride in common law and the Parliament."[315] Chinese-style patriotic education has consequently been portrayed as a mechanistic strategy geared toward producing "a politicized and particularistic nationalism, pragmatically tailored to the interest of

307 *Id.* at 53.

308 *Id.* at 53.

309 *See id.* at 54–73.

310 *See id.* at 55, 60, 67.

311 *See id.* at 60, 67.

312 *See id.* at 60–73; Zhao, *A Nation-State by Construction: Dynamics of Modern Chinese Nationalism, supra* note 157, at 218–31; Shirk, *supra* note 303, at 62, 164–66; Wang, *supra* note 303.

313 Zhao, *A Nation-State by Construction: Dynamics of Modern Chinese Nationalism, supra* note 157, at 230.

314 *Id.* at 230.

315 *Id.* at 230.

the ruling elite."[316] Ultimately, the harsh evaluation provided has been that by reducing nationalism to merely the sum of a party's policy preferences, the Chinese people have been deprived of "an inspired version of nationalism based on shared ideas and worthy principles.... Although the Chinese had one of the world greatest traditional civilizations, and they still have a tenaciously strong living culture of day-to-day customs and attitudes, they do not have anything resembling a shared body of ideals, principles, and values which could serve as a basis for the myths and symbols of worthy nationalism."[317]

Given this backdrop, the recent attempt to broaden and deepen national education in Hong Kong has generated a backlash similar in scope and vehemence to the one witnessed a decade earlier, in the wake of efforts to significantly tighten internal security regulations.[318] And, like on the earlier occasion, the pro-Beijing patron-client network in the territory has staged an unceremonious retreat in the face of strong grassroots pressures, effectively shelving the hastily promoted plan.[319] It should be emphasized that this affair may have had ramifications extending beyond the educational domain. The point is that successful implementation of mainland-type patriotic education, even in diluted form, could have fostered a psychological climate conducive to the alignment, whether partial or far-reaching, of Hong Kong's politico-legal institutions with those of China.

This decade-old pattern of action and reaction gives rise to four crucial theoretical observations. First, domestic political constellations and dynamics should not be considered the exclusive preserve of social scientists. It is apparent that the implementation of international law often hinges on how these factors are configured. International legal scholars cannot overlook them because such oversimplification may yield incomplete and unsatisfactory analytical accounts. The unitary actor hypothesis is a parsimonious and thus convenient conceptual tool, but one whose applicability is typically constrained, and meaningfully so, by institutional heterogeneity. This is inevitably the case in open and near-open societies, yet both hard and soft authoritarian regimes are also susceptible to factionalism and fragmentation.

316 *Id.* at 230.

317 Lucian W. Pye, "After the Collapse of Communism: The Challenge of Chinese Nationalism and Pragmatism", *in The Study of Modern China* 29, 35 (Eberhard Sandshneider ed., 1999).

318 *See* "Patriot Game: Teaching Hong Kongers How to be Patriotic Can Cut Both Ways", *supra* note 303.

319 *See id.*; "National Education a Lesson Learned for the HK Government", Asia Pacific News, *available at* http://www.channelnewsasia.com/stories/eastasia/view/1235425/1/.html (last visited Nov. 30, 2013).

In the specific Hong Kong context, it is clear that the amorphous pro-democracy movement, the "guardian" of the spirit of the Sino-British Joint Declaration and the Basic Law, is not merely an organizational channel for symbolic expression, but a societal force capable of influencing policy outcomes at critical junctures. By the same token, it is evident that the pro-Beijing patron-client network displays certain structural weaknesses that may impede its effectiveness. It is a traditional-style Chinese entity that is loosely connected and based as much on exchange relationships as on an unwavering commitment to an ideological ethos or some fundamental values. An illustration of its fragility was seen during the battle for and against national security legislation, when the Democratic Alliance for the Betterment of Hong Kong, a large and tactically focused political grouping normally content to toe the central and local government line (Table 1), opportunistically broke ranks with its partners upon realizing that support for the proposed measures could prove electorally costly.[320]

Second, the 2003 and 2012 Hong Kong experience highlights the drawbacks of the rational-comprehensive decision-making model as a vehicle for dissecting the implementation of international and constitutional law. It is evident that the powers that be in Beijing and their key supporters in the territory have consistently and seriously misread the mood in Hong Kong, the disruptive power of the opposition, and their own ability to handle intense political conflict in an intricate institutional setting where threats to prosperity and stability may have far-reaching consequences. The corollary is that it may often be necessary to venture beyond the realm of microeconomic-type narrow rationality and seek insights from academic disciplines that address individual and collective behavior from a cognitive perspective. This may require extending the theoretical search further than the basic satisficing construct—which places a heavy emphasis on constraints stemming from problems encountered in gathering, processing, and evaluating substantial quantities of information—and borrow from sources such as behavioral economics and cognitive psychology/science, where scholarly attention has shifted from mechanical difficulties in attaining decisional efficiency to persistent distortions resulting from the way issues are framed.[321] The blending of strict rationalist and such approaches (prospect theory and related formulations) is attracting growing interest in

---

320 *See* Petersen, *supra* note 301, at 53.

321 *See generally* Lucy F. Ackert and Richard Deaves, *Behavioral Finance: Psychology, Decision Making, and Markets* (2010); Jonathan Bendor, *Bounded Rationality and Politics* (2010); Edward Cartwright, *Behavioral Economics* (2011); Daniel Kahneman, *Thinking, Fast and Slow* (2011).

the field of international relations (mostly under the rubric of poliheuristic analysis),[322] but it has not made any significant inroads into the parallel sphere of international law.

Departures from rationality may not be a product of cognitive framing alone. The disorganized and misaligned pro-Beijing patron-client network may be a contributing factor. How else can one explain the decision to make a highly controversial book, entitled "The China Model," the pivot of the revamped national education curriculum?[323] This is a work whose "sections on modern history are a crude rehash of mainland propaganda, omitting any mention of the Cultural Revolution or the Tiananmen Square protests, and extolling the virtues of one-party rule: 'multiparty politics could victimize people, whereas concentrated political power creates a selfless government and stable society.'"[324] That is so out of tune with the mindset of the Hong Kong global metropolis, as well as the spirit of the Sino-British Joint Declaration and the Basic Law, that a strategic blunder of such magnitude must be attributed to structural incoherence that bears the hallmarks of the garbage-can model of policy making.

Third, the two ill-fated episodes of derailed mainlandization expose key limitations of the widely embraced, to the exclusion of alternative analytical accounts, transnational legal process theory. TLPT can be said to be underpinned by an inherently optimistic outlook, featuring a process in the course of which members of the international community interact with a host of benevolent socialization agents and internalize valuable norms conducive to the maintenance of a liberal world order. The relationship between Beijing and its principal Hong Kong allies with the vociferous pro-democracy movement,

---

322 *See generally* Steve Chan, "Judgment Heuristics and Prospect Theory: Practical Implications for Relations Across the Taiwan Straits", 3 *J.E. Asia Stud.* 55 (2003); Patrick James & Enyu Zhang, "Chinese Choices: A Poliheuristic Analysis of Foreign Policy Crises, 1950–1996", 1 *Foreign Pol'y Analysis* 31 (2005); Min Ye, "Poliheuristic Theory, Bargaining and Crisis Decision Making", 3 *Foreign Pol'y Analysis* 317 (2007); *Integrating Cognitive and Rational Theories of Foreign Policy Decision Making* (Alex Mintz ed., 2002); Nathan A. Feezer, *Chinese Crisis Decision Making: Using a Cybernetic Approach to Interpret and Predict Beijing's Behavior under Stress* (2010); Alex Mintz & Karl DeRouen, *Understanding Foreign Policy Decision Making* (2010); Nukhet A. Sandal *et al.*, "Poliheuristic Theory and Crisis Decision Making: A Comparative Analysis of Turkey with China", 44 *Canadian Journal of Political Science* 27–57 (2011); Kai He, *Decision Making during Crises: Prospect Theory and China's Foreign Policy Making after the Cold War* (2012).

323 *See* "Patriot Game: Teaching Hong Kongers How to be Patriotic Can Cut Both Ways", *supra* note 303.

324 *See id.*

amply and vividly observed in 2003 and 2012, does not conform to this pattern. It may more accurately be portrayed as an unproductive game of mistrust that inevitably culminates in breakdown and paralysis.[325] Little normative learning is taking place. Rather, the game seems to exhibit strong path dependence.

Fourth, the institutional architecture and operational drift, particularly facets that impinge on organizational capacity, do matter. This is not an endorsement of the managerial school, which primarily focuses on technical impediments to compliance with international law. It is evident that the fragmented pro-Beijing patron-client network, alienated from large segments of Hong Kong society, may face governance challenges. From an international legal and constitutional perspective, this may prove to be both a blessing and a curse. On the positive side, mainlandization of the politico-legal façade may encounter considerable headwinds. On the negative side, as shown elsewhere, initiatives consistent with the spirit of the Sino-British Joint Declaration and the Basic Law may not be implemented in a timely fashion or may remain frozen indefinitely.[326]

3 Curtailing Judicial Authority in Hong Kong

Periodic efforts to circumscribe judicial power in Hong Kong are another relevant dimension of the mainlandization strategy selectively explored here for purposes of partial conceptual illumination. These range from symbolic signaling to practical measures, whether modest or substantial in scope. An example of a symbolic but not insignificant gesture is a perplexing statement by Elsie Leung, a former Hong Kong Secretary for Justice, currently a Vice-Chairman of Beijing's Committee on the Basic Law and (for ideological or opportunistic reasons) a high-profile member of the regime's patron-client network, that Hong Kong judges do not properly grasp the nature of the relationship between the territory and China, followed by an equally perplexing stipulation that the one country-two systems blueprint, at the heart of the Sino-British Joint Declaration and the Basic Law, may not apply fully to Hong Kong's judiciary.[327]

A modest practical case in point is the non-extension beyond the official retirement age, a common procedure, of the tenure of Kemal Bokhari, a permanent judge of the Court of Final Appeal (CFA) and by far its most liberal

---

325 *See* Mushkat & Mushkat, *supra* note 297, at 766–80.

326 *See generally* Mushkat, *supra* note 266.

327 *See* "Hands Off Hong Kong's Judiciary", *Wall Street Asia*, Nov. 13, 2012, *available at* http://online.wsj.com/news/articles/SB10001424127887323894704578114352833047358 (last visited June 1, 2015).

member.[328] Justice Bokhari's parting shot, directed at Leung, was that clouds heralding a storm of unprecedented ferocity are gathering over the rule of law in Hong Kong.[329] His premature departure, by established standards, may suggest that, in the absence of countervailing trends, mainlandization may indeed chip away at judicial autonomy, a key pillar of the post-1997 politico-legal order rooted in the Sino-British Joint Declaration and the Basic Law.

A potentially more serious practical challenge to the rule of law is the tendency, infrequent but increasing, of the post-1997 Hong Kong government and the network in which it is embedded, operating in the shadow of its mainland patrons, to invoke in concrete terms, at politically intricate junctures, the specter of curtailing the authority of the CFA by seeking an interpretation of the Basic Law by the Standing Committee of China's National People's Congress (NPCSC).[330] This is not just a hypothetical scenario, but a course of action that has actually been followed.[331] The pattern may clearly be observed at the time

---

328 *See* Candy Chan, "Parting Shots", *The Standard*, Oct. 25, 2013, *available at* http://www.thestandard.com.hk/news_detail.asp?pp_cat=30&art_id=127672&sid=38012628&con_type=3 (last visited June 1, 2015).

329 *See id.*

330 *See generally Hong Kong's Constitutional Debate: Conflict over Interpretation*, *supra* note 267; Chen, *supra* note 267; Albert H.Y. Chen, "Constitutional Crisis in Hong Kong: Congressional Supremacy and Judicial Review", 33 *Int'l Law.* 1025 (1999); Po Jen Yap, "Interpreting the Basic Law and the Adjudication of Politically Sensitive Questions", 6 *Chinese J. Int'l L.* 543 (2007); Cora Chan, "Deference and the Separation of Powers: An Assessment of the Court's Constitutional and Institutional Competences", 41 *Hong Kong L.J.* 7 (2011); Todd Schneider, "David v. Goliath: The Hong Kong Courts and China's National People's Standing Committee", 20 *Berkeley J. Int'l L.* 575 (2012); Jie Cheng, "The Story of a New Policy", *available at* http://www.hkjournal.org/archive/2009_fall/1.htm (last visited Nov. 30, 2013); Danny Gittings, "Hong Kong's Courts Are Learning to Live with China", *available at* http://www.hkjournal.org/archive/2010_fall/2.htm (last visited Nov. 30, 2013); Hong Kong Bar Association, "The Necessity for Separate Legal Representation Arising from the Secretary for Justice's Request to the Court of Final Appeal on the Right of Abode of Children Born in Hong Kong to Non-Hong Kong Residents from Mainland China", Feb. 14, 2013, *available at* http://www.hkba.org/whatsnew/press-release/20130214-%20SJ%27s%20request%20for%20NPCSC%20interpretation%20in%20FDH%20case%20(E).pdf (last visited June 1, 2015); Thomas E. Kellogg, "Excessive Deference or Strategic Retreat? The Impact of Basic Article 158", *available at* http://www.hkjournal.org/archive/2008_spring/5.htm (last visited Nov. 30, 2013); Eddie Luk & Mary A. Benitez, "'Ask Beijing' Call Dismays Lawyers", *The Standard*, Dec. 14, 2013, *available at* http://www.thestandard.com.hk/news_detail.asp?art_id=129302&con_type=3 (last visited June 1, 2015).

331 *See* Cheng, *id.*

of writing.[332] The CFA itself may have recently complicated matters when a slim majority of the members involved decided, for the first time in the court's history, to ask for an authoritative mainland interpretation of the Basic Law in the case of *Democratic Republic of the Congo and Others v.* FG *Hemisphere Associates* LLC.[333]

The theoretical significance of encroachments on judicial autonomy lies in the relatively muted criticism and resistance, largely confined to academic and legal circles, they have provoked. The pro-Beijing patron-client network has consequently enjoyed a greater room for maneuver on this front than in the broader politico-legal domain. Importantly, this reflects the fact that, in this particular realm, the interests of the network and the public-at-large have roughly coincided at key points in time. The term "interests" is employed deliberately in this context because it implies that this is not, as often suggested,[334] merely an ideological conflict, revolving about the pace and scope of democratization,

---

332 *See generally* Hong Kong Bar Association, *supra* note 330; Luk & Benitez, *supra* note 330. *See also*, for an interim assessment, Anita Chiu & Patsy Moy, "Foreign Helpers' Plea for Permanent Residency Fails", Mar. 26, 2013, *available at* http://www.scmp.com/news/hong-kong/article/1199312/hong-kongs-top-court-rejects-domestic-helpers-appeal-permanent (last visited June 1, 2015); "The Lesson of Hong Kong's Maids", Mar. 26, 2013, Wall Street Journal Asia, *available at* http://online.wsj.com/news/articles/SB10001424127887324789504578382100145610908 (last visited Nov. 30, 2013).

333 *See generally* Cora Chan, "Reconceptualizing the Relationship between the Mainland Chinese Legal System and the Hong Kong Legal System", 6 *Asian J. Comp. L.* 1 (2011); Anne Butler, "Democratic Republic of the Congo v. FG Hemisphere Associates LLC: Hong Kong Conforms with China by Repudiating the Common Law Commercial Exception to Sovereign Immunity", 20 *Tul. J. Int'l & Comp. L.* 469 (2012); Cora Chan, "Reassessing the Boundaries of Judicial Autonomy in Hong Kong", 4 *Pub. L.* 601 (2012); Kathryn Crossley, "Case Analysis: Democratic Republic of the Congo and Ors v FG Hemisphere Associates LLC", June 17, 2011, *available at* http://asia.legalbusinessonline.com/news/analysis/106870/details.aspx (last visited Nov. 30, 2013); Paul Li & Nigel Sherman, "Controversial Ruling Sends Warning on Doing Business with Governments", Aug. 16, 2011, *available at* http://www.internationallawoffice.com/newsletters/detail.aspx?g=f075b515-81a0-4faa-ba61-404acd4ef6a9&redir=1 (last visited June 1, 2015). Anselmo Reyes, "On Two Supposed Immunity Problems with Hong Kong", Jan. 28, 2013, *available at* http://cjicl.org.uk/2013/01/28/on-two-supposed-immunity-problems-with-hong-kong-arbitration-awards-2/ (last visited June 1, 2015); Wu Chien-huei, "One Country Two State Immunity Doctrines: A Pluralistic Depiction of the Congo Case", Feb. 24, 2012, *available at* http://www.asiansil.org/publications/YSW%202012_14.pdf (last visited June 1, 2015).

334 *See generally* Lo, *Competing Chinese Political Visions: Hong Kong versus Beijing on Democracy*, *supra* note 269.

but one where parochial, rationalist-style factors are at play, even on the side perceived as uncompromisingly progressive.

The notion of a distinct Hong Kong identity is not without empirical foundation.[335] There is also some evidence, ranging from anecdotal to systematically derived, that local residents generally harbor negative attitudes toward mainlanders and people from several neighboring countries from which domestic helpers hail.[336] Any policy initiative to prevent them from becoming entrenched in the territory (e.g., by being granted the right of abode), is thus likely to be favorably received at grassroots level, rather than widely opposed, whatever the long-term implications for the rule of law.

The subdued reaction of the business community to the CFA decision in the case of *Democratic Republic of the Congo and Others v. FG Hemisphere Associates LLC* is more difficult to fathom. The implication is that, because sovereign immunity applies to States even when they are contracting in a purely commercial capacity, parties conducting business with governments and State-owned companies (SOEs) in the global Hong Kong metropolis may face challenges in enforcing judgments or arbitral awards in the territory, undermining its ability to perform international intermediation functions and reputation for offering a level playing field.[337]

The low-key response by the interests most palpably affected may be due to the judicial, as distinct from policy, context. The deeply-ingrained preference for restraint, firm ties to the bureaucratic establishment, and a view, realistic or otherwise, that the decision may not in practice materially impinge on commercial transactions may have also played a role in the process. What matters here are not the specific motives, but the fact that, unlike in other similar

335 *See generally* Gordon Mathews, Erik K.W. Ma & Tai-lok Lui, *Hong Kong, China: Learning to Belong to a Nation* (2008).

336 *See generally* Carol Jones, "Looking North: Hong Kong Images of Mainland Law and Order", 3 *Taiwan in Comp. Persp.* 99 (2011); Yu Hui Yan, "Imagination of the Self and the Other: Inter-Ethnic Attitudes between Filipino Domestic Helpers and their Employers", 5 *Hong Kong Anthropologist* 1 (2011); Te-ping Chen, "Hong Kong's 'Embarrassing' Racial Attitudes", Mar. 23, 2012, *available at* http://blogs.wsj.com/chinarealtime/2012/03/23/hong-kong%E2%80%99s-%E2%80%98embarrassing%E2%80%99-racial-attitudes/ (last visited Nov. 30, 2013); Mary K. Magistad, "Growing Rift between Hong Kong and Mainland China", Feb. 21, 2012, *available at* http://www.theworld.org/2012/02/hong-kong-mainland-china-rift/ (last visited Nov. 30, 2013).

337 *See generally* Chan, "Reconceptualizing the Relationship between the Mainland Chinese Legal System and the Hong Kong Legal System", *supra* note 332; Butler, *supra* note 332; Chan, "Reassessing the Boundaries of Judicial Autonomy in Hong Kong", *supra* note 332; Crossley, *supra* note 332; Reyes, *supra* note 332; Wu, *supra* note 332.

circumstances, meaningful conflict has not materialized. The corollary is that, in this particular case, the unitary actor hypothesis is not entirely irrelevant. More broadly speaking, the effectiveness of explanatory schemes may be situation dependent, meaning that an eclectic approach to theory construction may be called for and a "one-size-fits-all" type of a philosophy is unlikely to prove analytically fruitful.

IV Conclusion

The international legal space has undergone a fast-paced and marked analytical expansion in the past five decades or so. Multiple new conceptual schemes have emerged to account for and evaluate phenomena within its confines. The initial impetus for renewal originated within the field and progress has been sustained by momentum generated by students of international law and perhaps even stronger intellectual influences emanating from neighboring disciplines, notably international relations.

However, the pattern that has crystallized may be likened to the proverbial double-sided coin. On the one hand, we are blessed with a much deeper and a more nuanced perspective on international legal behavior, coupled with a better appreciation of the limitations of individual schools of thought and a greater willingness to challenge conventional wisdom. On the other hand, the various paradigms compete fiercely with each other and are typically regarded by proponents as all-encompassing. Synergistic relationships are conspicuous by their absence and scholars go to great lengths to assert the overwhelming superiority of their favorite constructs.

This attitude manifests itself across the entire theoretical spectrum. For instance, the authors of a highly sophisticated general rationalist treatise proceed to systematically rule out the validity of alternative explanatory models.[338] Similarly, in a fundamentally different segment of the international legal space, a writer who has examined Chinese compliance with international law, broadly and over time, is not content to establish the partial validity of transnational legal theory process theory, but for all intents and purposes deems it necessary

338 Jack L. Goldsmith & Eric A. Posner, *The Limitations of International Law* 4–10, 14–17 (2005). The manifold direct and indirect refutations of the arguments advanced in this book are equally one-sided. A recent example is Jens D. Ohlin, "Nash Equilibrium and International Law", 23 *Eur. J. Int'l L.* 915 (2012).

to discard the possibility that several other—less, more, or as important—forces might be at work in such a dynamic and intricate setting.[339]

The position taken in this paper is that, at the current juncture, no analytical framework is sufficiently robust to serve as a conceptual pivot in all circumstances and that a multi-pronged research strategy needs to be adopted. Moreover, the elements should not remain static, but vary from one situation to another, rendering the theoretical exploration of international law an eclectic undertaking, a realistic and not uncommon feature of scientific inquiry.[340] The implementation of the Sino-British Declaration, in a highly complex and fluid environment, arguably lends substantial support to this cautious and skeptical stance.

339 *See* Kent, *Beyond Compliance: China, International Organizations, and Global Security, supra* note 246, at 6–16, 245–48. *See also* Kent, *China, the United Nations, and Human Rights: The Limits of Compliance, supra* note 246, at 240–44.

340 *See, e.g.*, Rudra Sil & Peter J. Katzenstein, "Analytic Eclecticism in the Study of World Politics: Reconfiguring Problems and Mechanisms across Research Traditions", 8 *Persp. on Pol.* 411 (2010).

The "Duty" to Co-Operate for States Bordering Enclosed or Semi-Enclosed Seas

Erik Franckx and Marco Benatar

Table of Contents

I Introduction: The Importance of Co-Operation

As 2013 gradually comes to a close, recent events testify once more to the South China Sea's (SCS) reputation as a dispute prone region. In this part of the world, marred by quarrels over resources, insular entitlements and maritime delimitation, unilateral moves by any of the costal states have the potential to push tensions to the brink. It is only through co-operation that the SCS countries can extricate themselves from this quagmire in a just and mutually beneficial manner. Both the short-term avoidance of escalation as well as long-term solutions to the underlying sources of contention become attainable if this path is followed. Maritime-themed co-operation can occur in numerous areas ranging from fisheries to search & rescue. Past experiences from different regions of the globe have shown that successful collaborative instances in limited domains can generate spill-over effects that positively alter interstate relations across the board. Even in seas yet to be delimited due to opposing

* Research Professor, President of the Department of International and European Law, Director of the Centre for International Law, and Vice-Dean for Internationalization of the Faculty of Law and Criminology, Vrije Universiteit Brussel. Member of the Permanent Court of Arbitration.

** Doctoral Fellow, Research Foundation—Flanders (FWO). Member of the Department of International and European Law and the Centre for International Law, Vrije Universiteit Brussel.

 | DOI 10.1163/9789004306509_003

maritime claims, there is promising recent practice demonstrating that it is possible to work together on particular issues.[1]

From the jurist's point of view, there is much to be said for co-operation. One of the most notable aspects of contemporary international law is its fundamental change in nature. In the past century we witnessed, to use Friedmann's famous phraseology, a paradigm shift from a "law of co-existence" to a "law of co-operation."[2] Today, international law imposes a whole host of obligations to co-operate, which bring states "to act in good faith in pursuing a common objective and [take] into account the requirements of the other interested States."[3] The goals that are to be achieved vary greatly and the same goes for their sources, whether customary or conventional. In certain branches of the discipline, particularly international environmental law, obligations of this ilk have taken on paramount importance.[4] The UN Convention on the Law of the Sea (1982 Convention)[5] is anything but isolated from this general trend. Browsing through its many provisions will allow the reader to unearth a great number of such duties covering an impressive range of topics.[6]

II Article 123 of the 1982 Convention: Looking for Law in the Wrong Places

It should therefore come as no surprise that many a scholar unsettled by developments in the SCS has looked to the 1982 Convention as a fountainhead of

1 An excellent case in point is the Arctic, where regional states managed to conclude the Agreement on Cooperation on Aeronautical and Maritime Search and Rescue in the Arctic, May 12, 2011, http://library.arcticportal.org/1474/. Problems resulting from a failure to settle boundaries are set aside thanks to art. 3(2), which reads: "The delimitation of search and rescue regions is not related to and shall not prejudice the delimitation of any boundary between States or their sovereignty, sovereign rights or jurisdiction."

2 Wolfgang G. Friedmann, *The Changing Structure of International Law* (1964).

3 Tullio Scovazzi, *The Evolution of International Law of the Sea: New Issues, New Challenges*, 286 *R.C.A.D.I.* 39, 132–33 (2000).

4 Malgosia Fitzmaurice, *International Protection of the Environment*, 293 *R.C.A.D.I.* 9, 442 (2001).

5 United Nations Convention on the Law of the Sea, Dec. 10, 1982, 1833 U.N.T.S. 397 [hereinafter 1982 Convention].

6 *See* Moragodage C.W. Pinto, *The Duty of Co-Operation and the United Nations Convention on the Law of the Sea, in Realism in Law-Making: Essays on International Law in Honour of Willem Riphagen* 131 (Adriaan Bos & Hugo Siblesz eds., 1986) (offering a topology of co-operative duties *ratione loci* (areas under national jurisdiction; the high seas; landlocked and geographically disadvantaged states; the sea-bed beyond national jurisdiction) and *ratione materiae* (protection and preservation of the marine environment; marine scientific research; development and transfer of marine technology; archeological and historical objects found at sea).

binding obligations compelling coastal states to join forces in the pursuance of common goals. And indeed, this reflex is justified *prima facie* on two accounts: (1) all states with maritime/insular claims in the SCS are parties to the treaty: Brunei, Malaysia, the People's Republic of China, the Philippines and Vietnam;[7] and (2) a good number of obligations to co-operate stemming from the 1982 Convention are pertinent to problems besetting the region. Among the articles of the 1982 Convention invoked in support of the requirement to co-operate, some experts have uttered Article 123 in the same breath. This provision falls under Part IX, which reads as follows:

PART IX
ENCLOSED OR SEMI-ENCLOSED SEAS
Article 122
Definition

> For the purposes of this Convention, "enclosed or semi-enclosed sea" means a gulf, basin or sea surrounded by two or more States and connected to another sea or the ocean by a narrow outlet or consisting entirely or primarily of the territorial seas and exclusive economic zones of two or more coastal States.

Article 123
Cooperation of States bordering enclosed or semi-enclosed seas

> States bordering an enclosed or semi-enclosed sea should cooperate with each other in the exercise of their rights and in the performance of their duties under this Convention. To this end they shall endeavour, directly or through an appropriate regional organization:
>
> (a) to coordinate the management, conservation, exploration and exploitation of the living resources of the sea;

7 Dates of signature: Brunei (Dec. 5, 1984), Malaysia (Dec. 10, 1982), People's Republic of China (Dec. 10, 1982), Philippines (Dec. 10, 1982), Vietnam (Dec. 10, 1982); Dates of ratification/accession: Brunei (Nov. 5, 1996), Malaysia (Oct. 14, 1996), People's Republic of China (Jun. 7, 1996), Philippines (May 8, 1984), Vietnam (Jul. 25, 1994). Mention must be made of the Republic of China (Taiwan), which is also located in the SCS region and similarly puts forward claims of its own. However, its status under international law is debated, effectively barring it from acceding to the 1982 Convention. Any detailed treatment of this question would stray far beyond the scope of the present article.

(b) to coordinate the implementation of their rights and duties with respect to the protection and preservation of the marine environment;
(c) to coordinate their scientific research policies and undertake where appropriate joint programmes of scientific research in the area;
(d) to invite, as appropriate, other interested States or international organizations to cooperate with them in furtherance of the provisions of this article.

The geography of the SCS fits the description offered by Article 122, as a logical consequence of which Article 123 finds application. There seems to be broad consensus on this point. Opinions start to diverge however when we take a closer look at the actual impact of its terms. Our reading of Article 123 is such that its framing and wording do *not* imply autonomous, binding obligations and at best exert *weak* normative force. Having recourse to the *travaux préparatoires* does not suggest otherwise, quite to the contrary. Nor does the reigning regional atmosphere augur well for any shift in subsequent state practice coupled with *opinio juris*.

The choice of terminology notwithstanding, some scholars have adopted a different position, advocating greater legal significance for Article 123 or arguably hinting at duties that can be deduced therefrom. For instance, Hu, who sees promise in this clause, opines: "Part IX of the 1982 UNCLOS, especially Article 123, *was intended to provide an obligation of cooperation* on Parties bordering an enclosed or semi-enclosed sea to manage the activities occurring in their shared and common marine environment and to deal with their interrelations."[8] Townsend-Gault, taking a somewhat different approach, makes the case for a functional understanding of co-operation in maritime affairs. He writes:

> the choice of "legal" language [in Article 123, 1982 Convention] may be less important than it appears. Despite the absence of detailed provisions, it is surely of no small importance to note that the framers of UNCLOS singled out these marine areas for special attention. There must have been

8 Nien-Tsu Alfred Hu, "Semi-enclosed Troubled Waters: A New Thinking on the Application of the 1982 UNCLOS Article 123 to the South China Sea", 41 *Ocean Dev. & Int'l L.* 281, 304 (2010) (emphasis added).

> a cogent reason for creating the category of "enclosed and semi-enclosed seas," and enjoining certain forms of cooperation between their littorals.[9]

To this one can add other recent pieces that seem to imply binding requirements finding their origin in Article 123 by bringing up duties to co-operate and then referring to the latter provision in the following sentence.[10]

Such claims are not without precedent. Pinto, in his essay on the normative co-operative framework of the 1982 Convention, writes: "while the text [of Article 123] declares merely that such States '*should* co-operate,' there would seem to be no reason to interpret the articles as creating anything less than a legal duty of co-operation."[11] Another case in point is Pharand's view on Article 123 with respect to the Arctic:

> States have a special obligation to cooperate with each other when they border an "enclosed or semi-enclosed sea." ... The use of the word "should," instead of the usual "shall," normally indicates something short of a strict legal obligation. However, it must be noted that the object of the cooperation is so all encompassing that it would be virtually impossible to enforce, if a legal obligation really existed. What is important is that the same provision does impose a legal obligation on states to coordinate their efforts to attain certain specific objectives.[12]

Yet another example is Fleischer, who, in his treatment of the legal regime of fisheries, concludes that Article 123 contains an "obligation to co-operate in

9 Ian Townsend-Gault, "Maritime Cooperation in a Functional Perspective", *in Maritime Energy Resources in Asia: Legal Regimes and Cooperation* 7, 11 (Clive Schofield ed., 2012).

10 Shih-Ming Kao, Nathaniel Sifford Pearre & Jeremy Firestone, "Regional Cooperation in the South China Sea: Analysis of Existing Practices and Prospects", 43 *Ocean Dev. & Int'l L.* 283, 290–91 (2012); Jon M. Van Dyke, "Regional Cooperation in the South China Sea", at 1, The South China Sea: Cooperation for Regional Security & Development: Third International Workshop, Nov. 3–5, 2011, http://nghiencuubiendong.vn/trung-tam-du-lieu-bien-dong/doc_download/504-jon-van-dyke-regional-cooperation-in-the-south-china-sea (last visited June 1, 2015).

11 Pinto, *supra* note 6, at 140.

12 Donat Pharand, "The Arctic Waters and the Northwest Passage: A Final Revisit", 38 *Ocean Dev. & Int'l L.* 3, 53 (2007). It should be noted that the conclusion that Article 123 of the 1982 Convention applies to the Arctic is controversial. See Erik Franckx, *Maritime Claims in the Arctic: Canadian and Russian Perspectives* 240–243 (1993); Alexander Proelss & Till Müller, "The Legal Regime of the Arctic Ocean", 68 *Heidelberg J. Int'l L.* 651, 684–85 (2008).

the management and conservation of resources among States bordering an enclosed or semi-enclosed sea."[13]

We too subscribe to the view that co-operation is of the essence in the SCS region and can prove most valuable in easing tension, thereby creating an atmosphere amenable to compromise. However, putting laudable intentions and perceived practical necessity[14] aside, invoking Article 123 of the 1982 Convention as a *locus* of binding duties to flesh out co-operative regimes and the sort does not pass legal muster. This is not a mere technical nicety. Expanding the content of the provisions of the 1982 Convention beyond breaking point could be detrimental on a systemic level. Finalizing the text of what became the 1982 Convention necessitated concessions from all groups of states. Overly broad readings that do not find reasonable support in treaty interpretation run the risk of perturbing the "package deal" of 1982[15] which forms a fragile balance of opposing interests. The present article thus proposes to analyse Article 123 more closely with a view to discerning its scope and significance.

III An Analysis of Article 123 of the 1982 Convention

A *Hortatory or Mandatory?*

Whenever confronted with the need to interpret a treaty provision, the reference *par excellence* can be found in Articles 31–33 of the Vienna Convention

13 Carl A. Fleischer, "The New Régime of Maritime Fisheries", 209 *R.C.A.D.I.* 95, 139–40 (1988). Other examples include: Volker Röben, "The Southern Bluefin Tuna Cases: Re-Regionalization of the Settlement of Law of the Sea Disputes", 62 *Heidelberg J. Int'l L.* 61, 66 (2002) ("[T]he duty to cooperate, the 'Grundnorm' of international environmental law, codified in, *inter alia*, article 123 UNCLOS."); Thomas Dux, *Specially Protected Marine Areas in the Exclusive Economic Zone (EEZ): The Regime for the Protection of Specific Areas of the EEZ for Environmental Reasons under International Law* 109 (2011); Mary Ann Palma, Martin Tsamenyi & William R. Edeson, *Promoting Sustainable Fisheries: The International Legal and Policy Framework to Combat Illegal, Unreported and Unregulated Fishing* 153 (2010); Alberto A. Encomienda, "Marine Environmental Protection in the South China Sea: An UNCLOS Paradigm", *in Recent Developments in the Law of the Sea and China* 173, 173–75 (Myron H. Nordquist, John Norton Moore & Kuen-chen Fu eds., 2006).

14 Nathalie Ros, "La mer méditerranée: cas particulier et modèle avancé de gestion de la haute mer", 16 *Annuaire du Droit de la Mer* 33, 37–38 (2011).

15 James Harrison, *Making the Law of the Sea: A Study in the Development of International Law* 45 (2011).

on the Law of Treaties (VCLT).[16] As courts and tribunals have on numerous occasions authoritatively confirmed their customary nature,[17] determining whether the VCLT formally applies becomes an unnecessary exercise in the present analysis.

The first element invariably taken into consideration is the ordinary meaning to be given to the terms of the agreement. What is striking *in casu* is the

16 Vienna Convention on the Law of Treaties arts. 31–33, May 23, 1969, 1155 U.N.T.S. 331 [hereinafter VCLT].

> Art. 31: 1. A treaty shall be interpreted in good faith in accordance with the ordinary meaning to be given to the terms of the treaty in their context and in the light of its object and purpose. 2. The context for the purpose of the interpretation of a treaty shall comprise, in addition to the text, including its preamble and annexes: (*a*) any agreement relating to the treaty which was made between all the parties in connection with the conclusion of the treaty; (*b*) any instrument which was made by one or more parties in connection with the conclusion of the treaty and accepted by the other parties as an instrument related to the treaty. 3. There shall be taken into account, together with the context: (*a*) any subsequent agreement between the parties regarding the interpretation of the treaty or the application of its provisions; (*b*) any subsequent practice in the application of the treaty which establishes the agreement of the parties regarding its interpretation; (*c*) any relevant rules of international law applicable in the relations between the parties. 4. A special meaning shall be given to a term if it is established that the parties so intended.
> Art. 32: Recourse may be had to supplementary means of interpretation, including the preparatory work of the treaty and the circumstances of its conclusion, in order to confirm the meaning resulting from the application of article 31, or to determine the meaning when the interpretation according to article 31: (*a*) leaves the meaning ambiguous or obscure; or (*b*) leads to a result which is manifestly absurd or unreasonable.
> Art. 33: 1. When a treaty has been authenticated in two or more languages, the text is equally authoritative in each language, unless the treaty provides or the parties agree that, in case of divergence, a particular text shall prevail. 2. A version of the treaty in a language other than one of those in which the text was authenticated shall be considered an authentic text only if the treaty so provides or the parties so agree. 3. The terms of the treaty are presumed to have the same meaning in each authentic text. 4. Except where a particular text prevails in accordance with paragraph 1, when a comparison of the authentic texts discloses a difference of meaning which the application of articles 31 and 32 does not remove, the meaning which best reconciles the texts, having regard to the object and purpose of the treaty, shall be adopted.

17 *See, e.g.*, Iron Rhine Railway (Belg. v. Neth.), 27 R.I.A.A. 35, 62, para. 45 (2005) ("It is now well established that the provisions on interpretation of treaties contained in Articles 31 and 32 of the Convention reflect pre-existing customary international law [...]"). As regards the customary nature of art. 33 VCLT, see Richard K. Gardiner, *Treaty Interpretation* 16–17 (2008).

prevalence of non-committal language.[18] Although Article 123 stipulates co-operation and coordination for states bordering (semi-)enclosed seas, the terms used markedly soften the call to engage in such activities: "should cooperate" and "shall endeavour ... to coordinate." The difference between co-operation and co-ordination is not entirely clear, but the wording "to this end" suggests that co-ordination operates as a function of co-operation.[19] Lastly, the bordering states are called upon to "invite" others interested (states/international organizations) to co-operate and the word "appropriate" is used more than once. Neither of the latter two terms instils a sense of compulsory intent.

"Should" is one of the most commonly used forms of hortatory language and stands in stark contradistinction to "shall." Drawing implications from this difference has been wittily described as "the favourite international lawyer's game."[20] The French version of the text, one of the Convention's authentic languages, reads "devraient coopérer," which likewise connotes exhortation rather than obligation. As a generic term, this is how "should" is usually understood.[21]

---

18 This is not a rarity among treaties. *See* Appeal Relating to the Jurisdiction of the ICAO Council (Ind. v. Pak.), 1972 I.C.J. 46, 107, n.1 (August 18) (separate opinion of Judge Dillard): "[M]ultilateral treaties establishing functioning institutions frequently contain articles that represent ideals and aspirations which, being hortatory, are not considered to be legally binding except by those who seek to apply them to the other fellow."

19 There is doctrinal support to be found for this view. See Rüdiger Wolfrum, "Cooperation, International Law of", *in* 2 *Max Planck Encyclopedia of Public International Law* 783, 783, para. 2 (Rüdiger Wolfrum ed., 2012) (defining an obligation to co-operate as a duty "to enter into such *coordinated action* so as to achieve a specific goal" (emphasis added)). *See also* Mox Plant Case (Ire. v. U.K.), Proceedings Day 5 (Revised), 27 (June 17, 2003), http://www.pca-cpa.org/showfile.asp?fil_id=86.

20 Mox Plant Case (Ire. v. U.K.), Proceedings Day 5 (Revised), 23 (Jun. 17, 2003), http://www.pca-cpa.org/showfile.asp?fil_id=86.

21 This is not to say that "should" has never been interpreted as an obligation by international courts and tribunals. *E.g.*, Appellate Body Report, *Canada—Measures Affecting the Export of Civilian Aircraft*, para. 187, WT/DS70/AB/R (Aug. 20, 1999). Regarding Article 13(1) of the Understanding on Rules and Procedures governing the Settlement of Disputes (Annex 2, WTO Agreement):

> We note that Article 13.1 of the DSU provides that 'A Member *should* respond promptly and fully to any request by a panel for such information as the panel considers necessary and appropriate.' (emphasis added). Although the word 'should' is often used colloquially to imply an exhortation, or to state a preference, it is not always used in those ways. It can also be used 'to express a duty [or] obligation'. The word 'should' has, for instance, previously been interpreted by us as expressing a 'duty' of panels in the context of Article 11 of the DSU. Similarly, we are of the view that the word 'should' in the third sentence of Article 13.1 is, in the context of the whole of Article 13, used

Additionally, any claim to the contrary, i.e. attributing a special meaning to a treaty term, leads to a shift of the burden of proof.[22] With respect to Article 123 specifically, Ireland's position in the *Mox Plant Case* (Annex VII Tribunal) is quite telling. The underlying fact pattern centres on the UK's go-ahead to build and operate a complex to make mixed oxide fuel, rousing environmental concerns in Ireland.[23] In these proceedings, the applicant invoked, *inter alia*, a number of obligations under the 1982 Convention in an attempt to obtain a favourable Tribunal order compelling the UK to co-operate. Article 123 was one of the many provisions relied upon. However, in its Reply, Ireland actually agreed with the UK, contrary to what its interests would suggest, that the "should co-operate" passage "is expressed in hortatory, rather than mandatory, language."[24]

The passage "shall endeavour"[25] deserves some pause. The term "shall" is the classic illustration of mandatory language.[26] As pithily put by an arbitral tribunal in 2008: "The word 'shall' in treaty terminology means that what is provided for is *legally binding*."[27] Further substantiation of its compulsory nature is that if in doubt whether a document is a treaty or a memorandum

---

> in a normative, rather than a merely exhortative, sense. Members are, in other words, under a duty and an obligation to 'respond promptly and fully' to requests made by panels for information under Article 13.1 of the DSU.

Id. (footnotes omitted). For a trenchant critique, see Rambod Behboodi, " 'Should' Means 'Shall'. A Critical Analysis of the Obligation to Submit Information Under Article 13.1 of the DSU in the Canada—Aircraft Case", 3 *J. Int'l Econ. L.* 563 (2000).

22 Legal Status of Eastern Greenland (Den. v. Nor.), 1933 P.C.I.J., Ser. A/B, No. 53, 49 (Apr. 5): "if it is alleged by one of the Parties that some unusual or exceptional meaning is to be attributed to it [i.e. a conventional term], it lies on that Party to establish its contention."; Mojtaba Kazazi, *Burden of Proof and Related Issues: A Study on Evidence before International Tribunals* 227 (1996).

23 The facts surrounding the Mox Plant are noteworthy for prompting proceedings before multiple international jurisdictions: the International Tribunal for the Law of the Sea (ITLOS), an Annex VII (1982 Convention) Tribunal, an OSPAR (Convention) Tribunal and the European Court of Justice. For a brief overview, see Caroline E. Foster, *Science and the Precautionary Principle in International Courts and Tribunals* 44–49 (2011).

24 Mox Plant Case (Ire. v. U.K.), Reply of Ireland, 81–82, para. 7.17 (Mar. 7, 2003), http://www.pca-cpa.org/showfile.asp?fil_id=226.

25 In the French version: "s'efforcent."

26 This general observation holds true for the 1982 Convention. See Myron H. Nordquist et al., 3 *United Nations Convention on the Law of the Sea 1982: A Commentary* xliii–xliv ("Note on the Use of the Word 'Shall' ") (1995).

27 Wintershall Aktiengesellschaft v. Argentine Republic, para. 119, ICSID Case No. ARB/04/14, Award, 71 (Dec. 8, 2008).

of understanding, use of the term "shall" typically alludes to a desire to conclude a binding agreement.[28] However, one still has to account[29] for the term "endeavour," which, it is safe to assume, was intentionally added as a qualifying term.[30]

Here, a contextual interpretation sheds some further light. The OSPAR Tribunal took a sound approach in this regard:

> For the achievement of these aims the framers of the OSPAR Convention have carefully applied differential language to provide for stipulated levels of engagement of treaty obligations to achieve these objectives. There is a cascading standard of expression providing for the particular obligations imposed on a Contracting Party. For example, these are mandatory Provisions that provide for Contracting Parties:
>
> - to take some act ("shall apply", "shall include", "shall undertake", "shall co-operate" or "shall keep");
> - actively to work towards an objective ("take all possible steps", "implement programs", "carry out programs");
> - to deal with issues of planning for the objective ("establish programs", "adopt", "define", "draw up", "develop", "take account of"); and
> - to take measures ("take", "adopt", "plan", "apply", "introduce", "prescribe", "take into account").
>
> At a lesser level of engagement, other provisions provide for information to be dealt with ("collect", "access information") or that systems be set up ("provide for", "establish").

28 Anthony Aust, *Modern Treaty Law and Practice* 496 (2d ed. 2007).

29 *See* Anglo-Iranian Oil Co. Case (U.K. v. Iran), 1952 I.C.J. 93, 105 (July 22) (preliminary objection): "[A] legal text should be interpreted in such a way that a reason and a meaning can be attributed to every word in the text."

30 *Cf. e.g.*, Convention on Biological Diversity, art. 5, Jun. 5, 1992, 1760 U.N.T.S. 79: "Each Contracting Party shall, as far as possible and as appropriate, cooperate with other Contracting Parties, directly or, where appropriate, through competent international organizations, in respect of areas beyond national jurisdiction and on other matters of mutual interest, for the conservation and sustainable use of biological diversity."

Scovazzi, *supra* note 3, at 215, is critical of the implications of the qualified "shall cooperate" provision. He notes that "it does not say very much, being a mere invitation to co-operation" due to the hortatory formula " 'as far as possible and as appropriate', immediately followed by another 'where appropriate.' "

> When read as a whole (including the Annexes), it is plain to the Tribunal that the entire text discloses a carefully crafted hierarchy of obligations or engagement to achieve the disparate objectives of the OSPAR Convention. Those who framed the OSPAR Convention expressed themselves in carefully chosen, rather than in loose and general, terms . . .[31]

This "hierarchy of obligations" methodology is equally befitting in the present context. Viewed as a whole, the 1982 Convention similarly establishes a scale of duties articulating varying levels of normativity. The three most important expressions that can be identified in connection with co-operation are:[32]

- "shall cooperate"
- "shall promote international cooperation"
- "may cooperate"

Placed on this ladder, it seems reasonable to hold that "shall endeavour to coordinate" ranks below the binding "shall cooperate" yet above the patently permissive "may cooperate." Unfortunately, this does not conclusively put the matter to rest. We are in some sense left with the impression that Article 123 lingers in a legal twilight zone, necessitating further clarification.

B *Why Was Article 123 Added?*

The very fact that Part IX and in particular Article 123 exist has led some to believe that there must be legal significance behind it all.[33] Ireland too in the *Mox Plant* arbitration made a observation in this vein:

> Article 123 is not buried in the depths of UNCLOS. It stands in its own Part of UNCLOS . . . The very fact that UNCLOS singles out, uniquely, seas having that particular geographical configuration quite clearly indicates that this category of seas has some characteristic that demands special attention . . . What would be the point of singling out littoral States of enclosed and semi-enclosed seas for the imposition of particular duties

31 Access to Information under Article 9 of the OSPAR Convention (Ire. v. U.K.), 23 R.I.A.A. 59, 97, paras. 129–130 (2003).

32 Seokwoo Lee, "UNCLOS and the Obligation to Cooperate", *in Maritime Energy Resources in Asia: Legal Regimes and Cooperation* 23, 25 (Clive Schofield ed., 2012).

33 E.g. Townsend-Gault, *supra* note 9.

> of co-operation and co-ordination if they were not expected to take into account the particular characteristics of the seas that they share?[34]

Delving into the drafting history of the 1982 Convention will allow us to understand how Article 123 came to be and why. Even though Arts. 31 and 32 VCLT are structured in a step-by-step manner implying that recourse to preparatory works should only occur if the application of Article 31 leads to certain unsatisfactory results, in actuality many promote and effectively practice what is known as the "crucible" approach, i.e. fashioning interpretations in a "single combined operation" based on the variety of available techniques and factors.[35]

The *travaux préparatoires* yield two key insights. First of all, the choice of weak terminology was not fortuitous. It can be seen, to be more precise, as a reaction to several proposals[36] couched in mandatory language. The same can be said for Article 134 of the Informal Single Negotiating Text (ISNT/Part II) from 1975 (the precursor of today's Article 123), which read:

> States bordering enclosed or semi-enclosed seas *shall co-operate* with each other in the exercise of their rights and duties under the present Convention. To this end they *shall*, directly or through an appropriate regional organization:
>
> (a) *Co-ordinate* the management, conservation, exploration and exploitation of the living resources of the sea;
> (b) *Co-ordinate* the implementation of their rights and duties with respect to the preservation of the marine environment;
> (c) *Co-ordinate* their scientific research policies and undertake where appropriate joint programmes of scientific research in the area;
> (d) *Invite*, as appropriate, other interested States or international organizations to co-operate with them in furtherance of the provisions of this article.[37]

34 Mox Plant Case (Ire. v. U.K.), Reply of Ireland, 82–83, para. 7.22 (Mar. 7, 2003), http://www.pca-cpa.org/showfile.asp?fil_id=226.

35 Michael Waibel, "Demystifying the Art of Interpretation", 22 *Eur. J. Int'l L.* 571, 574–75 (2011); UN Conference on the Law of Treaties, Official Records, Documents of the Conference, U.N. Doc. A/Conf.39/11/Add.2, 39, para. 8 ("All the various elements, as they were present in any given case, would be thrown into the crucible, and their interaction would give the legally relevant interpretation.")

36 *See, e.g.*, the Iraqi proposals in Nordquist et al., *supra* note 26, at 357–58, 360–61.

37 UNCLOS III, U.N. Doc. A/CONF.62/WP.8/Part II (ISNT, 1975), IV Off. Rec. 152, 171, http://untreaty.un.org/cod/diplomaticconferences/lawofthesea-1982/docs/vol_IV/a_conf-62_wp-8_part-2.pdf (emphasis added).

Yet, by 1976, in a discernible turnaround, the terms had evolved. Article 130[38] of the Revised Single Negotiating Text (RSNT/Part II) now stipulated:

> States bordering enclosed or semi-enclosed seas *should co-operate* with each other in the exercise of their rights and duties under the present Convention. To this end they *shall endeavour*, directly or through an appropriate regional organization:
>
> (a) *To co-ordinate* the management, conservation, exploration and exploitation of the living resources of the sea;
> (b) *To co-ordinate* the implementation of their rights and duties with respect to the preservation of the marine environment;
> (c) *To co-ordinate* their scientific research policies and undertake where appropriate joint programmes of scientific research in the area;
> (d) *To invite*, as appropriate, other interested States or international organizations to co-operate with them in furtherance of the provisions of this article.[39]

The reason for this marked change is evinced by the Chairman of the Second Committee responsible for the drafting of the provision: "On the issue of enclosed and semi-enclosed seas, I have responded to the expressions of dissatisfaction with the provisions in the [ISNT] by making less mandatory the co-ordination of activities in such seas."[40]

Secondly, there was no intention to give additional rights or impose new obligations on states bordering (semi-)enclosed seas. The majority of participants were not eager to accord a special status to these maritime expanses. Therefore, the rights, jurisdiction, and obligations of the bordering states match those of other coastal states. Consequently, the passage in Article 123 calling upon states to co-operate "in the exercise of their rights and in the performance of their duties under this Convention" does not seem to add anything new to the generally applicable law of the sea regime.[41] Judge Anderson expressed a similar view in the *Mox Plant Case* before ITLOS:

---

38 Which is the follow-up of art. 134 ISNT/Part II.

39 UNCLOS III, U.N. Doc. A/CONF.62/WP.8/Rev.1/Part II (RSNT, 1976), V Off. Rec. 151, 172, http://untreaty.un.org/cod/diplomaticconferences/lawofthesea-1982/docs/vol_V/a_conf-62_wp-8_rev-1-part2.pdf (emphasis added).

40 Nordquist et al., *supra* note 26, at 362.

41 *See id.* at 365; Budislav Vukas, "Enclosed or Semi-Enclosed Seas", *in* 3 *Max Planck Encyclopedia of Public International Law* 415, 420–21, para. 22 (Rüdiger Wolfrum ed., 2012);

Turning to the content of article 123, it can be viewed in many ways as a particular application to the law of the sea of the general duty of States to cooperate, as laid down in Article 2 of the Charter of the UN, as well as wider duties of *voisinage*. Article 123 was cast in weak terms ("should" / "shall endeavour") *in order to safeguard the worldwide application of the Convention's provisions and its unified character.*[42]

C Devoid of Relevance?

Article 123 is not out of step with the general practice of treaty-law making. After all, conventions abound containing comparable weakly worded clauses lacking teeth. Coupled with the apparent reticence of the drafters to establish a robust arrangement for (semi-)enclosed seas, as demonstrated above, it remains uncertain what this article actually adds to the 1982 Convention. The three domains referenced by Article 123 have already been made the subject of other provisions which include binding co-operative duties.[43] This is above all the case for the protection and preservation of the marine environment, which besides the 1982 Convention, has received ample attention in many international and regional environmental treaties combating marine pollution. What significance then should we attribute to Article 123?

Firstly, the encouragement to join forces has *policy* relevance. The provision stipulates general directives, extending an invitation to states bordering (semi-)enclosed seas to work together.[44] The political legitimation it affords extends to forms of co-operation that exclude non-bordering states as well as in the three areas explicitly mentioned (as opposed to other domains e.g. navigation and maritime delimitation).[45]

But additionally, it can have some degree of *legal* bearing as regards areas that have received less attention in the 1982 Convention. Provisions of this type can be reflective of juridical principles of general international law.[46] Their

---

Tullio Scovazzi, "Implications of the New Law of the Sea for the Mediterranean", 5 *Marine Pol'y* 302, 307–08 (1981).

42 The Mox Plant Case (Ire. v. U.K.), Request for Provisional Measures, ITLOS, Case No. 10, 4 (Order of Dec. 3, 2001, Separate Opinion of Judge Anderson) (emphasis added).

43 *See, e.g.*, 1982 Convention, *supra* note 5, arts. 242–244 (marine scientific research), arts. 117–118 (marine living resources), arts. 197–201 (marine environment).

44 Laurent Lucchini & Michel Voelckel, *Droit de la Mer: Tome 1*, at 441 (1990).

45 Tullio Treves, "Action commune pour la protection de l'environnement marin—Rapport général", 3 *Revue de l'indemer* 71, 80 (1995). Naturally, the specific mention of living resources, the marine environment, and scientific research does not rule out collaboration in other areas among states bordering (semi-)enclosed seas.

46 See Alan Boyle, "Some Reflections on the Relationship of Treaties and Soft Law", 48 *Int'l & Comp. L.Q.* 901, 906–09 (1999).

interaction can engender legal consequences. Nonetheless, even if legally relevant, Article 123 is not an *autonomous* source of obligations. By way of illustration, Vukas, one of the most prolific writers on the topic of (semi-) enclosed seas, has held that a bordering state that consistently resists all attempts to enter into negotiations concerning one of the enumerated subject matters would be acting contrary to the latter clause.[47] A link should be made here to the ICJ's remarks concerning the need for negotiations to be "*meaningful*, which will not be the case when either [Party] insists upon its own position without contemplating any modification of it."[48] Another example can be found in the principle of good faith. Even if one accepts that Article 123 is simply a declaration of policy,[49] *bona fides* could require a state that has abandoned such declared policies to inform the other state(s) of its altered course if they have acted in reliance thereof.[50] If, in fact, states bordering (semi-) enclosed seas do head the call and conclude agreements to co-operate, good faith in the implementation of binding duties could necessitate a host of additional requirements e.g. providing correct information among other things.[51] Finally, Article 123 may come into play with respect to treaty interpretation as part of the "context" for the construal of other articles in the 1982 Convention.[52]

47 Budislav Vukas, "United Nations Convention on the Law of the Sea and the Polar Marine Environment", *in Protecting the Polar Marine Environment: Law and Policy for Pollution Prevention* 34, 42 (Davor Vidas ed., 2000). *See also* Janusz Symonides, "The Legal Status of the Enclosed and Semi-Enclosed Seas", 1984 *German Y.B. Int'l L.* 315, 327 (concluding that Article 123 prevents states from entering into agreements which are harmful to bordering states' interests, would appear harder to defend).

48 North Sea Continental Shelf (Fed. Rep. Germ./Neth.; Fed. Rep. Germ./Den.), 1969 I.C.J. 3, 47, para. 85 (Feb. 20) (judgment), and quoted in Gabčíkovo-Nagymaros Project (Hun./Slov.), 1997 I.C.J. 7, 78, para. 141 (Sept. 25) (judgment) (emphasis added).

49 If Article 123 were a source of legal obligations, one could readily rely on the principle *pacta sunt servanda*, which finds application in, *inter alia*, Article 26 of the VCLT ("Every treaty in force is binding upon the parties to it and must be performed by them in good faith."), Article 300 of the 1982 Convention ("States Parties shall fulfil in good faith the obligations assumed under this Convention…") and the Declaration on Principles of International Law concerning Friendly Relations and Co-operation among States in accordance with the Charter of the United Nations..

50 Mox Plant Case (Ire. v. U.K.), Memorial of Ireland, vol. 1, 144–145, paras. 8.30–8.33 (July 26, 2002), http://www.pca-cpa.org/showfile.asp?fil_id=224.

51 Vukas, *supra* note 47, at 42.

52 The preamble of an agreement, typically non-binding, is acknowledged as part of the context under Article 31 of the VCLT. *A fortiori* this would apply to treaty provisions as well.

IV Conclusion

In this article, we have argued that Article 123, construed in accordance with the interpretive techniques enshrined in the VCLT, does not constitute an autonomous source of fully-fledged obligations for states bordering (semi-)enclosed seas to co-operate as some seemingly suggest. Part IX of the 1982 Convention can indeed be considered a meagre result. This is all the more unfortunate in light of the geography of (semi-)enclosed seas, rendering them more susceptible to greater competition over maritime zones and resources as well as pollution.[53] However, this problem cannot be suitably solved by digressing from the path of legal rigour, by reading what is not written and disregarding the intention of the drafters of the 1982 Convention.

Consequently, we submit that one would be well advised to look elsewhere in the international law of co-operation. One need not look far. The 1982 Convention is not want for relevant obligations. With respect to all three subject matters singled out in Article 123, living resources,[54] marine environment[55] and scientific research,[56] there are duties incumbent upon states parties to the "constitution for the oceans." Other treaties can also provide solace, subject of course to ratification/accession. As for customary international law, the duty to co-operate is strongest in the realm of international environmental law, and thus of direct significance to one of the three topics addressed in Article 123, marine pollution. The ITLOS' statement in the *Mox Plant Case* is worth recalling here: "the duty to cooperate is a fundamental principle in the prevention of pollution of the marine environment under Part XII of the Convention and *general international law*."[57]

53 Hu, *supra* note 8, at 282.

54 *See, e.g.*, Elise A. Clark, "Strengthening Regional Fisheries Management—An Analysis of the Duty to Cooperate", 9 *New Zealand J. Pub. & Int'l L.* 223, 231–32 (2011).

55 *See, e.g.*, Louis B. Sohn, Kristen Gustafson Juras, John E. Noyes & Erik Franckx, *Law of the Sea in a Nutshell* 420–22 (2d ed. 2010).

56 *See, e.g.*, Yoshifumi Tanaka, "Obligation to Co-operate in Marine Scientific Research and the Conservation of Marine Living Resources", 65 *Heidelberg J. Int'l L.* 937, 940–45 (2005).

57 The Mox Plant Case (Ire. v. U.K.), Request for Provisional Measures, ITLOS, Case No. 10, para. 82 (Order of Dec. 3, 2001), reiterated in Case Concerning Land Reclamation by Singapore in and around the Straits of Johor (Malay. v. Sing.), Provisional Measures, ITLOS, Case No. 12, para. 92 (Order of Oct. 8, 2003) (emphasis added).

Countering Terrorism and Protecting Human Rights: An Asian International Legal Dimension

Irena Ilieva

Table of Contents

I Introduction

The region of Asia and the Pacific Ocean has been in the focus of interest of international relations and international law commentators for its dynamically developing processes, closely linked to the economic, strategic and political order emerging in the Asia-Pacific. Even in a small country like Bulgaria, there is a growing attention to important dimensions in the region in the period of globalization, seriously affecting the multipolar system of international relations.[1] The Asia-Pacific regionalism is studied from different points

---

* Professor, Institute for the State and the Law, Bulgarian Academy of Sciences; Professor, Law Faculty, Plovdiv University, Bulgaria. She is the author of books and studies related to the international protection of minorities on the Balkans; to their legal regulation in the European Union member states and Bulgaria; to women's rights in international law and EU Law; to equality of opportunities, religious rights and freedoms; to the problems of migration and asylum and the fight against international terrorism.

1 *See* Kyriak Tzonev, "Niakoi obshti polojenia, vliaeshti varhu vanshnata politika na asiatskite darjavi", 2 *Current Issues, Aspects and Perspectives of International Relations* 158 (2010) (in Bulgarian); Irena Ilieva, *Regionalni konvencii za borba sreshtu terorisma* 185–220 (2012); David Gosset, The Chinese Renaissance, Public Lectures 2009–2011, Republic of Bulgaria, Ministry of Foreign Affairs, Diplomatic Institute, at 17–26 (2012).

 | DOI 10.1163/9789004306509_004

of views (sustainability of growth and fuller participation in the World Trade Organization system,[2] regional international organizations,[3] geo-political aspects,[4] security and energy issues[5]).

With the end of the Cold War, the values of human rights and democracy have become universally accepted and the problems of human rights have lost their ideological history. The growing importance of the Asia-Pacific region was emphasized in the lecture of President B. Obama's national security advisor Thomas Donilon in his appearance at Asia Society New York on March 11, 2013. In it, he referenced to the speech delivered by President Obama in the Australian parliament in Canberra in 2011, which outlined the overarching objective of the United States in the region: to sustain a stable security environment and a regular order rooted in economic openness, peaceful resolution of disputes, and *the respect for universal rights and freedoms*.[6]

This article is aimed at studying and compairing approaches to countering terrorism according to two regional instruments of fighting terrorism in Asia: the Shanghai Convention on Combating Terrorism, Separatism and Extremism (2001) (SCCTSE) and the ASEAN Convention on Counter Terrorism (2007) (ACCT) in the context of the international protection of human rights. The analysis is focused on the main human rights such as the right of life, rights in police arrest/custody, detention conditions and treatment of prisoners, prohibition of torture.

The protection of human rights will be analyzed in two contexts. The first is the study of terrorism, based on the legal definitions in both conventions as serious violation of human rights, especially those of the victims. The second aspect is the standards for the protection of human rights with respect to the perpetrators or the potential suspects of terrorist crimes.

---

2 *See* Sujin Chan, "Beyond Special and Differential Treatment: Key Trends of Importance to East Asian Regionalism", 2010 *Chinese (Taiwan) Y.B. Int'l L. & Aff.* 1–21.

3 *See* Orlin Borisov, Irena Ilieva & Alexander Draguiev, *Regionalni mejdunarodni organi* 144–50 (2012).

4 Ariel Cohen, "The Dragon Looks West: China and the Shanghai Cooperation Organization" (Heritage Lectures, No. 961, Sept. 7, 2006), *available at* http://www.heritage.org/research/lecture/the-dragon-looks-west-china-and-the-shanghai-cooperation-organization (last visited June 1, 2015).

5 Gene Germanovich, "The Shanghai Cooperation Organization: A Threat to American Interests in Central Asia?", *China & Eurasia Forum Q.*, Spring 2008, at 19.

6 Thomas Donilon, "The United States and the Asia-Pacific in 2013", Mar. 11, 2013, http://asiasociety.org/new-york/complete-transcript-thomas-donilon-asia-society-new-york (last visited June 1, 2015).

The Special Rapporteur on the promotion and protection of human rights and fundamental freedoms while countering terrorism, Ben Emmerson, very clearly expressed the connection between the protection of the rights of victims and the rights of the alleged perpetrators of terroristic acts during the Secretary General's Symposium on International Counter-Terrorism Cooperation (September 19, 2011, New York): "It is essential that the protection of the rights of the victims of terrorism is seen as a genuine legal duty resting primarily on States, and that it is not misused as a pretext for violating the human rights of those suspected of terrorism, for taking emergency measures which provide for excessive and disproportionate executive powers, or for other essentially political purposes."[7]

The main thesis of this article is: although the two conventions contain different approaches to combating terrorism within the context of human rights protection, they represent a serious attempt of Asian countries to cope with the new challenges of the security environment, namely asymmetric threats such as terrorism. This thesis should be verified through the classical method of a positively legal analysis of the two conventions and within the context of the law of international organizations.

The dilemma "liberty or security" or sacrificing respect for human rights at the expense of the fight against the scourge of humanity—terrorism—became particularly acute after the terrorist attacks on September 11, 2001 against USA. It is authorized differently in the internal legal systems of the states. From the standpoint of international law, it is of great interest how this dilemma is solved in the activities of regional international organizations such as Shanghai Cooperation Organization (SCO)[8] and the Association of Southeast Asian Nations (ASEAN).[9]

---

7 Ben Emmerson, Speech for Secretary General's Symposium on International Counter-Terrorism Cooperation, Sept. 19, 2011, *available at* http://www.un.org/en/terrorism/ctitf/pdfs/sr_on_ct_and_hr_sg_symposium.pdf (last visited June 1, 2015).

8 As a reaction to the changing geopolitical situation in Central Asia, a forum emerged in 1996 in Shanghai—"The five of Shanghai," uniting Kazakhstan, Kyrgyzstan, China, the Russian Federation and Tajikistan. Two member states of the Forum: China and Russia are permanent members of the UN Security Council. In the mid-1990s China, Russia and several Central Asian countries resolved a series of border disputes, which ultimately led to the formation of a new multilateral security organization known as the "Shanghai Five." The logical result was the creation of the Shanghai Cooperation Organization (SCO) on June 15, 2001, whose members were the Russian Federation, Kazakhstan, Kyrgyzstan, China, Tajikistan and Uzbekistan. The status of observer states is granted to Afghanistan, India, Iran, Mongolia, Pakistan and the "dialogue partners" comprise Belarus, Turkey and Sri Lanka.

9 The Association of Southeast Asian Nations (ASEAN) was established on August 8, 1967 in Bangkok (Thailand) with the signing of the ASEAN Declaration by the founder states:

I need to emphasize that this article is not focused on the actual application and practice of the two conventions. Such an ambitious task is beyond the scope of this article for a number of reasons. First, it is necessary to collect jurisprudence from many countries of sufficient volume and reliability, which at this stage of the study is virtually impossible. Second, the diversity of the countries in the region and the language barrier prevents such an undertaking. Third, the region has no system for protecting human rights, similar to the European and Inter-American ones.

However, the author will discuss some features of the two leading countries of the Shanghai Cooperation Organization: Russian Federation and China. In terms of the protection of human rights, the two leading powers have a number of common approaches as well as significant differences. The latter is mainly related to the system of protecting human rights. Russia is a member of the Council of Europe and a party to the European Convention for the Protection of Human Rights and Fundamental Freedoms (ECHR).[10] In this regard, some references will be quoted to the case law of the European Court for Human Rights in the matter studied. The conclusions drawn are rather theoretical constructs on models of implementation of universal standards for the protection of human rights in various regions, mainly in the Asia-Pacific region and the European System for the Protection of Human Rights and Fundamental Freedoms.

China's position in relation to the foreign policy aspect of the protection of human rights has been the subject of research. As pointed out by Ming Wan: "Beijing adopted defensive human rights diplomacy. To avoid international isolation, the Chinese actively cultivated relations with neighboring nations. To fend off Western pressure, the government stood firm on the principle of sovereignty and noninterference in domestic affairs but remained flexible in making opportune concessions, such as release of prominent dissidents,

---

Indonesia, Malaysia, Philippines, Singapore and Thailand. Brunei Darussalam then joined on January 7, 1984, Vietnam on July 28, 1995, Lao PDR and Myanmar on July 23, 1997 and Cambodia on April 30, 1999. The set of aims and purposes set out in the ASEAN Declaration comprises: economic objectives (growth, cooperation for greater utilization of agriculture and industry, the expansion of trade, improvement of transportation, etc.), political-security aims (to promote regional peace and stability through respect for justice and the rule of the law in the relationship among countries of the region and adherence to the principles of the United Nations Charter, socio-cultural purposes (social progress and cultural development in the spirit of equality and partnership, to provide assistance to each other in the form of training and research facilities in the educational, professional, technical and administrative spheres).

10 Russia signed the ECHR on February 28, 1996 and ratified on May 5, 1998.

signing international human rights treaties, and publishing human rights white papers."[11]

II General Comparison of the Shanghai Convention on Combating Terrorism, Separatism and Extremism (SCCTSE) and the ASEAN Convention on Counter Terrorism (ACCT)

SCCTSE was signed on June 15, 2001 by the Republic of Kazakhstan, the People's Republic of China, the Kyrgyz Republic, the Russian Federation, the Republic of Tajikistan, and the Republic of Uzbekistan.[12] On September 14, 2001 the Permanent mission of Kazakhstan in the United Nations transmitted the text of the Declaration of Heads of Government of Member States of the SCO in connection with the terroristic acts carried out in the United States of America on September 11, 2001. In this document the Heads of Government stated: "We regard these barbaric acts as challenging the essential foundation of human civilization, the stability of society, the security of states and fundamental human rights, including the right to life ... This evil can be defeated only by the united efforts of all States ... The Member States of the SCO are taking active steps in that direction. Opposition to terrorism, extremism and separatism is one of the most important objectives of the Shanghai Convention on Combating Terrorism, Separatism and Extremism."[13]

The ACCT was done at Cebu, Philippines on January 13, 2007, signed by Brunei Darussalam, the Kingdom of Cambodia, the Republic of Indonesia, the Lao People's Democratic Republic, Malaysia, the Union of Myanmar, the Republic of the Philippines, the Republic of Singapore, the Kingdom of Thailand, and the Socialist Republic of Vietnam.[14]

---

11 Ming Wan, *Human Rights in Chinese Foreign Relations: Defining and Defending National Interests* 6 (2001).

12 Shanghai Convention on Combating Terrorism, Separatism and Extremism, June 15, 2001, *available at* http://www.sectsco.org/EN123/show.asp?id=68 (last visited June 1, 2015). The Convention entered into force on March 29, 2003.

13 United Nations, General Assembly, Note Verbale Dated 14 September 2001 from the Permanent Mission of Kazakhstan to the United Nations Addressed to the Secretary-General, U.N. Doc. A/56/364 (Sept. 17, 2001).

14 The ASEAN Convention on Counter Terrorism, Jan. 11, 2007, *available at* http://www.asean.org/news/item/asean-convention-on-counter-terrorism (last visited June 1, 2015). ACCT came into force on May 27, 2011, whereas Malaysia became the tenth Member State to deposit its instrument of ratification with the Secretary-General of ASEAN on January 11, 2013.

The first common feature of both conventions is the understanding that terrorism constitutes a threat to international peace and security. The ACCT highlights that terrorism is also threat to regional peace and stability.[15] The second common vision is the proclamation of the necessity of countering terrorism. The third characteristic of the conventions is the view that terrorism ("separatism and extremism" are also added in the SCCTSE) cannot be justified under any circumstances and cannot and should not be associated with any religion, nationality, civilization or ethnic group.[16] The fourth important common lineament is the observance of the principles of sovereignty, equality and territorial integrity of the states and non-interference in the internal affairs of the parties.[17] This recognizes that international cooperation and any measures undertaken to prevent and combat terrorism must comply with their obligations under international law, including the Charter of the United Nations.[18]

Cooperation in the area of prevention, identification and suppression of all forms of terrorist acts is the fifth common feature of both conventions.[19]

Although common features of both conventions might be evident, there are also some significant differences. They are related to the ways of implementing the cooperation in countering terrorism. According to the SCCTSE, the cooperation in countering terrorism shall be conducted through the *central competent authorities* of the parties, listed and notified to the Depositary

15 Shanghai Convention on Combating Terrorism, Separatism and Extremism, *supra* note 12, pmbl.; ASEAN Convention on Counter Terrorism, *supra* note 14, pmbl.

16 Shanghai Convention on Combating Terrorism, Separatism and Extremism, *supra* note 12, pmbl.; ASEAN Convention on Counter Terrorism, *supra* note 14, pmbl.

17 ASEAN Convention on Counter Terrorism, *supra* note 14, art. 3. The Shanghai Convention on Combating Terrorism, Separatism and Extremism does not contain this provision expressly, but it should be drawn by interpretation of Art. 9, Para. 6 concerning the request for assistance and the grounds for postponement or denial of this request.

18 According to the Plan of Action (annexed to the UN Global Counter-terrorism Strategy), the Member States of the United Nations decide to implement all General Assembly resolutions on measures to eliminate international terrorism, and relevant General Assembly resolutions on the protection of human rights and fundamental freedoms while countering terrorism. They recognize that international cooperation and any measures that are undertaken to prevent and combat terrorism must comply with their obligations under international law, including the Charter of the United Nations and relevant international conventions and protocols, in particular human rights law, refugee law and international humanitarian law. United Nations Action to Counter Terrorism, United Nations General Assembly Adopts Global Counter-Terrorism Strategy, http://www.un.org/en/terrorism/strategy-counter-terrorism.shtml (last visited June 1, 2015).

19 Shanghai Convention on Combating Terrorism, Separatism and Extremism, *supra* note 12, art. 2(1); ASEAN Convention on Counter Terrorism, *supra* note 14, pmbl.

within 60 days after the entry into force of the Convention.[20] The text is analogous to the disposition of Art. 3 of the Treaty on Cooperation among States of the Commonwealth of Independent States in Combating Terrorism (1999) (TCSCISCT).[21]

The cooperation among the central competent authorities is regulated by Art. 6 and comprises the following:

- exchange of information;
- execution of requests concerning operational search actions;
- development and implementation of agreed measures to prevent, identify and suppress acts referred to in Article 1, Para. 1 of the Convention, as well as mutual information on the results of their implementation;
- implementation of measures to prevent, identify and suppress, in their territories, acts referred to in Article 1, Para. 1 of the Convention, that are aimed against other Parties;
- implementation of measures to prevent, identify and suppress financing, supplies of weapons and ammunition or any other forms of assistance to any person and/or organization for the purpose of committing acts referred to in Article 1, Para. 1 of the Convention;
- implementation of measures to prevent, identify, suppress, prohibit or put an end to the activities aimed at training individuals for the purpose of committing acts referred to in Article 1, Para. 1 of the Convention;
- exchange of regulatory legal acts and information concerning practical implementation thereof;
- exchange of experience in the field of prevention, identification or suppression of acts referred to in Article 1, Para. 1 of the Convention;
- various forms of training, retraining or upgrading of their experts;
- conclusion, upon mutual consent of the Parties, of agreements on other forms of cooperation, including, as appropriate, practical assistance in suppressing acts referred to in Article 1, Para. 1 of the Convention and mitigating consequences thereof. Such agreements shall be formalized in appropriate protocols that shall form an integral part of the Convention.

The areas of cooperation according to Article 6 of the ACCT are based principally on *the prevention* (of the commission, financing of terrorist acts and

---

20 Article 4 of the Shanghai Convention stipulates an obligation for the state-parties to provide to the depositary a list of their central competent authorities responsible for the implementation of the Convention.

21 For analyses of the Treaty on Cooperation among States of the Commonwealth of Independent States in Combating Terrorism, see Ilieva, *supra* note 1, at 133–49.

movement of terrorists or terrorist groups), promotion of capacity-building and public awareness in efforts to counter terrorism, enhancing cross-border cooperation, intelligence exchange and sharing of information, developing regional databases, research, etc. An important disposition in the field of cooperation is that all activities and measures must be conducted *in conformity with the domestic laws of the respective Parties*.[22]

As a result of the regulations regarding the cooperation in countering terrorism, it can be inferred that there are different approaches of both international organizations (SCO and ASEAN). SCO adopts a more centralized and institutional approach that is rendered in the establishment of The Regional Anti-Terrorist Structure (RATS). The Executive Committee of the Regional Counter-Terrorist Structure (RCTS) of the SCO is a permanent body based in Tashkent, the capital of Uzbekistan. Its main tasks and duties are as follows:

- Maintaining working contacts with SCO members authorities and coordinating with international organizations tackling issues of fighting terrorism, separatism and extremism;
- Assistance in interaction among the member states in the preparation and staging of counter terrorist exercises at the request of concerned member states, preparation and conducting of such operation and other activities in the field of fighting terrorism, separatism and extremism;[23]
- Joint drafting of international legal documents concerning the fight against terrorism, separatism and extremism;
- Gathering and analyzing information coming to the RCTS from the member states, formation and filling of RCTS data bank;
- Joint formation of a system of effective response to global challenges and threats;
- Preparation and holding of scientific conferences and workshops, assistance in sharing experience in the field of fighting terrorism, separatism and extremism.[24]

22 *See generally* ASEAN Convention on Counter Terrorism, *supra* note 14, art. 6.

23 The last exercises "Peace Mission 2013" were conducted in August 2013 in the Ural Mountain (Russia) including 600 Chinese troops and 900 Russians. *See* Joshua Kucera, "Chinese Troops Exercise In Russia, But Where's Rest of the SCO?", Aug. 6, 2013, http://www.eurasianet.org/node/67350.

24 Shanghai Cooperation Organization, The Executive Committee of the Regional Counter-Terrorist Structure, http://www.sectsco.org/EN123/AntiTerrorism.asp (last visited June 1, 2015).

ASEAN adopts an approach that reflects the principles of contemporary international law as they are laid out in Art. 3 of the ACCT.[25] Meanwhile the formulations of "promote," "enhance," "strengthen," "encourage" are very likely to remain the wishes among Member States. Another important difference between the two approaches to cooperation in countering terrorism should be highlighted. This is the clearly expressed understanding of a complex approach in the fight against terrorism that encompasses the prevention of the causes of the phenomenon. This view was expressed by the Secretary-General of the UN Ban Ki-Moon at the Symposium on International Counter-Terrorism Cooperation, held in September 2011 in New York, who recognizes that terrorism cannot be combated only through security-related or law enforcement means: "Effective counter-terrorism requires a combination of social, educational, economic and political tools that target factors that make the terrorist option appear attractive. The strategy also recognises that human rights are an intrinsic part of the fight against terror, not an acceptable casualty of war." He added, and called on to "chart a course that reflects our determination to defeat terrorism and build a safer, more just and peaceful world for all."[26]

A similar understanding was expressed by the former Secretary-General of ASEAN Ong Keng Yong in his speech at the National Security Australia Conference 2005, held in Sydney on February 21, 2005: "We all know that terrorism cannot be eliminated through law enforcement and police actions alone. Deep-seated resentments arising from social inequality, poverty and lack of opportunities serve as fuel to terrorism propaganda. This is why I believe that a prosperous ASEAN, made possible through greater economic competitiveness and equality, is the most effective long-term measure against terrorism.

25 Article 3 of the ASEAN Convention: "The Parties shall carry out their obligations under this Convention in a manner consistent with the principles of sovereign equality and territorial integrity of States and that of non-interference in the internal affairs of other Parties."

26 "ASEAN, ASEAN Joins Hands with Global Community in Fighting Terrorism, Sept. 20, 2011, http://www.asean.org/news/asean-secretariat-news/item/asean-joins-hands-with-global-community-in-fighting-terrorism (last visited June 1, 2015). In commemoration of the fifth anniversary of the United Nations (UN) Global Counter-Terrorism Strategy, the UN Secretary-General's Symposium on International Counter-Terrorism Cooperation was organised by the UN Counter-Terrorism Implementation Task Force Office (CTITF) in partnership with the Executive Office of the Secretary-General and the constituent CTITF entities on September 20, 2011, at the United Nations headquarters in New York.

A citizenry trustful of its government and hopeful of the future is our best defence against those sowing hatred and destruction."[27]

III Comparison of the Legal Definitions of "Terrorism" in the Two Conventions

As I have pointed out in the introduction, the subjects studied are two conventions on fighting terrorism: the SCCTSE and the ACCT within the context of human rights.

According to Article 1 of the SCCTSE:

> 1. For the purposes of this Convention, the terms used in it shall have the following meaning:
>
> 1) "terrorism" means:
>   a. any act recognized as an offence in one of the treaties listed in the Annex to this Convention (hereinafter referred to as "the Annex") and as defined in this Treaty;
>   b. any other act intended to cause death or serious bodily injury to a civilian, or any other person not taking an active part in the hostilities in a situation of armed conflict or to cause major damage to any material facility, as well as to organize, plan, aid and abet such act, when the purpose of such act, by its nature or context, is to intimidate a population, violate public security or to compel public authorities or an international organization to do or to abstain from doing any act, *and prosecuted in accordance with the national laws of the Parties*;
>
> 2) "separatism" means any act intended to violate territorial integrity of a State including by annexation of any part of its territory or to disintegrate a State, committed in a violent manner, as well as planning and preparing, and abetting such act, and *subject to criminal prosecuting in accordance with the national laws* of the Parties;

27 Ong Keng Yong, ASEAN's Contribution to General Effort in Counter-Terrorism, Speech at the National Security Australia Conference 2005, Feb. 21, 2005, available at http://www.asean.org/resources/2012-02-10-08-47-56/speeches-statements-of-the-former-secretaries-general-of-asean/item/asean-s-contribution-to-regional-efforts-in-counter-terrorism (last visited June 1, 2015).

> 3) "Extremism" is an act aimed at seizing or keeping power through the use of violence or changing violently the constitutional regime of a State, as well as a violent encroachment upon public security, including organization, for the above purposes, of illegal armed formations and participation in them, *criminally prosecuted in conformity with the national laws* of the Parties.
>
> 2. This Article shall not affect any international treaty or any national law of the Parties, provides or may provide for a broader application of the terms used in this Article."

The ACCT only uses the technique of referencing to the existing universal counter-terrorism conventions.[28] The same approach may be found in the Inter-American Convention Against Terrorism (2002) and the South Asian Association for Regional Cooperation Convention on Suppression of Terrorism (1987).

The comparison of the definitions in the two conventions reveals different approaches with respect to the explanation of the term "terrorism." The Shanghai Convention applies a combined approach of referencing to the terrorist crimes listed in an annex to the Convention and providing a definition to the terms "separatism" and "extremism." The insertion of the term "extremism" is not a novelty in the international practice of the Russian Federation and the member states of the Commonwealth of Independent States which have taken part in the signing of the Resolution of the heads of member states of the Commonwealth of Independent States dated December 1, 2000 for the establishment of a Counter-terrorism center.[29] This Resolution resulted from the signing of the Treaty on Cooperation among States of the Commonwealth of Independent States in Combating Terrorism in Minsk on June 4, 1999.[30] A broad definition of "terrorism" is already formulated in the Treaty which includes both "domestic" and "international" terrorism, detailed are the forms of cooperation, including coordinated exchange of special antiterrorist units among stakeholders to provide practical assistance to counter acts of terrorism and combat their consequences (Article 5). The document repeatedly refers to cooperation between Member States in the fight against international terrorism and *other manifestations of extremism, including other manifestations of*

---

28 *See generally* ASEAN Convention on Counter Terrorism, *supra* note 14, art. 2.

29 For discussions concerning the establishment of the Centre, its structure, powers, tasks and functions, see Ilieva, *supra* note 1, at 149–56.

30 For analyses of the Treaty on Cooperation among States of the Commonwealth of Independent States in Combating Terrorism, see *id*, at 133–49.

extremism in the Member States and other countries. It also regulates the procedure for participation in the preparation and conducting of anti-terrorist command staff and operational-technical exercises organized by the Council of Heads of State of the CIS.[31] In that document, however, there is no legal definition of the term "extremism." The definition of "extremism" in SCCTSE, based on the notion of "statehood"[32] is an original contribution of the Convention to clarifying the nature of the phenomenon.[33]

Alexander Lukin assesses the combination of the definition of "terrorism" with those of "separatism" and "extremism" as positive and presents them as variations of the U.S. campaign against terrorism: "The SCO's approach to problems of international security, first of all, the struggle against terrorism, is much broader than that of the United States and its allies. While Washington puts emphasis on military strikes against international terrorist centers and attacks against states supporting terrorism (these may be any states unwelcome to Washington), the SCO nations see direct links between international terrorism, on the one hand, and separatism and religious extremism, on the other. So, while coordinating their actions with the U.S. in combating international terrorism, the SCO countries can act according to their own programs and in their own interests, closely linking this struggle with counteraction to separatism and Islamic extremism. Thus the SCO members seek to ensure their territorial integrity and the preservation of secular regimes in power in Central Asian countries."[34]

---

31 *Id.* at 150–52.

32 As James Crawford formulated, "[s]tatehood is now a protected status under international law, and to this extent sovereignity once achieved is entrenched." James Crawford, "Sovereignty as a Legal Value", *in The Cambridge Companion to International Law* 117, 120 (James Crawford & Martti Koskenniemi eds., 2012).

33 An interesting definition of "extremism" was suggested by Mohammed Alam:

> Extremism is primarily a course aimed at legal and religious norms, but beyond the established and accepted by society requirements to these norms. Extremism is a universal phenomenon, which affects all religions and political ideas and principles inherent in the respective political regimes. In particular, extremism exceeds moderation in religious behavior both in thought and in practical application, going beyond the boundaries of the principles that contribute to the understanding of religion and the interaction with it.

Mohammed Alam, "Terorismat—factori za razvitie, smisal i proiavi", *Mejdunarodni otnoshenia*, Dec. 2007, at 161.

34 Alexander Lukin, "The Shanghai Cooperation Organization: What Next?", *Russia in Global Affairs*, July-Sept. 2007, at 140, 142.

A new element in the SCCTSE is the introduction of a definition of the terms "separatism," "extremism" and "terrorism" and their incrimination in accordance with the domestic law of the member-states. This is particularly important for the implementation of the Convention, giving a broad discretion of states to resort to another interpretation by referring to the provisions of their national law (Argument in Art. 1, Para. 2). Thus the specific approach of the SCO member-states to combat all "Three Evils": separatism, extremism and terrorism, is clearly outlined.

The consistent application of this approach by the SCO member states is proved by a press release about a regular meeting of the Council of Ministers of Foreign Affairs of Shanghai Cooperation Organization (SCO) held in Cholpon-Ata (Kyrgyz Republic) on July 12–13, 2013. The meeting was also attended by the Secretary-General of SCO Dmitry Mezentsev and Director of the Executive Committee of the Regional Anti-Terrorism Structure of the SCO Zhang Sinfen. The press release stated: "Member states actively and purposefully oppose international terrorism, separatism and extremism, transnationally organized crime, illicit trafficking in narcotic drugs, psychotropic substances and their precursors, as well as weapons, ammunition and explosives, threats to information security, illegal migration, support further improving cooperation in these areas within regulatory framework."[35]

A significant difference between the two conventions exists with respect to the recall (non-recall) on the protection of human rights and with respect to the position of the provisions relating to the their protection. The Shanghai Convention does not expressly contain clauses on the protection of human rights. But that Convention shall not limit the right of the parties to conclude other international treaties on matters that constitute the subject of the Convention and do not contradict its purposes and object, nor shall it affect the rights and obligations of the parties under other international treaties to which they are parties, including the obligations under the international standard of human rights.

The review of the status of the main international instruments for human rights protection such as the International Convention on Civil and Political Rights(ICCPR), the Optional Protocol to the ICCPR, the Second Optional Protocol to the ICCPR, aiming at the abolition of the death penalty, the International Covenant on Economic, Social and Cultural Rights, the Convention against Torture and other Cruel, Inhuman or Degrading Treatment or Punishment shows that member states of SCO are generally countries that

35 Shanghai Cooperation Organisation, SCO Foreign Ministers Meet in Cholpon-Ata, July 13, 2013, *available at* http://www.sectsco.org/EN123/show.asp?id=439.

are part of these international instruments.[36] The exception is China that has signed ICCPR but has not ratified it. As pointed out by Ming Wan, this is due to "the preference for economic and social rights over civil and political right" in China.[37]

Unlike the Shanghai Convention, in the Preamble of the ACCT the member states recall the Charter of the United Nations and relevant principles of international law, the relevant international conventions and protocols relating to counter terrorism and relevant resolutions of the United Nations on measures aimed at countering international terrorism, *and reaffirm their commitment to the protection of human rights, fair treatment, the rule of law and due process*, as well as the principles enshrined in the Treaty of Amity and Cooperation in Southeast Asia done at Bali on February 24, 1976. Regardless of the techniques used, the incriminated offenses constitute serious violations of human rights considered in the light of the international standard for their protection and in particular—in the Universal Declaration on Human Rights (UDHR) and the ICCPR.

There is a worldwide consensus that terrorism constitutes a serious violation of human rights (particularly a violation of the right to physical integrity, life, freedom and security), and impedes socio-economic development through destabilization of the states. The interrelationship and indivisibility of civil, political, economic, social and cultural rights is also manifested in relation to preventing and combating terrorism.[38]

Acts intended to cause death or serious bodily injury constitute a serious violation of the right to life (Art. 3 of the UDHR, Art. 6 ICCPR), the prohibition of torture or cruel, inhuman or degrading treatment or punishment (Art. 5 of the UDHR, Art. 7 ICCPR), the right to liberty and security of the person (Art. 3 of the UDHR, Art. 9 ICCPR), the right to respect one's personal life (Art. 12 of the UDHR, Art. 17 ICCPR), etc.

The first duty of any state is to protect the lives of its citizens as well as of all individuals within its territory and subject to its jurisdiction. As I mentioned in the introduction, Russia is a member of the Council of Europe and a party to the ECHR (European Convention for the Protection of Human Rights).[39] This allows me to make some references to the European Court of Human Rights

36 *See* Annexes I, II, III, IV, V and VI.

37 Wan, *supra note* 11, at 20.

38 For more detailed discussions, see Martin Scheinin, Report of the Special Rapporteur on the Promotion and Protection of Human Rights and Fundamental Freedoms While Countering Terrorism, U.N. Doc. A/HRC/6/17 (Nov. 21, 2007).

39 *See supra* note 10.

in relation to the research topic on Russia, as well some conclusions about the different approaches of Russia and China. The case-law of the European Court for Human Rights provides some recent examples for the protection of the right to life of the victims of terroristic acts, especially the observance of the proportionality principle. The case *Finogenov and Others v. Russia*[40] concerned the siege in October 2002 of the "*Dubrovka*" theatre in Moscow by Chechen separatists and the decision to overcome the terrorists and liberate the hostages using gas.[41] The Court finds that there is no violation of Art. 2 concerning the decision to resolve the hostage crisis by force and use of gas, but finds violation of Article 2 concerning the inadequate planning and implementation of the rescue operation. In addition, there is violation of Article 2 concerning the ineffectiveness of the investigation into the allegations of the authorities' negligence in planning and carrying out the rescue operation, as well as the lack of medical assistance to hostages.

The constant practice of European Court for Human Rights emphasizes that States should not only refrain from the intentional and unlawful taking of life, but also *take appropriate steps to safeguard the lives of those within their jurisdiction, in particular by putting in place effective criminal law provisions backed up by law enforcement machinery*.[42] The absence of any direct State responsibility for the death of an individual does not exclude the applicability of Article 2.[43]

The case *Tagayeva and Others v. Russia*[44] is still pending and deals with an alleged breach of the State's obligations to protect life during hostage taking crisis in Beslan, North Osetia, Russia on September 1–3, 2004, when 331 persons died. The Russian government awarded compensation to the victims.[45]

40 Finogenov and others v. Russia, App. Nos. 18299/03 and 27311/03 (Eur. Ct. H.R. 2012).

41 *See* Ilieva, *supra* note 1, at 132.

42 L.C.B. v. U.K., App. No. 14/1997/798/1001 (Eur. Ct. H.R. 1998); Osman v. U.K., App. No. 87/1997/871/1083 (Eur. Ct. H.R. 1998).

43 Angelova and Iliev v. Bulgaria, App. No. 55523/00, para. 93 (Eur. Ct. H.R. 2007)

44 Tagayeva and Others v. Russia, App. No. 26562/07 (Eur. Ct. H.R. 2011).

45 *Id.* paras. 390–93. Pursuant to Russian Government order no. 1338-r of 11 September 2004, the victims of the terrorist act were awarded the following compensation: 100,000 Russian roubles (RUB) for each person who had been killed, RUB 50,000 for each person who had received serious and medium gravity injuries and RUB 25,000 for each person with minor injuries. Persons who had been the hostages but escaped unharmed received RUB 15,000 each. In addition, the families received RUB 18,000 for each deceased person in order to cover funeral expenses. The President of North Ossetia ordered, on 6 and 15 September 2004 (orders 58-rpa and 62-rp), the payment of RUB 25,000 in funeral costs to each person who had died, RUB 100,000 to each deceased, RUB 50,000 to each person who had suffered serious and medium injuries and RUB 25,000 to each of the other hostages.

Another large group of Court judgments refer to the events in Chechnya, particularly ill-treatment, disappearances, destruction of property, landmines, restriction on freedom of movement and lack of effective remedy. In most of the cases, at least one violation was found.[46]

In the case of *Aslakhanova and Others v. Russia* (18.12.2012), the Court indicated *general measures to be taken by Russia*. The case concerned the disappearances of eight men in Chechnya between March 2002 and July 2004, after having been arrested in a manner resembling a security operation. The Court found violations of Articles 2 (right to life), 3 (prohibition of torture and of inhuman or degrading treatment), 5 (right to liberty and security) and 13 (right to an effective remedy) in conjunction with Articles 2 and 3. The Court has regularly found violations of the same rights in similar cases in more than 120 judgments, resulting from the disappearances that have occurred in the Northern Caucasus since 1999. It concluded that the situation in the case of *Aslakhanova and Others* resulted from a *systemic problem* of non-investigation of such crimes, for which there was no effective remedy at national level.

The Court outlined two types of general measures under Article 46 (binding force and execution of judgments) to be taken by Russia to address those problems: to alleviate the continuing suffering of the victims' families; and, to remedy the structural deficiencies of the criminal proceedings. Without analyzing in detail the problem with the execution of these decisions, I would refer

---

The terrorist act in Beslan triggered a major humanitarian response, resulting in collections of significant sums of money. Pursuant to Ossetian Government decree no. 240 of November 17, 2004, the North Ossetian Ministry of labour and social development distributed the funds paid into their account devoted to humanitarian relief to the victims in the following manner: RUB 1,000,000 for each person who had died; persons who had received grave injuries were granted RUB 700,000; persons with medium gravity injuries received RUB 500,000 each; persons who had minor injuries or were among the hostages received RUB 350,000 each. In addition, each child who had lost their parents received RUB 350,000 and other persons who had been briefly detained but were not among hostages, received RUB 75,000 each. Similar sums were allocated to the families and victims among the servicemen of the FSB (Federalnaia Slujba bezopasnosti) and EMERCOM (Agency for Support and Coordination of Russian Participation in International Humanitarian Operations) who had been killed or wounded.

46 *See* Sambiyeva v. Russia, App. No. 20205/07 (Eur. Ct. H.R. 2011); Tashukhadzhiyev v. Russia, App. No. 33251/04 (Eur. Ct. H.R. 2011); Khashuyeva v. Russia, App. No. 25553/07 (Eur. Ct. H.R. 2011); Edilova v. Russia, App. No. 14662/07 (Eur. Ct. H.R. 2012); Khamzatov and others v. Russia, App. No. 31682/07 (Eur. Ct. H.R. 2012); Inderbiyeva v. Russia, App. No. 56765/08 (Eur. Ct. H.R. 2012); Kadirova and others v. Russia, App. No. 5432/07 (Eur. Ct. H.R. 2012); Shafiyeva v. Russia, App. No. 49379/09 (Eur. Ct. H.R. 2012); Umarovy v. Russia, App. No. 2546/08 (Eur. Ct. H.R. 2012); Umayevy v. Russia, App. No. 47354/07 (Eur. Ct. H.R. 2012).

to the findings of the Interim Report "National Compliance with Decisions of International Tribunals in Matters Involving Human Rights" of the Sofia Conference of the International Law Association: "Both the quality and quantity of Strasbourg jurisprudence in respect of the Russia Federation demonstrate that the application of the European Convention on Human Rights and its Protocols at the domestic level has a number of serious problems."[47]

In *Maskhadova and Others v. Russia* (06.06.2013) the Court held, among others, that there had been no violation of Article 2 concerning the death of *Aslan Maskhadov*, the Chechen separatist President, or the investigation into his death. This case essentially concerned the Russian authorities' refusal to return the bodies of the Chechen separatist President and Chechen insurgents to their families. In fact that decision confirmed the legality of the so-called terrorist sentence dated June 28, 2007 of the Constitutional Court of the Russian Federation concerning the request of the relatives of the rebels killed in Kabardino-Balkaria in October 2005 to have their bodies returned and against their anonymous burial (as analyzed by *Michael Geistlinger*).[48]

The brief review of the case law of the European Court of Human Rights in the studied mattershows the complexity of the problem of the respect for human rights in the fight against terrorism. The right to life competes in many cases with the use of force by the State in self-defense or defense of another (Article 2). The Strasbourg case-law is consequent in its jurisdiction: Article 2 § 2 justifies the use of force in self-defense only if it is "absolutely necessary."

Although there is no recall on human rights in the text of the Shanghai Convention, the problems associated with their protection have not been ignored. The issues concerning the exercise of human rights are discussed in the Concept of Cooperation Between Member States of the Shanghai Cooperation Organization in Combating Terrorism, Separatism, and Extremism (hereinafter referred to as the Concept). That document was adopted on June 5, 2005 by Resolution No. 1 of the Council of Heads of SCO Member States of the Shanghai Cooperation Organization. The Concept is fundamental to the development of a joint strategy and a system of measures for combating terrorism, separatism, and extremism as they are defined by the SCCTSE of June 15, 2001,

47 For a more detailed discussion, see International Law Association, "Report of the Seventy-Fifth Conference Held in Sofia, August 2012", at 209 (2012).

48 *See* Michael Geistlinger, "Minderheiten in Caukasus-Umsetzung von Mythen in Recht?", *in In Bewusstes Erinnern und Bewusstes Vergessen. Der Juristische Umgang mit der Vergangenheit in den Ländern Mittel- und Osteuropas* 152 (Angelika Nußberger & Caroline von Gall eds., 2011).

within the framework of the Shanghai Cooperation Organization. According to the General Provisions of this document, the "SCO member states proceed on the basis that terrorism, separatism, and extremism constitute a threat to international peace and security and impede the development of friendly relations between states and *the enjoyment of fundamental human rights and freedoms*."[49]

In the Shanghai Convention, a recall is made on the principles enshrined in the resolutions of the UN General Assembly and the UN Security Council, and on the basis of the abovementioned Concept, a conclusion may be drawn that there is a political unity on the principle that the Convention is to cooperate in the area of prevention, identification and suppression of acts referred to in Article 1, Para. 1 of this Convention (Art. 2). Particular emphasis has been placed on the fact that the states shall perform the said obligation in accordance with the other international obligations that they have assumed, and shall adhere to their domestic legislation (Art. 2, Para. 2). On the basis of that provision, a reasonable conclusion can be made that the performance of the obligations arising from the Shanghai Convention will comply with the obligation to observe the international standard on human rights and basic freedoms. The case-law of the European Court of Human Rights regarding Russia, which is briefly mentioned, shows that the implementation of the Shanghai Convention does not impair other international obligations of the Russian Federation, particularly in relation to the European Convention for the Protection of Human Rights (ECHR).

Additional argument for the above mentioned conclusion is the Concept itself: the SCO member states emphasize their adherence to the goals and principles of the United Nations and to other generally recognized principles and norms of international law concerning the maintenance of international peace, security, and the promotion of good-neighborly and friendly relations and cooperation between states. The SCO member states intend to actively participate in anti-terrorist actions conducted both under the aegis of the UN and within the framework of regional organizations. The necessity and degree of participation shall be in proportion to their national interests and international obligations. In the Convention, certain principles recognized by the international community have been incorporated into concrete provisions (Art. 3), namely, under no circumstances acts aimed at instigating a state of terror against society, a group of individuals, or a particular individual, should be subject to acquittal based upon political, philosophical, ideological, racial,

49 Concept of Cooperation Between SCO Member States in Combating Terrorism, Separatism, and Extremism, Feb. 15, 2012, http://www.fidh.org/Concept-of-Cooperation-Between-SCO.

ethnic, religious or any other similar considerations. Importantly, the above mentioned provision also states that the state-parties shall adopt analogous measures, *including in their own domestic legislation*.

The ACCT done at Cebu, Philippines on January 13, 2007 reaffirms the commitment of the member-states to protect human rights, fair treatment, the rule of law and due process. The ACCT is a significant achievement of ASEAN's counter-terrorism efforts as it serves as a framework for regional cooperation to counter, prevent and suppress terrorism and deepen counter-terrorism cooperation. The ACCT enhances the region's strategic role in the global strategy on counter-terrorism. The ACCT has now been ratified by all ten ASEAN Member States.

A different approach to countering terrorism and respecting human rights stands out in the preamble itself. The state-parties recall the Charter of the United Nations and the relevant principles of international law, the relevant international conventions and protocols relating to counter terrorism and the relevant resolutions of the United Nations on measures aimed at countering international terrorism, and reaffirming their commitment to protect human rights, fair treatment, the rule of law, due process as well as the principles enshrined in the Treaty of Amity and Cooperation in Southeast Asia done at Bali on February 24, 1976.

The philosophy of the convention connects aspects of the fight against terrorism combined with the protection of human rights, fair treatment, the rule of law and due process. Thus, the approach of the member states of ASEAN reflects the trends in the universal international legal framework for combating terrorism. In the Preamble of the ACCT the ASEAN member states expressed their deep concern about the grave danger posed by terrorism to innocent lives, infrastructure and the environment, regional and international peace and stability as well as to economic development. In this regard, the mutual relation between different human rights is conceptually regulated: the right to life, as well as economic and social rights.

In contrast to the lack of a crystalized common position on the protection of human rights in the SCCTSE, the ACCT very clearly reflects the conceptual difference and approach of ASEAN on the issue of regulating and observing human rights.

As *Termsak Chalermpalanupap*[50] points out, historically the concept of the protection of human rights in the ASEAN was proclaimed after the World

50 *See* Termsak Chalermpalanupap, "10 Facts about ASEAN Human Rights Cooperation", http://www.asean.org/images/archive/HLP-OtherDoc-1.pdf (last visited June 1, 2015). At the time of publishing the article Termsak Chalermpalanupap is Special Assistant to

Conference on Human Rights in Vienna June 14–25, 1993. "The six then Member States (Brunei Darussalam, Indonesia, Malaysia, the Philippines, Singapore, and Thailand) stated in the Joint *Communiqué* at the 26th ASEAN Ministerial Meeting (AMM) in Singapore, July 23–24, 1993 their collective view about human rights, which remains valid and relevant today": "The Foreign Ministers welcomed the international consensus achieved during the World Conference on Human Rights in Vienna, June 14–25, 1993, and reaffirmed ASEAN's commitment to and respect for human rights and fundamental freedoms as set out in the Vienna Declaration of June 25, 1993. They stressed that human rights are interrelated and indivisible comprising civil, political, economic, social and cultural rights. These rights are of equal importance. They should be addressed in a balanced and integrated manner and protected and promoted with due regard for specific cultural, social, economic and political circumstances. They emphasized that the promotion and protection of human rights should not be politicized."[51]

The Foreign Ministers agreed that ASEAN should coordinate a common approach on human rights and actively participate and contribute to the application, promotion and protection of human rights. They noted that the UN Charter had placed the question of universal observance and promotion of human rights within the context of international cooperation. They stressed that development is an inalienable right, and that the use of human rights as a conditionality for economic cooperation and development assistance is detrimental to international cooperation and could undermine an international consensus on human rights. They emphasized that the protection and promotion of human rights in the international community should take cognizance of the principles of respect for national sovereignty, territorial integrity and non-interference in the internal affairs of states. They were convinced that freedom, progress and national stability are promoted by a balance between the rights of the individual and those of the community, through which many individual rights are realized, as provided for in the Universal Declaration of Human Rights."

Thus, the conceptual framework for understanding human rights in ASEAN could be clearly distinguished from the one in SCO. ASEAN countries share the

---

the Secretary-General of ASEAN. He serves the HLP as a resource person of the ASEAN Secretariat. Views in this article are his own.

51 Joint Communiqué at the Twenty-Sixth ASEAN Ministerial Meeting (AMM) in Singapore, July 23–24, 1993, *available at* http://www.asean.org/news/item/joint-communique-of-the-twenty-sixth-asean-ministerial-meeting-singapore-23-24-july-1993 (last visited June 1, 2015)

concept of indivisibility and interrelatedness of civil, political, economic, social and cultural rights. With the entry of ASEAN Charter into force on December 15, 2008, the organization has strengthened its international legal framework for the protection of human rights. There is a reference to respect for and protection of human rights and fundamental freedoms in the Preamble, Arts. 1 and 2. Article 14 is a particularly important provision, since it envisages the establishment of the ASEAN human rights body.[52]

Since the Charter already entered into force on December 15, 2008, follow-up actions are undertaken to fulfill the commitment to promotion and protection of human rights, including the establishment of the ASEAN human rights body (AHRB), based on the relevant provisions in the Charter and the prevailing collective view of the ASEAN Foreign Ministers.

The ASEAN Intergovernmental Commission on Human Rights (AICHR)[53] was established on October 23, 2009. AICHR is a typical intergovernmental body with cross-cutting mandate that handles matters relating to human rights cooperation with other ASEAN bodies, external partners and stakeholders. The analysts of its activities, in my opinion, present the following tasks:

- Promotion and protection of human rights;
- Implementation of the ASEAN Human Rights Declaration;[54]
- Awareness and understanding of the ASEAN human rights instruments and mechanisms;
- Regular exchange of ideas among stakeholders and partners, dissemination of information on ASEAN Community Building and the ASEAN Human Rights Declaration, as well *other human rights instruments* to the wider ASEAN audience.

The adoption of ASEAN Human Rights Declaration, in my opinion, is a major step forward in the promotion and realization of human rights in the region, even though it is not a legally binding document.

---

52 Article 14 of the ASEAN Charter reads:
1. In conformity with the purposes and principles of the ASEAN Charter relating to the promotion and protection of human rights and fundamental freedoms, ASEAN shall establish an ASEAN human rights body.
2. This ASEAN human rights body shall operate in accordance with the terms of reference to be determined by the ASEAN Foreign Ministers Meeting.

53 ASEAN, ASEAN Intergovernmental Commission on Human Rights (AICHR), http://www.asean.org/communities/asean-political-security-community/category/asean-intergovernmental-commission-on-human-rights-aichr (last visited June 1, 2015).

54 ASEAN Human Rights Declaration, Nov. 18, 2012, *available at* http://aichr.org/?dl_name=ASEAN-Human-Rights-Declaration.pdf (last visited June 1, 2015).

IV The Protection of the Rights of the Alleged Perpetrators of Terroristic Acts

The ACCT has significant contribution to the second aspect of the study in this article: the standards for the protection of human rights with respect to the perpetrators or the potential suspects of terrorist crimes. Article 8 on "Fair Treatment" regulates an "Asian" standard for the protection of the persons taken into custody or regarding whom other measures or proceedings are carried out.

This provision guarantees *fair treatment according to the domestic law of the state party* in the territory of which that person is present as well the relevant international law, including international human rights law: "Any person who is taken into custody or regarding whom any other measures are taken or proceedings are carried out pursuant to this Convention shall be guaranteed *fair treatment*, including enjoyment of all rights and guarantees in conformity with the laws of the Party in the territory of which that person is present and applicable provisions of international law, including international human rights law" (Article 8, Para. 1).

Upon receiving information that a person who has committed or who is alleged to have committed an offence covered in Article 2 of this Convention may be present in its territory, the Party concerned shall take such measures as may be necessary under its domestic laws to investigate the facts contained in the information (Article 8, Para. 2). Therefore, the state-parties have the obligation to investigate the facts of the terrorist act committed under their domestic law.

Upon being satisfied that the circumstances so warrant, the Party in whose territory the offender or alleged offender is present shall take the appropriate measures under its domestic laws so as to ensure that person's presence for the purpose of prosecution or extradition (Article 8, Para. 3). The obligation to ensure the presence of the offender or alleged offender is also implemented under the domestic law of the country concerned.

According to Article 8, Para. 4, any person regarding whom measures referred to in Article 8 Para. 3 are being taken shall be entitled:

a. To communicate without delay with the nearest appropriate representative of the State of which that person is a national or which is otherwise entitled to protect that person's rights;
b. To be visited by a representative of that State;
c. To be informed of that person's rights under subparagraphs (a) and (b) of paragraph 4 of this Article.

The rights referred to in Article 8 Para. 4 shall be exercised in conformity with the laws and regulations of the Party in the territory of which the offender or alleged offender is present, subject to the provision that the said laws and regulations must enable full effect to be given to the purposes for which the rights accorded under Article 8 Para. 4 are intended. This provision is not new to the international legal framework for combating terrorism. Similar provisions are Article 6, Para. 4 of the International Convention Against the Taking of Hostages, Article 7, Para. 4 of the Convention for the Suppression of Unlawful Acts Against the Safety of Maritime Navigation, Article 7, Para. 4 of the International Convention for the Suppression of Terrorist Bombing, Article 9, Para. 4 of the International Convention for the Suppression of the Financing of Terrorism, and Article 10, Para. 4 of the International Convention for the Suppression of Acts of Nuclear Terrorism.

When a Party, pursuant to the present Article, has taken a person into custody, it shall immediately notify, directly or through the Secretary-General of ASEAN, the Parties which have established jurisdiction in accordance with paragraph 1 or 2 of Article 7, and if it considers it advisable, any other interested Parties, of the fact that such person is in custody and of the circumstances which warrant that person's detention. The Party which is carrying out the investigation referred to in paragraph 2 of Article 8 shall promptly inform the said Parties of its findings and shall indicate whether it intends to exercise jurisdiction over the said person (Article 8, Para. 6). The obligation of the Parties to mutually inform one another about the existing jurisdiction and the investigation creates certainty and predictability.

This disposition is in compliance with measure 3 of the Plan for Action annexed to the UN Global Counter—Terrorism Strategy: "To ensure the apprehension and prosecution or extradition of perpetrators of terrorist acts, in accordance with the relevant provisions of national and international law, in particular human rights law, refugee law and international humanitarian law. We will endeavor to conclude and implement to that effect mutual judicial assistance and extradition agreements, and to strengthen cooperation between law enforcement agencies."

The above provisions of the ACCT can be compared with the development of the rights of the alleged offender in the universal conventions for combating terrorism.

Initially the international legal framework for the rights of the alleged perpetrator at the universal level occurred indirectly: as correlative obligations of States.[55] For example, the obligation to notify the state of the nationality of the alleged perpetrator or the perpetrator (or if it is a stateless person, the

---

55 For detailed discussions on the rights of the alleged perpetrator, see Irena Ilieva, *International Law Problems of the Fight against International Terrorism* 202–09 (2005).

state in whose territory he resides), corresponds to the right of the person (Article 6, Para. 1, b. "c" of the Convention on the Prevention and Punishment of Crimes against Internationally Protected Persons, including Diplomatic Agents; Article 6, Para. 2, b. "d" of the International Convention Against the Taking of Hostages; Article 10, Para. 6 of the International Convention for the Suppression of Acts of Nuclear Terrorism). The obligation of the states under anti-terrorism conventions for fair treatment corresponds to the right of the alleged perpetrator or perpetrators of a terrorist offense to a fair trial (Article 9 of the Convention on the Prevention and Punishment of Crimes Against Internationally Protected Persons, Including Diplomatic Agents); Article 8, Para. 2 of the International Convention Against the Taking of Hostages; Article 12 of the Convention on the Physical Protection of Nuclear Material; Article 10, Para. 2 of the Convention for the Suppression of Unlawful Acts Against the Safety of Maritime Navigation, etc.).

Positively regulated rights of those suspected of terrorist offenses/crimes are found for the first time in the International Convention against the Taking of Hostages of 1979.

The rights of the alleged perpetrator are:

- to communicate without delay with the nearest appropriate representative of the State of which he is a national or which is otherwise entitled to establish such communication or, if he is a stateless person, the State in the territory of which he has his habitual residence
- to be visited by a representative of that State

The same amount of rights of the alleged perpetrator is arranged for in the Convention for the Suppression of Unlawful Acts Against the Safety of Maritime Navigation (Article 6, Para. 3). In the chronologically later adopted conventions is added thereto the right to be informed of these rights (Article 7(3) of the International Convention for the Suppression of Terrorist Bombing; Article 9(3) of the International Convention for the Suppression of the Financing of Terrorism, Article 10(3) of the International Convention for the Suppression of Acts of Nuclear Terrorism).

The rights to fair treatment are set forth in all universal anti-terroristic conventions (Article 12 of the Convention on the Physical Protection of Nuclear Material;[56] Article 14 of the International Convention for the Suppression

56 Convention on the Physical Protection of Nuclear Material art. 12, Mar. 3, 1980, 1458 U.N.T.S. 125. "Any person regarding whom proceedings are being carried out in connection with

of Terrorist Bombing;[57] Article 17 of the International Convention for the Suppression of the Financing of Terrorism;[58] Article 12 of the International Convention for the Suppression of Acts of Nuclear Terrorism.[59]

The comparison between the universal international legal framework and that of the ASEAN Convention shows similarities. Undoubtedly several rights are arranged for:

- To fair treatment;
- To communicate without delay with the nearest appropriate representative of the State of which that person is a national or which is otherwise entitled to protect that person's rights;
- To be visited by a representative of that State;
- To be informed of the above mentioned rights.

Yet the optional right to invite the International Committee of the Red Cross to communicate with and visit the alleged offender is missing. In the universal international legal framework it first appears in Article 6(6) of the

---

any of the offences set forth in Article 7 shall be guaranteed fair treatment at all stages of the proceedings."

57 International Convention for the Suppression of Terrorist Bombing art. 14, Dec. 15, 1997, 2149 U.N.T.S. 256.

> Any person who is taken into custody or regarding whom any other measures are taken or proceedings are carried out pursuant to this Convention shall be guaranteed fair treatment, including enjoyment of all rights and guarantees in conformity with the law of the State in the territory of which that person is present and applicable provisions of international law, including international law of human rights.

58 International Convention for the Suppression of the Financing of Terrorism art. 17, Dec. 9, 1999, 2178 U.N.T.S. 197.

> Any person who is taken into custody or regarding whom any other measures are taken or proceedings are carried out pursuant to this Convention shall be guaranteed fair treatment, including enjoyment of all rights and guarantees in conformity with the law of the State in the territory of which that person is present and applicable provisions of international law, including international human rights law

59 International Convention for the Suppression of Acts of Nuclear Terrorism art. 12, Apr. 13, 2005, 2445 U.N.T.S. 89.

> Any person who is taken into custody or regarding whom any other measures are taken or proceedings are carried out pursuant to this Convention shall be guaranteed fair treatment, including enjoyment of all rights and guarantees in conformity with the law of the State in the territory of which that person is present and applicable provisions of international law, including international law of human rights.

International Convention against the Taking of Hostages;[60] Article 7(5) of the International Convention for the Suppression of Terrorist Bombing;[61] Article 9(5) of the International Convention for the Suppression of the Financing of Terrorism;[62] Article 10(5) of the International Convention for the Suppression of Acts of Nuclear Terrorism.[63]

From the above comparative analysis, a reasonable conclusion can be drawn that the provisions of the ACCT meet the existing universal standard for the protection of the rights of those suspected of terrorist offenses/crimes, except for the right to invite the International Committee of the Red Cross to communicate with or visit the alleged offender.

It is noteworthy that the right for fair trial is missing. Indeed, as mentioned above, in the Preamble of the ACCT the member states *reaffirm their commitment to the protection of human rights, fair treatment, the rule of law and due process.* As Martin Scheinin points out in his Note of August 6, Protection of Human Rights and Fundamental Freedoms while countering terrorism, the fundamental principle of the right to a fair trial may not be subject to

60 International Convention against the Taking of Hostages art. 6(6), Dec. 17, 1979, 1316 U.N.T.S. 205. "The State which makes the preliminary inquiry contemplated in paragraph 1 of the article shall promptly report its findings to the States or organization referred to in paragraph 2 of the article and indicate whether it intends to exercise jurisdiction."

61 International Convention for the Suppression of Terrorist Bombing, *supra* note 57, art. 7(5).

> The provisions of paragraphs 3 and 4 shall be without prejudice to the right of any State Party having a claim to jurisdiction in accordance with article 6, subparagraph 1 (c) or 2 (c), to invite the International Committee of the Red Cross to communicate with and visit the alleged offender.

62 International Convention for the Suppression of the Financing of Terrorism, *supra* note 58, art. 9(5).

> The provisions of paragraphs 3 and 4 shall be without prejudice to the right of any State Party having a claim to jurisdiction in accordance with article 7, paragraph 1, subparagraph (b), or paragraph 2, subparagraph (b), to invite the International Committee of the Red Cross to communicate with and visit the alleged offender.

63 International Convention for the Suppression of Acts of Nuclear Terrorism, *supra* note 59, art. 10(5).

> The provisions of paragraphs 3 and 4 of the present article shall be without prejudice to the right of any State Party having a claim to jurisdiction in accordance with article 9, paragraph 1(*c*) or 2(*c*), to invite the International Committee of the Red Cross to communicate with and visit the alleged offender

derogation, and that any derogation must not circumvent the protection of non-derogable rights.[64]

The issue of fair treatment of the alleged perpetrator of a terrorist offense is closely connected with the observance of another fundamental right: the prohibition of use of torture and other forms of cruel, inhuman or degrading treatment, as well the ill treatment. The various uses of torture as counterterrorism strategy are analyzed by Adeno Addis[65] in his public lecture that he gave at Chuo University, Tokyo, Japan on July 21, 2009. He argued in detail that waterboarding, sleep deprivation, potentially injurious stress positions, continual intimidation by police dogs represent "torture" and are subject to the absolute prohibition under The Convention against Torture and Other Forms of Cruel, Inhuman or Degrading Treatment or Punishment.[66] The author classifies the various uses of torture: informational torture, confessional torture, punitive torture and intimidatory torture.[67] The focus of the edited version of the lecture is "informational torture" and the strong argumentation led to the conclusion that "torture would clearly not be an effective counterterrorism strategy."[68]

The problem of fair treatment is also linked to the right to be brought promptly before a judge or "other officer" after arrest. The last report on the situation of the detainees in Guantanamo Naval base, "the IACHR, the Working Group and the UN Special Rapporteurs stress that even in extraordinary circumstances, when the indefinite detention of individuals, most of whom have not been charged, goes beyond a minimally reasonable period of time, this constitutes a flagrant violation of international human rights law and in itself constitutes a form of cruel, inhuman, and degrading treatment. On this point, during its last period of sessions, the Inter-American Commission on Human Rights (IACHR) received specialized information on the severe and lasting physiological and psychological damage caused by the detainees' high degree of uncertainty over basic aspects of their lives, such as knowing whether or not they will be tried; whether they will be released and when; or whether they will see their family members again. This continuing state of suffering and

64 U.N. General Assembly, Protection of Human Rights and Fundamental Freedoms While Countering Terrorism, note by the Secretary General, U.N. Doc. A/63/223 (Aug. 6, 2008).

65 W. Ray Forrester Professor of Public and Constitutional Law, Tulane University School of Law.

66 Convention against Torture and Other Cruel, Inhuman or Degrading Treatment or Punishment, Dec. 10, 1984, 1465 U.N.T.S. 85. The Convention entered into force on 26 June 1987 after it had been ratified by 20 States. For the status of the Convention, see Annex VII.

67 *See also* "Amener le détenu a un état basique de dépendence", *Le Monde*, Apr. 25, 2009.

68 Adeno Addis, "Torture as a Counterterrorism Strategy", XLIV *Comp. L. Rev*. 129, 140 (2010).

uncertainty creates grave consequences such as stress, fear, depression, and anxiety, and affects the central nervous system as well as the cardiovascular and immunological systems."[69]

A recent judgment of the European Court for Human rights also deals with the interference between torture and ill treatment. The case *El-Masri v. "The former Yugoslav Republic of Macedonia"*[70] concerned the complaints of a German national of Lebanese origin that he had been a victim of a secret "rendition" operation during which he was arrested, held in isolation, questioned and ill-treated in a Skopje hotel for twenty-three days, then transferred to CIA agents who brought him to a secret detention facility in Afghanistan, where he was further ill-treated for over four months. The Court found Mr El-Masri's account to be established beyond reasonable doubt and held that "the former Yugoslav Republic of Macedonia" had been responsible for his torture and ill-treatment both in the country itself and after his transfer to the US authorities in the context of an extra-judicial "rendition."

The Court finds violation of Article 3 (prohibition of torture and inhuman or degrading treatment) of the Convention on account of the inhuman and degrading treatment to which the applicant was subject to while being held in a hotel in Skopje, on account of his treatment at Skopje Airport, which amounted to torture, and on account of his transfer into the custody of the United States authorities, thus exposing him to the risk of further treatment contrary to Article 3; violation of Article 3 on account of the failure of the former Yugoslav Republic of Macedonia to carry out an effective investigation into Mr. El-Masri's allegations of ill-treatment; violations of Article 5 (right to liberty and security) on account of his detention in the hotel in Skopje for 23 days and of his subsequent captivity in Afghanistan, as well as on account of the failure to carry out an effective investigation into his allegations of arbitrary detention; violation of Article 8 (right to respect for private and family life); and violation of Article 13 (right to an effective remedy).

69 Office of the United Nations High Commissioner for Human Rights, "IACHR, UN Working Group on Arbitrary Detention, UN Rapporteur on Torture, UN Rapporteur on Human Rights and Counter-Terrorism, and UN Rapporteur on Health Reiterate Need to End the Indefinite Detention of Individuals at Guatánamo Naval Base in Light of Current Human Rights Crisis", May 1, 2013, http://www.ohchr.org/EN/NewsEvents/Pages/DisplayNews.aspx?NewsID=13278&LangID=E.

70 El-Masri v. The former Yugoslav Republic of Macedonia, App. No. 39630/09 (Eur. Ct. H.R. 2012).

V Conclusion

The SCCTSE and the ACCT are a major contribution of the Asian-Pacific region in the struggle against terrorism. They are adopted in the framework of regional bodies, aiming at strengthening regional peace and security, a manifestation of the understanding of the state-parties as to the gravity of the crime "terrorism" and as to the need for mutual efforts and international regional cooperation in the fight against that scourge of humankind.

The two conventions incorporate different approaches with respect to the counteraction of terrorism. Whereas the SCCTSE makes a connection between counteraction against terrorism and the non-permission and incrimination of "separatism" and "extremism," the ACCT confines itself to making a reference to the crimes listed in the existing universal conventions on counteraction of terrorism.

The influence of the universal international law on the regional regulation of fighting against terrorism is most clearly manifested in the ACCT in comparison with the SCCTSE. This fact can be explained by the later adoption of the ACCT and the dynamically developing international law in the fight against terrorism.

This conclusion arises from the analysis of the two conventions in the light of the application of the international standard on protection of human rights. In the SCCTSE, there is no direct recall on the principle for the protection of human rights, whereas in the ACCT, apart from the direct proclamation of that principle in the preamble, substantial legal regulation exists with respect to the rights of the alleged perpetrator of a terrorist offense.

Member states of ASEAN also adopt the concept of interrelatedness and indivisibility of civil, political, economic, social and cultural rights. Nevertheless, the state-parties to the SCCTSE are aware of the significance of adhering to the principle that concerns the respect for human rights. This awareness has been evidenced in a political document, such as the Concept of Cooperation Between Member States of the Shanghai Cooperation Organization in Combating Terrorism, Separatism, and Extremism. That document was adopted on June 5, 2005 by Resolution No. 1 of the Council of Heads of SCO Member States of the Shanghai Cooperation Organization.

I need to emphasize that this article is not focused on the actual application and practice of the two conventions. However, we should not ignore the critical comments made by the non-governmental organization Human Rights Watch.[71] A significant weakness is the acceptance of the primacy of national

71 Joanne Mariner, Terrorism and Counterterrorism Program director at Human Rights Watch, said that SCO member states—which include Russia, China, Kazakhstan,

legislation in the incrimination of terrorist offence according to the SCCTSE. Another weakness is the lack of obligation for fair trial (upon the understanding of the jurisprudence of the European Court of Human Rights) for the perpetrators of terrorist crimes in the Shanghai Convention.

I am convinced that not knowing the principle of human rights protection and fundamental freedoms, as well as its actual lack of enforcement, is virtually a triumph of terrorists both at a global and regional level. Self-limitation of states and international organizations, as well as laying the problem of security above the one regarding the respect for human rights, is one of the objectives of international and domestic terrorism. In fact, this is a strong argument for terrorists all over the world to demonstrate and prove the weakness of the achievements in the field of international standards for human rights, the unsuitability of mechanisms for protecting human rights.

In this regard, it is essential that an inference should be drawn that the two conventions under surveillance re-establish some of the principles of the antiterrorist resolutions of the UN General Assembly, in particular that terrorism is not justifiable under any circumstances and therefore the states should combat it in all its forms and manifestations.

From the perspective of the law of the international organizations it can be concluded that the SCO and ASEAN are contributing to the contemporary multipolarity of the system of international relations. Following the adoption of the ASEAN Human Rights Declaration, the beginning of the emergence of a special "Asian" system of protection of human rights can be justified with a high degree of certainty. Although not legally binding, the Declaration is an important step towards the codification of this matter in the Asia Pacific. The analysis of the two conventions attests to the high degree of engagement of the Asian-Pacific states in the counteraction against terrorism and their indisputable contribution to the efforts of the international community.

Kyrgyzstan, Tajikistan, and Uzbekistan—have committed serious violations of human rights and humanitarian law in the name of counterterrorism. Of particular concern are SCO members' records with respect to extraditions, renditions, extrajudicial executions, treatment of terrorism suspects in police custody, and the treatment of religious dissidents and ethnic minorities, among others, who peacefully advocate independence. "Some SCO countries have conflated domestic dissent with terrorism, and used abusive means in combating it," said Joanne Mariner. "While constructive regional cooperation could play an important role in defeating terrorism, there is a good reason to worry that the organization simply reinforces members' worst practices." Human Rights Watch, "Eurasia: Uphold Human Rights in Combating Terrorism", June 15, 2006, http://www.hrw.org/news/2006/06/13/eurasia-uphold-human-rights-combating-terrorism.

VI Annexes

ANNEX I *Status of the International Convention on Civil and Political Rights as of September 16, 2013.*[72]

Member state of SCO	Signature	Ratification, accession (a), succession
Kazakhstan	2.12.2003	24.01.2006
Kyrgyzstan		7.10.1994 (a)
China	5.10.1998	
Russian Federation	18.03.1968	16.10.1973
Tadjikistan		4.01.1999 (a)

ANNEX II *Status of the International Convention on Civil and Political Rights as of September 16, 2013.*[73]

Member state of ASEAN	Signature	Ratification, accession (a), succession
Indonesia		23.02.2006 (a)
Malaysia		
Philippines	19.12.1966	23.10.1986
Singapore		
Thailand		29.10.1996 (a)
Brunei Darussalam		
Viet Nam		24.09.1982 (a)
Lao PDR	7.12.2000	25.09.2009
Myanmar		
Cambodia	17.10.1980	26.05.1992

72 Status of the International Covenant on Civil and Political Rights, *available at* http://treaties.un.org/Pages/ViewDetails.aspx?src=TREATY&mtdsg_no=IV-4&chapter=4&lang=en (last visited June 1, 2015).

73 Status of the International Convention on Civil and Political Rights, *available at* http://treaties.un.org/Pages/ViewDetails.aspx?src=TREATY&mtdsg_no=IV-4&chapter=4&lang=en (last visited June 1, 2015).

ANNEX III *Status of the Optional Protocol to the International Convention on Civil and Political Rights as of September 16, 2013.*[74]

Member state of SCO	Signature	Ratification, accession (a), succession
Kazakhstan	25.09.2007	30.06.2009
Kyrgyzstan		7.10.1994 (a)
China		
Russian Federation		1.10.1991 (a)
Tadjikistan		4.01.1999 (a)

ANNEX IV *Status of the Optional Protocol to the International Convention on Civil and Political Rights as of September 16, 2013.*[75]

Member state of ASEAN	Signature	Ratification, accession (a), succession
Indonesia		
Malaysia		
Philippines	19.12.1966	22.08.1989
Singapore		
Thailand		
Brunei Darussalam		
Viet Nam		
Lao PDR		
Myanmar		
Cambodia	27.09.2004	

74 Status of the Optional Protocol to the ICCPR, *available at* http://treaties.un.org/Pages/ViewDetails.aspx?src=TREATY&mtdsg_no=IV-5&chapter=4&lang=en (last visited June 1, 2015).

75 *Id.*

ANNEX V *Status of the Second Optional Protocol to the ICCPR, aiming at the abolition of the death penalty as of September 16, 2013.*[76]

State	Signature	Ratification, accession (a), succession
Kazakhstan		
Kyrgyzstan		6.12.2010
China		
Russian Federation		
Tadjikistan		
Indonesia		
Malaysia		
Philippines	20.09.2006	20.11.2007
Singapore		
Thailand		
Brunei Darussalam		
Viet Nam		
Lao PDR		
Myanmar		
Cambodia		

ANNEX VI *Status of the International Covenant on Economic, Social and Cultural Rights as of September 16, 2013.*[77]

Member state of SCO	Signature	Ratification, accession (a), succession
Kazakhstan	2.12.2003	24.01.2006
Kyrgyzstan		7.10.1994 (a)
China	27.10.1997	27.03.2001
Russian Federation	18.03.1968	16.10.1973
Tadjikistan		4.01.1999 (a)

76 Status of the Second Optional Protocol to the ICCPR, aiming at the abolition of the death penalty, *available at* http://treaties.un.org/Pages/ViewDetails.aspx?src=TREATY&mtdsg_no=IV-12&chapter=4&lang=en (last visited June 1, 2015).

77 Status of the International Covenant on Economic, Social and Cultural Rights, *available at* http://treaties.un.org/Pages/ViewDetails.aspx?src=TREATY&mtdsg_no=IV-3&chapter=4&lang=en (last visited June 1, 2015).

Member state of ASEAN	Signature	Ratification, accession (a), succession
Indonesia		23.02.2006
Malaysia		
Philippines	19.12.1966	7.06.1974
Singapore		
Thailand		5.06.1999
Brunei Darussalam		
Viet Nam		24.09.1982
Lao PDR	7.12.2000	13.02.2007
Myanmar		
Cambodia	17.10.1980	26.05.1992

ANNEX VII *Status of the Convention against Torture and other Cruel, Inhuman or Degrading Treatment or Punishment as of September 16, 2013.*[78]

State	Signature	Ratification, accession (a), succession
Kazakhstan		26.08.1998 (a)
Kyrgyzstan		5.09.1997 (a)
China	12.12.1986	4.10.1988
Russian Federation	10.12.1985	3.03.1987
Tadjikistan		11.01.1995 (a)
Indonesia	23.10.1985	28.10.1998
Malaysia		
Philippines		18.06.1986 (a)
Singapore		
Thailand		2.10.2007 (a)
Brunei Darussalam		
Viet Nam		
Lao PDR	21.09.2010	26.09.2012
Myanmar		
Cambodia		15.10.1992 (a)

78 Status of the Convention against Torture and other Cruel, Inhuman or Degrading Treatment or Punishment, *available at* http://treaties.un.org/Pages/ViewDetails.aspx?src=TREATY&mtdsg_no=IV-9&chapter=4&lang=en (last visited June 1, 2015).

The Delineation of Treaty-Making Powers between the Central Government of the People's Republic of China and the Special Administrative Region of Hong Kong

Björn Ahl

Table of Contents

I Introduction

This article investigates treaty-making by the People's Republic of China (China) and its Special Administrative Region of Hong Kong (HKSAR) with a focus on the delineation of treaty-making powers between the Central Government and the Region.[1] Though China is a unitary state,[2] the Region of Hong Kong enjoys far-reaching autonomy that allows it to maintain its capitalist system

* Associate Professor of Chinese Legal Culture, Institute of East Asian Studies, University of Cologne.

1 Part of this article is based on chapter two and the English summary of the author's book, *Björn Ahl*, Die Anwendung völkerrechtlicher Verträge in China [The Application of International Treaties in China], 2009, S. 67–122, 357–58.

2 Given that the Central Government does not exercise jurisdiction over the territory of Taiwan, China is also a divided state. Björn Ahl, "Taiwan", *in* 9 *The Max Planck Encyclopedia of Public International Law* 749 (Rüdiger Wolfrum ed., 2012).

 | DOI 10.1163/9789004306509_005

and own institutions, independent judicial authority and a legal system that is separate from Mainland China. The autonomy of the HKSAR includes the power to conclude certain international agreements on its own. This study of treaty-making powers takes a doctrinal approach. It analyses Chinese and HKSAR legislation including scholarly views and the relevant treaty-making practice.

Competences and procedures of treaty-making are crucial factors of a state's treaty-making practice. The modalities of participation of state organs in the treaty-making procedure determine the domestic effects of international treaties.[3] Legislative approval of a treaty can be regarded as a precondition of the validity or applicability of treaty norms under municipal law. It often depends on the state organ, which approves the conclusion of a treaty, if or where the treaty is published and how a treaty is ranked within the domestic hierarchy of norms. In Mainland China, treaties which are approved by the Standing Committee of the National People's Congress (NPC) are attached to the approval decision and published in the NPC Standing Committee's Official Gazette.[4] Such treaties have the rank of national statutes.[5]

---

3 John H. Jackson, "Status of Treaties in Domestic Legal Systems: A Policy Analysis", 86 *Am. J. Int'l L.* 310, 315 & 323 (1992); Thomas Cottier & Krista Nadakavukaren Schefer, "The Relationship between World Trade Organization Law, National and Regional Law", 1 *J. Int'l Econ. L.* 83, 115 (1998).

4 Zhonghua Renmin Gongheguo Renmin Daibiao Dahui Changwu Weiyuanhui Gongbao [Gazette of the Standing Committee of the National People's Congress of the People's Republic of China]; according to Treaty-making Law § 16 all treaties and agreements concluded according to the Treaty-making Law shall be published in Zhonghua Renmin Gongheguo Tiaoyueji [Treaty Series of the People's Republic of China] published by Zhonghua Renmin Gongheguo Waijiaobu [Foreign Ministry of China]. However, not all treaties have been included in the collection. *See* Jerry Z. Li & Sanzhuan Guo, "China", *in International Law and Domestic Legal Systems: Incorporation, Transformation, and Persuasion* 158, 179–80 (Dinah Shelton ed., 2011).

5 Hui Wu, "Tiao Yue Zai Wo Guo Guo Nei Fa Shang De Di Wei Ji Yu Guo Nei Fa Chong Tu De Yu Fang He Jie Jue [The Status of Treaties in Chinese Domestic Law: Avoiding and Resolving its Conflicts with Domestic Law]", *in Guo Ji Tiao Yue Yu Guo Nei Fa De Guan Xi* [*The Relationship between International Treaties and Municipal Law*] 124, 126 (Xiaoqing Zhu & Lie Huang eds., 2000). For an overview of China's approach to the application of international law in its domestic legal system and accounts of domestic implementation of treaties in China, see Björn Ahl, "Chinese Law and International Treaties", 39 *Hong Kong L. J.* 735, (2009); Peng-fei Zhu, "Jie Jue Guo Ji Tiao Yue Yu Guo Nei Fa Chong Tu Wen Ti De Xin Si Kao—Yi "Xian Fa" He "Di Jie Tiao Yue Fa" Wei Yi Ju [Thinking on Conflict Settlement of International Treaty and National Law- Based on Constitution and Law of Procedure of the Conclusion of Treaties]", 7(2) *Jiang Nan She Hui Xue Yuan Xue Bao* [*Journal of Jiangnan Social University*] 59 (2005); Xue

II Treaty-Making Powers of the Central State

According to Article 89(9) of the Chinese Constitution, the power to conclude treaties and agreements with foreign states is vested in the State Council.[6] Procedures and competences of treaty-making are provided for in detail in the Law of the People's Republic of China on the Procedure of Concluding International Treaties (Treaty-making Law) of 1990.[7] This law was modelled on a similar Soviet law of 1978.[8] Whereas other states make use of internal regulations, China has followed the practice of some socialist states to adopt a law to regulate details of how the Government conducts its external relations. The Ministry of Foreign Affairs (MFA) concludes treaties and agreements under the direction of the State Council.[9] The Treaty-making Law stipulates competences and authorization procedures for each step that precedes the conclusion of a treaty. Those steps include the proposal to conclude a treaty,

---

Hanqin & Jin Qian, "International Treaties in the Chinese Domestic Legal System", 8 *Chinese J. Int'l L.* 299 (2009); Keyuan Zou, "International Law in the Chinese Domestic Context", 44 *Val. U. L. Rev.* 935 (2010); Li & Guo, *supra* note 4, at 158.

6 Zhonghua Renmin Gongheguo Xianfa [Constitution of the People's Republic of China] (1982).

7 Zhonghua Renmin Gongheguo Dijie Tiaoyue Chengxu Fa [Law of the People's Republic of China on the Procedure of the Conclusion of International Treaties] (promulgated by the Standing Committee of the National People's Congress of the People's Republic of China, Dec. 28, 1990, effective Dec. 28, 1990), http://www.npc.gov.cn/wxzl/gongbao/2000-12/16/content_5004545.htm (last visited June 1, 2015). *See* Zihua Shen, "Wo Guo Tiao Yue Pi Zhun De Yun Zuo Ji Zhi [Procedure Mechanisms of Chinese Treaty Ratification]", 3 *Guojia Xingzheng Xueyuan Xuebao* [*Journal of the National Administrative Institute*] 69 (2012). It has been discussed to amend the Treaty-making Law, particularly in order to allocate the competences between state organs more clearly. For reference to the official amendment proposal and legal analysis, *see* Xinsheng Xie, Zhong Guo De Tiao Yue Di Jie Cheng Xu Yu Di Jie Quan [China's Treaty-Making Process and Treaty Making Power], 80 *Fa Xue Lun Tan* [*Legal Tribune*] 46 (2012).

8 O Poryadke Zaklyucheniya, Ispolneniya I Denonsatsii Mezhdunarodnykh Dogovorov SSSR [Law on the Procedure for the Conclusion, Performance, and Denunciation of International Treaties of the USSR], http://base.consultant.ru/cons/cgi/online.cgi?req=doc;base=ESU;n=1515 (last visited June 1, 2015); *see* "Lun Di Jie Guo Ji Tiao Yue De Gui Fan Hua [On the Formalization of the Conclusion of International Treaties]", *Fa Zhi Ri Bao* [Legal Daily], Jan. 27, 1991; Qichen Qian, Guan Yu Zhong Hua Ren Min Gong He Guo Di Jie Tiao Yue Cheng Xu Fa (Cao An) De Shuo Ming [Explanation of the Draft Law on the Procedure of Concluding International Treaties] (Aug. 30, 1990), *available at* http://www.npc.gov.cn/wxzl/gongbao/2000-12/27/content_5002493.htm.

9 Treaty-making Law § 3, cl. 4.

preparation of the treaty draft by the relevant department of the State Council in charge, as well as negotiation and determination of the final treaty text.[10]

International treaties are concluded either in the name of China, in the name of the Central People's Government (CPG), the State Council, or in the name of a department of the State Council such as a ministry, commission or another department directly under the State Council.[11] The competences to authorize treaty drafts and to sign full powers of representatives depend on this categorization.[12] However, the Treaty-making Law does not specify the conditions under which an international treaty is concluded in the name of the State, the Government or a ministry. Commentators suggest that only important political treaties and treaties that relate to the territory of China are concluded in the name of the State. If matters fall exclusively within the competence of a State Council department, the agreement can be concluded in the name of the department; in all other cases treaties should be concluded in the name of the Central Government.[13] In practice treaties that require approval by the Standing Committee of the NPC are generally concluded in the name of China.[14]

---

10 For a detailed analysis compare Xiaocheng Qin, *Zhong Hua Ren Min Gong He Guo Di Jie Tiao Yue De Xing Shi Yan Jiu* [*Study on the Forms of Treaties Concluded by the People's Republic of China*] (2003).

11 Treaty-Making Law § 4.

12 Treaty-Making Law §§ 5–6. *See also* Wang Tieya, *Guo Ji Fa* [*International Law*] 301 (2010).

13 Yiqin Zhang, "Jian Shu Wo Guo Di Jie Tiao Yue De Shen Pi Cheng Xu [Description of the Approval Procedure of Chinese Treaty-Making]", *in The Relationship between International Treaties and Municipal Law*, *supra* note 5, at 237, 243.

14 Treaties regarding criminal mutual assistance were often concluded in the name of China. For a comprehensive compilation of China's treaty activity *see* Lijiang Zhu & Chengyuan Ma, "Chinese Practice in Public International Law", 12 *Chinese J. Int'l L.* 363 (2012). Since the mid-1990s only a small number of treaties subject to legislative approval were concluded in the name of the Central Government. *See* Zhong Hua Ren Min Gong He Guo Zheng Fu He Lao Wo Ren Min Min Zhu Gong He Guo Zheng Fu Bian Jie Zhi Du Tiao Yue [Treaty between the Government of the People's Republic of China and the Government of the People's Democratic Republic of Laos on the Border System], China-Laos, Standing Comm. Nat'l People's Cong. Gaz (Dec. 3, 1993) No. 5, 59; Zhong Hua Ren Min Gong He Guo Zheng Fu, Chao Xian Min Zhu Zhu Yi Ren Min Gong He Guo Zheng Fu He E Luo Si Lian Bang Zheng Fu Guan Yu Que Ding Tu Men Jiang San Guo Guo Jie Shui Yu Fen Jie Xian De Xie Ding [Agreement between the Government of the People's Republic of China, the Government of the Democratic People's Republic of Korea and the Government of the Russian Federation on the Determination of Lines of Demarcation of the River Tumen as the Border between the Three States], Nov. 3 1998, China-N.Kor.-Russ., Standing Comm. Nat'l People's Cong. Gaz (1999) No. 3, 247.

If treaties are negotiated and signed in the name of China, the State Council authorizes the treaty drafts that are prepared and submitted by the MFA and/or the relevant State Council department.[15] Treaties signed in the name of the Central Government are prepared by the MFA or another State Council department in charge. The State Council authorizes the draft.[16] Agreements that are negotiated and signed in the name of a government department concerning matters within the functional competence of the department concerned are authorized by that department or in consultation with the MFA.[17]

A *Ratification of Treaties and External Representation of China*

As regards the external representation of China on the international plane, the current Constitution, unlike the Constitution of 1954,[18] does not explicitly assign the exclusive competence of external representation to the State President. Commentators often simply state that the power to make treaties is jointly exercised by the NPC Standing Committee, the State President and the State Council.[19] In practice, the State President represents China to conclude more important treaties; the President ratifies treaties in accordance with Article 81 of the Chinese Constitution.[20] Ministers of the State Council conclude less important treaties or agreements.[21] Some scholars view the State President as exercising only a "symbolic role" when ratifying treaties and suggest that the NPC Standing Committee should be responsible for the treaty ratification on the international level.[22] However, those scholarly views disregard

---

15 Treaty-Making Law § 5, cl. 1, sentence 1.

16 Treaty-Making Law § 5, cl. 1, sentence 2.

17 Treaty-Making Law § 5, cl. 1, sentence 3.

18 *See* Constitution of the People's Republic of China § 41 (1954).

19 Jinrong Li, *Guo Ji Fa* [*International Law*] 291 (2002); Jie Wu, *Xian Fa Jiao Cheng* [*Textbook on Constitutional Law*] 228 (1996); Wang, *supra* note 12, at 299.

20 Constitution of the People's Republic of China § 81 (1982), "The President of the People's Republic of China receives foreign diplomatic representatives on behalf of the People's Republic of China and, in pursuance of decisions of the Standing Committee of the National People's Congress, appoints and recalls plenipotentiary representatives abroad, and ratifies and abrogates treaties and important agreements concluded with foreign states."

21 *See* Constitution of the People's Republic of China § 89, cl. 9 (1982) and Treaty-Making Law § 3, cl. 1.

22 Xie, *supra* note 7, at 48–49; Hanfeng Chen et al., "Guoji Tiaoyue yu Guoneifa de Guanxi he zai Zhongguo de Shijian [The Relationship between International Treaties and Municipal Law and the Practice in China]", *in The Relationship between International Treaties and Municipal Law, supra* note 5, at 86, 95; Xu Lisha, "Lun Guo Ji Tiao Yue Zai Guo Nei Zhi Xing De Li Fa Shi Jian [On the Legislative Practice of the Domestic Execution of International

the requirements of intergovernmental intercourse as well as the text of the Chinese Constitution and ignore that the Secretary General of the Communist Party normally holds the office of State President. The reason for questioning the State President's external powers may be related to the inconsistency between the constitutional status of the President as the highest representative of the state in external matters on the one hand, and the constitutional status of the NPC and the NPC Standing Committee respectively as the highest state organs on the other hand. According to the wording of the Constitution and the current treaty practice, it is the State President who represents China on the international plane and ratifies treaties. Power of representation may be delegated to ministers of the State Council.

B *Legislative Approval*

The Constitution provides that the Standing Committee of the NPC decides on the ratification and abrogation of international treaties and important agreements concluded with foreign states.[23] Chinese legal doctrine defines the term of international treaties[24] and international agreements[25] both in a broad and a narrow sense. Whereas analysis and definition of the exact scope of these terms differ to some extent,[26] there is consensus that international treaties and agreements in their broadest sense denote any agreement under international law between states or other subjects of international law irrespective of the designation of the agreement. It is not required that the agreement is contained in one single document or that it is laid down in written form.[27] The narrow meaning of international treaties includes important agreements

---

Treaties], Hilaw.cn (Mar. 3, 2003), http://www.hicourt.gov.cn/theory/artilce_list.asp?id=903&l_class=2.

23 Constitution of the People's Republic of China § 67, cl. 14 (1982). The Constitution calls legislative approval of treaties by the NPC Standing Committee "decision on ratification" (Chinese: *Jue Ding Tong Wai Guo Di Jie De Tiao Yue de Pi Zhun*).

24 Chinese: *tiaoyue*.

25 Chinese: *xieding*.

26 Xie, *supra* note 7, at 47; Wang, *supra* note 12, at 295; Yifeng Chen, "The Treaty-making Power in China: Constitutionalization, Progress and Problems", 15 *Asian Y.B. Int'l L.* 43, 46, 49–50, 52 (2011); Li & Guo, *supra* note 4 at 163.

27 Tieya Wang, *Zhong Hua Fa Xue Da Ci Dian—Guo Ji Fa Juan* [*Comprehensive Legal Science Dictionary of China—Volume on International Law*] 547 (1996); Wang, *supra* note 12, at 294. For different forms of treaties accepted in Chinese practice, see Hungdah Chiu, *The People's Republic of China and the Law of Treaties* 14 (1972). With regard to non-written agreements, see Xiaocheng Qin, Oral International Agreements and China's Relevant Practice, 4 *Chinese J. Int'l L.* 465 (2005).

concerning political or economic matters that are concluded in written form and are subject to formal procedures including legislative approval such as treaties of alliance, border or neutrality treaties.[28] The Constitution applies the term of "treaty" in a narrow meaning in order to distinguish it from less important "agreements," which do not require the approval of the NPC Standing Committee. Agreements in a narrow sense denote less formal agreements on specific administrative or technical matters that require approval by the State Council or are concluded by a Department of the State Council without such approval requirement.[29]

According to the Treaty-making Law, treaties and important agreements are subject to legislative approval. Once the text of such an instrument has been signed, it is submitted to the State Council for examination and verification, and the State Council refers it to the NPC Standing Committee to take the decision on the approval of the treaty. Consequently, the State Council has the power to decide whether the relevant treaty falls within the category of "treaties and important agreements." Since the State Council is in a more powerful position in practice, the NPC Standing Committee's competence under the current constitution to overrule a decision of the State Council is only a theoretical option.[30] The Treaty-making Law provides that in particular the following treaties and agreements fall within this category: treaties of friendship and cooperation, treaties of peace and other treaties of a political nature, as well as treaties and agreements which contain stipulations inconsistent with the laws of China.[31] The purpose of the last section of this provision is to avoid inconsistencies between the contents of international treaties and the Chinese domestic legal system. The NPC Standing Committee can act in different ways to ensure conformity of treaties and municipal law: It can withhold approval, combine approval with the declaration of a reservation or adopt changes of domestic law.[32] It is also argued that approval by the NPC Standing Committee of a treaty that deviates from domestic law constitutes an implied amendment of the relevant national legislation due to the

28 Haopei Li, *Tiao Yue Fa Gai Lun* [*Introduction to Treaty Law*] 24 (1987); Wang, *supra* note 12, at 294, 296, 302.

29 Xianyu Yu, *Guo Ji Fa Lü Da Ci Dian* [*Comprehensive International Law Dictionary*] 159 (1995).

30 Chen, *supra* note 26, at 43–69; Zhu, *supra* note 5, at 61–62.

31 Further, the following treaties require treaties and agreements concerning territory and delimitation of boundary lines; treaties and agreements relating to judicial assistance and extradition; Treaty-making Law § 7.

32 Wu, *supra* note 5, at 129; Wang, *supra* note 12, at 302.

legislative character of the approval.[33] Given the informal consensus finding procedures prior to submission for approval of an international treaty to the NPC Standing Committee, it is unlikely that the Standing Committee will withhold its approval. In case there is no consensus among the state and party organs involved, the treaty will simply not be submitted to the NPC Standing Committee for approval. An example of such a situation of a treaty pending legislative approval after it has been signed is the International Covenant on Civil and Political Rights (ICCPR), which was initially signed by the Chinese government in 1998. However, it has not been submitted to the NPC Standing Committee for approval. Consequently, the accession of China to the ICCPR is still pending.[34]

Although the power of the NPC Standing Committee to participate in the treaty-making procedure has been gradually expanded,[35] the circumstances of the accession of China to the WTO revealed the relatively weak position of the NPC Standing Committee in relation to the executive. Article 67(14) of the Constitution stipulates that the President shall not ratify a treaty unless the Standing Committee of the NPC, after reviewing the treaty at one of its sessions, renders a decision to that effect. However, when acceding to the WTO, the Chinese government deposited the instrument of ratification only two days after signature, without the consent of the Standing Committee. Although the Standing Committee published a decision on the accession to the WTO, the decision referred only to the progress of the accession negotiations in general and was taken 15 months before the date of signature.[36] The intention was that the Standing Committee had, in this case, either taken an anticipated decision

33 Zewei Yang, *Guo Ji Fa Jiao Cheng* [*International Law Textbook*] 28 (1999); Ao Luo, "Lun Guo Ji Tiao Yue Zai Zhong Guo de Shi Yong [About the Application of International Treaties in China]", 26 *Fa Zhi Yu She Hui* [*Legal System and Society*] 13, 13 (2009).

34 It was said in an official statement of the State Council of 2005 that "[t]he Chinese government also signed the International Covenant on Civil and Political Rights in October 1998. At present, the Chinese government departments concerned are pressing on with their research and preparations, and when conditions are ripe, the State Council will submit a request to the Standing Committee of the NPC for examination and approval," *see* St. Council Information Office, Building of Political Democracy in China, http://www.china.org.cn/english/2005/Oct/145718.htm (last visited June 1, 2015).

35 Chen, *supra* note 26, at 51–52, counts 361 treaties that were subject to legislative approval before 2009. *Compare also* Chen, *supra* note 7, at 71.

36 *See* Quan Guo Ren Min Dai Biao Da Hui Chang Wu Wei Yuan Hui Guan Yu Wo Guo Jia Ru Shi Jie Mao Yi Zu Zhi De Jue Ding [Decision of the Standing Comm. Nat'l People's Cong. on the Accession of China to the World Trade Organization] (promulgated by the Stand. Comm. Nat'l People's Cong., Aug. 25 2000) 2001 Stand. Comm. Nat'l Cong. Gaz. 600.

on the accession or waived its power of decision regarding the ratification.[37] However, it is very doubtful whether the Chinese Constitution allows State organs to waive their powers or to delegate competences, as was the case for accession to the WTO. Some commentators therefore regard the accession of China to the WTO as a violation of the Chinese Constitution.[38]

When the NPC Standing Committee approves a treaty, the internal decision-making includes not only the delegates of the Standing Committee but involves other relevant actors of the Party-State in the process of informal decision-making.[39] Hence, the NPC Standing Committee's power to approve treaties is, in practice, not a genuine power of parliamentary participation and control.

III Treaty-Making Competence of Hong Kong

Although Hong Kong is an autonomous sub-entity of a unitary state, it arguably enjoys more extensive external autonomy than any other autonomous region.[40] The aspects that, apart from its treaty-making power, constitute Hong Kong's special international status include separate membership in international organizations, control of international shipping and air transportation, status as a separate customs territory with its own currency and system of taxation, issuing of Hong Kong Special Administrative Region passports and immigration control.[41] As was agreed upon in the Sino-British Joint Declaration, the Basic Law of Hong Kong vests the HKSAR with powers to conduct external affairs including the power to make treaties with foreign states.[42] The HKSAR

---

37 Minyou Yu, "Compliance with China's WTO Accession Agreement: A Chinese Lawyer's Perspective", *in Guo Ji Fa Wen Ti Zhuan Lun* [*International Law Issues Monograph*] 380, 408 (Shaping Shao ed., 2002); Xiangjun Kong, *WTO Fa Lu De Guo Nei Shi Yong* [*Domestic Application of WTO Law*] 146 (2002).

38 Naigen Zhang, *Guo Ji Fa Yuan Li* [*Theory of International Law*] 25 (2002).

39 Sebastian Heilmann, *Das politische System der Volksrepublik China* [*The Political System of the People's Republic of China*] 253 (2004).

40 Huaqun Zeng, "Unprecedented International Status: Theoretical and Practical Aspects of the HKSAR's External Autonomy", 9 *J. World Inv. & Trade* 249, 249 (2008).

41 Xiaobing Xu & George D. Wilson, "The Hong Kong Special Administrative Region as a Model of Regional External Autonomy", 32 *Case W. Res. J. Int'l L.* 1, 3–6 (2000).

42 *See* Joint Declaration of the Government of the United Kingdom of Great Britain and Northern Ireland and the Government of the Peoples Republic of China on the Question of Hong Kong with Annexes, Dec. 19, 1984, Gr. Brit.-H.K., § 3, cl. 10, Gr. Brit. T.S. No. 026 (1985), (Cd. 9543) [hereinafter Sino-British Joint Declaration]; Xianggang Jiben Fa [Basic Law] § 151; Xu & Wilson, *supra* note 41, at 1.

is not a state but a sub-entity of China; it has been often described as an entity *sui generis*.[43] Although Hong Kong is an organised political community under a government, it is not an entity that is in its external relations only bound by public international law and can avail itself of autonomous powers internally. The Basic Law provides that the Region is subordinated to the CPG and powers to exercise foreign affairs are vested in the CPG. The Region has no powers to give itself a constitution; the Central Authorities are responsible of amending the Basic Law.[44]

Although the HKSAR does not fulfil the prerequisites of statehood, the Region possesses relative legal personality in relation to specific rights and obligations under international law and its actions are insofar regulated directly by international rules.[45] However, Mainland Chinese commentators, in general, do not recognise the international legal personality of Hong Kong, although they accept a treaty-making competence of the Region.[46] It is argued that Hong Kong is neither a state nor has it any other international legal personality.[47] Based on the provision that the HKSAR is a local administrative region directly under the CPG, some commentators conclude that the Region is not even a partial subject of international law.[48] The reason for denying Hong Kong even

---

43 *See* Lorenz Langer, "Out of Joint? Hong Kong's International Status from the Sino-British Joint Declaration to the Present", 46 *Archiv des Völkerrechts* (AVR) [*Archive of Public International Law*] 309, 342 (2008).

44 Basic Law § 12, 13, 159.

45 "The subjects of law in any legal system are not necessarily identical in their nature or in the extent of their rights, and their nature depends upon the needs of the community. Throughout its history, the development of international law has been influenced by the requirements of international life…" Reparation for Injuries Suffered in the Service of the United Nations, Advisory Opinion, 1949 I.C.J. 174, 178 (Apr. 11); Xu & Wilson, *supra* note 41, at 35–37.

46 Gujie Yuan & Zhiqiao Qiu, "Xiang Gang, Ao Men Hui Gui Hou De Bu Fen Di Yue Quan Ji Tiao Yue Shi Yong [Partial Treaty-Making Competence and the Application of International Treaties in Hong Kong and Macau after the Handover]", *Hua Nan Shi Fan Da Xue Xue Bao, She Hui Ke Xue Bao* [*Journal of Huanan Normal University (Social Sciences Edition)*] 17, 18 (2001).

47 Shuying Liang, "Qian Xi Tiao Yue Zai Xiang Gang De Shi Yong [Examination of the Application of International Treaties in Hong Kong]", 1 *Zheng Fa Lun Tan* [*Tribune of Political Science and Law*] 104, 104, 108 (1999).

48 Guanping Yun & Yekun Zhong, *Zhong Hua Ren Min Gong He Guo Xiang Gang Te Bie Xing Zheng Qu Ji Ben Fa Gai Lun* [*Introduction to the Basic Law of the Hong Kong Special Administrative Region*] 306 (1993).

the status of a partial subject of international law may lie in the fear of harming the sovereignty of the nation.[49]

A Delineation of the HKSAR's Treaty-Making Power

A general rule on the delineation between the external powers of Hong Kong and the CPG is provided for in the chapter on the relationship between the Central Authorities and the HKSAR in Article 13, which introduces the distinction between "foreign affairs" powers of the CPG and "external affairs" to be exercised by the HKSAR.[50] Even though both terms do not seem to be significantly different, the corresponding terms in Chinese[51] indicate that the former relates to "quintessentially matters of state and international diplomacy," whereas the latter appears to be concerned with "economic and cultural matters."[52]

A more specific provision on treaty-making is laid down in the chapter on external affairs in Article 151 of the Basic Law.[53] According to the wording of Article 151, the HKSAR is vested with treaty-making powers in "appropriate

---

49 Yongping Ge, *Hongkong und die Europäische Union* [*Hong Kong and the European Union*] 267 (2003); Ge Yongping, Hong Kong's International Legal Status and Treaty-Making Competence, *in Iustitia et Pax: Gedächtnisschrift für Dieter Blumenwitz* 1098 (Gilbert Gorning et al. eds., 2008); Huaqun Zeng, "Initiative and Implications of Hong Kong's Bilateral Investment Treaties", 11 *J. World Inv. and Trade* 669, 694 (2010).

50 Basic Law § 13 reads:

> The Central People's Government shall be responsible for the foreign affairs relating to the Hong Kong Special Administrative Region.
>
> The Ministry of Foreign Affairs of the People's Republic of China shall establish an office in Hong Kong to deal with foreign affairs.
>
> The Central People's Government authorizes the Hong Kong Special Administrative Region to conduct relevant external affairs on its own in accordance with this Law.

51 Chinese: *Wai Jiao Shi Wu* and *Dui Wai Shi Wu*.

52 Yash Ghai, *Hong Kong's New Constitutional Order* 461 (1999). *See also* Sino-British Joint Declaration, *supra* note 42, § 3, cl. 10 (referring to Hong Kong's power to conclude treaties regarding economic and cultural matters).

53 Basic Law § 151 reads,

> The Hong Kong Special Administrative Region may on its own, using the name "Hong Kong, China," maintain and develop relations and conclude and implement agreements with foreign states and regions and relevant international organizations in the appropriate fields, including the economic, trade, financial and monetary, shipping, communications, tourism, cultural and sports fields.

The same wording can be found in the Sino-British Joint Declaration, *supra* note 42, Annex I Elaboration of the Government of the People's Republic of China of Its Basic Policies Regarding Hong Kong, XI Foreign Affairs.

fields." The list of matters mentioned in this article is not exhaustive but has only exemplary character. The Basic Law must be interpreted in order to determine the fields in which Hong Kong can conclude treaties, apart from those already explicitly listed in Article 151. An indication of how to interpret the notion of "appropriate fields" is the wording of Article 151 that terms treaties to be concluded by the HKSAR "agreements." The Chinese language version of the Basic Law, which prevails in case of a contradiction between the English and the Chinese versions of the Basic Law, uses the term *xieyi*.[54] This wording seems to relate to the general distinction between "treaties"[55] and "agreements."[56] If this distinction is regarded as crucial for the determination of the contents of agreements in the sense of Article 151, the HKSAR is prohibited from entering into politically important treaties.

The same result is achieved by taking into consideration the distinction in Article 13 of the Basic Law between "foreign affairs" and "external affairs." The competence of the Central Government in defence matters under Article 14 of the Basic Law implies that the HKSAR also has no treaty-making powers in the area of defence. Mainland Chinese commentators also conclude that Hong Kong's treaty-making competence only covers matters of a "non-political" nature.[57] In practice, prior approval of the CPG will always be sought in all unspecified fields, and when in doubt, the "mandate to negotiate" will be raised by the other party of the proposed agreement.

It has been proposed to apply the Mainland Chinese Treaty-making Law to Hong Kong in order to impose an approval procedure that subjects the

---

54 Pursuant to a decision of the National People's Congress Standing Committee, the Basic Law, the Chinese text shall prevail in case of discrepancy between the Chinese text and its English translation. Quan Guo Ren Min Dai Biao Da Hui Chang Wu Wei Yuan Hui Guan Yu Zhong Hua Ren Min Gong He Guo Xiang Gang Te Bie Xing Zheng Qu Ji Ben Fa Ying Wen Ben De Jue Ding [Decision of the National People's Congress Standing Committee on the English Text of the Basic Law of the Hong Kong Special Administrative Region] (promulgated by the Standing Comm. Nat'L People's Cong., Jun. 28, 1990), 1990 Standing Comm. Nat'l People's Cong. Gaz, 250.

55 Chinese: *Tiao Yue*.

56 Chinese: *Xie Yi*.

57 Zhiqiao Qiu, "Lun Xiang Gang, Ao Men Te Bie Xing Zheng Qu De Tiao Yue Di Jie Ji Shi Yong [On the Conclusion and Application of International Treaties in the Special Administrative Regions of Hong Kong and Macau]", 4 *Fu Jian Zheng Fa Guan Li Gan Bu Xue Yuan Xue Bao* [*Journal of the University of Politics and Law of Administrative Cadres in Fujian*] 37, 37–38 (2000); Yuan & Qiu, *supra* note 46, at 17–18.

conclusion of treaties by the HKSAR to prior scrutiny by the CPG.[58] However, this would formally require that the Treaty-making Law is included via a decision of the NPC Standing Committee in Annex III of the Basic Law, which sets out the national laws to be applied in the HKSAR. Further, Article 18(3) of the Basic Law provides that Laws listed in Annex III to the Basic Law shall be confined to those relating to defence and foreign affairs as well as other matters outside the limits of the autonomy of the Region as specified by the Basic Law.[59] Like other provisions of the Basic Law, Article 18(3) uses the concept of "foreign affairs" to refer to external relations powers outside the autonomy of the HKSAR. Hence, a national Treaty-making Law could only be made applicable in Hong Kong for matters of "foreign affairs." As foreign affairs lie within the exclusive competence of the CPG, there is no need to make the national Treaty-making Law applicable to Hong Kong.

After the handover in 1997, the HKSAR has on its own concluded bilateral investment promotion and protection agreements (BITs) and double taxation avoidance agreements under Article 151.[60] The HKSAR also concluded treaties in the areas of customs co-operation, maritime transportation and social security.[61] In 2011 and 2012, Hong Kong concluded free trade agreements with

58 Deming Huang & Wenjun Zuo, Guo Ji Fa Zhi Shi Ye Xia De Di Yue Quan [On Treaty Making Capacity from Perspective of International Rule of Law], *Gong Min Yu Fa* [*Citizen and Law*], Jan. 2011, at 4, 6

59 *See* Ghai, *supra* note 52, at 392–94.

60 The HKSAR concluded a bilateral investment promotion and protection agreement with Germany on Feb. 12, 1998, similar agreements have been concluded with Italy on Feb. 2, 1998 and Thailand on Apr. 12, 2006. For a full list, see Department of Justice of the Government of the Hong Kong Special Administrative Region, List of Investment Promotion and Protection Agreements, http://www.doj.gov.hk/eng/laws/table2ti.html (last visited June 1, 2015). Double taxation avoidance agreements were concluded with Germany on Jan. 17, 2005, Denmark on December 16, 2005 and Norway on January 11, 2005. For a full list, see Department of Justice of the Government of the Hong Kong Special Administrative Region, List of Double Taxation Avoidance Agreements, http://www.doj.gov.hk/eng/laws/table6ti.html (last visited June 1, 2015). On the conclusion of BITs by the HKSAR, see Zeng, *supra* note 49, at 669–96.

61 Agreement between the European Community and Hong Kong, China on Cooperation and mutual Administrative Assistance in Customs Matters, May 13, 1999, H.K.-E.U., http://www.doj.gov.hk/lawdoc/hk_ec_agreement.pdf (last visited June 1, 2015); Agreement between the Government of the Hong Kong Special Administrative Region of the People's Republic of China and the Cabinet of Ministers of Ukraine on Maritime Transport, Apr. 2, 2003, H.K.-Ukr., http://www.mic.gov.hk/eng/agreement/docs/ukraine_agreement.pdf (last visited June 1, 2015); Agreement on the Export of Social Insurance Benefits with the Netherlands, Dec. 1, 2003, H.K.-Neth., http://hongkong.nlconsulate.org/services/

the European Union and New Zealand as well as environmental and labour cooperation agreements.[62] Most of the agreements fall under the expressly listed categories of Article 151 such as economic, trade and financial areas. However, the agreements on social security, labour and environmental cooperation relate to the general category of "appropriate fields."

Whereas a comprehensive review of the agreements currently in force in general shows a restrictive approach of the Hong Kong Government in the exercise of treaty-making powers, it can be observed that Hong Kong has slightly expanded its treaty-making activity during the past few years by concluding treaties that go beyond the express matters of Article 151. However, international agreements on social insurance, labour and environment definitely fall within the "appropriate fields" of the external affairs of Hong Kong, as they have a close connection to the development of an international and sustainable local economy and do not touch on matters of relevance for the sovereignty of the Central State. The HKSAR has also gradually expanded the scope of agreements concluded with foreign states within the express matters of Article 151. While in the past most agreements were concluded in the areas of civil aviation, investment protection and juridical assistance in criminal matters, the focus has shifted to agreements on the avoidance of double taxation and free trade agreements.[63]

---

trade-and-economy/bilateral-agreements-netherlands---hong-kong.html (last visited June 1, 2015). The agreement between the Netherlands and Hong Kong on the export of social insurance benefits was signed in the names of the Governments of the Netherlands and the HKSAR of the People's Republic of China.

62 Free Trade Agreement between Hong Kong and the Member States of the European Free Trade Association, Oct. 1, 2012 and Nov. 1, 2012, H.K.-EFTA-States, http://www.tid.gov.hk/english/trade_relations/hkefta/text_agreement.html (last visited June 1, 2015); Hong Kong, China-New Zealand Closer Economic Partnership Agreement, Jan. 1, 2011, H.K.-N.Z., http://www.tid.gov.hk/english/trade_relations/hknzcep/text_agreement.html (last visited June 1, 2015); Environment Cooperation Agreement, Jan. 1, 2011, H.K.-N.Z., http://www.tid.gov.hk/english/trade_relations/hknzcep/files/HKNZ_ECA.pdf (last visited June 1, 2015); Memorandum of Understanding on Labor Cooperation, Jan. 1, 2011, H.K.-N.Z., http://www.doj.gov.hk/eng/laws/treaties.html#bf (last visited June 1, 2015). The environment cooperation agreement with New Zealand was signed by the Hong Kong Government Environmental Protection Department in the name of Hong Kong, China and by the Ministry for the Environment of New Zealand in the name of New Zealand.

63 As of March 2014 the number of avoidance of double taxation agreements amounted to 37, 24 of which were concluded after 2010. *See* Department of Justice of the Government of the Hong Kong Special Administrative Region, List of Double Taxation Avoidance Agreements, http://www.doj.gov.hk/eng/laws/table6ti.html (last visited June 1, 2015). *See also* Wan Pun Lung, "Application and Conclusion of Treaties in the Hong Kong Special

The practice after 1997 indicates that agreements on the establishment of representations of international organisations in Hong Kong were concluded between the Central Government and the relevant international organisation pursuant to Article 152(1) of the Basic Law.[64] The CPG's competence may be based on the fact that the agreements confer on the representations and their personnel in Hong Kong certain privileges and immunities falling within "foreign affairs." Although under Article 152(2) the HKSAR may, using the name Hong Kong, China, participate in international organisations not limited to states. It appears that the discretion lies with the Central Government depending on the subject matters of the agreements and whether participation in the agreements is limited to states. For example, Hong Kong is a member of the WTO in its capacity as a separate customs territory by virtue of Article 116 of the Basic Law,[65] and it became a "non-state member" of the International Civil Aviation Organization in 2010.[66] According to current practice, the host country agreement with the international organization is concluded by the CPG

Administrative Region of the People's Republic of China: Sixteen Years of Practice", 12 *Chinese J. Int'l L.* 589, 611 (2013).

64 Agreement Between the Government of the People's Republic of China and the Commission of the European Communities Concerning the Maintenance of the Office of the Commission of the European Communities in the Hong Kong SAR of the People's Republic of China, Jul. 1, 1997, H.K.-Eur. Comm., http://www.doj.gov.hk/lawdoc/bilateral/aeio_1e.pdf (last visited June 1, 2015); Host Country Agreement Between the Government of the People's Republic of China and the Bank for International Settlements Relating to the Establishment and Status of a Representative Office of the Bank for International Settlements in the Hong Kong SAR of the People's Republic of China, May 11, 1998, China-Int'l. Mon. Fund, http://www.doj.gov.hk/lawdoc/bilateral/aeio_3e.pdf (last visited June 1, 2015).

65 Article 116 reads:

> The Hong Kong Special Administrative Region shall be a separate customs territory. The Hong Kong Special Administrative Region may, using the name "Hong Kong, China", participate in relevant international organizations and international trade agreements (including preferential trade arrangements), such as the General Agreement on Tariffs and Trade and arrangements regarding international trade in textiles.
>
> Export quotas, tariff preferences and other similar arrangements, which are obtained or made by the Hong Kong Special Administrative Region or which were obtained or made and remain valid, shall be enjoyed exclusively by the Region.

66 Constitutional and Mainland Affairs Bureau of the Government of the Hong Kong Special Administrative Region, International Intergovernmental Organisations not limited to States, http://www.cmab.gov.hk/en/issues/external2.htm (last visited June 1, 2015).

and a memorandum of administrative agreement is signed by the Hong Kong Government and the international organization.[67]

B *Treaty-Making Power Subject to Authorization*

Different from Article 151, the provisions of Articles 96, 133 and 155 of the Basic Law provide a treaty-making power of the Region which can only be exercised upon approval by the Central Government. The conclusion of treaties by the Region is conditional upon "the assistance or authorisation of the Central People's Government."[68] It is concluded from the context that "to assist" and "to authorise" are not alternative options but that an authorisation is required in all circumstances. Hong Kong may rely on the assistance of the Central Government in order to enter into treaty negotiations with a foreign government. In practice, the HKSAR is required to obtain authorisation in order to enter into negotiations with a foreign government and also needs to obtain further authorisation of the finalized text of the agreement before the agreement may become binding on Hong Kong.

Pursuant to Article 96, the HKSAR may enter, with the assistance or authorisation of the CPG, into agreements with foreign states on reciprocal juridical assistance such as agreements for the mutual enforcement of judgements and arbitral awards, taking of evidence overseas and extradition arrangements.[69] Hong Kong has concluded numerous agreements on mutual legal assistance, surrender of fugitive offenders and transfer of sentenced persons pursuant to Article 96.[70]

As of 2014 Hong Kong had signed over 60 air service agreements with foreign states.[71] Air service agreements under Article 133 of the Basic Law concern air services between Hong Kong and foreign states. Such agreements are the responsibility of the HKSAR Government but require "specific authorizations" of the CPG. Authorization is effected by the MFA on a case-by-case basis

---

67 Lung, *supra* note 63, at 611.

68 Basic Law §§ 96, 155.

69 Ghai, *supra* note 52, at 464.

70 For an overview of treaties concluded by the HKSAR *see* Department of Justice of the Government of the Hong Kong Special Administrative Region, List of Fugitive Offenders Agreements, http://www.doj.gov.hk/eng/laws/table4ti.html (last visited June 1, 2015).

71 Department of Justice of the Government of the Hong Kong Special Administrative Region, List of Air Services Agreements and Air Services Transit Agreements, http://www.doj.gov.hk/eng/laws/table1ti.html (last visited June 1, 2015).

approving the conclusion of a specific air service agreement by the HKSAR Government with a certain foreign government.[72]

Different from the establishment of official and semi-official economic and trade missions, which only have to be reported to the CPG, the establishment of foreign consular and other official or semi-official missions in Hong Kong requires the approval of the Central Government.[73] It is questionable whether the Region or the Central Government has the power to conclude a bilateral consular agreement. Although the conclusion of a consular agreement does not fall into the external affairs ambit of Article 151 of the Basic Law due to the political significance of such agreements, it could be argued that the approval of establishing a consular mission in Hong Kong pays enough respect to the sovereignty of the state and includes the authorisation to enter into the relevant consular agreement. However, consular agreements are in practice concluded by the Central Government and their application is extended to the HKSAR.[74]

C *Restrictions of the Treaty-Making Power of the Central Government in Relation to Hong Kong*

There are generally two ways in which an international treaty or agreement becomes binding on the HKSAR. Treaty obligations of the HKSAR either arise as a result of the exercise of Hong Kong's own power to conclude agreements under Article 151 of the Basic Law or as a result of the decision of the CPG to apply an international treaty to Hong Kong to which China is or becomes a party. Normally, international treaties become binding upon each party in respect of its entire territory.[75] However, China's practice in regard to Hong Kong is different given that treaties to which China is a party are not necessarily applicable to the HKSAR but require a specific decision of the CPG in order

72 *See, e.g.*, Agreement between the Government of the HKSAR of the People's Republic of China and the Government of the Kingdom of Saudi Arabia Concerning Air Services, Jul. 27, 2006, H.K.-Saudi Arabia, http://www.doj.gov.hk/lawdoc/ASASAUDIARABIAe.pdf (last visited June 1, 2015).

73 Basic Law § 157, cl. 1.

74 Compare the consular agreements after July 1, 1997 with Australia of September 15, 2000, Canada of March 11, 1999, Cambodia January 12, 2011, India of July 28, 2001, Japan of February 16, 2010 and New Zealand April 23, 2006, the Russian Federation of October 23, 2003, and Vietnam of July 26, 2000. See Department of Justice of the Government of the Hong Kong Special Administrative Region, List of Consular Agreements, http://www.doj.gov.hk/eng/laws/table8ti.html (last visited June 1, 2015).

75 Vienna Convention of the Law of Treaties art. 29, May 22, 1969, 1155 U.N.T.S. 18232.

to become binding in relation to the territory of the Region.[76] According to Article 153(1) of the Basic Law, the CPG decides on the application of treaties to which China is or becomes a party in accordance with the "circumstances and needs of the Region, and after seeking the views of the government of the Region." Hence, the Basic Law provides for a specific consultation procedure between the CPG and the Hong Kong government as a precondition for the applicability of international treaties concluded by the CPG to the territory of the HKSAR. This procedural requirement implies a restriction of the CPG's treaty-making power in relation to the HKSAR.

The Basic Law also provides for a power of the Region to participate in the treaty-making of the Central Government. Pursuant to Article 150 of the Basic Law, representatives of the HKSAR may participate in negotiations at the diplomatic level as members of the delegation of the Central Government, if the negotiations directly affect the Region.[77] Chinese commentators have described this power as a "restricted power of diplomatic negotiations" of the HKSAR.[78] The power to participate is viewed to be restricted in various aspects: it is only the Central Government that may take the initiative to conduct negotiations with foreign governments and the CPG has discretion whether or not to allow participation of the Region, even if the negotiations affect the Region. Moreover, representatives of the HKSAR may not, as members of a delegation of the CPG, hold the views of the Region.[79] In practice, different views of representatives of the CPG and the Region will be solved in informal meetings before the start of the negotiations and both sides will agree on a concerted action. It then depends on various factors such as the expertise of the individual delegation members whether a member from Beijing or from Hong Kong will lead parts or all of the negotiations. Hence, the participation of the HKSAR in treaty negotiations of the CPG operates in a practical way that makes best use of expertise and resources of both the Region and the Central Government. Here, practice appears to be in sharp contrast with the abovementioned restrictive scholarly views that attempt to reduce any impact that the Government of the HKSAR may have on foreign affairs of China.

---

76 Lung, *supra* note 63, at 591.

77 Compare the similar wording of the Sino-British Joint Declaration, *supra* note 42, at Annex I Part XI. It has been regarded as a mistake to incorporate a provision about the participation of the HKSAR in diplomatic affaires in the chapter on the external affairs of the HKSAR. *See* Roda Mushkat, "Foreign, External and Defence Affairs", *in The Basic Law and Hong Kong's Future* 248, 252 (Peter Wesley-Smith & Albert Chen eds., 1988).

78 Yun & Zhong, *supra* note 48, at 311; Chinese: *You Xian de Wai Jiao Tan Pan Quan.*

79 *Id.*

The conclusion of air service agreements providing air services between other parts of China and other states and regions with stops at the HKSAR and air services between the HKSAR and other states and regions with stops at other parts of China falls within the competence of the CPG.[80] In concluding such agreements, the CPG is required to take into account the special conditions and economic interests of the HKSAR. Moreover, Hong Kong Government representatives may participate in air service agreement negotiations as members of the Central Government delegation.[81] This procedural requirement for the conclusion of air service agreements by the CPG also implies a restriction of the CPG's treaty-making power in relation to the HKSAR.

IV Conclusion

The conditions of domestic treaty application relate not only to existing treaty obligations but also to the participation of different state organs in the treaty-making process. As regards the external representation of China on the international plane, the existing ambiguity is associated with the fact that the current Constitution, unlike the Constitution of 1954, does not explicitly assign the exclusive competence of external representation to the State President. However, taking into account that the Constitution is dominated by the principle of concentration rather than separation of powers, there may be no need for a clear delineation of the competence of external representation. In practice, the State President represents China to conclude more important treaties; the President ratifies treaties in accordance with Article 81 of the Constitution. Ministers of the State Council conclude less important treaties or agreements. The discussion about the scope of the external representation power of the State President reveals how much Chinese constitutional law is still influenced by the concept of collective state leadership in the area of external representation. The reason for scholars to question the State President's external powers may be connected with the inconsistency between the constitutional status of the President as the highest representative of the state in external matters on the one hand, and the constitutional status of the NPC and the NPC Standing Committee respectively as the highest state organs on the other hand. Hence, some scholars view the State President as exercising only a "symbolic role" when ratifying treaties and suggest that the NPC Standing Committee should be responsible for the treaty

80 Basic Law § 132, cl. 1.

81 Basic Law § 132, cl. 2, 3.

ratification on the international plane. However, the scholarly proposals disregard the requirements of intergovernmental intercourse as well as the text of the Chinese Constitution. Moreover, these suggestions ignore the fact that the Secretary General of the Communist Party regularly holds the office of State President.

Although the power of the NPC Standing Committee to participate in the treaty-making process has been gradually expanded, the circumstances of the accession of China to the WTO revealed the relatively weak position of the NPC Standing Committee in relation to the executive. When the NPC Standing Committee approves a treaty, internal decision-making includes not only the delegates of the Standing Committee but also involves other relevant actors of the Party-State in the process of informal decision-making. Therefore, the NPC Standing Committee's power to approve treaties is, in practice, not a genuine power of parliamentary participation and control.

The HKSAR is vested with a separate power to conclude international treaties. The treaty-making competence is provided for in the Basic Law of Hong Kong and the underlying international treaty, the Joint Declaration. The Central Government retains the competence to conclude treaties in the fields of defence and foreign affairs. Chinese scholars have made various attempts to interpret Hong Kong's treaty-making power restrictively. In practice, the Region exercises its treaty-making power independently and is not subject to the proposed limitations by the CPG. In particular, the practice of the past years indicates that the HKSAR has gradually expanded the scope of agreements concluded under Article 151 of the Basic Law. Some agreements such as those on the avoidance of double taxation and free trade fall within the express matters of Article 151, while agreements on social insurance, labor and environment cannot be subsumed under the express fields in which the HKSAR has the power to conclude agreements. However, such agreements belong to the "appropriate fields" of the external affairs of Hong Kong as they have a close connection to the development of an international and sustainable local economy.

Apart from Hong Kong's power to conclude agreements on its own, it can also participate in treaty negotiations of the CPG. Practice in this regard indicates that scholarly suggestions to restrict this kind of participation do not play any significant role. Further, it is found that the provisions of the Basic Law that require the CPG to take into account the needs of Hong Kong and to consult its views when it decides on the application of an international treaty to the HKSAR do in fact restrict the treaty-making power of the CPG in relation to Hong Kong.

States, Governments, and Collective Recognition

Jure Vidmar

Table of Contents

I Introduction

The act of recognition in international law is a complicated relationship between law and politics; "a political act that has legal consequences."[1] Contemporary debate has been predominantly dealing with the act of recognition of states, the legal effects of which remain controversial, while the act of recognition of governments has become virtually obsolete. With regard to states, it seems to be generally-accepted that recognition is declaratory

---

* Leverhulme Early Career Fellow in the Faculty of Law and Research Fellow of St John's College, University of Oxford; Extraordinary Lecturer, Centre for Human Rights, Faculty of Law, University of Pretoria; Visiting Fellow, Harvard Law School. The author's research is supported by the Early Career Fellowship of the Leverhulme Trust.

1 Robert McCorquodale, "The Creation and Recognition of States", *in Public International Law: An Australian Perspective* 184, 193 (Sam Blay, Ryszard Piotrowicz & Martin Tsamenyi eds., 2005).

 | DOI 10.1163/9789004306509_006

and, as such, not required for the existence of a state.[2] With regard to governments, international practice is said to have accepted the Estrada doctrine whereby recognition of new foreign governments is not granted explicitly.[3] But some recent international practice negates these theoretical axioms.

The wide international acceptance of Kosovo's unilateral declaration of independence may well have had constitutive effects.[4] In the context of recognition of governments, we have witnessed clear collective departures from the Estrada doctrine in the example of Libya.[5] What significance does this have for the concept of recognition in contemporary international law? What are the legal effects of recognition of states and governments where the international community acts collectively? Ultimately, what significance does the recent practice of recognition have for the legal status of Taiwan?

This paper considers recent international practice on recognition of states and governments and identifies the avenues of granting recognition collectively. In so doing, it determines the legal relevance and irrelevance of international recognition and draws the conceptual difference between the concepts of collective recognition of states and governments in contested territorial situations.

II Recognition of States: Always Declaratory Always Political?

A *Declaratory Recognition*

Writers on recognition have traditionally distinguished between the constitutive and declaratory theories. In the constitutive view, recognition is "a necessary act before the recognized entity can enjoy an international

2 *See*, e.g., David Harris, *Cases and Materials on International Law* 131 (2010).

3 This doctrine is named after the Mexican minister of foreign affairs Genaro Estrada who, in 1930, made a proclamation on behalf of Mexico that its government in the future shall issue "no declaration in the sense of grants of recognition, since [Mexico] considers that such a course is an insulting practice and one which, in addition to the facts that it offends sovereignty of other nations, implies that judgment of some sort may be passed upon the internal affairs of those nations by other governments, inasmuch as the latter assume, in effect, an attitude of criticism when they decide, favourably or unfavourably, as to the legal qualifications of foreign regimes." Estrada Doctrine (1930), *reprinted in* Brad Roth, *Governmental Illegitimacy in International Law* 137–38 (1999).

4 *See* Jure Vidmar, "Explaining the Legal Effects of Recognition", 61 *Int'l & Comp. L.Q.* 361, 379–82 (2012).

5 *See infra* note 138.

personality."[6] Accordingly, it is claimed that statehood depends on recognition.[7] However, a state may be recognized by some states but not by others and this is the main problem of the constitutive approach.[8] Since there is no central international authority for granting recognition, such an entity at the same time has and does not have an international personality.[9] It is then unclear how many and whose recognitions need to be granted in order to successfully create a state. Most contemporary writers have thus adopted the view that recognition is declaratory,[10] that is, "merely a political act recognizing a pre-existing state of affairs."[11] The recognizing states only acknowledge a pre-existing situation. But not even this explanation is without difficulties.

In the absence of a central authority for determining whether or not a certain entity is a state, this duty needs to be performed by (existing) states.[12] Hersch Lauterpacht argued that once the statehood criteria are met, foreign states have a *duty* to grant recognition.[13] However, this position is generally rejected, as no such duty exists in international law.[14] And in the absence of a duty to recognize, Lauterpacht's constitutive approach does not work. Essentially, if recognition is constitutive, while no *duty* exists to grant recognition, we may have entities that are recognized as states by some states but not by others. We are then back to the original deficiency of the constitutive theory and still do not objectively know whether or not they are states.

International practice confirms that non-recognized states may indeed exist. Such are the examples of the Federal Republic of Yugoslavia (FRY) and Macedonia. The international involvement channeled through the European Community (EC) led to the pivotal opinion that the Socialist Federal Republic of Yugoslavia (SFRY) no longer existed and the new states had emerged in the

---

6 Martin Dixon, Robert McCorquodale & Sara Williams, *Cases and Materials in International Law* 154 (2011).

7 Thomas Grant, *The Recognition of States: Law and Practice in Debate and Evolution* 2 (1999).

8 James Brierly, *The Law of Nations* 138 (1963).

9 *Id.*

10 *See* Harris, *supra* note 2, at 145.

11 *Id.*

12 *Cf. supra* note 6.

13 *See* Hersch Lauterpacht, *Recognition in International Law* 65–66 (1948).

14 Hans Kelsen, *General Theory of Law and State* 223 (1999); Kristina Marek, *Identity and Continuity of States in Public International Law* 137 (1968); *See* Stefan Talmon, *Kollektive Nichtanerkennung Illegaler Staaten* [*Collective Non-Recognition of Illegal States*] 103 (2004).

absence of an applicable claim to territorial integrity.[15] This position was subsequently accepted in the practice of states and U.N. organs.[16] It is significant that the FRY and Macedonia remained universally non-recognized for some period, yet in the absence of an applicable counterclaim to territorial integrity, there was no doubt that they were states. Since the predecessor state no longer existed, what else would they be?

The FRY was an unusual example because it denied that it was a newly-created state and instead claimed continuity with the legal personality of the SFRY.[17] The controversy was thus actually about state succession rather than statehood. But despite being non-recognized, the FRY appeared before the ICJ in the Bosnia Genocide case.[18] The ICJ implicitly[19] and the Badinter

---

15 Opinion No. 1 of the Arbitration Commission of the Peace Conference on Yugoslavia, *reprinted in* Snezana Trifunovska, *Yugoslavia through Documents: From Its Creation to Its Dissolution* 415–16 (1994).

16 *See* S.C. Res. 757, pmbl. para. 10, U.N. Doc. S/RES/757 (May 30, 1992); S.C. Res. 777, para. 1, U.N. Doc. S/RES/777 (Sept. 19, 1992).

17 The Federal Republic of Yugoslavia's claim to the SFRY's international personality is evident from submissions of both Serbia and Montenegro to the E.C. in response to the invitation to apply for recognition, as expressed by the E.C. Declaration. Declaration on Yugoslavia (EC) (Dec. 16, 1991) para. 3 [hereinafter EC Declaration]. In his reply on December 23, 1991, Serbia's Foreign Minister recalled that Serbia acquired "internationally recognized statehood at the Berlin Congress of 1878 and on that basis had participated in the establishment in 1918 of the Kingdom of Serbs, Croats and Slovenes which became Yugoslavia [and concluded that Serbia] is not interested in secession." Roland Rich, "Recognition of States: The Collapse of Yugoslavia and the Soviet Union", 4 *Eur. J. Int'l L.* 36, 47 (1993). Montenegro's Foreign Minister, in his response on December 24, 1991, also declined the E.C.'s invitation to apply for recognition and recalled the international personality that Montenegro had prior to joining the Yugoslav state formations. *Id.* The issue was also referred to in Opinion 11 of the Badinter Commission: "There are particular problems in determining the date of state succession in respect of the Federal Republic of Yugoslavia because that state considers itself to be the continuation of the Socialist Federal Republic of Yugoslavia rather than a successor State." Opinion No. 11 of the Arbitration Commission of the Peace Conference on Yugoslavia (July 16, 1993), *reprinted in* Trifunovska, *supra* note 15, at 1017, para. 7.

18 *See* Application of Convention on Prevention and Punishment of Crime of Genocide (Bosn. & Herz. v. Yugoslavia), Preliminary Objections, 1996 I.C.J. 595, 596 (July 11) [hereinafter Bosnia Genocide case].

19 In the Bosnia Genocide case, the ICJ took the position that the FRY became a party to the Genocide Convention, to which the SFRY was previously a party, on the day when it adopted its new constitution. Bosnia Genocide case, para. 17. This implicitly means that, in the view of the ICJ, the FRY became a state on April 27, 1992. *See id.*

Commission explicitly[20] pronounced that the FRY became a state on April 27, 1992, the day of the adoption of its new constitution.

Although the Badinter Commission recommended its recognition in 1992, Macedonia remained unrecognized by the EC member states until December 16, 1993, and even then it was recognized under a compromise name: The Former Yugoslav Republic of Macedonia (FYR Macedonia).[21] Prior to recognition by the EC, the FYR Macedonia had already become a member of the U.N. on April 8, 1993.[22] The reason for non-recognition was Greece's objection to its constitutional name—Macedonia.[23] The EC did not extend recognition due to internal policy matters, but this policy was applied almost universally, given that only Bulgaria, Turkey, and Lithuania granted recognition under the original name before admission of the FYR Macedonia to the U.N.[24] The lack of universal recognition for Macedonia does not mean that Macedonia was not a state in that period. It is merely an example of political non-recognition.[25] It should be noted that in its Opinion 11, the Badinter Commission held that Macedonia became a state on November 17, 1991, the day when it adopted a new constitution proclaiming independence.

---

20 *See* Opinion No. 11 of the Arbitration Commission of the Peace Conference on Yugoslavia, *reprinted in* Trifunovska *supra* note 15 (stating that the FRY became a state on the day when it adopted its constitution).

21 James Crawford, *The Creation of States in International Law* 398 (2d ed. 2006).

22 G.A. Res. 47/225, U.N. Doc. A/RES/47/225 (Apr. 8, 1993) (admission of Macedonia to U.N. membership).

23 *See* Grant, *supra* note 7, at 158.

24 *See* Rich, *supra* note 17, at 52 (1993) (arguing that the E.C.'s policy of non-recognition of Macedonia had been virtually universalized but there were a few exceptions).

25 On May 1 and 2, 1992, the E.C. and its member states adopted the Declaration on the Former Yugoslav Republic of Macedonia, in which it was held that they were "willing to recognise that State as a sovereign and independent State, within its existing borders, and under a name that can be accepted by all parties concerned." Declaration on the Former Yugoslav Republic of Macedonia, Informal Meeting of Ministers of Foreign Affairs, Guimaracs, May 1–2, 1992, *reprinted in* Christopher Hill & Karen E. Smith, *European Foreign Policy: Key Documents* 376 (2000). The use of the term "state" rather than, for example, "entity", clearly implies that Macedonia's attributes of statehood were not a subject of dispute; rather, the E.C. did not want to enter into relations with Macedonia under its constitutional name. In this context, see also Matthew C.R. Craven, "What's in a Name? The Former Yugoslav Republic of Macedonia and Issues of Statehood", 16 *Aust. Y.B. Int'l L.* 199, 207–18 (1995) (arguing that non-recognizing states did not deny Macedonia's statehood).

These examples show that in some circumstances declaratory theory indeed works. But examples such as Kosovo, where legal circumstances differ, pose a challenge to the conventional declaratory approach.

B *The Constitutive Effects of Collective Recognition*

Predominantly settled by ethnic Albanians, the territory of Kosovo came under the *de facto* rule of Serbia in 1912.[26] After the First World War it became an autonomous entity within Serbia and retained this legal status in the subsequent Yugoslav state formations.[27] In 1989, Serbia suspended its autonomy, which resulted in an escalated ethnic conflict.[28] A decade of tensions led to a grave humanitarian situation and NATO intervention in 1999.[29] A detailed analysis of these events is beyond the scope of this article,[30] but on June 10, 1999, the Security Council, acting under Chapter VII of the U.N. Charter, adopted Resolution 1244, which put the territory of Kosovo under the regime of international territorial administration.[31]

The preamble to Resolution 1244, *inter alia*, reaffirms "the commitment of all Member States to the sovereignty and territorial integrity of the Federal Republic of Yugoslavia and other states of the region, as set out in the Final Act of Helsinki and Annex 2."[32] The Resolution's operative paragraphs, however, created a situation in which the FRY exercised no sovereign powers in Kosovo.[33]

---

26 *See* Noel Malcolm, *Kosovo: A Short History* 252 (1998) (discussing how Kosovo came under Serbian rule).

27 *See id.* at 264. This did not only apply to Kosovo Albanians but also to Albanians living in other parts of the Kingdom of Serbs, Croats, and Slovenes (later called Yugoslavia). *See id.*

28 *Id.* at 344.

29 *See* Dino Kritsiotis, "The Kosovo Crisis and NATO's Application of Armed Force against the Federal Republic of Yugoslavia", 49 *Int'l & Comp. L.Q.* 330, 330 (2000).

30 For more background on these events, see Bruno Simma, "NATO, the UN and the Use of Force: Legal Aspects", 10 *Eur. J. Int'l L.* 1, 10 (1999); Antonio Cassese, "*Ex Iniuria ius Oritur*: Are We Moving Towards International Legitimation of Forcible Humanitarian Countermeasures in the World Community?", 10 *Eur. J. Int'l L.* 23, 24 (1999); Christine Chinkin, "Kosovo: A 'Good' or 'Bad' War?", 93 *Am. J. Int'l L.* 841, 844 (1999); Kritsiotis, *supra* note 29, at 340 (analyzing the illegality of the use of force against the FRY).

31 S.C. Res. 1244, U.N. Doc. S/RES/1244 (June 10, 1999). Resolution 1244 refers to the FRY but now applies to Serbia. *See* Constitutional Charter Serbia and Montenegro art. 60.

32 *Id.* pmbl. para. 10.

33 The Resolution initially demanded "that the Federal Republic of Yugoslavia put an immediate and verifiable end to violence and repression in Kosovo, and begin and complete verifiable phased withdrawal from Kosovo of all military, police and paramilitary forces according to a rapid timetable." *Id.* para. 3. It allowed for the return of "an agreed number of Yugoslav and Serb military personnel" after the withdrawal. *Id.* para. 4. However,

Eventually, an international attempt was made to secure approval from the parent state and confirm Kosovo's path to independence through a Security Council resolution, following a pattern similar to that in the example of East Timor. After this attempt failed, a group of states decided to lead Kosovo to independence without Serbia's consent and without a Security Council resolution.[34] There is also evidence that Kosovo declared independence with the prior approval of a number of states who had also promised recognition in advance.[35] When Kosovo declared independence on February 17, 2008, the act attracted significant international support.[36]

But recognition is far from being universal. It is therefore questionable whether this attempt at state creation through recognition has been successful. Furthermore, it may well be that recognition actually created the ambiguity with regard to Kosovo's legal status. Before the recognitions were granted, it was clear that Kosovo was not a state. This is now unclear and remains unclear even after the Kosovo Advisory Opinion in which the ICJ avoided any reference to Kosovo's legal status.[37]

Is Kosovo a state? If so, would it be a state without the recognition which has been granted by a high number of states? If recognition is always declaratory, why should Kosovo be a state now when it was not after the declaration of

---

as follows from Annex 2, to which the commitment to territorial integrity expressed in the preamble refers, this return was merely symbolic and the number of personnel was severely limited. *See Id.* Annex 2, paras. 6, 10 n. 1. The Resolution further decided to deploy "international civil and security presences" (*id.* para. 5), requested "the Secretary-General to appoint, in consultation with the Security Council, a Special Representative to control implementation of the international civil presence, and ... to coordinate closely with the international security presence" (*id.* para. 6), and authorized "Member States and relevant international organizations to establish the international security presence in Kosovo" (*id.* para. 7).

34 *See, e.g.*, Dan Bilefski & Nicholas Wood, "Talks on Kosovo's Future Stagnate", *N.Y. Times*, Dec. 8, 2007, at A6 (citing the willingness of world leaders to move to "the next phase" following the failure of negotiations); Dan Bilefski, "U.S. and Germany Plan to Recognize Kosovo", *N.Y. Times*, Jan. 11, 2008, at A9 (noting that both the United States and Germany planned to recognize Kosovo and would be urging the rest of Europe to do so as well).

35 Bilefski, *supra* note 34.

36 *Id.*

37 The ICJ specifically observed that the question posed to the Court did "not ask whether or not Kosovo has achieved statehood." Accordance with International Law of the Unilateral Declaration of Independence in Respect of Kosovo, Advisory Opinion, 2010 I.C.J. 141, para. 51 (July 22) [hereinafter Kosovo Advisory Opinion].

independence in 1991?[38] At the time only Albania granted recognition,[39] while recognition has been granted by a hundred states since the 2008 declaration of independence.[40] It is difficult to ignore such a high number of recognitions, but what implications does it have for Kosovo's legal status?

One could try to reformulate the deficiency of the constitutive theory and ask the well-known question from the other direction: how many and whose *withholdings* of recognition are necessary such that an entity is *not* considered a state? Is Kosovo a state because it has been recognized by a hundred states, or is it not a state because it has been recognized *only* by a hundred states? This dilemma illustrates the problem of the constitutive approach, yet it also illustrates that it is precisely the high number of recognitions which has led to the situation in which Kosovo's legal status is ambiguous. A high number of recognitions does not necessarily clarify the legal status but can create at least an ambiguity. Consequently, recognition does not always have purely declaratory effects, especially not when it is granted collectively.

When one accepts that recognition could, under some circumstances, create a state, one runs into the basic problem of the constitutive theory: how many and whose recognitions are necessary? Does the concept of collective recognition provide for a way out of this vicious circle?

Writing about Kosovo, Weller suggests that recognition would need to be *widespread* if it were to have state-creative effects.[41] And Crawford refers to historic practice to conclude that *collective* recognition can indeed serve as a tool of a less formalized collective state creation.[42] If recognition is universal or near-universal, it can have the effects of a collective state creation. However, what if it is only "widespread," yet not near universal, as is currently the case with Kosovo? In this case recognition creates ambiguity with regard to the legal status of a territory, and this ambiguity is sometimes overcome over a longer period of time.[43]

---

38 The unofficial parliament of Kosovo Albanians issued a declaration of independence on September 22, 1991. *See* Marc Weller, "Modesty Can Be a Virtue: Judicial Economy in the ICJ Kosovo Opinion", 24 *Leiden J. Int'l L.* 127, 129 (2011).

39 *See* Crawford, *supra* note 21, at 408.

40 As of June 13, 2013, Kosovo has been recognized by 100 states. *See* Who Recognized Kosova as an Independent State, Kosovo Thanks You, http://www.kosovothanksyou.com (last visited Jun. 15, 2013).

41 Weller, *supra* note 38, at 129–30.

42 Crawford, *supra* note 21, at 141.

43 Vidmar, *supra* note 3, at 378–79.

Although recognition of states is generally a declaratory act, collective recognition can have the effects of a collective state creation. But recognition in this case needs to be virtually universal, otherwise widespread (collective) recognition can lead to ambiguity with regard to the legal status of a territory. At the same time, under some circumstances foreign states have a duty to withhold recognition. What are these circumstances and what bearing does this have for the legal status of an independence-seeking entity?

C *The Duty to Withhold Recognition*

The duty to withhold recognition is triggered by violations of certain fundamental norms of international law. This section traces the development of such a duty and ultimately considers whether the unilateral character of a claim for independence triggers an obligation to withhold recognition.

In 1974, the officers of the Greek Cypriot National Guard, which was backed by Greece, overthrew the central government of Cyprus.[44] In response, Turkey militarily intervened and established an effective Turkish entity in Northern Cyprus.[45] Turkey maintained that the intervention aimed to protect Turkish Cypriots;[46] however, the Security Council adopted Resolution 353 which condemned the intervention.[47] The Turkish Republic of Northern Cyprus (TRNC) declared independence on November 15, 1983,[48] that is, after negotiations on a possible federal arrangement between the Turkish and Greek Cypriot entities failed.[49]

Upon the proclamation of independence of the TRNC, the Security Council adopted Resolution 541 which, inter alia, called upon "all States to respect the sovereignty, independence, territorial integrity and non-alignment of the Republic of Cyprus,"[50] and called upon "all States not to recognise any Cypriot state other than the Republic of Cyprus."[51] While Resolution 541 was not adopted under Chapter VII of the UN Charter, the TRNC was not recognized by any state other than Turkey.[52] It is generally accepted that Turkey's illegal use of force in Cyprus created international territorial illegality and foreign states have a duty not to recognize such a situation.

---

44 *See* David Raič, Statehood and the Law of Self-Determination 123 (2002).

45 *Id.*

46 *Id.*

47 S.C. Res. 353, U.N. Doc. S/RES/353 (July 29, 1974).

48 *See* Raic, *supra* note 44, at 123.

49 *Id.*

50 S.C. Res. 541, U.N. Doc. S/RES/541 (Nov. 18, 1983), para. 6.

51 *Id.* para. 7.

52 *See* Crawford, *supra* note 21, at 144.

On November 11, 1965, the government of Southern Rhodesia issued the Unilateral Declaration of Independence (UDI).[53] This was done despite the fact that both the General Assembly and the Security Council adopted a set of resolutions in which the white-minority government, due to the exclusion of the black population from political participation, was proclaimed as non-representative of the entire population of Southern Rhodesia and was thus held not to be the right authority to declare independence.[54] The Security Council called on the United Kingdom (UK) not to decolonize Southern Rhodesia and on other states to withhold recognition.[55]

Upon the issuing of the UDI, the U.N. organs continued the initiative for collective non-recognition. Resolution 2024 of the General Assembly condemned "the unilateral declaration of independence made by the racialist minority in Southern Rhodesia"[56] and recommended the matter to the Security Council.[57] The Security Council adopted Resolution 216, in which it condemned "the unilateral declaration of independence made by a racist minority in Southern Rhodesia."[58] It further decided "to call upon all states not to recognize this illegal racist minority regime in Southern Rhodesia and to refrain from rendering any assistance to this illegal regime."[59] This Resolution was followed by Resolution 217, in which the Security Council condemned "the usurpation of power by a racist settler minority in Southern Rhodesia and [regarded] the declaration of independence by it as having no legal validity,"[60] and called upon "all States not to recognize this illegal authority and not to entertain any diplomatic or other relations with it."[61]

All states, including apartheid South Africa,[62] complied with the resolutions and "Rhodesia was at no stage recognized by any State."[63] This was the

---

53 John Dugard, *Recognition and the United Nations* 90 (1987). The UDI included a provision that the government of Southern Rhodesia would act as the representative of the Queen: UDI, s 2 (1)(b). However, in 1970, Southern Rhodesia proclaimed itself a republic: *Id.* 90–91.

54 *See* G.A. Res. 1747 (XVI), U.N. Doc. A/RES/1747 (XVI) (June 27, 1962); S.C. Res. 202, U.N. Doc. S/RES/202 (May 6, 1965), G.A. Res. 2022 (XX), U.N. Doc. A/RES/2022 (XX) (Nov. 5, 1965).

55 *See* S.C. Res. 202, paras. 3–5.

56 G.A. Res. 2024 (XX), U.N. Doc. A/RES/2024 (XX) (Nov. 11, 1965), para. 1.

57 *Id.* para. 3.

58 S.C. Res. 216, U.N. Doc. S/RES/216 (Nov. 12, 1965), para. 1.

59 *Id.*

60 S.C. Res 217, U.N. Doc. S/RES/217 (Nov. 20, 1965), para. 3.

61 *Id.* para. 6.

62 Dugard, *supra* note 53, at 91 (arguing "South Africa, with which Rhodesia maintained diplomatic relations and close economic and political ties, refrained from according express recognition to Rhodesia").

63 *Id.* at 91.

legal situation despite the fact that there was no doubt that Southern Rhodesia met the traditional criteria for statehood.[64] None of the relevant resolutions directly invoked Chapter VII of the UN Charter, although references to international peace and security were made. The legal status of some of the resolutions may thus be questionable;[65] however, in the absence of an explicit reference to Chapter VII of the UN Charter, the resolutions were probably not legally binding.

Upon Southern Rhodesia's proclamation of a republic on March 18, 1970,[66] the Security Council, acting under Chapter VII of the UN Charter, adopted Resolution 277, in which it decided "that Member States shall refrain from recognizing this illegal regime or from rendering assistance to it."[67] The call for the non-recognition of Southern Rhodesia thus doubtlessly became legally binding, although full compliance had already been achieved after previous, non-binding, resolutions.[68] The Security Council and General Assembly Resolutions on Southern Rhodesia avoided the use of the term "state," or even "illegal" or "illegally-created" state. The reason for this avoidance needs to be sought in the purpose of these resolutions, namely preventing Southern Rhodesia from acquiring statehood. The Security Council and the General Assembly obviously did not want to cause any ambiguity, which could have resulted if the term "state" were used.[69]

Southern Rhodesia was thus an effective entity which could not become a state due to its illegal creation, whereby the territorial illegality was determined by racism and denial of the right of self-determination. Similar considerations underlie the gaining of quasi-independence of the South African Homelands: Transkei,[70] Bophuthatswana,[71] Venda[72] and Ciskei.[73] Even before the declaration of independence of the four Homelands, the General Assembly Resolutions 2671F[74] and 2775E[75] held that the Homeland policies were expressions of apartheid and were against the right of self-determination.

---

64 *Id.*

65 *Id.* at 95.

66 *Id.* at 92–93.

67 S.C. Res. 277, U.N. Doc. S/RES/277 (Mar. 18, 1970), para. 2.

68 *Cf. supra* notes 54–61.

69 Dugard, *supra* note 53, at 94.

70 Status of Transkei Act 100 (Oct. 26, 1976).

71 Status of Bophuthatswana Act 89 (Dec. 6, 1977).

72 Status of Venda Act 107 (Sept. 13, 1979).

73 Status of Ciskei Act 110 (Dec. 4, 1981).

74 G.A. Res. 2671 F, U.N. Doc. A/RES/2671 F (Dec. 8, 1970), para. 3.

75 G.A. Res. 2775, U.N. Doc. A/RES/2775 (Nov. 29, 1971).

After the declaration of independence of Transkei, the General Assembly adopted Resolution 31/6A in which it called upon "all Governments to deny any form of recognition to the so-called independent Transkei and to refrain from having any dealings with the so-called independent Transkei or other Bantustans."[76] The General Assembly thus held that the creation of the Homelands was a pursuance of racist policies (rather than a real expression of the right of self-determination) and called for non-recognition. This view was subsequently confirmed by Security Council Resolutions 402[77] and 407,[78] and also by General Assembly Resolutions 37/43[79] and 37/69A after the admission to quasi-independence of the three other Homelands.[80]

None of these Security Council Resolutions was adopted under Chapter VII of the UN Charter. Nonetheless, the full compliance of third states was achieved. Further, the fact that the Security Council did not act under Chapter VII of the UN Charter "does not necessarily mean that States [were] not under any legal obligation to withhold recognition of the Homeland-States."[81] The character of norms violated in the case of the South African Homelands may arguably be that of *jus cogens* and, consequently, states may have been "under a general legal obligation to withhold recognition of such an illegality."[82]

While it can be generally concluded that the violation of the right of self-determination and the pursuance of racist policies were the sources of the illegality of the state creations in the case of the South African Homelands, it also needs to be noted that these cases may serve as examples of limitations on state creations with the consent of a parent state. In other words, even if the parent state waives its claim for territorial integrity, the entity will nevertheless not become a state where it would emerge in breach of certain fundamental norms of international law, in particular those of a *jus cogens* character.

The duty to withhold recognition has also been defined as an obligation *erga omnes* in the International Law Commission (ILC) Articles on State Responsibility.[83] Article 41(2) provides that "no State shall recognize as lawful a situation created by a serious breach [of *jus cogens*] nor render aid or assistance

76 G.A. Res. 31/6 A, U.N. Doc. A/RES/31/6 A (Oct. 26, 1976), para. 3.

77 S.C. Res. 402, U.N. Doc. S/RES/402 (Dec. 22, 1976).

78 S.C. Res. 407, U.N. Doc. S/RES/407 (May 25, 1977).

79 G.A. Res. 37/43, U.N. Doc. A/RES/37/43 (Dec. 3, 1982).

80 G.A. Res. 37/69 A, U.N. Doc. A/RES/37/69A (Dec. 9, 1982).

81 DUGARD, *supra* note 53, at 102.

82 *Id.*

83 Responsibility of States for Internationally Wrongful Acts, G.A. Res. 56/83, Annex, arts. 40 & 41, U.N. Doc. A/RES/56/83/Annex (Dec. 12, 2001) [ILC Articles on State Responsibility].

in maintaining that situation."[84] It also specifies that states owe an obligation *erga omnes* to withhold formal or implied recognition of an effective territorial situation created in breach of *jus cogens*.[85] Pursuant to the Commentary on the ILC Articles on State Responsibility, norms of *jus cogens* character include the prohibition of illegal use of force, the right of self-determination, and the prohibition of racial discrimination.[86]

Although the association of illegality in the context of the obligation to withhold recognition with the concept of *jus cogens* remains somewhat controversial,[87] the ICJ has given its cautious acknowledgement in the Kosovo Advisory Opinion.[88] International law clearly demands that under some circumstances states owe an obligation *erga omnes* to withhold recognition.[89] At the same time, nothing in the doctrine or non-recognition practice suggests that an obligation to withhold recognition applies where independence is declared without the consent of a parent state, or that an obligation *erga omnes* would apply because of the unilateral character of a declaration of independence.[90] Indeed, the principle of territorial integrity of states cannot be seen as an absolute right of states or even as a norm of *jus cogens*.[91]

That the obligation to withhold recognition does not apply simply because an attempt at secession is unilateral also follows from Reference

---

84 *Id.* art. 41(2).

85 ILC Articles on State Responsibility, Commentary on art. 41.

86 ILC Articles on State Responsibility, Commentary on art. 40.

87 Stefan Talmon, "The Duty Not to 'Recognize as Lawful' a Situation Created by the Illegal Use of Force or Other Serious Breach of a *Jus Cogens* Obligation: An Obligation Without Real Substance?", *in The Fundamental Rules of the International Legal Order: Jus Cogens and Obligations Erga Omnes* 103 (Christian Tomuschat & Jean-Marc Thouvenin eds., 2006) (arguing that only a very few *jus cogens* norms could be relevant in the context of state creation and that violation of such norms does not result in an entity not being a state).

88 Kosovo Advisory Opinion, para. 81 (holding that "declarations of independence" may be illegal where it is "connected with the unlawful use of force or other egregious violations of norms of general international law, in particular those of a peremptory character (*jus cogens*)").

89 *See* McCorquodale, *supra* note 1.

90 *See* Jure Vidmar, "Conceptualizing Declarations of Independence in International Law", 32 Oxford J.L. Stud. 153, 166 (2011) (arguing that the unilateral nature of a declaration of independence does not underlie territorial illegality that triggers an *erga omnes* obligation to withhold recognition).

91 *See* Anne Peters, "Statehood After 1989: 'Effectivités' Between Legality and Virtuality", *in* 3 *Select Proceedings of the European Society of International Law* 171, 179 (James Crawford & Sarah Nouwen eds., 2012) (arguing that territorial integrity of states is not a peremptory norm of international law).

re: Secession of Quebec (the Quebec case), where the Supreme Court of Canada pronounced that:

> The ultimate success of... a [unilateral] secession would be dependent on recognition by the international community, which is likely to consider the legality and legitimacy of secession having regard to, amongst other facts, the conduct of Québec and Canada, in determining whether to grant or withhold recognition.[92]

This holding can only be based on the underlying position that the unilateral character of secession does not trigger an obligation to withhold recognition. Rather, the neutrality of international law with respect to unilateral secession affects even the act of recognition. Where an entity tries to emerge as an independent state, international law does not prescribe that recognition needs to be either granted or withheld.

D *Recognition of States and Taiwan*

Thus far it has been established that the emergence of a new state against the wishes of its parent state is not illegal under international law, but it is very unlikely. Where an attempt at secession is unilateral, recognition can have constitutive effects. But in such circumstances it would need to be virtually universal. Recognition that is widespread, yet not universal, creates an ambiguity with regard to the legal status of a territory. Furthermore, if collective recognition could not create a state, why would it be necessary for international law to develop the obligation to withhold recognition in the situations of territorial illegality?

The ambiguity with regard to the legal status could be ended by subsequent admission of the secessionist entity to U.N. membership; however, practice shows that no state has been admitted to the U.N. against the competing claim to territorial integrity by its parent state. This does not necessarily mean that such an entity may not be a state. At the same time, in the absence of U.N. membership, there exists no objective international indicator that would end the ambiguity and objectively demonstrate an entity's statehood.

If Taiwan declared independence, this would *not* be an internationally wrongful act. Following the Kosovo Advisory Opinion, a unilateral declaration of independence as such does not offend any norm of international law.[93] The law of state responsibility only demands international non-acceptance

---

92 Reference re: Secession of Quebec, [1998] 2 S.C.R. 217, para. 155 (Can.).

93 Kosovo Advisory Opinion, para. 81.

of an effective situation created in breach of a *peremptory* norm of international law.[94] Unlike Southern Rhodesia and the TRNC, Taiwan is *not* marked by such a breach. Taiwan would only seek to emerge as a new state unilaterally, which is not illegal per se; that is, if a breach of a peremptory norm, such as racism and illegal use of force, is not attached to the situation. Following the Quebec case reasoning and the Kosovo state practice, the ultimate success of Taiwan's unilateral declaration of independence would depend on international recognition.

This section has demonstrated that international law would not require other states to withhold recognition of Taiwan. No obligation *erga omnes* in the sense of Article 41 of ILC Articles of State Responsibility would apply here. At the same time, foreign states would have no legal obligation to recognize Taiwan. Their decisions on recognition would be eminently political. It is thus highly unlikely that many states would recognize Taiwan if it declared independence unilaterally. And in the absence of a widespread recognition, Taiwan's legal status would be neither changed nor clarified. For these reasons, issuing a formal declaration of independence would bring no immediate benefit. It would not be illegal under international law, but it would probably remain ineffective, as international recognition is unlikely to be widespread. Taiwan will thus likely to continue to claim that the Republic of China has always been independent, so no new declaration of independence is necessary.[95] But this claim may have implications under the law governing recognition of governments (rather than the law governing recognition of states).

III Recognition of Governments

While it cannot be expected that Taiwan's legal status could be clarified through the concept of state recognition in the near future, the significance of the newest developments in the sphere of the recognition of governments still needs to be considered. The act of recognition of governments is even more controversial, as, unlike the recognition of states, it is not a one-time act.[96] This opens the possibility of much more frequent politicization of this type of recognition

---

94 *Cf. supra* notes 85–86.

95 *See* Responses to Questions Submitted by Deutsche Welle: Lee Teng-hui President Republic of China, July 9, 1999, http://www.fas.org/news/taiwan/1999/0709.htm (last visited June 1, 2015).

96 *See* McCorquodale, *supra* note 1, at 198.

than the recognition of states. Recognition of governments can thus become "a political tool for reaching foreign policy goals."[97]

Where the change of a government occurs in accordance with constitutional provisions of the state in question, the new government would not become subject to recognition. This is different where a new government usurps power against the constitutional provisions.[98] For example, if a government changes after democratic elections, the new government will be automatically accepted without an international enquiry into its legitimacy.[99] This may be different where a democratic government is overthrown in a coup.[100]

The practice of explicit recognition of governments has declined and most governments now resort to the "Estrada Doctrine," which perceives an explicit declaration of recognition of governments as an insulting practice that interferes with the internal affairs of other states. In contrast with an explicit act of recognition, the approach of the "Estrada Doctrine" is less formal and "confines itself to the maintenance or withdrawal... of... diplomatic agents, and to the continued acceptance... of... accredited diplomatic agents."[101] This doctrine was quietly accepted even by the United States with the Department of State statement in 1977.[102]

A *Non-Explicit Recognition of Governments*

Although the practice of explicit recognition of governments has declined, there is significant practice of factual non-recognition of governments. Such practice has been identified in three types of situations:

> [1] [There exist] [t]wo or more local *de facto* authorities each claiming to be the only legitimate government of a (recognized) State... [2] the government of a State claims to continue to be the government of a part of the State's territory that has *de facto* seceded... [3] an authority in exile claims to be the government of a State which is under the effective

97 M.J. Peterson, *Recognition of Governments: Legal Doctrine and State Practice* 3 (1997).

98 Harris, *supra* note 2, at 156.

99 *Id.*

100 *See generally* Jean d'Aspremont, "Responsibility for Coups in International Law", 18 *Tul. J. Int'l & Comp. L.* 451 (2010).

101 Harris, *supra* note 2, at 156.

102 *Id.*, at 159. The United States Department of State argued that "establishment of relations does not involve approval or disapproval but merely demonstrates a willingness on our part to conduct affairs with other governments directly." US Department of State statement (1977), reprinted in Harris, *supra* note 2, at 159.

> control of a colonial power, a belligerent occupant or its local puppet, or an authority which came to power by *coup d'état* or revolution.[103]

In the absence of explicit recognition in such situations, actions of states imply their views with regard to the problem of which government is considered to be the legitimate representative of a certain state.[104]

Important clarification on the acceptance of governmental authority stems from the practice of U.N. organs. The Taiwan-based Government of the Republic of China initially represented China in the UN.[105] In 1971, however, the General Assembly adopted Resolution 2758[106] which recognized:

> [T]he representatives of [the Government of the People's Republic of China] as the only legitimate representatives of China [and expelled] the representatives of [the Government of the Republic of China (Taiwan)] from the place which they unlawfully [occupied] at the United Nations and in all the organizations related to it.[107]

The underlying reason for the General Assembly's pronouncement was the fact that the Government of the Republic of China controlled only a fraction of the Chinese territory and thus could not make a legitimate claim to represent the entire Chinese state.[108] It needs to be noted here that internationally China is thus seen as one state and the Government of the Peoples' Republic of China a legitimate representative of that state. Since a change of a government does not change the identity of the state under international law,[109] it follows that under international law the Peoples' Republic of China also continues the international personality of the pre-1949 China.

Although recognition of governments should not be conflated for recognition of states, there are several other instances which indicate that acceptance of a certain authority as being the legitimate government of an entity could be perceived as recognition of the entity as a state. The racist government of

103 Stefan Talmon, *Recognition of Governments in International Law: With Particular Reference to Governments in Exile* 7–8 (1998).

104 *Id.*

105 Crawford, *supra* note 21, at 200.

106 G.A. Res 2758, U.N. Doc. A/RES/2758 (Oct. 25, 1971).

107 *Id.* para. 4.

108 Crawford, *supra* note 21, at 200.

109 This is a well-established principle that follows from the Tinoco Arbitration. See The Tinoco Claims Arbitration (Great Britain v. Costa Rica) (1923) 1 R.I.A.A. 369.

Southern Rhodesia was internationally illegitimate and resulted in universal non-recognition of Southern Rhodesia as a state.[110] The situation with the South African homelands[111] was similar, and so was collective non-acceptance of the Turkish puppet-government in Northern Cyprus which has resulted in the Turkish Republic of Northern Cyprus not being recognized as a state.[112] Likewise, recognition of the Republic of China can have implications of acceptance of Taiwan as being an independent state.

An illustrative example is also the Iraqi occupation of Kuwait in 1990. Non-recognition of the Kuwaiti government as the only legitimate government of Kuwait after the Iraqi occupation could be implied acceptance of the Iraqi annexation. Although the Kuwaiti government was ineffective in the territory of this state, the Security Council acted under Chapter VII, condemned the occupation and proclaimed the Government of Kuwait to be the only legitimate government of that territory.[113]

In sum, governmental legitimacy is traditionally rooted in effective control over the territory. Yet this doctrine is not unqualified. It is well-established in international law that an effective governmental authority will be denied its legitimacy in situations of territorial illegality. Now it needs to be considered what limitations are on the effective-control principle beyond territorial illegality.

B *Collective Denial of Legitimacy to the Taliban Government in Afghanistan*

Acting under Chapter VII of the UN Charter, the Security Council adopted Resolution 1363, in which it insisted:

> [T]hat the Afghan faction known as the Taliban, which also calls itself the Islamic Emirate of Afghanistan, comply promptly with its previous resolutions ... take appropriate effective measures to ensure that the *territory under its control* is not used for terrorist installations and camps.[114]

110 *Id. See also* Jericho Nkala, *The United Nations, International Law, and the Rhodesian Independence Crisis* 57 (1985).

111 *See supra* notes 44–64.

112 S.C. Res. 353, U.N. Doc. S/RES/353 (July 20, 1974); S.C. Res. 541, U.N. S/RES/541 (Nov. 18, 1983), para. 6.

113 *See* S.C. Res. 661, U.N. Doc. S/RES/661 (Aug. 6, 1990).

114 S.C. Res. 1267, U.N. Doc. S/RES/1267 (Oct. 15, 1999), para. 1 (emphasis added).

With the formulation "the Afghan faction known as the Taliban", which also calls itself "the Islamic Emirate of Afghanistan"[115] (rather than the Government of Afghanistan), the Security Council implied that it did not see the Taliban government as the legitimate authority of Afghanistan.

The Security Council, in several instances, further invoked obligations of "the Taliban, as well as other Afghan factions."[116] This indicates that the Taliban government did not exercise an effective control over the territory of Afghanistan. The authority of the Taliban government of Afghanistan was, therefore, also partly denied on the grounds of non-effectiveness. This was further affirmed in subsequent resolutions where the Security Council stated that the Taliban were obliged to comply with duties imposed by international law, while it strictly avoided using the term "the government of Afghanistan." Instead, terms such "the Afghan faction known as the Taliban,"[117] "the Taliban authorities",[118] "the territory of Afghanistan under Taliban control,"[119] were used, or it was demanded that "the Taliban [and not 'the government of Afghanistan'] comply"[120] with previous resolutions. These pronouncements indicate that the denied legitimacy of the Taliban government was partly rooted in the lack of effective control over the entire territory of Afghanistan. But this was certainly not the only consideration.

Security Council Resolution 1378, *inter alia*, condemned "the Taliban for allowing Afghanistan to be used as a base for the export of terrorism by the Al-Qaida network and other terrorist groups";[121] expressed deep concern about "serious violations by the Taliban of human rights and international humanitarian law";[122] and further gave "its strong support for the efforts of the Afghan people to establish a new and transitional administration leading to the formation of a government, both of which: [i] should be broad-based, multi-ethnic and fully representative of all the Afghan people and committed to peace with Afghanistan's neighbors; [ii] should respect the human rights of all Afghan people, regardless of gender, ethnicity or religion; [and] [iii] should respect Afghanistan's international obligations."[123]

---

115 *Id.*

116 *See* S.C. Res. 1214, U.N. Doc. S/RES/1214 (Dec. 8, 1998) para. 1.

117 *See* S.C. Res 1267, U.N. Doc. S/RES/1267 (Oct. 15, 1999) para. 1.

118 *See* S.C. Res 1333, U.N. Doc. S/RES/1333 (Dec. 19, 2000) pmbl.

119 *See* S.C. Res. 1363, U.N. Doc. S/RES/1363 (July 30, 2001) para. 3(b).

120 *See* S.C. Res. 1333, *supra* note 118, paras.1, 2.

121 S.C. Res. 1378, U.N. Doc. S/RES/1378 (Nov. 14, 2001) pmbl.

122 *Id.*

123 *Id.*, para. 1.

The Security Council thus denied legitimacy of the Taliban government in Afghanistan based on its grave human rights violations and threats to international peace, and expressed its support for a change of government. The Security Council's measures against the Taliban authorities in Afghanistan were a collective response to serious breaches of internationally protected human rights and involvement in international terrorism, combined with the lack of effective control. Indeed, it needs to be noted that, with regard to Afghanistan, the Security Council did not challenge a government that would be effective in the entire territory of that state.

C Libya: Collective Action through the Security Council and a Deviation from "Estrada"

Security Council Resolutions 1970 and 1973 on Libya were adopted under Chapter VII of the UN Charter: the Security Council identified the existence of a threat to international peace and security and drew a number of legal consequences such as travel ban,[124] asset freezing,[125] referral to the International Criminal Tribunal,[126] and arms embargo.[127] In order to protect civilians, the Security Council authorized the use of all necessary means, which can be seen as a euphemism for the use of force.[128] But it explicitly excluded "a foreign occupation force of any form on any part of Libyan territory."[129]

The Resolutions are not concerned with the choice of a political system. Resolution 1970, for example, urged the Libyan authorities to "[a]ct with the utmost restraint, respect human rights and international humanitarian law, and allow immediate access for international human rights monitors."[130] Resolution 1973 condemned "the gross and systematic violation of human rights, including arbitrary detentions, enforced disappearances, torture and summary executions."[131] Unlike the relevant resolutions on Afghanistan,[132] the resolutions on Libya did not explicitly deny legitimacy of the sitting government. Nor did it call for a regime change, even when the Benghazi-based government of the National Transitional Council was already in control

124 S.C. Res. 1970, U.N. Doc. S/RES/1970 (Feb. 26, 2011), para. 15.

125 *Id.* paras. 17–21.

126 *Id.* paras. 4–8.

127 *Id.* paras. 9–14.

128 *See* Christian Henderson, "International Measures for the Protection of Civilians in Libya and Cote D'Ivoire", 60 *Int'l & Comp. L.Q.* 767, 770–71 (2011).

129 S.C. Res. 1973, U.N. Doc. S/RES/1973 (Mar. 17, 2011), para. 4.

130 S.C. Res. 1970, *supra* note 124, para. 2(a).

131 S.C. Res. 1973, *supra* note 129, pmbl., para. 4.

132 *See supra* notes 116–21.

of large parts of Libyan territory at that time. Indeed, the language used in the resolutions on Afghanistan clearly disputed legitimacy of the Taliban government,[133] while the resolutions on Libya referred to the Gaddafi government as "the Libyan authorities."[134] Moreover, the resolutions on Libya did not call for a regime-change; the authorization of the use of force was limited to the protection of civilian population.[135]

Nevertheless, the government-change in Libya clearly was not only a domestic but an internationalized issue.[136] It is debatable whether the international support for the National Transitional Council overstepped the Security Council's mandate, and at which point the international involvement should have stopped.[137] As argued above, an internationalized government-change was not authorized by the applicable Security Council resolutions and neither was a requirement expressed for an enactment of a particular political system.

In the case of Libya, a number of states departed from the Estrada doctrine and decided to grant explicit recognition to the National Transitional Council.[138] This is a notable exception to the general practice developed over the past decades. The recognizing states clearly expressed preferences to one of the competing authorities, and their decisions were rooted in human rights considerations and a grave humanitarian situation. Indeed, for many states the Gaddafi government lost its legitimacy by the escalation of abusiveness against its people.

It is nevertheless notable that recognition of the competing authority did not come before the National Transitional Council managed to establish a degree of control over parts of the Libyan territory. In other words, governmental legitimacy was not denied to a firmly-established and entirely effective government. It was rather that the international community progressively shifted toward one of the competing authorities, neither of which was in effective control over the entire territory of Libya. Still, the Gaddafi government was in control of the capital and several governmental institutions, so it seemed

133 *Id.*

134 *See supra* note 130.

135 *See* Henderson, *supra* note 128, at 772.

136 *See generally* Mehrdad Payandeh, "The United Nations, Military Intervention, and Regime Change in Libya", 55 *Va J. Int'l L.* 355 (2012).

137 *Id.*

138 *See* Dapo Akande, "Recognition of Libyan National transitional Council as Government of Libya", *EJIL Talk!* (July 23, 2011), http://www.ejiltalk.org/recognition-of-libyan-national-transitional-council-as-government-of-libya. *See also* Stefan Talmon, "Recognition of the Libyan National Transitional Council", *ASIL Insights* (June 16, 2011), http://www.asil.org/insights110616.cfm.

to have had a better claim on the basis of effectiveness. But it lost this claim due to gross and systematic human rights violations and grave humanitarian situation.

Libya was thus a situation in which two competing authorities claimed to be the legitimate government of the state. Neither of them was in effective control of the entire territory of Libya. A number of states decided to grant an explicit recognition to the National Transitional Council on the basis of the Gaddafi government's record of gross human rights violations. It is, however, very unlikely that the competing authority would have been recognized, if it did not control part of the territory and demonstrate the capability of taking full control over Libya.

D *Recognition of Governments and its Implications for Taiwan*

The traditional test for the governmental authority is effective control over the territory of a state. There are certain limitations to this, and governments have been stripped of their representative legitimacy on the basis of abusiveness toward their own people. In response to the developments in Libya, some states departed from the Estrada doctrine. This resulted from a combination of a loss of effective control over part of the territory and a record of gross and systematic human rights violations. However, as cautioned by Talmon, gross and systematic violations of human rights do not automatically de-recognize a government internationally or make it "less of a government."[139] This only happens through international action. The present paper has demonstrated that such an action can be channeled either through the Security Council's binding powers or by the institute of recognition of governments.

While gross and systematic human rights violations may constitute a threat to international peace and thus trigger the Security Council's action under Chapter VII of the UN Charter, such measures are not triggered by the absence of democratic elections alone. Recognition of governments in the "pre-Estrada sense" has not been re-established.[140] However, there is some evidence of collective non-recognition or de-recognition of governments. Some effective governments were denied recognition because they were deemed illegitimate due to their unconstitutional establishments by overthrowing democratically-elected ones. Such were the examples of Haiti[141] and Sierra

139 Stefan Talmon, "De-Recognition of Colonel Qaddafi as Head of State of Libya?", 60 *Int'l & Comp. L.Q.* 759, 765 (2011).

140 *Cf. supra* note 3.

141 *See* S.C. Res. 940, U.N. Doc. S/RES/940 (July 31, 1994), para. 4 (authorizing the use of force to reverse the coup).

Leone.[142] And in other situations foreign states had to choose which competing authority they would recognize as the government of a certain state, where neither one was fully in effective control of the territory of the state in question. In these circumstances gross abuses of human rights may influence the choice of the authority challenging the incumbent authority.

No example exists in collective practice that would deny legitimacy to a firmly-established non-democratic government, based solely or predominantly on its non-democratic nature. As the example of the Taliban government in Afghanistan shows, the legitimacy of a government may be questioned on the basis of threats to international peace and grave violations of human rights; but not on the basis of non-democratic practices.

International practice thus demonstrates that effective control over the territory is still the fundamental basis for legitimate governmental authority. This may be challenged by collective action through the Security Council or collective de-recognition of one governmental authority and recognition of another one. Both scenarios are highly unlikely in the situation of the China/Taiwan relations.

Although Taiwan has abandoned its position for the Republic of China to be the legitimate government of China as a whole, it continues to claim continuity with independence, that is, statehood of the Republic of China prior to 1949.[143] This may well be the most politically expedient claim that Taiwan can make at the moment, but its problem is that the identity of the Chinese state has never changed in international law. In other words, no new state emerged in 1949, only the government of an *existing* state had changed. And in 1971 it was confirmed that the government of the Peoples' Republic had a more plausible claim to be the government of China. The decisive factor underlying such an international perception was effective control over the territory which remains an important test even in contemporary international law.

IV Conclusion

Taiwan is in an ambiguous international legal position which also tests the coherence of some traditional concepts in international law: recognition of states, recognition of governments, and continuity with the international

---

142 S.C. Res. 1132, U.N. Doc. S/RES/1132 (Oct. 8, 1997), para. 1 (condemning the coup in Sierra Leone and calling for restoration of the democratically elected government).

143 *See* Responses to Questions Submitted by Deutsche Welle: Lee Teng-hui President Republic of China, July 9, 1999, *supra* note 95.

personality. Although recognition of states is, in principle, a declaratory act, when granted collectively—and universally or near-universally—it is capable of having constitutive effects. This can happen where an entity seeks to emerge as a state unilaterally. International law does not prohibit either declaring independence unilaterally or granting recognition to a secession-seeking entity. But foreign states only very rarely and rather exceptionally grant recognition to such an entity. Kosovo is the only recent example where recognition may have constituted a state, and even with a hundred recognitions its legal status remains objectively ambiguous. Collective recognition can have the effects of a collective state creation. But where recognition is not virtually universal, such an entity can be a state for some states but not for others.

If Taiwan declared independence, this would not be an internationally illegal act, but rather an internationally neutral act. And neither would collective recognition of Taiwan be illegal. Collective recognition would be very unlikely and recognition certainly would not be universal or near-universal. Therefore, if Taiwan sought statehood, this unilateral path would unlikely be effective. It is true that recognition of Taiwan would not be illegal, but international law—at the same time—creates no obligation to grant recognition. The decision on granting recognition is political, which does not work in Taiwan's favor. Despite the decline of explicit recognition of governments in contemporary international law, the act is still present in contemporary international law and affairs, sometimes silently and sometimes directly.

With the prospect of an explicit declaration of independence being ineffective, Taiwan will likely continue to stand on the position that the Republic of China has always been independent. However, this does not clarify Taiwan's legal status and does not imply that Taiwan is a state. The legal status of the Chinese territory did not change in 1949, so this is not a case of there being two states: the Republic and the Peoples' Republic. Rather, there was a change of government in one state, while the identity of the Chinese state remained the same under international law. Making a claim for continuity with the pre-1949 Government of the Republic of China is thus not a claim for statehood. There has always only been one statehood—that of China—the rest is about governments, not states.

The solution of the Taiwan question could theoretically lie in declaration of independence, that is, by making an explicit claim for separate statehood. International acceptance of such a claim could follow via recognition, but in order for such a declaration to be effective, recognition would need to be near-universal. Since recognition depends on political considerations, such a scenario is very unlikely. Taiwan should thus refrain from unilateral acts, as they are unlikely to yield any results in terms of clarification of its legal status.

Do *Jus Cogens* Norms Invalidate State Immunity? International Restorative Justice and Japanese War Compensation Cases

Tomoko Yamashita

Table of Contents

---

* JSPS Postdoctoral Research Fellow, Kyoto University; Ph.D., LL.M., and LL.B., Kobe University; Master Complémentaire en droit international, Université libre de Bruxelles (Belgium). This article is based on the author's presentation at the 2013 ILA-ASIL Asia-Pacific Research Forum, May 15–16, 2013. The author would like to express her deepest gratitude to all the professors and colleagues for their helpful comments and suggestions and to the Konosuke Matsushita Memorial Foundation for its research grant given for this work.

 | DOI 10.1163/9789004306509_007

I Introduction

War compensation is a social problem in the sense that its legally correct answer does not always placate the demands of social justice.[1] Governments consider the problem of war reparations to be "solved" by the conclusion of peace treaties. In this case, Japan considers that economic aid to its neighbouring developing countries (at least at that time) constitutes a kind of apology for past military aggression and that such a solution is also desirable (at least at that time) by the dictatorial political leaders of these countries for the purpose of re-establishing a "future-oriented" relationship with Japan.[2] However, even though almost 70 years has passed since the end of WWII, the suffering of victims has never ceased and some of them continue to claim compensation.

An analysis of private war compensation cases brought before Japanese domestic courts draws our attention to an interesting feature that reflects the changing political situation in East Asia. The first of such claims was brought by Japanese citizens in the 1950s against the Japanese government who had waived the possibility of obtaining compensation from the Allied Powers. The second was brought between the 1970s and 1990s by Japan's former colonial subjects, especially the Taiwanese people and Korean residents in Japan who served as former Japanese military personnel or civil servants but could not benefit from Japan's public pensions for the bereaved or for their disabilities, which were only granted to Japanese citizens. The third was from the late 1980s to the early 1990s, brought by a variety of foreign victims who suffered from illegal acts carried out by the Japanese imperial army or enterprises during WWII.[3]

In the wake of the end of the Cold War, the latest manifestation, backed by a grassroots movement of lawyers, has witnessed a subtle political change.[4] For example, the Japanese government affirmed that individual rights to compensation could not be deprived by the conclusion of peace treaties. In 1991, the then Director of the Treaties Bureau of the Ministry of Foreign Affairs of

1 Pierre d'Argent, *Les réparations de guerre en droit international public* 3–4 (2002).

2 Zhihui Yang, "From War Reparation to Postwar Reparation", *in Toward a History beyond Borders: Contentious Issues in Sino-Japanese Relations* 402–03 (Daqing Yang et al. eds., 2012).

3 Masahiko Asada, "Nippon ni okeru sengo hosyo to kokusaiho [War Compensation in Japan and International Law]", 1321 *Jurist* 26 (2006). For more detailed English commentaries about past Japanese jurisprudence on war victims, see Masahiro Igarashi, "Post-War Compensation Cases, Japanese Courts and International Law", 43 *Japanese Ann. Int'l L.* 45 (2000); Shin Hae Bong, "Compensation for Victims of Wartime Atrocities: Recent Developments in Japan's Case Law", 3 J. *Int'l. Crim. Justice* 187 (2005).

4 Masatoshi Miyasaka, "Saikosai heisei 19 nen 4 gatsu 27 nichi daini shohotei hanketsu [Judgment of April 27, 2007, Supreme Court of Japan]", 1346 *Jurist* 78 (2007).

Japan (MOFA) stated at *Sangiin* [the House of the Councillors of the Diet] that Article 2(1) of the 1965 ROK–Japan Agreement does not extinguish individual rights to claim compensation but that this provision means that the States have agreed not to exercise diplomatic protection for this issue.[5] In addition, official records concerning the forced migration and labour of Chinese people during WWII, which were secretly studied by the MOFA in 1946 despite having been claimed as lost by the ministry itself, were found by journalists in 1993 in private archives. Copies had secretly been kept by researchers who engaged in the MOFA's fact finding mission of 1946 or taken to the Tokyo Overseas Chinese General Assembly.[6] These detailed reports were prepared by the MOFA in order to defend Japanese war criminals at the International Military Tribunal for the Far East[7] and the MOFA recognised them as official documents.[8] According to these official records, the number of Chinese people drafted to Japan was 38,935, working in 135 worksites run by 35 enterprises. However, the directors of only two worksites were actually accused of being war criminals, because of a policy change of the occupation of the Allied Powers led by the United States in the course of the Cold War and the Chinese Civil War.

Even though an important detail was admitted by the Supreme Court of Japan in affirming the substantive existence of individual rights to litigate for war compensation (*Song et al. v. Nishimatsu Construction Co.*, 27 April 2007), unfortunately, all the demands of war victims have been unsuccessful before Japanese domestic courts. The reasons have always been procedural: the statute of limitations provided in the Civil Code and the notorious, old doctrine of *Kokka-Mutouseki* (the non-responsibility of the State) that prevailed in pre-war Japan.[9] From an international legal point of view, it is the so-called "waiver of

---

5 For the official opinion of the Japanese government (expressed by Shunji Yanai, the then Director of the Treaties Bureau of the MOFA), see Minutes of *Yosan-iinkai* [the Budgetary Committee] at *Sangiin*, 121st session of the Diet, No. 3, Aug. 27, 1991, *available at* http://kokkai.ndl.go.jp/SENTAKU/sangiin/121/1380/12108271380003a.html [in Japanese].

6 To know how and why the reports were found in 1993, see NHK Reporters Group, *Maboroshi no gaiko houkokusho: tyugokujin kyousei renkou no kiroku* [*Non-Existent Diplomatic Reports: Records of Forced Migration of Chinese People*] (1994).

7 For the accused cases, see GHQ/SCAP Records, *Legal Section, Records Pertaining to Rules and Procedures Governing the Conduct of Japanese War Crimes Trials, Atrocities Committed against Chinese Laborers, and Background Investigations of Major Japanese War Criminals*, NMII Entry No. 292.

8 MOFA (Japan), *Kajin roumusha shurou jijyou tyousa houkokusyo* [*Chinese Labourers' Working Conditions Survey Report*]. For a short summary of this report, see NHK, *supra* note 6, 228–44.

9 According to the *Kokka-Mutbseki* doctrine, "the government is not responsible to its citizens for damages caused by the acts that it performs in the exercise of official authority at private

claims" clause in the peace treaties and special agreements concluded with Japan that block individual victims from obtaining compensation for their suffering during WWII. As a result, South Korean victims are now using Korean domestic courts in order to obtain private war compensation from Japanese enterprises that had, at a practical level, complied with the forced migration and labour policy of the government during the war. Indeed, courts have started to rule in their favour, starting with the judgment of the Supreme Court on 24 May 2012 (*Gap et al. v. Mitsubishi Heavy Industries Ltd.* case).

Against this backdrop, this article discusses the question of whether *jus cogens* norms can invalidate procedural obstacles in international law, the "waiver of claims" and State immunity, in order to realise international restorative justice, especially in the case of war crimes under international humanitarian law. As this largely involves sensitive political issues, the main purpose of this article is to provide a legal platform for future arguments among stakeholders. By classifying the opinions and interpretations of each judiciary for Japanese war compensation cases, it considers the theoretical question of whether the *jus cogens* norm could invalidate State immunity and other difficulties.

In seeking the meaning of the "waiver of claims" through private war compensation claims brought before Japanese domestic courts, the first chapter considers why such a renunciation is considered to be justified only because of a nationality link between the State and its nationals: what was waived (II-A) and under which conditions (II-B). The second chapter focuses on attempts by several national courts, especially those of "victim States," to overcome these procedural defaults from the *jus cogens* perspective. The Italian–German disputes that resulted in the ICJ's *Jurisdictional Immunities* case should be seen as posing a question against a State's absolute jurisdictional immunity in the case of a *jus cogens* violation (III-A). A possible solution was formulated from another perspective. It was actually the judgment of the South Korean Supreme Court mentioned above that formulated a solution from another perspective, which circumvented troublesome arguments concerning State immunity theory and directly accused the private companies who engaged in forced labour during WWII (III-B).

---

law." Shin, *supra* note 3, 188. This logic was completely abandoned after the enforcement of the State Redress Act (Act No. 125 of 1947). For the English text, see Japanese Law Translation Database System, http://www.japaneselawtranslation.go.jp/ (last visited Mar. 12, 2015).

II The Nature of "Waiver of Claims" in Japanese Jurisprudence

The ICJ's Advisory Opinion on the *Legal Consequences of the Construction of a Wall* confirmed the existence of a State's "obligation to make reparation for the damage caused to all the natural or legal persons concerned" in customary international law.[10] However, such an obligation could be invalidated at the procedural level by the "waiver of claims" found in peace treaties.

Waiver" in general terms can be defined as a "manifestation of the will by a subject of international law with the intention to renounce a right or claim."[11] It is essentially a unilateral legal act of a State that expresses, commonly in international treaty, its motivation to abandon or diminish a right protected by international law.[12] It needs to be manifested in an explicit way and should be considered to be a kind of valid consent of the right-holder precluding the wrongfulness of the act and preventing the subsequent possibility of arguing for international responsibility.[13]

As will be shown below, the principal peace treaties and special agreements concluded with Japan stipulate that the concerned States waived all their compensation claims and those of their nationals arising out of the war or out of actions taken because of the existence of a state of war. Such provisions prevent private persons from seeking reparations against the other State with a view to stabilising international political relations after WWII. In other words, the most disadvantaged individuals are those that suffered during the war because the possibility of suing the responsible State is blocked by their own State. However, a question arises as to why a State could renounce the rights or claims of private persons without their consent, just because they were its nationals.

A *Object: What Was Waived?*

Lauterpacht rightly states that "[t]he orthodox positivist doctrine has been explicit in the affirmation that only States are subjects of international law."[14]

10 Legal Consequences of the Construction of a Wall in the Occupied Palestinian Territory, Advisory Opinion, 2004 I.C.J. 136, paras. 152–53 (July 9, 2004).

11 Isabel Feichtner, "Waiver", *M.P.E.P.I.L.*, para. 3 (online ed., last updated Oct. 2006).

12 Jean Salmon, *Dictionnaire de droit international* 968–69 (2001); Gian C. Venturini, "La portée et les effets juridiques des attitudes et des actes unilatéraux des Etats", 112 *Recueil des Cours* 394 (1964); Eric Suy, *Les actes unilatéraux en droit international public* 153–55 (1962).

13 Andrea Gattini, *La renonciation au droit d'invoquer la responsabilité, in Völkerrecht als Wertordnung: Festschrift für Christian Tomuschat* 317, 319–20 (Pierre-Marie Dupuy et al. eds., 2006).

14 Hersch Lauterpacht, *International Law* 489 (1975).

From this position, a State has been able to arbitrarily reject the legal capacity of its citizens and limit their access to domestic and international courts as a corollary of its sovereignty. Regardless of the claimants' nationality, Japanese domestic courts tend to justify the "waiver of claims" based on orthodox positivist approach of diplomatic protection.[15] In *Nishimatsu Construction Ltd.*, the Supreme Court noted that "a State has the power, on the basis of its sovereignty over its nationals, to dispose of claims including those held by individuals upon the conclusion of a peace treaty to terminate a war."[16]

In order to determine the object of the waiver in the 1951 San Francisco Treaty, it is necessary to analyse *Shimoda et al.* because the reasoning of the judgment contains very detailed elements on the waiver of individual claims.[17] Brought by Japanese victims of the atomic bombings by the United States of Hiroshima and Nagasaki, this case is also known as the first judicial decision in the world that recognised the illegality of nuclear weapons. In placing international responsibility on the Japanese government, which had waived claims against the Allied Powers by accepting Article 19(a) of the 1951 San Francisco Treaty, the plaintiffs insisted that this waiver was an unlawful expropriation contrary to Article 29(3) of the Constitution[18] and Article 1(1) of the State Redress Act.[19]

In its judgment, the Tokyo District Court first denied the plaintiff's allegation that an individual who suffered injury by an act contrary to international law had a claim for damages in international law against the State that caused the injury. The Court was of the view that "in order for a person to be a subject

---

15 *Mavrommatis Palestine Concessions* (Greek v. U.K.), 1924 P.C.I.J. (ser. A) No. 2, at 12 (Aug. 30) (introducing the traditional theory that "[b]y taking up the case of one of its subjects and by resorting to diplomatic action or international judicial proceedings on his behalf, a state is in reality asserting its own rights—its right to ensure, in the person of its subjects, respect for the rules of international law").

16 Saikō-Saibansho [Sup. Ct.] Apr. 27, 2007, Nishimatsu Construction Ltd. v. Li Xiang et al., 51 *Japanese Y.B. Int'l L.* 518, 526 (2008).

17 Tōkyō Chihō Saibansho [Tōkyō Dist. Ct.] Dec. 7, 1963, Shimoda et al. v. State of Japan, 8 *Japanese Ann. Int'l L.* 626 (1964).

18 Article 29 of the Constitution stipulates the following: "Private property may be taken for public use upon just compensation therefore." For the English text, see Japanese Law Translation Database System, *supra* note 9.

19 State Redress Act, Act No. 125 of 1947, *supra* note 9, art. 1(1) (stipulating that "[w]hen a public officer who exercises the public authority of the State or of a public entity has, in the course of his/her duties, unlawfully inflicted damage on another person intentionally or negligently, the State or public entity shall assume the responsibility to compensate therefore.")

of rights in international law, he must be able to assert his rights and be bound by his duties in his own name" and "there is in general no way open to an individual who suffers injuries from an act of hostility contrary to international law to claim damages on the level of international law" except in cases where the treaty so provides (as it had done in certain prior agreements that established an international tribunal accessible to individuals).[20] However, unfortunately, such a provision cannot be found in the 1951 San Francisco Treaty and, furthermore:

> There is no example where individual claims for damages were recognized in customary international law at any time prior to the Japanese Peace Treaty. Accordingly, it does not follow that the Japanese Peace Treaty admitted Japanese nationals' claims for damages in international law and accordingly made them the object of a waiver. What were waived in article 19 (a) of the Japanese Peace Treaty were Japanese nationals' claims under the municipal laws of Japan and of the Allied Powers.[21]

This view, which restricted an individual's capacity in international law, was relevant, especially in the world before the 1945 UN Charter. As Anzilotti explains, in those days, an individual used to be considered to be an object of international law and a mere component of a State's property.[22] In other words, only domestic law can recognise the suffering of individuals because they are kept under the absolute personal jurisdiction of the State based on their nationality, which gives rise to rights and obligations between the individual and the State under municipal law.[23] Nationality "constitutes a translation into juridical terms of the individual's connection with the State which has made him its national," as a kind of "formal relationship" between natural persons and a State.[24] Based on this political philosophy, which involves relations of allegiance and protection, individuals' rights and obligations are determined by the States to which they belong.[25] A State can bring a claim of

20 Shimoda et al., 8 *Japanese Ann. Int'l L.*, at 636–38, para. III (3).

21 *Id.* at 642, para. IV (6).

22 Dionisio Anzilotti, "La responsabilité internationale des états à raison des dommages soufferts par des étrangers", 13 *Revue Générale de Droit International Public* 5, 8–9, para. 3 (1906).

23 Zsuzsanna Deen-Racsmany, "Diplomatic Protection and International Criminal Law: Can the Gap Be Bridged?", 20 *Leiden J. Int'l L.* 909, 911 n.8 (2007).

24 Nottebohm Case (Liech. v. Guat.), 1955 I.C.J. 4, 23 (Apr. 6).

25 Salmon, *supra* note 12, 727; Oliver Dörr, "Nationality", *M.P.E.P.I.L.* paras. 4–5 (online ed., last updated Nov. 2006).

diplomatic protection when its national is injured by another State; however, in this case, international law only perceives the damages suffered by the State and not by the individual.[26] In his report to the ILC in 1956, Garcia-Amador pointed out that "individuals are left in a very precarious position" because it is considered "simply as a right vested in the State" under the system.[27] As a Special Rapporteur charged with drafting articles on diplomatic protection, Bennouna explained in 1998 that this arbitrariness was an established customary rule of international law according to which a "State has a 'procedural' right to bring an international claim in order to protect its nationals when they have suffered injury as a result of a violation of international law, hence, the State may agree to limit that right or even to waive it in its treaty practice with other countries."[28]

Such a procedural right of the State to bring an international case, namely diplomatic protection claim, could be renounced by the inter-governmental conclusion of peace treaties. However, what seems problematic is that according to the Tokyo District Court, the private claims of individuals under municipal laws were also "waived" by Article 19(a) of the 1951 Treaty. Obviously, the "waiver" here is not exactly the same meaning as that mentioned above, since private claims were not "waived" by the right-holders but by their national State. Indeed, as will be seen below, Japanese judiciary itself seems to have recently found this understanding to be illogical and has slightly changed its attitude towards later claims brought by non-Japanese people. Indeed, it has come to recognise that a private claim under municipal law cannot be renounced but inactivated by the renunciation of the State's rights for diplomatic protection in peace treaties.

B *Conditions: How Has It Been Waived?*

Since the conclusion of the 1951 San Francisco Treaty, Japan has gradually concluded bilateral peace treaties with those States that did not participate in the San Francisco Conference. The negotiations of bilateral agreements with

26 Anzilotti, *supra* note 22, at 10, para. 4.

27 Alain Pellet, "The Second Death of Euripides Mavrommatis? Notes on the International Law Commission's Draft Articles on Diplomatic Protection", 7 *L. & Prac. of Int'l Ct. & Tribunals* 33, 42, para. 17 (2008).

28 Mohamed Bennouna, "Preliminary Report on Diplomatic Protection", para. 49, U.N. Doc. A/CN.4/484 (1998); Riccardo Pisillo-Mazzeschi, "International Obligation to Provide for Reparation Claims", *in State Responsibility and the Individual: Reparation in Instances of Grave Violations of Human Rights* 145–50 (Albrecht Randelzhofer & Christian Tomuschat eds., 1999).

China and Korea were suspended until the 1960s and 1970s because of political difficulties even though most civilian victims were residents of these countries. Three main legal frameworks have emerged as peace treaties with Japan in *lato sensu*: 1) the 1951 San Francisco Treaty, 2) the 1965 agreements with Korea and 3) the settlements with China, which are especially complicated in relation to the legal status of the Republic of China (ROC) and the People's Republic of China (PRC). As each instrument provides different conditions for the "waiver of claims," this section examines whether such an arbitrary disposal of individual rights was illegal.

1 1951 Peace Treaty with Japan (San Francisco Treaty)

Japan is often compared with the Federal Republic of Germany (FRG), which compensated victims of Nazi persecution through its domestic legislations (*Wiedergutmachen*). However, a simple comparison is difficult, because the division of Germany after WWII made the situation very complex and forced the FRG not to settle the issue of inter-governmental war "reparation" until today.[29] For Japan, the situation is much simpler because of a State-to-State lump-sum peace treaty concluded in San Francisco with 48 out of 55 States in 1951.[30] In this way, the 1951 San Francisco Treaty became *the* source of private compensation claims for damages caused by the Japanese government during the war.[31]

The 1951 Treaty contains all the traditional provisions of a modern peace treaty such as those related to territorial, political, financial and economic issues.[32] The enemies of Japan during WWII, the Allied Powers, explicitly abandoned the possibility of their nationals being able to sue Japan in Article 14(b) of the Treaty:

> b) Except as otherwise provided in the present Treaty, the Allied Powers waive all reparations claims of the Allied Powers, other claims of the Allied Powers and their nationals arising out of any actions taken by

---

29 D'Argent, *supra* note 1, at 127–233. Concerning the individual reparations issue, the German Democratic Republic (East Germany) refused to accept such a responsibility until Apr. 12, 1990, just before the Reunification.

30 Peace Treaty with Japan and the Allied Powers, Sep. 8, 1951, 136 U.N.T.S. 45 [hereinafter San Francisco Treaty].

31 Mika Hayashi, "Peace Treaty with Japan (1951)", para. 3, *M.P.E.P.I.L.* (online ed., last updated July 2009).

32 Rainer Hofmann, "Compensation for Personal Damages Suffered during World War II", para. 9, *M.P.E.P.I.L* (online ed., last updated Feb. 2013).

> Japan and its nationals in the course of the prosecution of the war, and claims of the Allied Powers for direct military costs of occupation.

With regard to this provision, a controversy was aroused by ex-Dutch prisoners of war and civilian detainees. In asking for compensation for maltreatment by the Japanese Imperial Army in the Dutch East Indies (now part of Indonesia), the plaintiffs insisted that a waiver of individual rights was not explicitly mentioned in this provision. However, the Tokyo High Court rejected this assertion because:

> The appropriate interpretation of this would be that the claim of a national of an Allied Power as an individual was also "abandoned" by the Allied Powers, and that the substantive claim of nationals of the Allied Powers has also been dissolved.[33]

The reasoning of the Tokyo High Court takes a very dualistic positivist approach in international law. In this case, as will be seen below, the plaintiffs' argument concerning Article 3 of the 1907 Hague Convention IV was also denied by the Court because the provision does not explicitly mention such a possibility. A slight change from *Shimoda et al.* can be found here on the point that the Court said private war compensation claims were "abandoned" by the 1951 San Francisco Treaty, based on the will of States at the municipal law level.

2 Bilateral Agreements outside the 1951 San Francisco Treaty

Even though Korea and China were not invited to the 1951 San Francisco Conference, the Treaty took into account the fact that a large proportion of the victims were their nationals. This is evident from the fact that Article 21 of the 1951 San Francisco Treaty qualifies Korea and China as "beneficiaries" of its provisions.[34]

---

33 Tōkyō Kōtō Saibansho [Tōkyō High Ct.] Oct. 11, 2011, Lapré et al. v. State of Japan, 45 *Japanese Ann. Int'l L.* 144, 145 (2002). Around the same time, British citizens asked for compensation using the same logic. *See* Tōkyō Dist. Ct. Nov. 26, 1998, Titherington et al. v. State of Japan, 46(2) *Shomu Geppo* [*Monthly Bulletin on Law Suits*] 73 (2000).

34 Article 21 stipulates that "Notwithstanding the provisions of Article 25 of the present Treaty, China shall be entitled to the benefits of Articles 10 and 14(a)2; and Korea to the benefits of Articles 2, 4, 9 and 12 of the present Treaty."

a Agreements between Korea and Japan

The legal reason why Korea did not take part in the 1951 San Francisco Treaty was because it used to be part of Japan; therefore, it could not be at war with Japan as a result of the Japan–Korea Annexation Treaty of 22 August 1910, which extended Japanese sovereignty over the country.[35] The situation did not allow Korea to come to the Conference of 1951 since another war had broken out in the peninsula at that time, after which it was finally divided into two countries, the Democratic People's Republic of Korea (DPRK) and the Republic of Korea (ROK). Even though the armistice in 1953 put into force a ceasefire for the Korean War, it took time for them to conclude peace treaties with Japan for WWII due to the Cold War.

(1) The ROK

As both countries were in the United States-led West bloc, the peace treaty between South Korea and Japan could be concluded relatively early in 1965; this was entitled the Treaty on Basic Relations between the ROK and Japan (the 1965 ROK–Japan Treaty on Basic Relations).[36] Because this Treaty did not mention war compensation, another special agreement for the war compensation issue was created, namely the Agreement between Japan and the Republic of Korea Concerning the Settlement of Problems in Regard to Property and Claims and Economic Cooperation (the 1965 ROK–Japan Agreement).[37] This Agreement stipulates the waiver of war compensation claims between both States and their nationals and states that Japan should provide economic assistance and launch yen loans-financed projects for Korean economic development in return. The issue of private war reparations is stipulated in Articles 2(1) and (3) of the 1965 Korea–Japan Agreement:

> Article II
>
> 1. The Contracting Parties confirm that [the] problem concerning property, rights and interests of the two Contracting Parties and their nationals (including juridical persons) and concerning claims between the Contracting Parties and their nationals, including those provided for

35 D'Argent, *supra* note 1, at 285, 290–93.

36 Treaty on Basic Relations between Japan and the Republic of Korea, June 22, 1965, 583 U.N.T.S. 45.

37 Agreement Between Japan and the Republic of Korea Concerning the Settlement of Problems in Regard to Property and Claims and Economic Cooperation, June 22, 1965, 583 U.N.T.S. 173.

> in Article IV, paragraph (a) of the Treaty of Peace with Japan signed at the city of San Francisco on September 8, 1951, is settled completely and finally.
>
> ...
>
> 3. Subject to the provisions of paragraph 2, no contention shall be made with respect to the measures on property, rights and interests of either Contracting Party and its nationals which are within the jurisdiction of the other Contracting Party on the date of the signing of the present Agreement, or with respect to any claims of either Contracting Party and its nationals against the other Contracting Party and its nationals arising from the causes which occurred on or before the said date.

Instead of renouncing claims, Article 2(1) of the Agreement confirms that the "problem concerning property, rights and interests of... their nationals... is *settled completely and finally*."[38] The question was whether this slight difference from the 1951 San Francisco Treaty leads to a different answer for private war compensation claims.

The answer from the Supreme Court of Japan was in the negative in the judgment on 29 November 2004. The plaintiffs claimed compensation for their intolerable suffering and for unpaid wages as civilian workers in the Japanese Imperial Army during WWII. Indeed, some women among them were treated as "comfort women"—sex slaves for the Army.[39] By recalling the judgment of the Tokyo High Court, the Supreme Court rejected their request by stating that:[40]

> Articles 2(1) and (3) of the 1965 Agreement stipulates that both Japan and the ROK agree that they will not exercise diplomatic protection over the "properties, rights, and interests and other claims" held by themselves and their citizens that are all kinds of substantive rights that have any

---

38 *Id.* art. 2(1) (emphasis added).

39 For a detailed analysis of Japanese jurisprudence concerning "comfort women", see Igarashi, *supra* note 3, at 54–71; Shin, *supra* note 3, at 188 n.2. *See also* Gay J. McDougal, "Systematic Rape, Sexual Slavery and Slavery-Like Practices during Armed Conflict", U.N. Doc. E/CN.4/Sub.2/1998/13. A peoples' tribunal as a civil and social movement of NGOs took place in 2000. Christine M. Chinkin, "Women's International Tribunal on Japanese Military Sexual Slavery", 95 *Am. J. Int'l. L.* 335 (2001).

40 Sup. Ct. Nov. 29, 2004, Park et al. v. State of Japan, 1879 Hanrei Jiho 58 (2004). The text of this judgment is largely a citation of the judgment of July 20, 2003 of the Tōkyō High Court. The latter's English translation is available at 47 *Japanese Ann. Int'l L.* 203 (2004).

> property values on legal grounds and that what type of domestic measures should be adopted is left entirely to each nation's government respectively.

An important aspect should not be overlooked here; the Supreme Court confirmed that what was waived in this provision was only the right of diplomatic protection of the States; private claims existing at a domestic law level were not renounced by the Agreement. Indeed, this view is consistent with that of the Japanese government expressed by a Director of the MOFA in 1991.[41] The Supreme Court continued in this paragraph by stating that their claims were, unfortunately, not admissible in light of the 1965 Act No. 144, an implementing measure of the 1965 Agreement.[42] Nevertheless, it should be noted that this slight development can be contrasted with the *Dutch East Indies* case, where the Tokyo High Court supported a total waiver of private claims in light of Article 14 of the San Francisco Treaty. In fact, the judiciary appears not to have adhered to the subtle terminological difference in each peace treaty and seems to have assimilated all the claims into the same framework. As will be seen later, this forefeeling was affirmed by the Supreme Court in 2007 in the case involving plaintiffs who were Chinese nationals.

(2) The DPRK

Since the DPRK and Japan still have no official diplomatic relations, no case has yet been brought by North Korean citizens before Japanese tribunals. In 2002, the Prime Minister of Japan visited the DPRK for the first time and the two governments issued a joint statement providing for the waiver of claims between the two populations.[43] However, there has been no subsequent development of relations because political difficulties arose after the visit.

b *Bilateral Settlement between China and Japan*

Among the other countries, the legal situation concerning China is extremely complicated. Due to the Chinese Civil War, China was not invited to the 1951 San Francisco Conference. Hence, Japan concluded a peace treaty in 1952

41 Minutes of *Yosan-iinkai* at *Sangiin, supra* note 5.

42 Act on Measures in Relation to the Property Rights of the Republic of Korea and Others Incidental to Enforcement of Article 2 of the "Agreement Between Japan and the Republic of Korea Concerning the Settlement of Problems in Regard to Property and Claims and Economic Cooperation" (Act No. 144 of 1965) [in Japanese].

43 Japan–DPRK Pyongyang Declaration, Sept. 17, 2002, *available at* http://www.mofa.go.jp/region/asia-paci/n_korea/pmv0209/pyongyang.html.

(1952 Taipei Treaty) with the ROC, which was led by the Chinese Nationalist Party even though it had already withdrawn to Taiwan at that time after the establishment of the PRC in 1949.[44] With the General Assembly of the United Nations switching its recognition of "China" in 1971,[45] a Joint Communiqué by Japan and the PRC was issued in 1972 whereby the Minister of Foreign Affairs,[46] Masayoshi Ohira, explained at a press conference that the 1952 Taipei Treaty had lost its *raison d'être*, thus losing any future applicability.[47]

In fact, the legality and validity of the 1952 Taipei Treaty has always been denied by the PRC,[48] while Japan, in its political dialogue, has always insisted that it is not legally possible to conclude another peace treaty with "China" and, as such, the 1952 Taipei Treaty is applicable over the PRC.[49] Contrary to what Minister Ohira alleged, the Japanese government seems to consider that the "China" of the 1952 Taipei Treaty switched to the PRC after the 1972 Joint Communiqué of Japan and the PRC.[50]

Although the 1978 Treaty of Peace and Friendship between Japan and the PRC (1978 Beijing Treaty) was entitled so,[51] it cannot be defined as a "peace treaty" in *stricto sensu* at least at the time of its conclusion—it was rather the 1972 Joint Communiqué that can been considered as such.[52] In fact, the 1978

---

44 Treaty of Peace and Friendship between Japan and the Republic of China, Apr. 27, 1952, 138 U.N.T.S. 38.

45 G.A. Res. 2758 (XXVI), UN Doc. A/RES/2758 (XXVI) (Oct. 25, 1971).

46 Joint Communiqué of the Government of Japan and the Government of the People's Republic of China, Sept. 27, 1972, available at http://www.mofa.go.jp/region/asia-paci/china/joint72.html.

47 *See* Masahiko Asada, "Nikka heiwa jyoyaku to kokusaiho (1) [The Peace Treaty between Japan and the Republic of China in an International Legal Perspective (1)]", 147(4) *Hogaku Ronso* [*Kyoto Law Review*] 1, 4 (2000).

48 Yang, *supra* note 2, at 381–82.

49 For a detailed analysis, see id. at 373–97; Masaya Inoue, *Nicchu kokko seijyouka no seijishi* [*Political History of Diplomatic Normalization between China and Japan*] 41–73, 526–36 (2010).

50 For the official opinion of the Japanese government expressed by Masuro Takashima (the then Director of the Treaties Bureau of the MOFA), see Minutes of *Naikaku-iinkai* [the Committee of the Cabinet], *Shugiin* [House of Representatives], 71st session of the Diet, Jul. 26, 1973, http://kokkai.ndl.go.jp/SENTAKU/syugiin/071/0020/main.html [in Japanese] (last visited Mar. 12, 2015).

51 Treaty of Peace and Friendship between Japan and the People's Republic of China, Aug. 12, 1978, 1225 U.N.T.S. 257.

52 According to Kuriyama (the then Director of the Treaties Division, Treaties Bureau of the MOFA), "it was the view commonly shared by the leaders of the two Governments that as the issues arising from the past abnormal state of affairs between the two countries were

Beijing Treaty does not mention the problems relating to WWII; its preamble merely confirms that the Joint Communiqué is the basis for relations between the two countries.

For this problem, it is the Supreme Court of Japan in *Nishimatsu Construction Ltd.* that proposed a final legal solution.[53] In this case, Chinese appealers asked for compensation for their suffering due to forced labour in Japan at the factory of Nishimatsu Construction Ltd. during WWII. At that time, the Japanese government promoted Chinese and Korean immigration to supplement the labour force in Japan in collaboration with private companies involved in heavy industry. Nishimatsu Construction Ltd. received a large number of Chinese workers under the government's direction.

(1) The Nature of the 1972 Joint Communiqué between Japan and the PRC

The legal relationship between the 1952 Taipei Treaty with the ROC and the 1972 Joint Communiqué with the PRC will now be examined. The Supreme Court expressed its doubts over whether the ROC's control over China was effective enough in 1952 to conclude a peace treaty in the name of "China." The Supreme Court accepted Japan's position, which recognised the ROC as representing China because the PRC was not seen as the sole legitimate representative of China until 1971, when the General Assembly of the United Nations adopted Resolution 2758 (XXVI). However, the Supreme Court stated that:

> We cannot firmly conclude that Article 11 of the Japan-ROC Peace Treaty and Protocol providing for war reparations and the waiver of claims, including claims held by individuals, are applicable to the mainland of China which was never placed under the control of the government of the Republic of China after the conclusion of the treaty.[54]

As for the PRC, the governments of the PRC and Japan did not choose to conclude a new peace treaty and only issued a reciprocal unilateral declaration

---

dealt with in the Communiqué, a treaty of peace and friendship should not be of such a backward looking nature as to reopen these issues." Takakazu Kuriyama, "Some Legal Aspects of the Japan-China Joint Communiqué", 17 *Japanese Ann. Int'l L.* 42, 50 (1973).

53 Nishimatsu Construction Ltd., 51 *Japanese Y.B. Int'l L.*, at 518–32. The whole sentence is available at 61 *Minshu* [Official Civil Case Reports of the Supreme Court] (3) 1188 (2007). Another judgment was rendered on the same day concerning the issue of "comfort women" (Second phase, 1435 *Saibansho Jiho* [Bulletin of the Court] 12 (2007), but this article only argues the former case because the same logic is employed in both cases.

54 *Nishimatsu Construction Ltd.*, 51 *Japanese Y.B. Int'l L.*, at 528, para. (3) C.

named the Joint Communiqué.[55] This was the only solution for the diplomatic normalisation between the two governments because Japan insisted that it could not conclude another peace treaty in *stricto sensu* with "China." If Japan had signed another peace treaty, this would have meant that the state of war with "China" had continued until 1972, which would have caused many problems in relation to the application of international as well as domestic law.[56] However, the exact legal status of the 1972 Joint Communiqué is still unclear. Some authors have argued that the nature of the 1972 Communiqué should be decided based on the content and context of each provision.[57] Given the preparatory work, the Supreme Court judged that:

> [T]he Japan-China Joint Communiqué constitutes a peace treaty in its substance, and the joint Communiqué cannot be considered as providing, as regards war reparations and the disposition of claims, arrangements that are different from those under the Framework of the San Francisco Peace Treaty . . . the People's Republic of China obviously considered it as creating an international legal effect. It is obvious that it could at least have the legal status of a unilateral declaration made by the People's Republic of China.[58]

The Supreme Court affirmed that the 1972 Joint Communiqué was a *de facto* peace treaty between Japan and the PRC in the more general framework of the 1951 San Francisco Treaty, which created a single war settlement system with Japan after WWII. What is interesting is that the Supreme Court admitted the independent and simultaneous existence of the 1951 Taipei Treaty and the 1972 Joint Communiqué, contrary to the official view of the Japanese government, which considered the 1972 Joint Communiqué to be an *amendment* of the 1952 Taipei Treaty.

---

55 "The Communiqué is of course, politically, an extremely important document . . . Yet, both the Japanese and Chinese sides . . . agreed that a joint communiqué would be the proper form to record the results of the summit talks." Kuriyama, *supra* note 52, 50–51.

56 Inoue, *supra* note 49, 526–36. The relationship between the ROK and the PRC has been contended since 1967, concerning the possession of a student's dormitory in Kyoto (Koka-ryo) whose owner is simply registered as "China." *Cf.* Sup. Ct, Mar. 27, 2007, Koka-ryo Case, 51 *Japanese Y.B. Int'l L.* 512 (2008).

57 Masahiko Asada, "Nikka heiwa jyoyaku to kokusaiho (4) [The Peace Treaty between Japan and the Republic of China in an International Legal Perspective (4)]", 152(4) *Hogaku Ronso* [*Kyoto Law Review*] 1, 4–5 (2002). *See also* Asada, *supra* note 47.

58 Nishimatsu Construction Ltd., 51 *Japanese Y.B. Int'l L.*, at 529, para. (4) B; 531, para. C.

The more important point is the fact that this view, which was based on "the framework of the San Francisco Peace Treaty," was a new idea that had never before been proposed, even at a doctrinal level.[59] In this way, "China," a mere beneficiary under the meaning of Article 21 of the 1951 San Francisco Treaty, was incorporated into the system as a whole.[60] All provisions of the 1951 Treaty may be interpreted in favour of "China," as a third State in the convention whose assent should be presumed as long as the contrary is not indicated, unless the treaty provides otherwise.[61] Therefore, the consent of "China" is not necessarily required, at least in an explicit way at the date of the conclusion of the 1951 Treaty, since it should be "presumed" when the tribunals interpret the provisions.

In spite of the innovativeness of the idea, a doubt arises from this conclusion of the Supreme Court. Japan had an obligation to conclude a bilateral peace treaty with "China" in light of Article 26 of the 1951 San Francisco Treaty but this expired "three years after the entry into force of the present Treaty" (during 1955). At the time of the declaration of the 1972 Joint Communiqué, such an obligation no longer existed. With this in mind, the question that can be asked is how the 1951 San Francisco Treaty and the 1972 Joint Communiqué were legally linked. The reasoning of the Supreme Court is not at all clear on this point, but its motivation is probably rooted in regret over the absence of "China" at the San Francisco Conference, given its political importance after WWII within the framework of the United Nations.

(2) Integral Framework of the 1951 San Francisco Treaty

In view of the preparatory work, the Supreme Court examined the will of the PRC government and confirmed "Paragraph 5 of the Japan-China Joint Communiqué as a provision establishing all post-war arrangements covering not only war reparations but also the disposition of claims."[62] The Supreme Court then developed the argument of the "Framework of the San Francisco Peace Treaty":

> Considering that the purpose of the waiver of claims under the Framework of the San Francisco Peace Treaty is to prevent issues concerning claims from being brought up in individual and ex-post-civil litigation, the term

59 Masahiko Asada, "Nisimatsu kensetsu jiken tyugokujin ianpu niji sosyo [Chinese Comfort Women v. Nishiatsu Construction Co. (Second phase)", 1993 *Hanrei Jiho* 164, 171 (2007) [in Japanese].

60 San Francisco Treaty, *supra* note 30, art. 21.

61 *Cf.* Vienna Convention on the Law of Treaties, art. 36(1), May 23, 1969, 1155 U.N.T.S. 331.

62 Nishimatsu Construction Ltd., 51 *Japanese Y.B. Int'l L.*, at 530, para. (4) B (c).

> "waiver of claims" in this context should be understood to mean not to extinguish substantive claims but to extinguish the ability to litigate such substantive claims.[63]

The most remarkable phrase is that the "waiver of claims" of peace treaties has the simple effect of extinguishing "the ability to litigate such substantive claims." Although the difference between "substantive claims" and "ability to litigate such substantive claims" must be specified, it is still outstanding because lower instance courts have generally considered that the "waiver of claims" in peace treaties deprives private persons of their rights to claim before the courts. However, the Supreme Court here admitted the possible existence of such rights at primary rule even though such rights cannot be redressed because of procedural limits. However, it still seems better to admit the existence of "substantive claims" since legal solutions can be achieved by the modification of procedural rules, for example, by special legislation or a new treaty that introduces remedial measures in favour of individual victims. In fact, the same argument is implied in the opinion of the Japanese government regarding Article 2(1) of the 1965 ROK–Japan Agreement that was submitted to *Nishimatsu Construction Ltd.* under Article 14(b) of the 1951 San Francisco Treaty: "it is relevant to understand that the waiver of claims does not mean to extinguish claims substantially but to only *inactivate* function of the claims which allows a resort to the courts."[64]

In sum, the Supreme Court considered that all post-war arrangements should be dealt with under the same framework. In this way, it can be said that the Supreme Court modified *de facto* the incorrect reasoning of the Tokyo High Court mentioned above by stating that the "waiver of claims means the extinction of competence to litigate the claims."[65] However, even though an important detail was approved by the Supreme Court, which affirmed the substantive existence of individual rights to litigate for war compensation, all demands were ultimately dismissed for procedural reasons.

III *Jus Cogens* Norms and State Immunity

In the preceding section, the "waiver of claims" in peace treaties with Japan was identified by Japanese judiciary as a State's action to deprive individuals

63 *Id.* at 526, para. (2) C.

64 Nishimatsu Construction Ltd., 61 *Minshu*, at 1198, para. 3. This part of the judgment is only available in Japanese.

65 Nishimatsu Construction Ltd., 51 *Japanese Y.B. Int'l L.*, at 531, para. C.

of the possibility or competence to sue responsible States in domestic courts. It is a mere procedural obstacle to recover damages suffered by individuals by extinguishing their "ability to litigate such substantive claims." As a next step, an analysis must be carried out to consider how individual claimants could circumvent this obstacle. It appears, in fact, much easier for the victims to obtain judgement in their favour in their home country, even though there exist established procedural rules that may block their claims. Some domestic courts have already ruled in this way by denying jurisdictional immunity accorded to foreign states or the validity of the "waiver of claims" clause. However, from a consensual positivist approach, the violation of a rule of *jus cogens* does not automatically deprive the wrongdoing state or its officials of their immunity under customary international law.[66] The reasoning of these national judgments thus needs to be scrutinised to consider whether such exceptions in the case of *jus cogens* violations could reasonably challenge the classic international view of State immunity.

A *Do* **Jus Cogens** *Violations Invalidate a State's Jurisdictional Immunity?*

A peremptory norm of general international law is a norm accepted and recognised by the entire international community as a norm from which no derogation is permitted and which can be modified only by a subsequent norm of general international law having the same character.[67] The idea of *jus cogens* norms was hardly conceivable in the first part of the 20th century since at that time the will of States was accepted as paramount.[68] Some examples of *jus cogens* norms are suggested in the commentary to Article 50 of the ILC Draft Articles on the Law of Treaties: an unlawful use of force contrary to the principles of the UN Charter; the performance of any other criminal act under international law; the commission of acts, such as trade in slaves, piracy or genocide; violations of human rights; the equality of States; or the principle of self-determination.[69] Peremptory norms cannot be modified or amended

66 S.A.G. Talmon, "*Jus Cogens* after Germany v. Italy: Substantive and Procedural Rules Distinguished", 25 *Leiden J. Int'l L.* 979, 990 (2012); A. Orakhelashvili, "Jurisdictional Immunities of the State (Germany v. Italy; Greece Intervening)", 106 *Am. J. Int'l L.* 609, 612 (2012). *See* Arrest Warrant of 11 April 2000 (Dem. Rep. Congo v. Belg.), 2002 I.C.J. 3, 24, para. 58 (Feb. 14).

67 Vienna Convention on the Law of Treaties, *supra* note 61, art. 53.

68 Jochen A. Frowein, "Ius Cogens", *M.P.E.P.I.L.*, para. 3 (online ed.; last updated on Jan. 2009).

69 Commentary to Article 50 of the ILC Draft Articles on the Law of Treaties with Commentaries (1966), UN Doc. A/6309/Rev.1, 177, 7 GAOR 21st Session Supp 9, 20. A/6309/Rev.1 (F) (A/21/9) (1966), para. 3.

by the will of States because they are intrinsically superior and cannot be dispensed with through standard inter-State transactions.[70] Having its roots in the natural law doctrine, the concept of *jus cogens* is, therefore, not comprehensible through a strict positivist approach, but rather aimed at each legal subject to interdict the derogation from a general legal regime.[71] Among such norms, the only example confirmed by the ICJ is the prohibition of genocide;[72] however, several peremptory norms are supposed to exist in the present international legal order.

1 Human Rights Exception

Provided that the protection of core human rights was a peremptory norm at the time of WWII, the derogation from State immunity was discussed in two ways by the national courts of Greece and Italy.

In *Distomo*, the Court of Cassation of Greece affirmed in 2000 that:

> the exception to the immunity rule should apply where the offences for which compensation is sought (especially crimes against humanity) did not target civilians generally, but specific individuals in a given place who were neither directly nor indirectly connected with the military operations.[73]

In carrying out "cruel murders" that targeted the population of the village of Distomo, Germany "had tacitly waived" its jurisdictional immunity because the acts over which it was being sued "were carried out by its organs in contravention of the rules of *jus cogens* (Article 46 of the Regulations on the Laws and Customs of War Annexed to the Fourth Hague Convention of 1907) and did not have the character of acts of sovereign power."[74] In this respect, the main argument of the Greek Court of Cassation relied on the "tacit waiver" of jurisdictional immunity in the case of crimes against humanity committed as *acta jure imperii*.

In the sense that it denies the *jure imperii* nature, this argument may be similar to that of the US Court of Appeals in *Siderman de Blake et al.* which noted

---

70 Alexander Orakhelashvili, *Peremptory Norms in International Law* 8 (2006).

71 *Id.* at 36–38; Robert Kolb, "Théorie du ius cogens international", 36 *Rev. Belge de Droit Int'l* 5, 14 (2003).

72 Armed Activities on the Territory of the Congo (New Application: 2002) (Dem. Rep. Congo v. Rwanda), 2006 I.C.J. 6, 26, para. 64 (Feb. 3).

73 Distomo et al. v Germany, 129 I.L.R. 513, 519 (Ct. Cassation 2000) (Greece).

74 *Id.* at 520–21.

that "[i]nternational law does not recognise an act that violates *jus cogens* as a sovereign act."[75] However, the Greek Court's view is not supportable since, as mentioned above, the waiver of rights and claims always needs to be explicit; otherwise, it may infringe on one of the fundamental principles in the international legal order, namely the equality and independence of sovereignty.

The judgment in *Distomo* was also criticised by the judgment of the Court of Cassation of Italy in 2004 according to which "it is improbable that a State which commits serious violations intends to renounce those benefits from which it derives immunity from jurisdiction, prerogatives which make it very difficult, if not altogether impossible, to establish guilt."[76] This case was brought by an Italian national, Ferrini, who had been arrested in August 1944 and deported to Germany where he was detained and forced to work in a munitions factory until the end of WWII. The Italian Court of Cassation condemned such a deportation and subjection to forced labour as a war crime, which it assumed was prohibited by customary international law at the time given that it was committed in light of Article 6(b) of the Charter of the International Military Tribunal of Nuremberg as signed in London on 8 August 1945 as well as the judgment of the Tribunal, which affirmed that it was a flagrant violation of the 1907 Hague Convention IV.[77] The Italian Court of Cassation, therefore, contended that, "in respect of particularly serious criminal activities, now attaches [sic] to the protection of fundamental human rights over and above the protection of State interests through the recognition of immunity from foreign jurisdiction."[78] Although which norms were peremptory in character was not discussed (both norms could be *jus cogens*), the Court affirmed that the protection of fundamental human rights was superior to State immunity in the normative hierarchy of international law. According to the Italian Court, no immunity was available for Germany in spite of the *jure imperii* character of the concerned human rights violations.

This Italian view is very comprehensible, since the acts of mass executions and destruction of property by German forces indisputably constituted sovereign acts, as also confirmed by the German Supreme Court (*Bundesgerichtshof*).[79] This may be logical if one doubts the existence of State immunity as customary law after the absolute understanding of immunity

75 Siderman de Blake et al. v. Argentina, 965 F.2d 699, para. 58 (9th Cir. 1992).

76 Ferrini et al. v. Germany, 128 I.L.R. 658, 668, para. 8.2 (Ct. Cassation 2004) (It.).

77 *Id.* at 666, para. 7.2.

78 *Id.* at 673, para. 10.2.

79 Distomo et al. v. Germany, BGH-III ZR 245/98, paras. B.I.2.a & B.I.V.2.b (Fed. Sup. Ct. 2006) (Ger.)

has been replaced by the idea of restrictive immunity. However, the importance of State immunity as a normative guarantee for the equality and independence of the sovereignty of each State, one of the fundamental principles in international law, cannot be ignored. In fact, only these cases mentioned above have ever denied immunity for a foreign State sued in respect of human rights violations committed within the context of exercising State authority under international law. Even though some support has been expressed by the US and UK courts, the concerned foreign countries always benefited from the immunity accorded by national immunity legislation.[80] Additionally, after *Distomo*, the Special Supreme Court of Greece found in another case that in the present state of development of international law, Germany was entitled to State immunity.[81] Hence, even under a restrictive immunity principle, it is still doubtful, at least with regard to the time of WWII, whether a *jus cogens* norm invalidates a State's jurisdictional immunity.

2 State Immunity on the Basis of Sovereign Equality

International courts appear to disagree with the human rights exception of State immunity. The ICJ has actually answered this question in the *Jurisdictional Immunity* brought by Germany because of the aforementioned Greek and Italian cases.[82]

In this case, Italy insisted that "a State which fails to perform its obligation to make reparation to the victims of grave violations of international humanitarian law, and which offers those victims no effective means of claiming the reparation to which they may be entitled, would be deprived of the right to invoke its jurisdictional immunity before the courts of the State of the victims' nationality."[83] However, the ICJ denied this argument in stating that:

> State practice in the form of judicial decisions supports the proposition that State immunity for *acta jure imperii* continues to extend to civil proceedings for acts occasioning death, personal injury or damage to property committed by the armed forces and other organs of a State in the conduct of armed conflict, even if the relevant acts take place on the

---

80 Rosanne Van Alebeek, *The Immunity of States and Their Officials in International Criminal Law and International Human Rights Law* 313–14 (2008).

81 Margellos et al. v. Germany, 129 I.L.R. 525, 531–33, paras. 14–15 (Special Sup. Ct. 2002) (Greece).

82 Jurisdictional Immunities of the State (Ger. v. It., Greece intervening), 2012 I.C.J. 99, paras. 33–35 (Feb. 3).

83 *Id.* para. 45.

> territory of the forum State. That practice is accompanied by *opinio juris*, as demonstrated by the positions taken by States and the jurisprudence of a number of national courts which have made clear that they considered that customary international law required immunity. The almost complete absence of contrary jurisprudence is also significant, as is the absence of any statements by States in connection with the work of the International Law Commission regarding State immunity and the adoption of the United Nations Convention or, so far as the Court has been able to discover, in any other context asserting that customary international law does not require immunity in such cases.[84]

This conclusion corresponds to the traditional idea of inter-State law, which sees the rule of State immunity holding an important position in international law and international relations because it is a fundamental principle of the international legal order that derives from the principle of the sovereign equality of States provided in Article 2, paragraph 1, of the Charter of the United Nations.[85] Due to this:

> [T]he Court considers that customary international law continues to require that a State be accorded immunity in proceedings for torts allegedly committed on the territory of another State by its armed forces and other organs of State in the course of conducting an armed conflict.[86]

As the ICJ noted, this opinion was also confirmed by the *Kalogeropoulou* case of the European Court of Human Rights in the same context. In this case, the Greek courts ordered Germany to pay damages to the applicants but the Minister of Justice refused to allow the applicants to enforce the judgment against German property. The applicants alleged that this refusal should be regarded as an unjustified interference contrary to Article 6 §1 of the European Convention of Human Rights, which gives everyone the right to have any claim relating to his or her civil rights and obligations brought before a court or tribunal. The Court, however, stated that this "right of access to the courts is not absolute, but may be subject to limitations" that pursue a legitimate aim if there is a "reasonable relationship of proportionality between the means

84 *Id.* para. 77.
85 *Id.* para. 57.
86 *Id.* para. 78.

employed and the aim sought to be achieved."[87] Here, it is not important to decide whether the first infringement was a violation of the *jus cogens* rule or not since granting "sovereign immunity to a State in civil proceedings pursues the legitimate aim of complying with international law to promote comity and good relations between States."[88]

Indeed, this attitude has been repeatedly confirmed by the European Court of Human Rights for *acta jure imperii*.[89] The reasoning of international courts articulates the mainstream thinking of present international law concerning State immunity. Instead, their approach seems simplistic at best based on natural law dogma, to the effect that the rules of sovereign immunity are useful, reasonable and necessary and hence a part of international law.[90] This conclusion thus contradicts our basic sense of justice over the suffering of the weakest (i.e. the victims). Indeed, the Italian Constitutional Court refused to implement the ICJ's judgment, stating that it is contrary to the Italian Constitution (precisely, the guarantee of access to a court).[91] This point leads us further towards a consideration of the possible options for realising international restorative justice because international courts did not tackle the core question in a straightforward way, that is, whether a *jus cogens* violation invalidates jurisdictional immunity.

B *Do* Jus Cogens *Violations Invalidate the "Waiver of Claims"?*

Theoretically, a right to compensation is not an appendage to a procedural right to remedy, nor is it simply "understood" as an obligation to respect, but it rather exists as an individual right arising from a substantial breach of the obligation, which must be enjoyed by individuals, to respect the right to an effective remedy in a domestic legal system.[92] Although it seems to be very difficult to distinguish a procedural right from a substantive right to individual

---

87 Kalogeropoulou and others v. Greece & Germany, App. No. 59021/00, para. D(a) (Eur. Ct. H.R. 2002).

88 *Id.*

89 *E.g.*, Al-Adsani v. U.K., App. No. 35763/97, para. 56 (Eur. Ct. H.R. 2001); Fogarty v. U.K., App. No. 37112/97, para. 36 (Eur. Ct. H.R. 2001).

90 Orakhelashvili, *supra* note 66, at 612–15.

91 Judgment No. 238–2014 (Constitutional Ct. 2014) (It.), English translation available at http://www.cortecostituzionale.it/documenti/download/doc/recent_judgments/S238_2013_en.pdf (last visited Jan. 15, 2015).

92 Pierre d'Argent, "Le droit de la responsabilité internationale complété? Examen des principes fondamentaux et directives concernant le droit à un recours et à réparation des victimes de violations flagrantes du droit international des droits de l'homme et de violations graves du droit international humanitaire", 51 *Ann. fr. de dr. int'l* 27, 43 (2005).

remedies, this argument principally corresponds to that of the primary rule and the secondary rule proposed by Roberto Ago at the ILC.[93] The main difficulty of the "waiver of claims" is whether individuals are substantive right-holders at the international level. If they were established as such, it would be possible for them to accuse a State of illegality by arbitrarily "waiving" their rights in peace treaties. In this respect, the question is whether there is any difference between the violation of "normal" individual/human rights and of human rights protected by *jus cogens* norms.

1 Article 3 of the 1907 Hague Convention IV

Some authors suggest that Article 3 of the 1907 Hague Convention IV creates a right of redress for individuals who have suffered damage as a result of violations of *jus in bello*, and that this right is directly applicable even in domestic law. It states that:

> A belligerent party which violates the provisions of the said Regulations shall, if the case demands, be liable to pay compensation. It shall be responsible for all acts committed by persons forming part of its armed forces.

In *Dutch East Indies* mentioned above, three eminent international lawyers submitted their expert opinions to the Tokyo District Court and the Tokyo High Court in favour of the plaintiffs who argued that private war compensation should be included in Article 3 of the 1907 Hague Convention IV.[94] According to Kalshoven, the minutes of the Second Peace Conference at The Hague in 1907 that led to the adoption of this convention indicated that States intended to compensate individuals directly and promptly for damages suffered as a result of violations of *jus in bello*.[95] In his view, the term "compensation" in Article 3 was formulated in a way that "drafters may have been thinking solely of the damage or injury caused to individual persons" but "the wording of the

93 Roberto Ago, "First Report on State Responsibility", U.N. Doc. A/CN.4/217 and Add.1, *reprinted in* [1969] 2 Y.B. Int'l L. Comm'n 125; Roberto Ago, "Second Report on State Responsibility", U.N. Doc. A/CN.4/233, *reprinted in* [1970] 2 Y.B. Int'l L. Comm'n 177.

94 Frits Kalshoven, "Article 3 of the Convention (IV) Respecting the Laws and Customs of War on Land, Signed at the Hague, 18 October 1907: Expert Opinion Submitted to the Tokyo District Court on Cases by Ex-allied Power POWs and Civilian Detainees", *reprinted in War and the Rights of Individuals: Renaissance of Individual Compensation* 38 (Hisakazu Fujita et al. (eds), 1999).

95 Frits Kalshoven, "State Responsibility for Warlike Acts of the Armed Forces", 40 *Int'l & Comp. L.Q.* 827, 830–32 (1991).

second sentence of Article 3 is broad enough to cover the case of State responsibility as well."[96]

This view is also supported by David and Greenwood. By emphasising the direct applicability of *jus in bello* to human rights issues, David confirms that private persons have rights to remedy for their war damages, based on the resolution of the General Assembly concerning the conflict of the former Yugoslavia[97] and "the entire philosophy behind the exhaustion of local remedies" before the implementation of the responsibility of the State.[98] Greenwood refers to an ICJ judgment in 1992 concerning *Certain Phosphate Lands in Nauru* and argues that "there is no limitation period in international law by which claims become time barred after a specified period of time."[99] However, all of these arguments were rejected by the Tokyo District Court as well as by the Tokyo High Court. With regard to the preparatory work of Article 3 of the 1907 Hague Convention IV, the Tokyo High Court rejected his reasoning, stating that:

> Though Article 3 of the Hague Convention is about the liability of a defaulting State to compensate, it does not explicitly describe the recipient of this compensation. There also are no procedural provisions regarding how an individual might file a suit against that State for compensation. There also are no procedural provisions regarding how an individual might file a suit against that State for compensation. Moreover, as has already stated, under international law at the time of the conclusion of the Hague Convention, in principle the subjects of international law were States. Individuals are recognized as subjects of international law only exceptionally, when there are concrete provisions in international law regarding their rights and obligations.[100]

This understanding seems relevant in the view of authors such as d'Argent, who states that the preparatory work shows that States have

96 Kalshoven, *supra* note 94, at 38.

97 G.A. Res. 49/196, U.N. Doc. A/RES/49/196 (Dec. 23, 1994).

98 Eric David, "The Direct Effect of Article 3 of the Fourth Hague Convention of 18th October 1907 respecting the Laws and Customs of War on Land: Expert Opinion Submitted to the Tokyo District Court on Cases by Ex-Allied Power POWs and Civilian Detainees", *reprinted in War and the Rights of Individuals, supra* note 94, at 54–55, paras. 8–10

99 Christopher Greenwood, "Rights to Compensation of Former Prisoner of War and Civilian Internees under Article 3 of Hague Convention No. IV, 1907: Expert Opinion submitted to the Tokyo District Court on cases by Ex-allied Power POWs and Civilian Detainees", *reprinted in id.* at 69 para. 31.

100 Lapré. v. State of Japan, 45 *Japanese Ann. Int'l L.*, at 145.

no interest in establishing a principle of State responsibility in favour of individuals.[101] Because "the preparatory work is only supplementary to treaty interpretation,"[102] it is still controversial at a doctrinal level; therefore, further analysis is required in this respect.

Another case before the Tokyo High Court was also argued by using the Hague Convention IV. In this case, Hong Kong residents demanded compensation for pecuniary losses since the conversion of their Hong Kong dollars into Japanese military currency had become invalid after WWII. The reasoning of the Tokyo High Court was based on the issue of the international personality of individuals:

> [T]he Hague Convention has no stipulations or terms that recognize the ability of individuals to demand compensatory damages directly from a State, In addition, Article 1 of the Hague Convention ... aims to realize the purposes of the Convention by making the Contracting States issue such instructions. In accordance with the foregoing, Article 3 of the Hague Convention should be interpreted, from its wording itself, to provide State responsibilities between States, not individual rights for compensation.[103]

Indeed, these judgments are consistent with US decisions, for example those in *Goldstar* (*Panama*) *SA*[104] and *Princz*.[105] It is true that inferring the existence of "individual rights" only from Article 3 of the 1907 Hague Convention IV is very difficult, especially in the legal order before the UN Charter of 1945.[106] It should be noted that the adoption of the Additional Protocol I of 1977, a joint reading with the Hague Convention IV, made it possible for individuals to obtain private war compensations. The commentary on Article 91 issued by the ICRC mentions this as follows:

---

101 D'Argent, *supra* note 1, at 784.

102 Tōkyō Dist. Ct. Nov. 30, 1998, Lapré et al. v. State of Japan, 42 *Japanese Ann. Int'l L.* 143, 149 (1999), English translation *reprinted in reprinted in War and the Rights of Individuals, supra* note 94, at 104.

103 Tōkyō High Ct. Feb. 8, 2001, Ngo et al. v. State of Japan, 45 *Japanese Ann. Int'l L.* 144 (2002). The Supreme Court rejected the final appeal by the Judgment of Oct. 16, 2001 of the third Chamber.

104 Goldstar (Panama) SA v. United States, 967 F.2d 965 (4th Cir. 1992).

105 Princz v. Federal Republic of Germany, 26 F.3d 1166 (D.C. Cir. 1994).

106 Hofmann, *supra* note 32, paras. 26–28.

> Those entitled to compensation will normally be Parties to the conflict or their nationals, though in exceptional cases they may also be neutral countries, in the case of violation of the rules on neutrality or of unlawful conduct with respect to neutral nationals in the territory of a Party to the conflict.[107]

Although this formulation seems to confirm existing rights under international humanitarian law, it is still doubtful whether these developments after WWII can be applicable to the incidents during the war. Individuals are, today, undoubtedly right-holders and are entitled to access to justice at least at the national level. Moreover, their rights are guaranteed by international human rights law as it directly confers rights and obligations on individuals to the extent that those rights and obligations are incorporated into the domestic law of the State."[108] However, as the customary right of individuals to reparation remains controversial,[109] it is unfortunately difficult to allow such a right in this situation where only Article 3 of the Hague Convention IV applies.

2 Avoid Suing a Sovereign Power? Cases before the South Korean Courts

In the context of Japanese war compensation cases, those from Korea cannot be ignored. From a legal perspective, a remarkable decision was made on 24 May 2012 in *Gap et al. v. Mitsubishi Heavy Industries Ltd.* The claimants were Korean citizens residing in the ROK, but had been treated as Japanese citizens during the Japanese Occupation Period. They were sent to Japan under the National Service Draft Ordinance of 8 July 1939 (Ordinance No. 451) and were forced to work in Japanese factories whose ownership passed down to Mitsubishi Heavy Industries Ltd.

Paragraph 6 of the decision deals with the question of whether the 1965 ROK–Japan Agreement extinguished the possibility of individual claims. The Korean government's views are cited as follows:

> [T]he ROK government released parts of the documents regarding the Claims Agreement [sic: the 1965 ROK–Japan Agreement], established

107 International Committee of the Red Cross, *Commentary on the Additional Protocols of 8 June 1977 to the Geneva Conventions of 12 August 1949*, at 1056 (Yves Sandoz, Christophe Swinarski & Bruno Zimmermann eds., 1987).

108 Eric David, *Principes de droit des conflits armé* 705, para. 4.43 (4th ed. 2008).

109 Christine Evans, *The Right to Reparation in International Law for Victims of Armed Conflict* 39 (2014).

> the 'Public-Private Joint Committee on the Follow-up Measures after the Public Release of ROK–Japan Negotiations Documents (hereinafter the "Public-private Joint Committee")' on Aug. 26, 2005. Additionally, the government publically announced that 'the Claims Agreement was not signed to claim compensation for Japan's colonial rule, but to resolve financial and civil receivable and liability issues between the two nations, in accordance with Article IV of the San Francisco Treaty. The crimes against humanity committed by the Japanese government and military, such as the comfort women in the Japanese army, were not resolved by the Claims Agreement. Neither were issues of Koreans forcibly relocated and abandoned at Sakhalin or atomic bomb victims included in the Agreement; therefore the Japanese government's legal responsibilities remain'.[110]

This official opinion of the government was also supported by the Supreme Court of ROK. In adopting the main argument of the Busan High Court,[111] the Supreme Court stated that:

> In Claims Agreement negotiation, Japanese government did not acknowledge colonial rule's unlawfulness and denied legal compensation for forced mobilization victims. ROK and Japanese government did not agree on the nature of Japanese Korean peninsula rule. In this circumstance, claim rights for tort against humanity involving Japanese government power or colonial rule tort damages were not addressed in Claims Agreement. Thus, Plaintiffs' damages claim rights have not expired due to Claims Agreement.[112]

In other words, forced labour constituted a "tort against humanity" and the illegality of the colonisation of Korea by Japan from 1910 to 1945 can be considered to be a legal basis to invalidate the "waiver of claims" of the 1965 ROK–Japan Agreement in this respect. The claimants sought the payment of accrued wages for the period and compensation for the violation of international law,

---

110 Supreme Court [S. Ct.], 2009Da22549 (Gap et al. v. Mitsubishi Heavy Industries Ltd), para. 1.H., May 24, 2012 (S. Kor.), *translated in* Supreme Court Library of Korea, http://library.scourt.go.kr/jsp/html/decision/9-240hkh2012.5.24.2009Da22549.htm (last visited Mar. 12, 2015).

111 Busan High Court, 2007Na4288 (Gap et al. v. Mitsubishi Heavy Industries Ltd.), Feb. 3, 2009.

112 S. Ct., 2009Da22549, para. 4.C (S. Kor.).

which is not explicitly specified but may be customary international law in general terms. The reason why ILO Convention No. 29 (Forced Labour Convention, 1930), which was ratified by Japan on 21 November 1932, is not mentioned here may be that Korea was not a party to the Convention until recently. At the time of its conclusion, Korea had already been "annexed" to Japan and did not have any power to conclude a treaty in its own name. By insisting on the illegality of the colonisation of Korea, both the claimant and the Supreme Court could not argue a violation of Convention No. 29.

It is also interesting that the Court employed different terminology: "tort against humanity" for forced labour and "crime against humanity" for "comfort women." The latter case was left unresolved by the Claims Agreement. In other words, the Supreme Court suggested that the prohibition of a crime against humanity was a *jus cogens* norm that invalidated the provisions of the 1965 ROK–Japan Agreement insofar as it concerned "comfort women." The Supreme Court continued by saying that even though the 1965 ROK–Japan Agreement was concluded:

> [A] country may not expire a citizen's individual right to claim without consent of an individual citizen by treaty where a diplomatic protection right is abandoned. It is against the principle of modern law. If a country may expire citizen's individual right to claim by treaty under the international law, unless explicitly expressed in the treaty, citizen's individual right to claim cannot be seen as expired together with the country's diplomatic protection right since the country and individual citizen are separate legal entity.[113]

This is the most progressive part of this decision, as it shows how modern law requires the consent of individual citizens when a State invalidates their individual rights. Given that individual rights need to be realised through conventional measures in the international sphere, it should be taken into consideration that they are referring to individual rights at the domestic level. This is evident from the argument over procedure, which made no mention of the 1907 Hague Convention IV, the international human rights protected by the Convention or customary law. In conclusion, the Court stated that:

> Even if Plaintiff's' rights to claim are subject to Claims Agreement, the individual right to claim itself did not expire just based on Claims Agreement as a matter of course. With Claims Agreement, ROK's

113 *Id.*

> diplomatic protection right for claims was abandoned. ROK lost the means to protect the pertinent right diplomatically if it expired within Japan by Japanese measures. Thus, Plaintiffs' rights to claim against Defendant had not expired due to Claims Agreement. Plaintiffs may exercise the rights against Defendant.[114]

Although the Supreme Courts of both the ROK and Japan agreed that individual rights to claim were not extinguished by the 1965 ROK–Japan Agreement, their conclusions differed as to whether the claims were acceptable at a preliminary level. This is because of the different interpretations of "claims" in the 1965 Agreement. Japan's Supreme Court distinguished between a procedural right and a substantive right, while the ROK's Supreme Court considered that the concept of "claims" in the Agreement should be indivisibly united. Indeed, these differences are not essentially juridical but rather political as a result of the ambiguous and compromissory terminology used in Article 2(1) of the 1965 ROK–Japan Agreement, which only stated that the "problem concerning property, rights and interests of … their nationals … is settled completely and finally" instead of waiving all reparation claims of nationals as it had done in Article 14(b) of the 1951 San Francisco Treaty.

In the judgment of 24 May 2012, the Supreme Court quashed the decision of the plaintiff who had lost at Busan High Court. In the remand, Busan High Court ordered on 30 July 2013 Mitsubishi Heavy Industry Ltd. to pay compensation to the plaintiffs. The first Korean decision that ordered a Japanese private company (Nippon Steel & Sumitomo Metal Corp.) to distribute war compensation was handed down just 20 days before this judgment at Seoul High Court.[115] Increasingly, the Korean Courts seem to be ruling in favour of victims in private war compensation claims against Japanese private entities.

IV Conclusion

In order to resolve the current political difficulties in East Asia, both dynamic legal thinking and rigorous interpretation are needed. Concerning private war compensation litigations, it should be noted that the view supported

---

114 *Id.*

115 Choe Sang-Hun, "South Korean Court Tells Japanese Company to Pay for Forced Labor", *N.Y. Times*, July 30, 2013, at A9, available at http://www.nytimes.com/2013/07/31/world/asia/south-korean-court-tells-japanese-company-to-pay-for-forced-labor.html (last visited Mar. 12, 2015).

by Japanese courts and the government is principally based on the classic approach to State-to-State war settlement. This view can be legally justified even when *jus cogens* violations have taken place because, as Talmon points out, States cannot validly consent to the breach of an obligation arising under *jus cogens* but this does not exclude a valid "waiver of the consequences of the breach in terms of responsibility."[116] However, this should not be considered to be Japan recognising as lawful a situation created by serious humanitarian breaches during WWII. It is indeed problematic that the government of Japan only started to take measures after the 1990s through the initiative of former Prime Ministers who publicly expressed their regret for the country's actions in WWII. The government appears to be providing relatively constructive measures for former "comfort women," since it is still receiving strong attention from international human rights bodies.[117] The Japanese government established the Asian Women's Fund based on the statement of Prime Minister Tomiichi Murayama on 31 August 1994, expressing once more his "profound and sincere remorse and apologies" with regard to the "comfort women" issue and stating his desire to find "an appropriate way which enables a wide participation" of Japanese people in order to share such feelings of apology and remorse.[118] Nevertheless, such efforts often come to nothing because of indiscreet statements from right-wing politicians (actually, most Korean women victims of sexual abuse by the Japanese Imperial Army have refused to receive compensation from the Fund). On this issue, it is worth noting that the Assembly of the Kyoto Prefecture issued a letter of opinion after a majority vote on 26 March 2013, which strongly urged the government of Japan to solve the problem of "comfort women" as soon as possible by carrying out further investigations and issuing additional apologies, necessary restitution and compensation to victims.[119] In the course of municipal initiatives,[120] this is the first

116 Talmon, *supra* note 66, at 997.

117 *E.g.*, Committee on Economic, Social and Cultural Rights, Concluding Observations on the Third Periodic Report of Japan, para. 26, U.N. Doc. E/C.12/JPN/3 (May 16, 2011); Replies of Japan to the List of Issues, paras. 35–38, UN Doc. E/C.12/JPN/Q/3/Add.1 (Apr. 17, 2013).

118 The Asian Women's Fund, http://www.awf.or.jp/ (last visited Mar. 12, 2015).

119 The letter of opinion is addressed to the Prime Minister, the Chairpersons of the House of Representatives and of the House of Councillors, the Ministers of Internal Affairs, Foreign Affairs, Education, Culture, Sports, Science and Technology and Health, Labor and Welfare, and the Chief Cabinet Secretary. Assembly of Kyoto Prefecture, http://www.pref.kyoto.jp/gikai/html/joho/documents/1302_ik_5.pdf (last visited Mar. 15, 2015) [in Japanese].

120 The letters of opinion for "comfort women" victims have already submitted to the Japanese government by the following local governments: in 2008, Takarazuka City

official opinion expressed at the prefectural level and it was followed by the Assembly of the Shimane Prefecture on 26 June 2013.[121] These opinion letters are not legally binding but they are still remarkable for how they criticise the reluctance of the government of Japan.[122]

On the other hand, the problem of forced labour seems to be less of a concern compared with the "comfort women" issue. From a dynamic perspective, the decision of the Korean Supreme Court in 2012 is remarkable since it suggests that any existing treaty, including a peace treaty, becomes void when it is in conflict with the prohibition of a crime against humanity, with connotations for peremptory norms. However, the most problematic aspect is that the real perpetrator, a foreign State, cannot be accused in respect of its own responsibility. A problem remains as to when the effective execution procedure of judgments rendered by domestic courts should be taken into account; however, it is evident that human dignity constitutes a fundamental value of the international community, which may serve as a reasonable way to settle past crimes at tribunals. It is still doubtful how effective the Korean judgment should be since it is only a solution for forced labour cases where the responsible company still survives to this day. Moreover, it is not possible to sue the other perpetrator, the Japanese government, which ordered these companies to follow its policy of forced labour and which took no measures to rectify this situation after the war. In order to confront and solve the whole problem, a new foundation specialised in the forced labour issue should be modelled on

(Mar. 28), Kiyose City (June 25) & Sapporo City (Nov. 7); in 2009, Fukuoka City (Mar. 25), Minoh City (June 22), Mitaka City (June 23), Koganei City (June 24), Kyotanabe City (June 29), Ikoma City (Sept. 11), Sennan City (Sept. 25), Kokubunji City (Oct. 1), Nagaokakyo City (Dec. 14), Funabashi City (Dec. 14), Kunitachi City (Dec. 18) & Tagawa City (Dec. 22); in 2010, Fujimino City (Mar. 16), Okayama City (Mar. 19), Abiko City (Mar. 23), Muko City (Mar. 24), Nakijin Village (Mar. 25), Suita City (Mar. 26), Sakai City (Mar. 29), Otaru City (June 21), Nishitokyo City (June 21), Nanjo City (June 21), Yomitan Village (June 22), Tomigusuku City (June 22), Tarama Village (June 24), Ichinoseki City (June 25), Takatsuki City (June 28), Shibetsu City (Sept. 16), Hokuei Town (Sept. 24), Yawata City (Sept. 29), Hakodate City (Sept. 30), Kizugawa City (Oct. 1) & Osaka City (Oct. 13); in 2011, Miyashiro Town (Sept. 28); in 2012, Uji City (June 27) & Koryo Town (Sept. 26); in 2013, Joyo City (June 27).

121 The Assembly of the Shimane Prefecture, http://www.pref.shimane.lg.jp/gikai/ugoki/gikai_kako/H2506/h2506_giin_gian_06.html (last visited Mar. 12, 2015) [in Japanese].

122 Article 99 of the Local Autonomy Act stipulates that a local assembly may submit its opinion to the Diet and the offices of the Japanese government.

the "Remembrance, Responsibility and Future" concept launched by German industry and the German government.[123]

This article does not follow up another important argument regarding the denial of jurisdictional immunity arising in the case of the inexistence of alternative remedies.[124] In addition to *jus cogens* violations, such a lack of alternative remedies may link the question of State immunity with diplomatic protection *in* order to pursue the effective protection of fundamental human rights. This is because a complex analysis is required to answer our fundamental question, namely why victims cannot ask for compensation for their suffering even though such suffering was not their fault but was undeniably the result of the expression of the ego of a State, in "lifting" State immunities at tribunals that are the most accessible for victims. In fact, in his report for the ILC Articles on Diplomatic Protection, Dugard proposed in Article 4(1) that:

> Unless the injured person is able to bring a claim for such injury before a competent international court or tribunal, the State of his/her nationality has a legal duty to exercise diplomatic protection on behalf of the injured person upon request, if the injury results from a grave breach of a jus cogens norm attributable to another State.[125]

This provision was proposed as a *lex ferenda*; however, it was severely criticised at the ILC for its lack of *opinio juris* and was thus deleted from the outcome.[126] In this vein, a State that waived private claims against the responsible State should be responsible for not invoking diplomatic protection for their nationals. As we have seen, even though the Italian Court's argument only constitutes a *lex ferenda* in the present international legal order and although it gives preference to fundamental human rights over State immunity, the accumulation of such State practices might be useful to discover *jus cogens* in war compensation cases. On this point, the Constitutional Court of the ROK rendered a highly suggestive judgment: in light of the ROK's Constitution and the dispute settlement clause contained in the 1965 ROK–Japan Agreement, it is the State's

123 Stiftung "Erinnerung, Verantwortung und Zukunft", http://www.stiftung-evz.de/start.html (last visited Mar. 12, 2015).

124 For discussions of this issue, see *e.g.*, Jones v. Saudi Arabia, [2004] EWCA Civ 1394; [2005] Q.B. 699.

125 John Dugard, First Report on Diplomatic Protection, paras. 75–93, U.N. Doc. A/CN.4/506 (Mar. 7, 2000).

126 Report of the International Law Commission to the General Assembly, *reprinted in* [2000] 2 Y.B. Int'l L. Comm'n 78, paras. 450–51, U.N. Doc. A/CN.4/SER.A/2000/Add.1 (Part 2)/Rev.1.

duty to solve the problem of individual war compensation, and its omission may infringe on the fundamental rights of its nationals.[127] The obligation to provide diplomatic protection seems to be emerging at the national level.

Although lawyers have struggled to secure victims' interests, if the government does not take any action at a legislative level, the individual compensation problem cannot be solved. As I noted at the beginning, war compensation is a social problem in the sense that its legally correct answer does not always placate the demands of social justice. In this respect, the idea of restorative justice is a noteworthy approach that shows the highest rates of victim satisfaction and offender accountability, as it focuses on the dialogue among victims, offenders and the involved community. It *has* firstly emerged out of the context of juvenile delinquencies,[128] but it also appears to be useful for considering war compensation cases as a social problem. The following contention by Fujita gets to the point at the core of war compensation:

> The fact that enormous cases have been brought by foreign victims—and the number of cases and plaintiffs should be going to increase enormously in future—shows that how immense damages caused by Japan during the war to people of pacific countries (especially East Asian and South-East Asian countries) were and suggests that this problem has not yet been "solved"; it is now meaningless to insist at courts that the problem has "solved by State-to-State agreement such as peace treaty." At least, the victims, regardless of whether they are individuals or States, do not think that the problem has been "solved"; in other words, Japan is far from "meeting" real (international) responsibility, therefore, "international" disputes still exist between foreign victims and Japan.[129]

The process of restorative justice should be weighted in favour of the most disadvantaged as soon as possible.

---

127 Constitutional Court of Korea, 23–2(A) KCCR 366, 2006Hun-Ma788 (Victims of "Comfort Women" v. ROK), Aug. 30, 2011 (S. Kor.).

128 Howard Zehr, *Changing Lenses: A New Focus for Crime and Justice* (1990).

129 Hisakazu Fujita, "Sengo Hosyo no Riron Mondai [Theoretical problem of War Compensation]", 15 *Kokusai Jinken* [*Human Rights International*] 3 (2004) [the original text is in Japanese and translated here by the author].

The Prospects for the Sino-Philippine Arbitration on the South China Sea (U-Shaped Line) Dispute

Michael Sheng-ti Gau

Table of Contents

* LL.M. (Cambridge), LL.M. (King's College London), Ph.D. (Leiden). Professor of International Law, Institute for the Law of the Sea, National Taiwan Ocean University. This Special Report is dedicated to celebrate the 70-year birthday of Professor Dr. Tzu-Wen Lee (李子文), who tutored the author in 1985–1986 for the Philip C. Jessup International Law Moot Court Competition. The author is grateful to the reviewers for their comments. The opinions expressed here do not represent those of any government agencies. Email: mikegau97@msn.com.

 | DOI 10.1163/9789004306509_008

I Introduction

On January 22, 2013, the Philippines invoked Article 287 and Annex VII of the United Nations Convention on the Law of the Sea (UNCLOS)[1] and presented a diplomatic notification to initiate arbitration against China.[2] As said by the Notification and Statement of Claim (the Notification),[3] the goal is "to seek a peaceful and durable resolution of the dispute in the West Philippine Sea (WPS)" between these two States. The Philippines challenged against China's claims and entitlement to the eastern part of South China Sea (SCS) enclosed by the "nine-dash-line," requesting the Arbitral Tribunal to declare the area as its exclusive economic zone (EEZ) and continental shelf.[4] Five groups of claims were presented by the Notification:

Firstly, China's rights concerning the SCS maritime areas are those established by UNCLOS only and consist of the territorial sea, the contiguous zone, the EEZ and the continental shelf. China's maritime claims therein based on the "nine-dash line (U-Shaped Line)"[5] contravene UNCLOS and are invalid.[6] Secondly, the Mischief Reef (美濟礁), McKennan Reef (西門礁), Gaven Reef (南薰礁) and Subi Reef (渚碧礁) are submerged features not above sea level at high tide, and should not be deemed as islands or rocks according to Article 121 of UNCLOS. None of them are located on China's continental shelf. Rather, the Mischief and McKennan Reefs are part of the Philippines' continental shelf. China's occupation of these four maritime features and construction activities

1 United Nations Convention on the Law of the Sea, Dec. 10, 1982, 1833 U.N.T.S. 3 (1982) [hereinafter UNCLOS].

2 For the official explanations of the Philippines, see Institute for Maritime and Ocean Affairs, Statement by the Secretary of DFA on the UNCLOS Arbitral Proceedings against China. http://www.imoa.ph/press-releases/statement-by-secretary-of-foreign-affairs-albert-del-rosario-on-the-unclos-arbitral-proceedings-against-china-to-achieve-a-peaceful-and-durable-solution-to-the-dispute-in-the-wps/ (last visited Mar. 10, 2015).

3 *See* Notification and Statement of Claims, issued by Department of Foreign Affairs of Republic of the Philippines in Manila to the Embassy of the People's Republic of China in Manila, at 1, para. 1, Serial No. 13-0211, Jan. 22, 2013, https://www.dfa.gov.ph/index.php/component/docman/doc_download/56-notification-and-statement-of-claim-on-west-philippine-sea?Itemid=546 (last visited Mar. 10, 2015) [hereinafter Notification].

4 *Id.* paras. 31 (Section III: The Philippines' Claims) & 41 (Section V: Relief Sought).

5 The term "nine-dash line" is interchangeable with "U-Shaped Line" and "eleven-dash line." For various names of this line, *see* Keyuan Zou, "China's U-Shaped Line in the South China Sea Revisited", 43 *Ocean Dev. & Int'l L.* 18 (2012).

6 *See* Notification, *supra* note 3, paras. 31 (first and second claims), 41 (first to third reliefs).

thereon are unlawful and should be terminated.[7] Thirdly, Scarborough Shoal (黃岩島), Johnson Reef (赤瓜礁), Cuarteron Reef (華陽礁), and Fiery Cross Reef (永暑礁) should be considered as rocks under Article 121(3), and may only generate state entitlement to the territorial sea. Having unlawfully claimed maritime entitlements beyond twelve nautical miles (M) *from* these features, China should refrain from preventing Philippine vessels from exploiting the living resources in waters adjacent to Scarborough Shoal and Johnson Reef, and from undertaking other activities inconsistent with UNCLOS at or in the vicinity of these features.[8] Fourthly, the Philippines is entitled under UNCLOS to a 12-M territorial sea, a 200-M EEZ, and a continental shelf measured from its archipelagic baselines. China has unlawfully claimed and exploited the living and non-living resources in this EEZ and continental shelf, and prevented the Philippines from exploiting the living and non-living resources therein.[9] Fifthly, China has unlawfully interfered with the Philippines' exercise of its navigational rights and other rights under UNCLOS within and beyond the Philippines' EEZ. China should desist from these unlawful activities.[10]

On February 19, 2013, China officially refused to join the litigation,[11] based on, *inter alia*, its 2006 Declaration[12] covering the disputes brought by the Philippines and depriving the Arbitral Tribunal of necessary jurisdiction to entertain the case. The default rules[13] were applied to establish the arbitral tribunal. On June 25, 2013, the fifth arbitrator was appointed and the arbitral tribunal was established (the Tribunal).

The first meeting of the Members of the Tribunal was held on July 11, 2013, when they decided to use the Permanent Court of Arbitration (PCA)

7 *Id.* paras. 31 (third to fifth claims), 41 (fourth to seventh reliefs).

8 *Id.* paras. 31 (sixth and seventh claims), 41 (eighth and ninth reliefs).

9 *Id.* paras. 31 (eighth and ninth claims), 41 (tenth and eleventh reliefs).

10 *Id.* paras. 31 (tenth claims), 41 (twelfth and thirteenth reliefs).

11 *See* Statement Made by the Spokesman of the Foreign Ministry of China, Feb. 9, 2013, http://www.fmprc.gov.cn/eng/xwfw/s2510/2511/t1015317.shtml (last visited Mar. 10, 2015).

12 On August 25, 2006 China made a written declaration according to Article 298 of UNCLOS. It reads: "The Government of the People's Republic of China does not accept any of the procedures provided for in Section 2 of Part XV of the Convention with respect to all the categories of disputes referred to in paragraph 1 (a) (b) and (c) of Article 298 of the Convention." United Nations Ocean & Law of the Sea, Declarations and Statements, http://www.un.org/Depts/los/convention_agreements/convention_declarations.htm#China upon ratification (last visited Mar. 10, 2015).

13 UNCLOS, *supra* note 1, Annex VII, art. 3(e).

as Registry.[14] On August 27, 2013, the Tribunal adopted the PH-CN Rules of Procedure (ROP) for this arbitration and issued the first Procedural Order to fix March 30, 2014 as the deadline for the Philippines to submit its Memorial (the Memorial). The Tribunal directed the Philippines to fully address all issues in the Memorial, including matters relating to the jurisdiction of the Tribunal, the admissibility of the Philippines' claims, and the merits of the dispute.[15]

As directed, the Philippines presented the Memorial consisting of 15 Submissions which largely maintain the structure of the Notification. In the Memorial the Tribunal is requested to adjudge and declare that:

(1) China's maritime entitlements in the SCS, like those of the Philippines, may not extend beyond those permitted by UNCLOS;
(2) China's claims to sovereign rights and jurisdiction, and to 'historic rights', with respect to the maritime areas of the SCS encompassed by the so-called 'nine-dash line' are contrary to UNCLOS and without lawful effect to the extent that they exceed the geographic and substantive limits of China's maritime entitlements under UNCLOS;
(3) Scarborough Shoal generates no entitlement to an EEZ or continental shelf;
(4) Mischief Reef, Second Thomas Shoal and Subi Reef are low-tide elevations (LTES) that do not generate entitlements to a territorial sea, EEZ or continental shelf, and are not features that are capable of appropriation by occupation or otherwise;
(5) Mischief Reef and Second Thomas Shoal are part of the EEZ and continental shelf of the Philippines;
(6) Gaven Reef and McKennan Reef (including Hughes Reef) are LTES that do not generate entitlement to a territorial sea, EEZ or continental shelf, but their low-water line may be used to determine the baseline from which the breadth of the territorial sea of Namyit and Sin Cowe, respectively, is measured;
(7) Joshson Reef, Cuarteron Reef and Fiery Cross Reef generate no entitlement to an EEZ or continental shelf;
(8) China has unlawfully interfered with the enjoyment and exercise of the sovereign rights of the Philippines with respect to the living and non-living resources of its EEZ and continental shelf;

14 For the information released by the PCA, see PCA, The Republic of the Philippines v. The People's Republic of China, http://www.pca-cpa.org/showpage.asp?pag_id=1529 (last visited Mar. 10, 2015).

15 *Id.*

(9) China has unlawfully failed to prevent its nationals and vessels from exploiting the living resources in the EEZ of the Philippines;
(10) China has unlawfully prevented Philippine fishermen from pursuing their livelihoods by interfering with traditional fishing activities at Scarborough Shoal;
(11) China has violated its obligations under UNCLOS to protect and preserve the marine environment at Scarborough Shoal and Second Thomas Shoal;
(12) China's occupation of and construction activities on Mischief Reef: (a) violate the provisions of UNCLOS concerning artificial islands, installations, and structures; (b) violate China's duties to protect and preserve the marine environment under the Convention; and (c) constitute unlawful act of attempted appropriation in violation of the Convention;
(13) China has breached its obligation under UNCLOS by operating its law enforcement vessels in a dangerous manner causing serious risk of collision to Philippine vessels navigating in the vicinity of Scarborough Shoal;
(14) Since the commencement of this arbitration in January 2013, China has unlawfully aggravated and extended the dispute by, among other things: (a) Interfering with the Philippines' rights of navigation in the waters at, and adjacent to, Second Thomas Shoal; (b) Preventing the rotation and resupply of Philippine personnel stationed at Second Thomas Shoal; and (c) Endangering the health and well-being of Philippine personnel stationed at Second Thomas Shoal.
(15) China shall desist from further unlawful claims and activities.[16]

To echo the above-mentioned Philippine claims, the US Department of State released on December 5, 2014 its serial study on "Limits in the Seas No. 143" entitled "China: Maritime Claims in the SCS" that questioned each of China's possible SCS maritime claims with the U-Shaped Line.[17] Simultaneously, the "Statement of the Ministry of Foreign Affairs of Viet Nam for the attention

16 Through an interview with a Philippine scholar, the author obtains the information about the fifteen Submissions made by the Philippine Government against China for this arbitration.

17 US Dept. of State Bureau of Oceans & Int'l Envtl. & Sci. Affairs, "China: Maritime Claims in the South China Sea" (Limits in the Sea, No. 143), http://www.state.gov/documents/organization/234936.pdf (last visited Mar. 14, 2015).

of the Tribunal in the Proceedings between the Republic of the Philippines and the People's Republic of China" was received by the Tribunal.[18] As said by the press, this Vietnamese document supported the Philippine position that the Tribunal has jurisdiction over the disputes presented.[19] On December 7, 2014 the "Position Paper of the Government of the PRC on the Matter of Jurisdiction in the SCS Arbitration Initiated by the Republic of the Philippines (the Position Paper)" was released. Arguing that the Tribunal has no jurisdiction over the disputes, the Position Paper however was neither meant to be a Counter-Memorial by China,[20] nor treated as such by the Tribunal.[21] This made Article 25(2) of ROP[22] applicable. Accordingly, the Tribunal gave the Philippines a list of questions to be answered before March 15, 2015 in the form of Further Written Argument. China is also requested to provide its comments on such Philippine supplemental arguments by June 15, 2015.[23] China did not respond as requested. Then the hearing took place on July 7–13, 2015 in Peace Palace in the Hague, to address the jurisdictional objections raised by China's Position Paper as well as other jurisdictional and admissibility issues. As said

18 *See* Press Release by the Tribunal, Dec. 17, 2014, http://www.pca-cpa.org/showfile.asp?fil_id=2846 (last visited Mar. 14, 2015).

19 Camille Diola, "Int'l tribunal Seeks More Arguments from Philippines", *The Philippine Star*, Dec. 18, 2014, http://www.philstar.com/disputed-seas/2014/12/18/1404065/intl-tribunal-seeks-more-arguments-philippines (last visited Mar. 14, 2015).

20 "China's Position Paper on South China Sea", *China Daily*, Dec. 7, 2014, http://www.chinadaily.com.cn/china/2014-12/07/content_19037946.htm (last visited Mar. 14, 2015).

21 *See* Press Release of the Tribunal, *supra* note 18.

22 Article 25(2) of the ROP reads:

> In the event that a Party does not appear before the Arbitral Tribunal or fails to defend its case, the Arbitral Tribunal shall invite written arguments from the appearing Party on, or pose questions regarding, specific issues which the Arbitral Tribunal considers have not been canvassed, or have been inadequately canvassed, in the pleadings submitted by the appearing Party. The appearing Party shall make a supplemental written submission in relation to the matters identified by the Arbitral Tribunal within three months of the Arbitral Tribunal's invitation. The supplemental submission of the appearing Party shall be communicated to the non-appearing Party for its comments which shall be submitted within three months of the communication of the supplemental submission. The Arbitral Tribunal may take whatever other steps it may consider necessary, within the scope of its powers under the Convention, its Annex VII, and these Rules, to afford to each of the Parties a full opportunity to present its case.

ROP, http://www.pca-cpa.org/showfile.asp?fil_id=2504 (last visited Mar. 14, 2015).

23 This is requested by the Procedural Order No. 3 of the Tribunal issued on December 17, 2014. *Supra* note 18.

by the 6th Press Release by the PCA dated on July, 13, the award on the part of jurisdiction will be produced by the end of 2015.[24]

The goal of this arbitration, as declared by the Philippines, is to facilitate the resolution of the Sino-Philippine SCS disputes, through settling certain legal issues by the Tribunal without being barred by the 2006 China's Declaration.[25] However, doubts remain that the facilitative role of this Tribunal with limited subject-matter jurisdiction[26] may not serve the goal eventually. Two questions should be asked here. If the Philippines loses the case in the merits, will it lose legal grounds to counter China's activities as identified by the Memorial? If the Philippines wins in the merits phase, will China become legally unjustified to carry on those activities as contested? Both answers seem negative, based on the author's preliminary study on the Notification.[27] To provide a detailed

---

24 *See* the 4th Procedural Order of the Tribunal issued on April 22, 2015 available at: file:///D:/Documents%20and%20Settings/user/My%20Documents/Downloads/PH-CN%20-%20 20150422%20-%20Press%20Release%20No.%204%20(ENG)%20(5).pdf. *See* the 5th press release issued for the hearing on July 7, 2015, available at: file:///D:/Documents%20 and%20Settings/user/My%20Documents/Downloads/PH-CN%20-%2020150707%20 -%20Press%20Release%20No.%205%20(ENG).pdf. *Also see* the 6th press release issued on July 13, 2015 available at: file:///D:/Documents%20and%20Settings/user/My%20 Documents/Downloads/PH-CN%20-%2020150713%20-%20Press%20Release%20 No.%206%20(4).pdf (last visited July 18, 2015).

25 On January 22, 2013, the Secretary of Foreign Affairs of the Philippines, Mr. Albert del Rosario, made a statement in a press conference which explained the initiation by the Philippines of an arbitral proceedings against China to achieve a peaceful and durable solution to the dispute in the WPS (South China Sea). "Statement: The Secretary of Foreign Affairs on the UNCLOS Arbitral Proceedings against China, January 22, 2013", Jan. 22, 2013, http://www.gov.ph/2013/01/22/statement-the-secretary-of-foreign-affairs-on-the-unclos-arbitral-proceedings-against-china-january-22–2013/ (last visited Mar. 10, 2015).

26 *See* Andreas Zimmermann & Jelena Bäumler, "Navigating Through Narrow Jurisdictional Straits: The Philippines—PRC South China Sea Dispute and UNCLOS", 12 *L. & Prac. Int'l Ct. & Tribunals* 431 (2013); Ted L. McDorman, "The South China Sea: The U-Shaped Line, Islands and the Philippine-China Arbitration", 2013 *German Y.B. Int'l L.* 33; *The South China Sea Arbitration: A Chinese Perspective* (Stefan Talmon & Bing Bing Jia eds., 2014); Mincai Yu, "China's Responses to the Compulsory Arbitration on the South China Sea Dispute: Legal Effects and Policy Options", 45 *Ocean Dev. & Int'l L.* 1 (2014); Sienho Yee, "The South China Sea Arbitration (The Philippines v. China): Potential Jurisdictional Obstacles or Objections", 13 *Chinese J. Int'l L.* 663 (2014); Mincai Yu, "China's Informal Participation in the Annex VII Philippines v. China Arbitral Tribunal's Proceedings", 30 *Int'l J. Marine & Coastal L.* 54 (2015).

27 Michael Sheng-ti Gau, "The Sino-Philippine Arbitration of the South China Sea Nine-Dash-Line Dispute: Applying the Rule of Default of Appearance", 28 *Ocean Y.B.* 81 (2014).

examination of this fundamental issue so as to evaluate the efficacy[28] of this arbitration, the following sections will provide the available legal arguments for the losing party to justify the continuation of its disputed yet over-ruled actions. As the Philippine Submissions will be divided into four groups for the sake of discussion, the examination of the possible legal arguments will be made in each of the groups. Most importantly, the general principle of *res judicata* embodied by Article 296 of UNCLOS will be discussed and then applied in support of these contentions throughout the examination.

II The *Res Judicata* Principle and its Application to the Disputes Constituted by the Philippine Submissions

Entitled "finality and binding force of decisions", Article 296 of UNCLOS reads: "1. Any decision rendered by a court or tribunal *having jurisdiction* under this section shall be final and shall be complied with by all the parties *to the dispute.* 2. Any such decision shall have no binding force except between the parties and *in respect of that particular dispute*".[29] Article 11 of Annex VII to UNCLOS[30] and Article 26(2) of ROP[31] restate this rule of *res judicata* that is also a general principle of law recognized by civilized nations.[32]

Clearly, the finality and binding force of decisions cannot be established without two conditions. *First*, the dispute must fall within the subject-matter jurisdiction of the tribunal.[33] *Second*, the dispute must have been presented to the tribunal for settlement. Sometimes the tribunal is presented with a

---

28 In the very first case which came before the Permanent Court of International Justice, it was decided that the PCIJ neither could nor should contemplate the possibility of its judgment not being complied with. See PCIJ, S.S. "Wimbledon", 1923 P.C.I.J. (ser. A) No. 1, at 32 (Aug. 17). *See* Bin Cheng, *General Principles of Law as Applied by International Courts and Tribunals* 339, 356 (1953).

29 UNCLOS, *supra* note 1, art. 296.

30 Article 11 (Finality of Award) of Annex VII to UNCLOS reads: "The award shall be final and without appeal, unless the parties to the dispute have agreed in advance to an appellate procedure. It shall be complied with by the parties to the dispute." UNCLOS, *supra* note 1, Annex VII, art. 11.

31 Article 26(2) of PH-CN Rules of Procedure adopted on August 27, 2013, reads: "Pursuant to Article 11 of Annex VII to the Convention, the award shall be final and without appeal, unless the Parties agree in advance to an appellate procedure. It shall be complied with by the Parties." Rules of Procedure, *supra* note 22, art. 26(2).

32 Cheng, *supra* note 28, 336.

33 Stefan Talmon, "The South China Sea Arbitration: Is There a Case to Answer?", *supra* note 26, at 15, 26–53.

dispute that allegedly goes beyond the scope of the tribunal's subject-matter jurisdiction. Then most likely the tribunal will have to address the preliminary dispute concerning whether it has jurisdiction over the dispute.[34] When the answer to this preliminary question is held to be negative, the tribunal will refrain from determining the merits. Consequently, the dispute in merits will be left unsettled. On the other hand, any dispute, whether within or beyond the scope of the tribunal's jurisdiction, will remain unresolved if it is *not* presented to the tribunal for its resolution.

In this Sino-Philippine Arbitration, the situation is more complicated where the two Parties have disputes of multiple layers in the SCS.[35] While the disputes on the surface layer have been presented to the Tribunal for settlement, the inner layers (the core) disputes are neither within the subject-matter jurisdiction of the Tribunal nor brought to the Tribunal by the Philippines.[36] Being no-less-important and hotly debated, the issue whether the Tribunal has jurisdiction to try the surface disputes submitted[37] is *not* the focus of this paper. The author rather intends to address the part of un-presented core disputes

---

34 UNCLOS, *supra* note 1, art. 288(4). *Also see* ROP, *supra* note 22, art. 20(1).

35 Michael Sheng-ti Gau, *supra* note 27, at 121. The real Sino-Philippine SCS disputes are four-fold: (i) territorial disputes over Scarborough Shoal and all the maritime features within Philippines' KIG, which is part of China's Nansha Islands; (ii) disputes concerning legal capability of certain reefs or rocks in China's Nansha Islands to establish the territorial sea, the EEZ, and the continental shelf; (iii) disputes concerning the legality under UNCLOS of China's possible historical rights claims within the U-shaped line; and (iv) disputes concerning maritime boundary delimitation for the overlapping Sino-Philippine maritime claims.

36 Paragraph 7 of the Notification reads:

> "The Philippines does not seek in this arbitration a determination of which Party enjoys sovereignty over the islands claimed by both of them. Nor does it request a delimitation of any maritime boundaries. The Philippines is conscious of China's Declaration of 25 August 2006 under Article 298 of UNCLOS, and has avoided raising subjects or making claims that China has, by virtue of that Declaration, excluded from arbitral jurisdiction."

Para. 40 then reads:

> "It follows that the Philippines' claims do not fall within China's Declaration of 25 August 2006, because they do not: concern the interpretation or application of Articles 15, 74, and 83 relating to sea boundary delimitation; involve historic bays or titles within the meaning of the relevant provisions of the Convention; concern military activities or law enforcement activities; or concern matters over which the Security Council is exercising functions assigned to it by the UN Charter."

Notification, *supra* note 3, at 3 & 16.

37 This issue has been discussed by a few papers and official statements. *See supra* notes 20, 26–27.

and explore the consequences of such incomplete submission of disputes by the Philippines.

Given the situation of none-submission of core disputes, can the award *settle* the Sino-Philippine confrontations reflected by the Philippine Submissions? Will the confrontations go on instead? If so, what may justify such protraction of clashing policies, claims, and actions in the SCS? Is it because the unsettled core disputes constitute the *real* causes of conflict? How can the *res judicata* principle apply (or not be violated) in such a scenario?

In this connection, the authoritative study by Professor Bin Cheng (鄭斌) is inspiring. According to him, *res judicata* has two effects: (1) "that which is *res judicata* is definitive"; and (2) "what has been finally decided by a tribunal is binding upon the parties".[38] More important is the *limits* of such principle, "[it] applies only where there is *identity of... the question at issue*".[39] In the words of Article 296 of UNCLOS, any decision rendered by a tribunal having jurisdiction under Section 2 of Part XV shall have no binding force except... *in respect of that particular dispute*.[40] In other words, *res judicata* principle is "to prevent legal principles accepted by the Court in a particular case from being binding... *in other disputes*",[41] and "what is not *res judicata* between the parties has *no* authoritative and binding effect".[42]

Perhaps this very principle, as analyzed by Professor Bin Cheng, can be applied to explain, if not to justify, the possible outcome of this arbitration that is the lingering row. To be submitted, no matter which Party wins the case in the merits phase, the losing Party will not be stripped of legal grounds to carry on its disputed yet over-ruled actions. It is probably based on the

38 Cheng, *supra* note 28, at 337–38.

39 This was held by the British-United States Claims Arbitral Tribunal (1910), as quoted by Bin Cheng, *id.* 339–40.

40 The identity of "that particular case", as one of the conditions of *res judicata*, means "the matter in that dispute" or "the same question at issue". It covers both "the object" and "the grounds of the claim" of that dispute. "[W]here new rights are asserted, there is a new case which ought not to be barred by a previous decision even if the parties and the object be identical." "In the case of the Compagnie generale de l'Orenoque (1905), it was decided that counter-claims, as well as claims that might be presented by way of setoff, constituted independent actions. Even though they could have been pleaded in a previous action, if in fact they were not presented and considered, subsequent action upon them was not precluded by the previous decision." *See* various decisions cited by Bin Cheng, *id.* nn. 16–17, 341, 343, 345–47.

41 *See id.* at 341, n.22 (summarizing the PCIJ's position).

42 *Id.* at 341.

unaffected and undefeated claims of the losing Party for territorial sovereignty over SCS maritime features or/and for maritime delimitation in the SCS region. Such un-interrupted behaviors would not do violence to the award and could even conform to the *res judicata* principle for four reasons. *First*, the core Sino-Philippine territorial and maritime delimitation disputes rather constitute the *causes of* the confrontations reflected by the Philippine Submissions. *Second*, such core disputes are undoubtedly beyond the subject-matter jurisdiction of the Tribunal and have not been brought to the Tribunal for settlement in the first place. *Third*, the legality of claims of either Party in such core disputes shall not be adjudged by the Tribunal. *Fourth*, no matter which award the Tribunal may give in the merits, there can be no *res judicata* between the Parties over such core disputes. The potential legal arguments to be advanced by the losing Party are substantiated as follows.

A *The Legality Dispute of the U-Shaped Line Indicated in Submissions 1–2*

1 Philippines' Possible Arguments When Losing the Case

In case that the award is not in favor of the Philippines with respect to Submissions 1–2, the Philippines will probably not lose its legal grounds for complaining. The continued condemnation against China's U-Shaped Line by the Philippines will be fully expected and justified, due to the following reasons.

First, it could be argued by the Philippines that the Tribunal is not authorized to settle the Sino-Philippine territorial disputes[43] with respect to *all* the maritime features in the Kalayaan Islands Group (KIG) and Scarborough Shoal, not limited to those nine maritime features identified in Submissions 3–7. Hence, the award of the Tribunal may neither affect nor dismiss Philippine territorial claims to these maritime features, including those islands within the KIG that are considered capable of generating territorial water, EEZ and continental shelf according to Article 121 of UNCLOS. By the same token, the award may not be interpreted as upholding China's competing territorial claims with regard to those maritime features and islands. As a consequence, from Philippine perspectives, it is impossible for the award to vindicate China's claim for any maritime entitlement to territorial waters, EEZ, and continental shelf in the WPS that may be generated by these islands. The U-Shaped Line as

43 *See* Notification, *supra* note 3, para. 3. *Also see* Robert C. Beckman & Clive H. Schofield, "Defining EEZ Claims from Islands: A Potential South China Sea Change", 29 *Int'l J. Marine & Coastal L.* 208 (2014).

the boundary of China's *maritime claim* remain baseless, as China is not even entitled to have any maritime zones under UNCLOS legal regime within the WPS in the first place.

Second, the original version of the U-Shaped Line indicated on the Location Map of the South China Sea Islands (南海諸島位置圖) published by the Republic of China Government in 1947[44] (see Figure 1 of this paper) may not be justifiably kept by China in its official map according to the award in favor of China. It is because that such an award does not serve to endorse China's competing territorial claims over the maritime features lying within the U-Shaped Line. Since all or part of these maritime features have been claimed by other States (including the Philippines, Vietnam and/or Malaysia) the legality of the U-Shaped Line to mark the whereabouts of *China's* territories in the SCS remains doubtful. In other words, the maintenance of the original version of the U-Shaped Line by China remains legally questionable even if China wins the case.

2 China's Possible Arguments When Losing the Case

On the other hand, should the award be given in favor of the Philippines, China will probably be justified for its non-deletion of the U-Shaped Line for the following reasons.

First, China may contend that, as the Tribunal is unauthorized to settle Sino-Philippine territorial disputes in SCS region, the award may not be construed as overruling China's much older and comprehensive territorial claims for all the maritime features within the U-Shaped Line drawn in the 1947 Map. As this map indicates China's SCS territorial claims,[45] the legal effect of the U-Shaped Line within this map may neither be affected nor be denied by the award. As a result, such (older) version of U-Shaped Line can be kept on the map without legal problems.

Second, concerning the *advanced* version of the U-Shaped Line allegedly used by China as the boundary of its *maritime claims* in SCS seen by the Philippines,[46] it can also stay under any outcome of this litigation. This is because the U-Shaped Line must be and has been removed after maritime

44 *See* US Dept. of State Bureau of Oceans & Int'l Envtl. & Sci. Affairs, *supra* note 17, at 3. *See also* Bing Bing Jia and Stefan Talmon, "Introduction", *in The South China Sea Arbitration*, *supra* note 26, at 1, 4.

45 Gau, *supra* note 27, 100–04.

46 *See* Philippines' Submission 2, *supra* note 16.

boundaries between China and other SCS bordering State are drawn.[47] In other words, this version of the U-Shaped Line or *deletion of this line* is part of the overall maritime boundary delimitation settlement. The issue of the U-Shaped Line is therefore *concerning* the application of Articles 74(1)[48] and 83(1)[49] of UNCLOS.

The key issue here is the interpretation of the term "concerning" as the second word in Article 298(1)(a)(i).[50] The ordinary meaning to be given to the term[51] "concern" as a verb is:[52] (1) have relation to, (2) *affect*,[53] and (3) be of

---

47 Keyuan Zou, "Maritime Boundary Delimitation in the Gulf of Tonkin", 30 *Ocean Dev. & Int'l L.* 235, 245–46, 248 (1999). *See also* Keyuan Zou, *infra* note 56.

48 Article 74(1) of UNCLOS reads: "The delimitation of the exclusive economic zone between States with opposite or adjacent coasts shall be effected by agreement on the basis of international law, as referred to in Article 38 of the Statute of the International Court of Justice, in order to achieve an equitable solution." UNCLOS, *supra* note 1, art 74(1).

49 Article 83(1) of UNCLOS reads: "The delimitation of the continental shelf between States with opposite or adjacent coasts shall be effected by agreement on the basis of international law, as referred to in Article 38 of the Statute of the International Court of Justice, in order to achieve an equitable solution." *Id.* art.83(1)

50 Article 298(1)(a)(i) of UNCLOS reads:

> 1. When signing, ratifying or acceding to this Convention or at any time thereafter, a State may, without prejudice to the obligations arising under section 1, declare in writing that it does not accept any one or more of the procedures provided for in section 2 with respect to one or more of the following categories of disputes:
> (a)(i) disputes concerning the interpretation or application of articles 15, 74 and 83 relating to sea boundary delimitations, or those involving historic bays or titles, provided that a State having made such a declaration shall, when such a dispute arises subsequent to the entry into force of this Convention and where no agreement within a reasonable period of time is reached in negotiations between the parties, at the request of any party to the dispute, accept submission of the matter to conciliation under Annex V, section 2; and provided further that any dispute that necessarily involves the concurrent consideration of any unsettled dispute concerning sovereignty or other rights over continental or insular land territory shall be excluded from such submission;

Id. art. 298(1)(a)(i)

51 Vienna Convention on the Law of Treaties arts. 31–32, May 23, 1969, 1155 U.N.T.S. 331.

52 Oxford Advanced Learner's Dictionary of Current English (A S Hornby ed., 3d ed. 1980).

53 As confirmed by the ICJ in the Greece v. Turkey, the meaning of the term "concern" as a verb can be interpreted as "affect".

> In the present case, moreover, quite apart from the question of the status of the above-mentioned Greek islands for the purpose of determining Greece's entitlement to continental shelf, the Court notes that during the hearings in 1976 the Greek Government referred to a certain straight base-line claimed by Turkey which is, however, contested

importance to. Therefore, the term "concerning" should be interpreted as (1) having relation to or *relating to*,[54] (2) affecting, and (3) being important to. It follows that any dispute *relating to, affecting, or important to* the application of Article 74(1) and 83(1) should be considered as *concerning* the application of these two articles and caught by Article 298(1)(a)(i). To be noted, both Articles 74(1) and 83(1) explicitly address delimitation agreements concluded by disputing parties. Moreover, as ITLOS said in Bangladesh v. Myanmar, these two provisions also apply to judicial and arbitral delimitation decisions.[55] In other words, any dispute affecting, important to, and relating to the application of these two provisions to the maritime delimitation *judicial settlement* will also be covered by Article 298(1)(a)(i).

Here, the original (1947) eleven-dash line, the 2009 nine-dash line (see Figure 2 of this paper), and the present (2012) ten-dash line all seem to be relating to, affecting, important to, and concerning maritime boundary delimitation

---

> by Greece. Although it recognized that the resulting discrepancy between the Greek and Turkish views of the limits of Turkey's territorial sea in the area is not great, it observed that the discrepancy 'obviously *affects* the question of the delimitation of the continental shelf'. The question of the limits of a State's territorial sea, as the Greek Government itself has recognized, is indisputably one which not only relates to, but *directly concerns* territorial status.

Aegean Sea Continental Shelf Case (Greece v. Turk.), 1978 I.C.J. 3, 37, para. 89. (italic added).

54 The term "relating to" has been interpreted by the ICJ in Aegean Sea Continental Shelf Case as "emanating from" and "being an automatic adjunct of".

> The question for decision is whether the present dispute is one 'relating to the territorial status of Greece', not whether the rights in dispute are legally to be considered as 'territorial' rights; and a dispute regarding entitlement to and delimitation of areas of continental shelf tends by its very nature to be one relating to territorial status.... In short, continental shelf rights are legally both an emanation from and an automatic adjunct of the territorial sovereignty of the coastal State. It follows that the territorial regime—the territorial status—of a coastal State comprises, *ipso jure*, the rights of exploration and exploitation over the continental shelf to which it is entitled under international law. A dispute regarding those rights would, therefore, appear to be one which may be said to 'relate' to the territorial status of the coastal State.

Id. at 36, para. 86.

55 *See* Dispute Concerning Delimitation of the Maritime Boundary between Bangladesh and Myanmar in the Bay of Bengal (Bangladesh v. Myanmar), Judgment of 14 March 2012, para. 183. The judgment is available online:
Dispute Concerning Delimitation of the Maritime Boundary between Bangladesh and Myanmar in the Bay of Bengal (Bangl. v. Myan). Case No. 16, Judgment of Mar. 14, 2012, http://www.itlos.org/fileadmin/itlos/documents/cases/case_no_16/C16_Judgment_14_03_2012_rev.pdf (last visited Mar. 10, 2015).

between China and other States with opposite coasts, based on (1) the diplomatic practice by China for its negotiations with Vietnam concerning the disputes in the Gulf of Tonkin, (2) one of the dashes between Taiwan and the Philippines, and (3) another one dash between Taiwan and Japan.

For the original U-Shaped Line or eleven-dash line on the 1947 Map, there were two dashes between China's Hainan Island and Vietnam. These two dashes were removed in 1960s. The PRC Government did not explain the reason. Based on his long-time observation, Professor Zou Keyuan is of the opinion that such removal might have been related to the transfer of the sovereignty over the Bai Long Wei (or Bach Long Vi) Island in the Gulf of Tonkin from China to Vietnam.[56] If Professor Zou's observation is correct, then those two dashes would have a bearing on China's territorial claim while not directly related to China's maritime claims. Still, an indirect impact would be produced upon maritime boundary delimitation between China and Vietnam as Bai Long Wei Island would most probably *affect and be important to* the process of delimitation in Vietnam's favor.[57] If Professor Zou's observation is not true, the fact that those two dashes were removed before China and Vietnam reached maritime boundary delimitation agreement in the Gulf of Tonkin[58] would strongly suggest that those two dashes were previously used by China as a provisional maritime claim. Making the dashes *negotiable or even dispensable* will doubtlessly facilitate the Sino-Vietnam maritime boundary delimitation negotiation. Put differently, after drawing Sino-Vietnamese maritime boundary in the Gulf of Tonkin, the maintenance of those two dashes, if acting as China's maritime claim, would be not only redundant but confusing. In any case, those two dashes between China's Hainan Island and Vietnam should be deemed either indirectly or directly *relating to, important to, affecting*, and *concerning* maritime delimitation between China and Vietnam.

There is another dash between Taiwan and the Philippines which appears in both the 1947 Map and the 2009 Map, the latter of which is attached to the 2009 China's Note Verbale (NV).[59] In addition, the U-Shaped Line appearing

56 Keyuan Zou, *Law of the Sea in East Asia: Issues and Prospects* 50 (2005).

57 Zou, *supra* note 47, 248 (1999).

58 The Sino-Vietnam Agreement on the Delimitation of the Territorial Sea, Exclusive Economic Zone and Continental Shelf in the Beibu Gulf (which is also called Gulf of Tonkin) was signed on December 25, 2000 and entered into force on June 30, 2004. *See* Keyuan Zou, "The Sino-Vietnamese Agreement on Maritime Boundary Delimitation in the Gulf of Tonkin", 36 *Ocean Dev. & Int'l L* 13 (2005).

59 Mission of the People's Republic of China to the United Nations, NV, CML/17/2009, May 7, 2009, *available at* http://www.un.org/Depts/los/clcs_new/submissions_files/mysvnm33_09/chn_2009re_mys_vnm_e.pdf; Mission of the People's Republic of China to the

in the Map of Sansha City of Hai-Nan Province (中華人民共和國海南省三沙市地圖) published in November 2012 by Starmap Publisher (星球地圖出版社) in China has one more dash between Taiwan and Japan. It is well-known that the maritime boundary between Taiwan and the Philippines and the boundary between Taiwan and Japan are yet to be drawn. It will be unbelievable if these two dashes represent Taiwan-Philippine and Taiwan-Japan maritime boundaries. However, when the time comes for such boundary to be drawn after agreements are reached by the parties concerned, such dashes most probably will be removed, if used as a provisional maritime claim by China. Thus, it seems fair to say that the U-Shaped Line or the present ten-dash line drawn by PRC, if used to indicate China's provisional maritime claim, would be relating to, important to, affecting, and *concerning* sea boundary delimitation between China on the one hand and other States with opposite coasts on the other hand.

Covered by Article 298(1)(a)(i), the legality issue of the U-Shaped Line, if treated as the provisional boundary of China's maritime claim in the SCS, would be precluded from adjudication by the Tribunal in accordance with the 2006 China's Declaration. Since it is legally impossible for the award to address such an issue, non-deletion of the U-Shaped Line, as China's provisional maritime claim, cannot be inconsistent with the award and *res judicata* principle.

B *The Dispute Concerning Legal Status of Certain Maritime Features and China's Trespass to Philippine EEZ Identified by Submissions 3–9*

1 Philippines' Possible Arguments When Losing the Case

In case that the Philippines loses in the part of disputes constituted by Submissions 3–9, it will mean that the Tribunal declares that according to Article 121 of UNCLOS: (1) Scarborough Shoal, Johnson Reef, Cuarteron Reef, and Fiery Cross Reef may generate EEZ and continental shelf; (2) Mischief Reef, Second Thomas Shoal, Subi Reef, Gaven Reef and McKennan Reef may at least generate territorial water; (3) *consequently*, China also has EEZ and continental shelf in SCS so as to justify its interference with enjoyment and exercise of Philippine sovereign rights with respect to living and non-living natural resources within Philippine EEZ and continental shelf in the WPS; and (4) China's protection given to its nationals and vessels when exploiting the living resources in Philippine EEZ and continental shelf becomes lawful because such exploitation also occurs in China's EEZ and continental shelf.

United Nations, NV, CML/18/2009, May 7, 2009, *available: at* http://www.un.org/Depts/los/clcs_new/submissions_files/vnm37_09/chn_2009re_vnm_c.pdf (last visited Mar. 10, 2015).

When such possible result occurs, the following legal reasons remain available for the Philippines to justify its continued counter-actions against China.

The Philippines (together with Vietnam and Malaysia) may probably argue that even if those maritime features can be considered as islands under Article 121 of UNCLOS so as to be capable of generating maritime zones like territorial water, EEZ and/or continental shelf, such benefit does not accrue to China. As just discussed, this is because, from Philippine view, China does not have sovereignty over these features and China's territorial claims over these features cannot be endorsed by the award of this Tribunal. China's territorial claims over all the maritime features in the Spratly Islands Group and Scarborough Shoal are contested by the Philippines, Vietnam, and Malaysia, while the award of this Tribunal does not settle such disputes. China's maritime entitlements to EEZ and continental shelf in the WPS thus lack legal foundation. It is not possible for China and the Philippines to have any overlapping EEZ and continental shelf claims in the WPS, as China has none. In such a vast maritime area deemed as Philippine EEZ and continental shelf, China's interference with the enjoyment and exercise of Philippine sovereign rights with respect to the living and non-living resources of the Philippines cannot be justified even by the award in favor of China. By the same token, China's protection given to its nationals and vessels that exploit the living resources in the Philippine EEZ remains unjustified.

2 China's Possible Arguments When Losing the Case

On the other hand, should China lose in the part of disputes constituted by Submissions 3–9, it will mean that the Tribunal declares that: (1) Scarborough Shoal, Johnson Reef, Cuarteron Reef, and Fiery Cross Reef may not generate EEZ and continental shelf for China (and for any other State); (2) Mischief Reef, Second Thomas Shoal, Subi Reef, Gaven Reef and McKennan Reef may not even generate territorial water for China (and for any other State); (3) *consequently*, China has no EEZ and continental shelf in the WPS so as to justify China's interference with the enjoyment and exercise of Philippine sovereign rights with respect to living and non-living natural resources within Philippine EEZ and continental shelf in the WPS; and (4) in the same maritime area China's protection given to its nationals and vessels when exploiting the living resources in Philippine EEZ and continental shelf becomes unlawful.

Under such circumstances, it can be expected that China will not stop its disputed actions. It will probably offer the following legal justifications.

First, China may contend that it is pointless for the Philippines to bring Submissions 3–7 to the Tribunal for settlement, as China does not rely on those nine maritime features *individually* to claim maritime entitlements under UNCLOS legal regime. What has been used by China to claim EEZ and continental shelf in the eastern part of SCS enclosed by the U-Shaped Line is the *entire* Spratly Islands Group,[60] which includes at least 12 non-rock islands legally capable of generating EEZ and continental shelf[61] for China according to Article 121 of UNCLOS. In other words, no disputes[62] can be constituted by Submissions 3–7 for the Tribunal to entertain in the first place. Therefore, the Tribunal must refrain from entertaining such *moot* dispute.

Second, even if China uses those nine maritime features to claim EEZ and continental shelf, China at the same time relies on other maritime features, including non-rock islands, in the Spratly Islands Group to justify such maritime zonal claims. As the Tribunal may not deny China's territorial claims over, *inter alia*, those 12 non-rock islands, the award cannot be construed as dismissing its maritime entitlements to EEZ and continental shelf in the WPS that such islands may generate.

Third, since China has unaffected and undefeated maritime entitlements to EEZ and continental shelf in the WPS, it becomes undeniable that Chinese and Philippine EEZ and continental shelf claims *overlap* in such a vast maritime area. In other words, between China and the Philippines there is a maritime boundary delimitation dispute in WPS.

Fourth, the Tribunal is powerless to draw the maritime boundary for China and the Philippines so as to settle the above-mentioned Sino-Philippine maritime boundary delimitation dispute.[63] It follows that the award cannot be

---

60 Mission of the People's Republic of China to the United Nations, NV, CML/8/2011, Apr. 14, 2011, available at http://www.un.org/Depts/los/clcs_new/submissions_files/mysvnm33_09/chn_2011_re_phl_e.pdf (last visited Mar. 10, 2015).

61 Beckman & Schofield, *supra* note 43, 210–211. The 12 non-rock islands are (1) Taiwan-occupied Itu Aba; (2) Philippines-occupied Thitu Island, West York Island, Northeast Cay, Nanshan Island, Loaita Island; and (3) Vietnam-occupied Spratly Island, Southwest Cay, Sin Cowe Island, Sandy Cay, Namyit Island, and Amboyna Cay.

62 In the judgment of *The Mavrommatis Palestine Concessions*, the Permanent Court of International Justice has defined a dispute as "a disagreement on a point of law or fact, a conflict of legal views or of interests between two persons." The Mavrommatis Palestine Concessions, 1924 P.C.I.J. (ser. A), No. 2, at 11 (Aug. 30). Seen as an elaboration of such a definition, J.G. Merrills said that, "a dispute may be defined as a specific disagreement concerning a matter of fact, law or policy in which a claim or assertion of one party is met with refusal, counter-claim or denial by another." *See* J.G. Merrills, *International Dispute Settlement*, 1 (4th ed. 2005). A.V. Lowe and J. Collier also describe the dispute as "a specific disagreement relating to a question of rights or interests in which the parties proceed by way of claims, counter-claims, denials and so on." *See* J. Collier & A.V. Lowe, *The Settlement of Disputes in International Law: Institutions and Procedures* 1 (1999).

63 *See supra* note 36.

interpreted as a settlement of such overlapping maritime zonal disputes. In short, the Sino-Philippine boundary line in the SCS remains missing even after this Tribunal gives its award.

Fifth, before the boundary line is drawn, what is being complained by the Philippines in its Submissions 8–9 will not end. It is simply a reflection or symptom of the competition out of mutually exclusive overlapping maritime zonal claims. The Sino-Philippine maritime confrontations will continue as such core (maritime boundary delimitation) dispute remains unsettled. For China as the losing party in this arbitration, it is still justified to invoke its undefeated EEZ and continental shelf entitlement in the WPS to support its disputed interference under Submission 8 and protective activities opposed by Submission 9, as long as these activities occur in the area within 200 M from any non-rock island within the Spratly Islands Group. In fact, what have been contested by the Philippines in the entire arbitration in terms of Sino-Philippine maritime confrontations happened in the EEZ and continental shelf generated by those non-rock islands within the Spratly Islands Group, except for those incidents occurring in the territorial water surrounding Scarborough Shoal. Table 1 and Figure 3 of this paper demonstrate that such Chinese maritime entitlements to EEZ and continental shelf *reach* the location of Reed Bank and eight of those China-occupied maritime features (excluding Scarborough Shoal).

C The Maritime Confrontations in the Water Adjacent to Scarborough Shoal under Submissions 10–11 and 13

1 Philippines' Possible Arguments When Losing the Case

In case the Philippines loses with respect to its Submissions 10–11 and 13, it will mean that the Tribunal declares that: (1) China's prevention of Philippine fishermen from their livelihoods by interfering with latter's traditional fishing activities at Scarborough Shoal is not unlawful; (2) China has not violated its obligations under UNCLOS to protect and preserve the marine environment at Scarborough Shoal; and (3) China has not breached its UNCLOS obligations by operating its law enforcement vessels in a dangerous manner causing serious risk of collision to Philippine vessels navigating in the vicinity of Scarborough Shoal.

Under such circumstances, the Philippines will still have legal justifications to continue its verbal objections and physical counter-measures against China's no-longer-disputed actions in the waters adjacent to Scarborough Shoal, for the following reasons.

First, as the Sino-Philippine territorial dispute over Scarborough Shoal and the territorial water thereof remains unsettled by the award of the Tribunal, Philippine sovereignty over this "rock" and its territorial water remains unaffected. The award cannot be construed as endorsing China's competing territorial claim, otherwise it would mean that the Tribunal has made an *ultra vires* decision. The Tribunal will be wise enough not to do this.

Second, in the situation that the Philippines has territorial sovereignty over Scarborough Shoal and its territorial water, what is left for China as a non-coastal State will be the *right of innocent passage* under UNCLOS legal regime.[64] Pursuant to innocent passage rules, any non-coastal State (including China) has no right to prevent local (Philippine) fishermen from conducting fishing activities, including traditional fishing activities. Such prevention is incompatible with the basic idea of *passage* as defined by Article 18 of UNCLOS.[65] Moreover, such prevention, as it has no direct bearing on passage, should be considered prejudicial to the peace, good order or security of the Philippines (as the coastal State) in accordance with Article 19(2)(l) of UNCLOS.[66] Once China resumes its preventive actions as indicated by Submission 9 after this

64 *See* UNCLOS, *supra* note 1, arts. 17–21.

65 Article 18 (Meaning of passage) of UNCLOS reads:

> 1. Passage means navigation through the territorial sea for the purpose of: (a) traversing that sea without entering internal waters or calling at a roadstead or port facility outside internal waters; or (b) proceeding to or from internal waters or a call at such roadstead or port facility.
> 2. Passage shall be continuous and expeditious. However, passage includes stopping and anchoring, but only in so far as the same are incidental to ordinary navigation or are rendered necessary by *force majeure* or distress or for the purpose of rendering assistance to persons, ships or aircraft in danger or distress.

Id. art. 18.

66 Article 19 (Meaning of innocent passage) of UNCLOS reads:

> 1. Passage is innocent so long as it is not prejudicial to the peace, good order or security of the coastal State. Such passage shall take place in conformity with this Convention and with other rules of international law.
> 2. Passage of a foreign ship shall be considered to be prejudicial to the peace, good order or security of the coastal State if in the territorial sea it engages in any of the following activities: (a) any threat or use of force against the sovereignty, territorial integrity or political independence of the coastal State, or in any other manner in violation of the principles of international law embodied in the Charter of the United Nations; (b) any exercise or practice with weapons of any kind; (c) any act aimed at collecting information to the prejudice of the defence or security of the coastal State; (d) any act of propaganda aimed at affecting the defence or security of the coastal State; (e) the launching, landing or taking on board of any aircraft; (f) the launching, landing or taking on board of any military device; (g) the loading or unloading of any commodity, currency or person contrary to the customs, fiscal, immigration or sanitary laws and regulations of the coastal State; (h) any act of wilful and serious pollution contrary to this Convention; (i) any fishing activities; (j) the carrying out of research or survey activities; (k) any act aimed at interfering with any systems of

arbitration, the Philippines can still lawfully take actions against China's activities that are inconsistent with the innocent passage rules.

Third, from Philippine perspectives China may only have the right of innocent passage when its law enforcement and fishing vessels find themselves in the water adjacent to Scarborough Shoal. China's law enforcement vessels have no right to interfere with Philippine law enforcement vessels that try to enforce Philippine fisheries rules against Chinese fishing vessels harvesting in such Philippine territorial water. To begin with, the fishing activities conducted by Chinese fishing vessels in this Philippine territorial water violate the rules of innocent passage according to Article 19(2)(i).[67] Moreover, when such Chinese vessels have done something harmful to the marine environment in such Philippine territorial water, Philippine law enforcement vessels have every right to prevent and punish such activities according to Article 21(1)(d)–(f).[68] China's law enforcement vessels will doubtlessly violate international law when (1) taking actions to protect its own fishing vessels that have violated Philippine fisheries rules and (2) interfering with Philippine law enforcement activities. It will then justify Philippine condemnation and counter-measures, irrespective of the award in favor of China concerning Submission 11.

Fourth, since in the water adjacent to Scarborough Shoal China as non-coastal State only has the right of innocent passage under UNCLOS, the actions of Chinese law enforcement vessels to block the way of Philippine vessels while causing near-collision incidents will be considered to be prejudicial to the peace, good order or security of the Philippines as the coastal State. This is because that such actions of China are not having any direct bearing on passage in accordance with Article 19(2)(l) of UNCLOS.[69] Again, it will justify Philippine condemnation and counter-measures, irrespective of the award in favor of China concerning Submission 13.

---

communication or any other facilities or installations of the coastal State; (L) any other activity not having a direct bearing on passage.

Id. art. 19.

67 *Id.*

68 Article 21(1)(d)–(f) (Laws and regulations of the coastal State relating to innocent passage) of UNCLOS reads: "1. The coastal State may adopt laws and regulations, in conformity with the provisions of this Convention and other rules of international law, relating to innocent passage through the territorial sea, in respect of all or any of the following: … (d) the conservation of the living resources of the sea; (e) the prevention of infringement of the fisheries laws and regulations of the coastal State; (f) the preservation of the environment of the coastal State and the prevention, reduction and control of pollution thereof;" *Id.* art 21(1)(d)–(f).

69 *See supra* note 66.

2 China's Possible Arguments When Losing the Case

On the other hand, should China lose in this arbitration with respect to Philippine Submissions 10–11 and 13, China will probably refuse to cease the disputed actions. The following justifications may probably be invoked by China.

First, as the Tribunal is powerless to settle Sino-Philippine territorial dispute over, *inter alia*, Scarborough Shoal, the validity of China's territorial claim over this "rock" and its adjacent water remain unchallenged by the award of this Arbitration. In this area the status of China as a coastal State remains unaffected, whereas the Philippines may only have the right of innocent passage under UNCLOS legal regime. While exercising the right of innocent passage in this Chinese territorial water surrounding Scarborough Shoal, Philippine fishing vessels may not conduct fishing activities in accordance with Article 19(2)(i)[70] of UNCLOS, including traditional fishing. It would justify China's continuous prevention against the exercise of Philippine traditional fishing in such area.

Second, for the award in favor of the Philippines with respect to Submission 11, China may probably argue that it is only acceptable if the premise of the award is that *the water adjacent to Scarborough Shoal is China's territorial water*. China may be willing to follow the rules of UNCLOS, if any, for the coastal State to protect and preserve the marine environment in its territorial water and will probably be ready to rectify any mistakes committed in its own territorial water. On the other hand, China perhaps will not accept any judicial decision on this submission premised on treating it as a non-coastal State. China may argue that any award by the Tribunal may not be interpreted as denying China's territorial claim over Scarborough Shoal and its adjacent water, based on the reason already mentioned. China has legal grounds to differ if considered to be in breach of rules of marine environmental protection under UNCLOS, while being treated as *a non-coastal State*. It will be especially so if China is required to demand its fishing vessels harvesting in the water adjacent to Scarborough Shoal to yield themselves to the law enforcement actions by the Philippine government vessels there (which only enjoy innocent passage). China's continued actions that have been opposed by Submission 11 will be justified in such a scenario.

Third, for the award in favor of the Philippines with respect to Submission 13, China may probably point out the on-going Sino-Philippine competition for occupying Scarborough Shoal and its adjacent water that the Tribunal may ignore throughout the litigation due to Philippines' omission both in its

---

70 *Id.*

Memorial and the hearing. China, as the one getting upper hand only recently, has been vigilant about the danger of its territory being lost again to the Philippines. No matter what kind of operation carried out by the Philippines, be it by civilians[71] or officials, through fishing boats or law enforcement vessels, either navigable or immobile,[72] China's reactions may be primarily for maintaining its territorial integrity by holding on to the maritime features it has recovered. The rules to be followed by China's law enforcement vessels, in this context, turn out to be the limitations imposed by the principle of self-defense under the United Nations Charter and customary international law.[73] Clearly, the real dispute to be constituted by Submission 13 has been removed from the subject-matter jurisdiction of the Tribunal,[74] as it falls within the scope of disputes concerning military activities covered by Article 298(1)(b)[75] and

---

71 The Philippine civilian, Cloma, who was an owner of a fishing company and director of the Philippine Maritime Institute, sailed to Spratly Islands and "discovered" Kalayaan Islands (the Freedomland) in May 1956. Then in December 1974, President Marcos of the Philippines received a document from Cloma transferring all the rights of Tomas Cloma & Associates in "Freedomland" to the Philippine Government. In June 1978 President Marcos issued a decree officially claiming part of the Spratly Islands and making it a municipality in Palawan province. The area claimed was almost identical with Cloma's claim. *See* Shicun Wu, *Solving Disputes for Regional Cooperation and Development in the South China Sea: A Chinese Perspective* 127–28 (2013). *See also* Jia & Talmon, *supra* note 44, at 6.

72 On Second Thomas Shoal, the Philippines uses an immobile warship, BRP Sierra Madre, to occupy that maritime feature since 1999. *See* Darshana M. Baruah, "Second Thomas Shoal: The New Battleground", *The Diplomat*, Apr. 30, 2014, http://thediplomat.com/2014/04/second-thomas-shoal-the-new-battleground/ (last visited Mar. 17, 2015).

73 For the two authoritative treatments of this topic, see D.W. Bowett, *Self-Defense in International Law* (1958). And see Ian Brownlie, *International Law and the Use of Force by States* (1963). *Also*, "Although the Convention does not contain express provisions on the use of force in the arrest of ships, international law, which is applicable by virtue of article 293 of the Convention, requires that the use of force must be avoided as far as possible and, where force is unavoidable, it must not go beyond what is reasonable and necessary in the circumstances. Considerations of humanity must apply in the law of the sea, as they do in other areas of international law" M/V Saiga (No. 2) (St. Vincent v. Guinea), Case No. 2, Judgment of July 1, 1999, https://www.itlos.org/fileadmin/itlos/documents/cases/case_no_2/merits/Judgment.01.07.99.E.pdf, para. 155.

74 *See supra* note 36. This dispute was not even submitted by the Philippines to the Tribunal in the first place.

75 Article 298(1)(b) of UNCLOS reads:

1. When signing, ratifying or acceding to this Convention or at any time thereafter, a State may, without prejudice to the obligations arising under section 1, declare in writing that it does not accept any one or more of the procedures provided for in section 2

therefore caught by the 2006 China's Declaration. Since the Tribunal has no power to try such kind of dispute in the first place, the award may not be construed as dismissing China's legal positions for conducting such military activities. If China decides to take further actions of this nature, it should not be considered as non-compliance of the award and Article 296, either.

D *The Maritime Confrontation in Mischief Reef and Second Thomas Shoal under Submissions 11–12 and 14*

1 Philippines' Possible Arguments When Losing the Case

With respect to the Sino-Philippine maritime confrontations in Mischief Reef and Second Thomas Shoal, in case that the Philippines *loses* in Submissions 11–12 and 14, it would mean that the Tribunal declares that:

(11) China has *not* violated its obligations under UNCLOS to protect and preserve the marine environment at Second Thomas Shoal;

(12) China's occupation of and construction activities on Mischief Reef did *not* (a) violate the provisions of UNCLOS concerning artificial islands, installations and structures; (b) violate China's duties to protect and preserve the marine environment under UNCLOS; and (c) constitute unlawful acts of attempted appropriation in violation of UNCLOS; and

(14) China has *not* unlawfully aggravated and extended the dispute by (a) interfering with the Philippines' rights of navigation in the waters at, and adjacent to, Second Thomas Shoal; (b) preventing the rotation and resupply of Philippine personnel stationed at Second Thomas Shoal; and (c) endangering the health and well-being of Philippine personnel stationed at Second Thomas Shoal.

It is submitted that, under such circumstances, the Philippines will not stop its opposition and counter-actions against China and will probably offer the following legal justifications.

To begin with, the Philippines may probably contend that the award of the Tribunal may not be interpreted as endorsing China's territorial water, EEZ and

---

with respect to one or more of the following categories of disputes: ... (b) disputes concerning military activities, including military activities by government vessels and aircraft engaged in non-commercial service, and disputes concerning law enforcement activities in regard to the exercise of sovereign rights or jurisdiction excluded from the jurisdiction of a court or tribunal under article 297, paragraph 2 or 3;

UNCLOS, *supra* note 1, art. 298(1)(b).

continental shelf claims in the WPS. It is because of the limited subject-matter jurisdiction of the Tribunal that the award may not be interpreted as *upholding* China's territorial claims over all the maritime features in the Spratly Islands Group and Scarborough Shoal, including those islands capable of generating territorial water, EEZ and continental shelf under Article 121 of UNCLOS. Therefore, the award cannot affect the Philippines' position that China does not have maritime entitlements to territorial water, EEZ and continental shelf in the WPS. Being LTEs, Mischief Reef and Second Thomas Shoal are incapable of generating even territorial waters. Located within 200 M from Philippines' archipelagic baselines, they are part of the Philippines' continental shelf. These two LTEs are not standing on China's continental shelf, as China has none. To be added, the award may not be construed as denying the Philippines' territorial claims over the maritime features in the KIG. Therefore, the Philippines' continental shelf and EEZ to be generated from those islands within KIG over which the Philippines enjoy territorial sovereignty can also reach Mischief Reef and Second Thomas Shoal (see Table 1 and Figure 3 of this paper).[76]

Second, it follows that China, as a non-coastal State, has no grounds to construct artificial islands, installations and structures on Mischief Reef in accordance with Articles 60 and 80[77] of UNCLOS, as it is not within China's EEZ and continental shelf. On the other hand, the right of the Philippines to conduct such activities may not be dismissed by the award. Furthermore, the Philippines as the coastal State is entitled to have the exclusive right to authorize and regulate the construction, operation and use of (China-built) installations and structures which *may interfere with* the Philippines' exercise of its rights as the coastal State in the zone, pursuant to Article 60(1)(c).[78] Therefore, the Philippines will be legally justified not only for its continuous objection raised in its Submission 12, but also for its interference with China's activities on Mischief Reef.

---

76 To be noted, the Philippines claims territorial sovereignty over maritime feature within KIG, including Itu Aba Island, Thitu Island, and West York Islands. *See* Jia & Talmon, *supra* note 44, at 6.

77 Article 80 (Artificial islands, installations and structures on the continental shelf) of UNCLOS reads: "Article 60 applies *mutatis mutandis* to artificial islands, installations and structures on the continental shelf." UNCLOS, *supra* note 1, art. 80.

78 Article 60(1)(c) (Artificial islands, installations and structures in the exclusive economic zone) of UNCLOS reads: "1. In the exclusive economic zone, the coastal State shall have the exclusive right to construct and to authorize and regulate the construction, operation and use of: . . . (c) installations and structures which may interfere with the exercise of the rights of the coastal State in the zone." *Id.* art. 60(1)(c).

Third, for the part of protecting and preserving the marine environment of Mischief Reef and Second Thomas Shoal under Submissions 11 and 12(b), what have been disputed are the actions by China's law enforcement vessels which prevented their Philippine counterpart from enforcing Philippine laws upon Chinese fishing vessels conducting activities *harmful* to marine environment in Philippine EEZ. From Philippine perspectives, those Chinese fishing vessels are harvesting in the Philippines' (but not China's) EEZ. Therefore, China should ensure that its fishing vessels follow Philippine fisheries laws and regulations pursuant to Article 58(3).[79] When fishing activities endanger Philippine marine environment, Philippine law enforcement vessels have every right to detain and punish these fishing vessels in accordance with Article 56(1)(a)[80] and 56(1)(b)(iii).[81] Such right of the Philippines may not be dismissed by the award in any way. China as a non-coastal State has the duty to comply with the obligation under Article 58(3) to have due regard to the rights of the Philippines and to comply with the laws and regulations adopted by the Philippines. When China fails to observe such obligations, the Philippines' counter-actions will be legally justified. Even the award of this Arbitration in China's favor cannot be interpreted as depriving the Philippines of such rights.

Fourth, for the part of Submission 14, the Philippines may contend that, as the coastal State whose EEZ and continental shelf extend to Second Thomas

---

79 Article 58(3) (Rights and duties of other States in the exclusive economic zone) of UNCLOS reads:

> 3. In exercising their rights and performing their duties under this Convention in the exclusive economic zone, States shall have due regard to the rights and duties of the coastal State and shall comply with the laws and regulations adopted by the coastal State in accordance with the provisions of this Convention and other rules of international law in so far as they are not incompatible with this Part.

Id. art. 58(3).

80 Article 56(1)(a) (Rights, jurisdiction and duties of the coastal State in the exclusive economic zone) of UNCLOS reads:

> 1. In the exclusive economic zone, the coastal State has: (a) sovereign rights for the purpose of exploring and exploiting, conserving and managing the natural resources, whether living or non-living, of the waters superjacent to the seabed and of the seabed and its subsoil, and with regard to other activities for the economic exploitation and exploration of the zone, such as the production of energy from the water, currents and winds.

Id. art. 56(1)(a).

81 Article 56(1)(b)(iii) (Rights, jurisdiction and duties of the coastal State in the exclusive economic zone) of UNCLOS reads: "1. In the exclusive economic zone, the coastal State has: ... (b) jurisdiction as provided for in the relevant provisions of this Convention with regard to: ... (iii) the protection and preservation of the marine environment." *Id.* art. 56(1)(b)(iii).

Shoal, the Philippines has the *exclusive right* to construct artificial island, installations and structures on Second Thomas Shoal under Article 60 and 80 of UNCLOS. *A fortiori*, it is justified for the Philippines to place any facility less permanent than artificial island, installations and structures on this LTE, not to mention that the ship BRP Sierra Madre was not intentionally placed on this LTE by the Philippines. Since the Philippines as the coastal State has the *exclusive* jurisdiction over such ship on this LTE, including jurisdiction with regard to health and safety laws and regulations pursuant to Article 60(2),[82] the Philippines will still be legally justified to exercise jurisdiction over the actions of China's vessels that are endangering the health and safety of the personnel on the ship BRP Sierra Madre after this Arbitration. Even the award by the Tribunal in favor of China cannot be interpreted as precluding the Philippines from exercising such an *exclusive* right and jurisdiction.

2 China's Possible Arguments When Losing the Case

On the other hand, should China lose the case with respect to the Philippines' Submissions 11–12 and 14, it can be expected that China will not cease its disputed actions, either. The possible legal justifications for China to put forth are as follows.

First, China may probably argue that the award cannot be interpreted as dismissing China's maritime entitlements to EEZ and continental shelf in the WPS, due to the Tribunal's limited subject-matter jurisdiction as discussed above. Moreover, China's EEZ and continental shelf generated by the Spratly Islands Group *as a whole* and by certain islands *individually* within the Spratly Islands Group can reach Mischief Reef and Second Thomas Shoal (see Table 1 and Figure 3 of this paper). Therefore, these two maritime features, even if considered as LTEs by the award, are part of China's EEZ and continental shelf. China's status as a coastal State in the waters surrounding these two LTEs cannot be affected or overruled by the award whose legally binding force does not reach this matter.

Second, Mischief Reef and Second Thomas Shoal, as LTEs, fall within the overlapping area claimed as EEZ and continental shelf by both China and the Philippines. Since the Tribunal is not authorized to draw maritime boundary for both China and the Philippines in such overlapping area, the award cannot be interpreted as denying these LTEs as part of China's EEZ and continental shelf.

---

82 Article 60(2) (Artificial islands, installations and structures in the exclusive economic zone) of UNCLOS reads: "... 2. The coastal State shall have exclusive jurisdiction over such artificial islands, installations and structures, including jurisdiction with regard to customs, fiscal, health, safety and immigration laws and regulations." *Id.* art. 60(2).

Third, as the award cannot deny Mischief Reef as part of China's EEZ and continental shelf, China will probably be justified to exercise its exclusive rights under Articles 60(1)–(2) and 80 of UNCLOS as a coastal State for this LTE. Therefore, China's continuous activities of occupying and constructing artificial islands, installations, and structures on Mischief Reef are neither unlawful, nor inconsistent with the award in the Philippines' favor regarding Submission 12.

Fourth, for the part of protecting and preserving the marine environment of Mischief Reef and Second Thomas Shoal under Submissions 11 and 12(b), the targets of complaint are the actions taken by China's law enforcement vessels which prevented their Philippine counterpart from enforcing Philippine laws upon Chinese fishing vessels conducting activities allegedly *harmful* to marine environment in the waters adjacent to these two LTEs. From China's viewpoint, those Chinese fishing vessels are harvesting in China's (but not Philippine) EEZ. For the part of possible environmental damage caused by the fishing vessels, China perhaps may express its willingness to exercise its jurisdiction with regard to the protection and preservation of the marine environment according to Article 56(1)(b)(iii), and to rectify any mistakes ever committed. However, for the part of obstruction of Philippine law enforcement activities as the core of these two submissions, China may probably insist on the unaffected validity of its actions against the Philippines. This is because in such area of China's EEZ and continental shelf, it is China (but not the Philippines) that has the sovereign right for the purpose of exploring and exploiting, conserving and managing the natural resources, whether living or non-living, of the waters superjacent to the sea-bed and of the sea-bed and its subsoil in accordance with Article 60(1)(a).[83] Besides, since China has jurisdiction with regard to the protection and preservation of the marine environment in China's EEZ and continental shelf according to Article 56(1)(b)(iii), it will be justifiable for China to insist on exercising jurisdiction over its own fishing vessels, if not upon Philippine fishing vessels as well. In such kind of overlapping EEZ and continental shelf, it will be better for China to exercise jurisdiction over its own fishing vessels. To ask China to yield to the Philippines in letting the Philippines' law enforcement vessels exercise jurisdiction over Chinese fishing vessels will be itself aggravating and extending the disputes, instead of lessening the tensions between the two parties.

---

83 Article 60(1)(a) (Artificial islands, installations and structures in the exclusive economic zone) of UNCLOS reads: "1. In the exclusive economic zone, the coastal State shall have the exclusive right to construct and to authorize and regulate the construction, operation and use of: (a) artificial islands." *Id.* art. 60(1)(a).

Fifth, for the part of China's obstruction of Philippines' law enforcement vessels in the waters surrounding Mischief Reef and Second Thomas Shoal as disputed by the Philippines in Submissions 11 and 12(b), China may probably argue that the award cannot be interpreted as denying the legality of such actions of China. This is because the 2006 China's Declaration has, *inter alia*, precluded the jurisdiction of the Annex VII-Tribunal to try disputes concerning law enforcement activities in regard to the exercise of sovereign rights or jurisdiction excluded from the jurisdiction of this Tribunal under Article 297(3).[84] To be noted, what may be excluded by Article 297(3)(a) covers any dispute relating to the sovereign rights of the coastal State with respect to the living resources in the EEZ or the exercise of such sovereign rights.[85] Since the jurisdiction of this Tribunal to try such dispute has been excluded by the joint operation of the 2006 China's Declaration, Article 298(1)(b), and Article 297(3)(a), the award of the Tribunal cannot be interpreted as affecting or overruling the legal positions of China in such a dispute. With its validity unchallenged by the award, China's obstruction activities against its Philippine counterpart (which are law enforcement actions by nature), once resumed, cannot be considered as non-compliance of the award.

Sixth, for the continued actions complained by the Philippines' Submission 14, China may probably offer the following justifications. To begin with, as Second Thomas Shoal cannot be denied by the award as part of the continental shelf and EEZ pertaining to China, it is not unlawful for China to exercise the exclusive right under Articles 60(1)(c) and 80 of UNCLOS to authorize and regulate the construction, operation and use of installations and structures which may interfere with the exercise of China's rights as the coastal State in the zone. *A fortiori*, anything less permanent than installations and structures that *may* interfere with China's exercise of its rights as the coastal State may not be placed or erected there unless being authorized and regulated by China. It follows that the Philippine ship the BRP Sierra Madre sitting on Second Thomas Shoal may be regulated by China as the coastal State

84 *See supra* note 75, art. 298(1)(b).

85 Article 297 (Limitations on applicability of section 2) of UNCLOS reads: "... 3. (a) Disputes concerning the interpretation or application of the provisions of this Convention with regard to fisheries shall be settled in accordance with section 2, except that the coastal State shall not be obliged to accept the submission to such settlement of any dispute relating to its sovereign rights with respect to the living resources in the exclusive economic zone or their exercise, including its discretionary powers for determining the allowable catch, its harvesting capacity, the allocation of surpluses to other States and the terms and conditions established in its conservation and management laws and regulations." UNCLOS, *supra* note 1, art. 297.

of the EEZ and continental shelf reaching this LTE. Moreover, Article 60(2) of UNCLOS[86] empowers China to have exclusive jurisdiction over such artificial islands, installations, and structures that may interfere with the exercise of China's right as the coastal State in the zone, including jurisdiction with regard to *immigration* laws and regulations. Applying such legal provisions to the Philippine ship, China will be fully justified to interfere with the Philippines' actions for the purpose of rotation and re-supply of Philippine *personnel* stationed at Second Thomas Shoal.

III Conclusion

One of the outstanding events in international dispute settlement in 2013 is the Sino-Philippine Arbitration on the South China Sea (U-Shaped Line) Disputes. This arbitration is extra-ordinary for several reasons. *First*, a whole set of complicated disputes with multiple layers have caused the confrontations, part of which are wished (by the Philippines) to be settled through this arbitration. *Second*, not every part of the disputes has been submitted to the Tribunal for settlement. *Third*, the core disputes (territorial disputes and maritime boundary delimitation disputes) have not been submitted to the Tribunal for resolution. *Fourth*, had the Philippines submitted such core disputes, the Tribunal would not have entertained them due to its limited subject-matter jurisdiction. *Fifth*, the Philippines initiated this arbitration against the will of China, which declared shortly afterwards that it will not participate in this arbitration, due to, *inter alia*, that the disputes submitted go beyond the scope of Tribunal's jurisdiction.

So far, academic papers on this subject have focused on the "surface disputes" *submitted* to the Tribunal and discussed whether such part of disputes fall within the subject-matter jurisdiction of the Tribunal. If eventually the answer is affirmative, China's possible non-compliance with the unfavorable award in the merits phase may probably be seen as a breach of Article 296 of UNCLOS to which China is a Contracting Party. However, if this is a problem, it is not merely China's problem. As discussed by this paper, this is *not* an issue of violating Article 296, but rather a common phenomenon for both Parties that even conforms to *res judicata* principle and Article 296.

To prove this point, this paper looks at *the missing part* of the disputes that have not been submitted to the Tribunal, i.e. the core disputes. This paper finds out that such core disputes constitute the real causes of the Sino-Philippine

86 *See supra* note 82.

confrontations reflected by the Philippine Submissions. In other words, mere submission of surface disputes by the Philippines does not help to even reduce the confrontations. This has been confirmed by all the potential arguments for the losing Party (be it China or the Philippines) to justify the continuation of its disputed SCS claims, and law enforcement, if not military, activities.

On the other hand, this paper applies the *limits* of the *res judicata* principle embodied by Article 296, as analyzed by Professor Bin Cheng, to the unsubmitted core disputes which will (and shall) go un-adjudged by the Tribunal. In other words, the award shall refrain from determining or rejecting the legality of claims and activities by either Party made in such core disputes. As Professor Bin Cheng puts it, "what is not *res judicata* between the parties has no authoritative and binding effect"[87] and *res judicata* principle is "to prevent legal principles accepted by the Court in a particular case from being binding… *in other disputes*".[88] Therefore, the continuous behavior of the losing Party based on its unaffected territorial or maritime boundary delimitation claims will not do violence to the award on the surface disputes submitted. Such *"non-compliance by appearance"* will be consistent with the *res judicata* principle, especially the *limits* of such a general principle.

Last but not the least, should the Philippines lose in this arbitration in the merits phase, its highly expected continuation of complaining and countermeasures against China's territorial and maritime claims and actions in the SCS will not violate Article 296. This would then contradict with the declared "goal" of Philippine initiation of this arbitration in the very beginning.[89] Perhaps China's non-participation in this essentially unappealing arbitration becomes comprehensible this way.

87 *See supra* note 42 and accompanying text.

88 *See supra* note 41 and accompanying text.

89 *Supra* note 24.

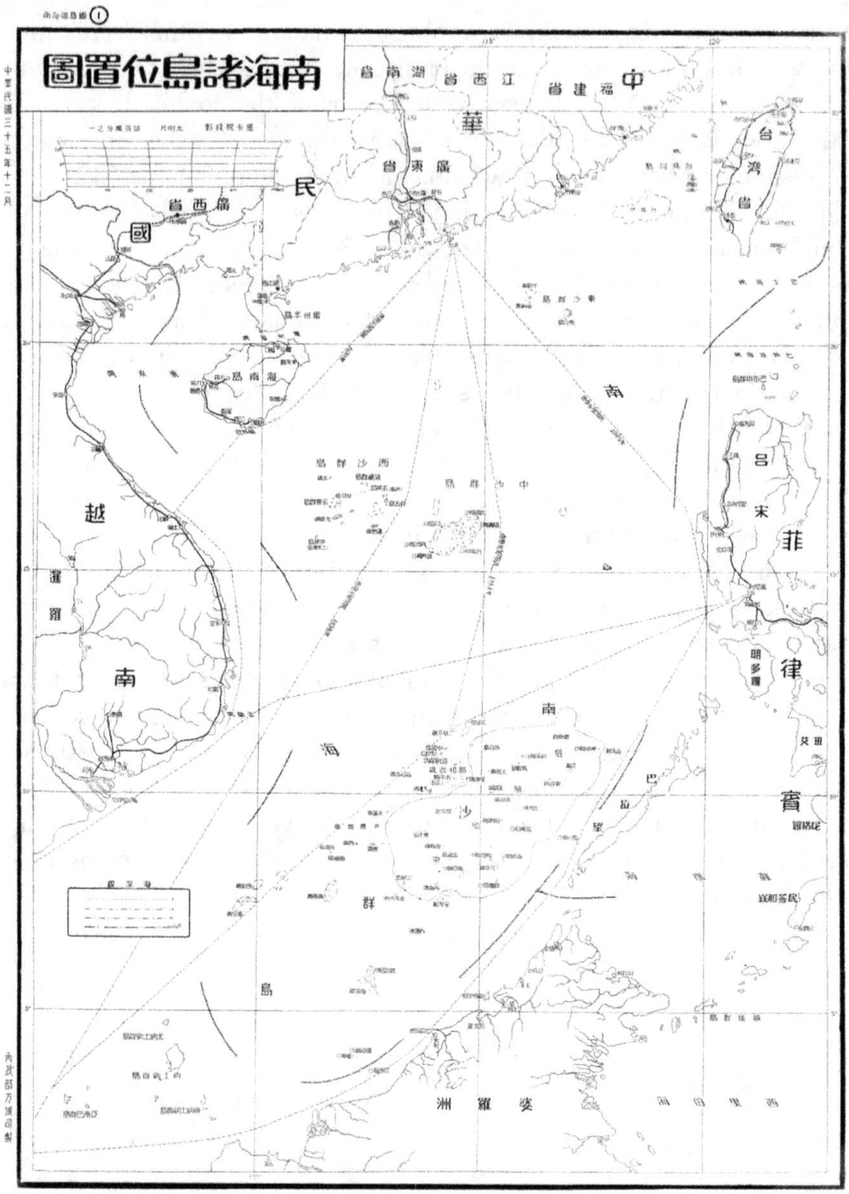

FIGURE 1 *The 1947 China's location map of the SCS islands.*
SOURCE: DRAWN BY THE DIVISION OF TERRITORY & BOUNDARY, MINISTRY OF THE INTERIOR, DECEMBER 1946 (THE 35TH YEAR OF THE REPUBLIC OF CHINA), ROC GOVERNMENT (PUBLISHED IN DEC. 1947)

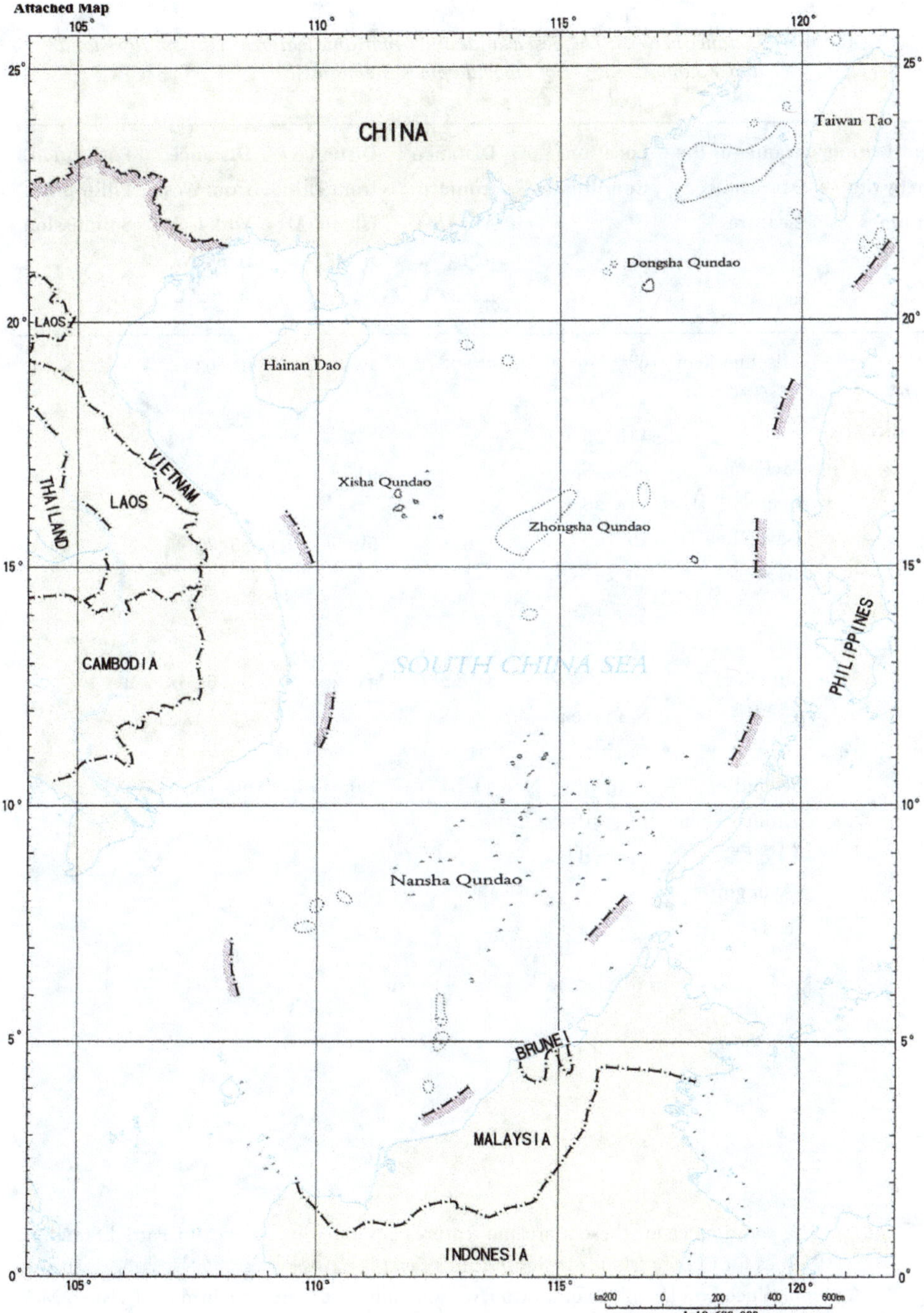

FIGURE 2 *China's SCS map with the nine-dashed line in its 2009 NV.*
SOURCE: CHINESE (PRC) GOVERNMENT RELEASED IN 2009 IN ITS NV DELIVERED TO THE UN

TABLE 1 *Distance between 3 biggest islands and 9 maritime features in the Spratly Islands under Submissions 3–7 of the Philippines' Memorial*

Categorization Given by the Philippines	Names of the Maritime Features	Location Coordinates[90]	Distance[91] from Itu Aba (M) 10°23' N, 114°22' E	Distance from Thitu Island (M) 11°06' N, 114°17' E	Distance from West York Is(M) 11°05' N, 115°02' E	Position in Philippines' Submission
Low-tide elevation Under UNCLOS Article 13	Mischief Reef 美濟礁	9°52'–9°56' N, 115°30'–115°35' E	77–78	114	91–93	4–5, 12, 14
	McKennan Reef 西門礁	9°54' N, 114°28' E	42	91	101	6
	Gaven Reef 南熏礁	10°10'–10°13' N, 114°13'–114°15' E	7–9	56–58	75–77	6
	Subi Reef 渚碧礁	10°54'–10°56' N, 114°04'–114°07' E	21–22	31–32	63–65	4
	Second Thomas Shoal 仁愛礁 (Ayungin Reef)	9°39'-9°48' N, 115°51'–115°54' E	90–91	125–128	99–104	11, 14

90 The coordinates for these maritime features are based on the List of Partial Standard Names for China's Islands in South China Sea (我國南海諸島部分標準地名). It was reproduced on Unanhai.com, http://www.unanhai.com/nhzddm.htm (last visited Mar. 10, 2015).

91 The distances are calculated by the Latitude/Longitude Distance Calculator provided by the National Weather Service, National Hurricane Center of National Oceanic and Atmospheric Administration (http://www.nhc.noaa.gov/gccalc.shtml).

Categorization Given by the Philippines	Names of the Maritime Features	Location Coordinates	Distance from Itu Aba (M) 10°23' N, 114°22' E	Distance from Thitu Island (M) 11°06' N, 114°17' E	Distance from West York Is(M) 11°05' N, 115°02' E	Position in Philippines' Submission
Rocks Under UNCLOS Article 121(3)	Johnson Reef 赤瓜礁	9°42' N, 114°17' E	49	98	110	7
	Cuarteron Reef 華陽礁	8°51'–8°52' N, 112°50'–112°53' E	143–145	181–182	211–213	7
	Fiery Cross Reef 永暑礁	9°30'–9°40' N, 112°53'–113°04' E	86–114	120–143	153–181	7
	Reed Bank 禮樂灘	11°06'–11° 55' N, 116°22'–117°20' E	128–193	121–181	71–132	

SOURCE: DRAWN AND CALCULATED BY THE AUTHOR WITH THE HELP OF NOAA WEBSITE.

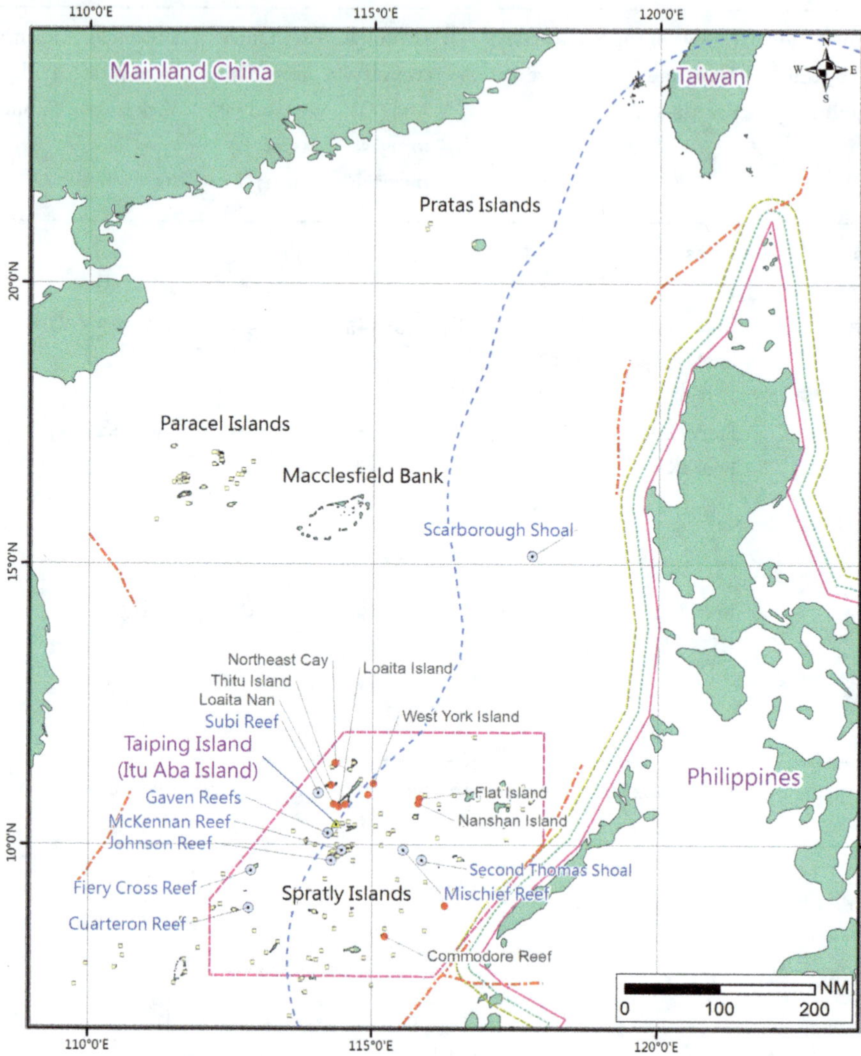

FIGURE 3 *Maritime features occupied by PRC,*[92] *Taiwan,*[93] *and Philippine*[94] *governments.*

92 The Frog-egg like features are occupied by Beijing Government and identified by Submissions 3–7 of the Philippine Memorial.

93 Taiping Island (Itu Aba) is occupied by Taiwan.

94 Thitu Island, West York Island, Northeast Cay, Nanshan Island, Loaita Island, Flat Island, Loaita Nan, and Commodore Reef are occupied by the Philippines.

Contemporary Practice and Judicial Decisions of the Republic of China (Taiwan) Relating to International Law, 2013

Compiled by Chun-i Chen, Pasha L. Hsieh, Pei-Lun Tsai, Chun-Liang Lai, I-Hon Hsiao, and Kai-Chih Chang, with the Assistance of Lee & Li Attorneys-at-Law

Explanatory Note

Items reported here primarily cover the period of 2013. This report does not claim to be exhaustive for the period it intends to cover, and the compilers will add more items when available in future volumes.

Items included in this report are classified according to the following sections:

I	International Law in General
II	Subjects of International Law
III	International Organizations
IV	Individuals
V	Territory and Territorial Jurisdiction
VI	State Responsibility
VII	The Law of the Sea, Environment, Health, and Aviation
VIII	The Law of Treaties
IX	Diplomatic, Consular and Similar Relations
X	Peaceful Settlement of International Disputes
XI	Arms Control, Use of Force and International Criminal Law
XII	International Economic Relations
XIII	Private International Law
XIV	Others

 | DOI 10.1163/9789004306509_009

I International Law in General

Foreign Policy Report, 8th Congress of the Legislative Yuan, 3rd Session (March 18, 2013)

On March 18, 2013, the Minister of Foreign Affairs, Mr. David Y. L. Lin was invited by the Foreign and National Defense Committee of the Legislative Yuan to report on the foreign policy of the Republic of China. The report is as follows:[1]

I Foreword

It is an honor for me to present a briefing on the most recent activities of the Ministry of Foreign Affairs (MOFA) to the Foreign and National Defense Committee. On behalf of MOFA and all my colleagues, I would like to take this opportunity to extend my appreciation to President Wang Jin-pyng and all other members of the Legislative Yuan for their staunch support of our work, and to congratulate President Wang on his successful trips to the United States in January and the Republic of Korea (ROK) in February of this year.

The aim of the foreign policy of the Republic of China (Taiwan) is to safeguard national sovereignty and security and create an international environment that is conducive to national development. Since 2008, the government has promoted the "viable diplomacy" policy in an effort to consolidate the foundation for protecting sovereignty, expanding international space, and sustaining national development. Today, the ROC enjoys solid relations with 23 diplomatic allies, with which we share frequent high-level interactions. With the United States, Japan, members of the European Union, Southeast Asian nations, Australia, New Zealand, and other non-diplomatic partner countries, we have forged cooperative relations in the areas of security, economy, trade, tourism, technology, culture, aviation, agriculture, and fishery.

In order to maintain the momentum of viable diplomacy and build public trust, MOFA will continue to monitor international developments, formulate counterstrategies, allocate resources, clarify our policies, and thereby create a friendly, convenient, and beneficial global environment.

Today, I will discuss the opportunities and challenges in the current international political and economic climate, the progress and concrete successes we have achieved with viable diplomacy, as well as our priorities and future prospects. Your comments and suggestions are very much appreciated.

---

1 Ministry of Foreign Affairs (MOFA), Foreign Policy Report, 8th Congress of the Legislative Yuan, 3rd Session (March 18, 2013), *available at* http://www.mofa.gov.tw/en/News_Content3.aspx?n=4BAF9BD5400A05D9&s=C609F113A313275F.

II Opportunities and Challenges in the Current International Climate

1 *The International Political and Economic Landscape, and Strategic and Security Developments in East Asia*

(1) Maintaining Dynamic and Stable Systems in East Asia

The bilateral and multilateral free trade systems established by East Asian countries over the past two decades have evolved into mechanisms for cooperation and reciprocity. Traditional competition for power has given way to a pursuit of economic strength, as most parties refuse to allow disputes to undermine these systems or affect the economic scale and international division of labor that have resulted from their institution.

Peace in East Asia lies in the dynamic equilibrium between power, nationalism, and economic interests. Beginning in 2012, a series of sovereignty disputes over the East China Sea and the South China Sea have arisen. Leadership transitions have taken place in mainland China, Japan, as well as the Koreas. Each of these countries has striven to maintain domestic stability by taking a hard-line approach externally. Conflict has flared between mainland China and Japan around the Diaoyutai Islands. North Korea has launched the Unha-3 satellite and conducted nuclear tests. Although nationalist sentiment has risen, fortunately, all parties have exercised restraint out of concern for their economic interests. Free trade agreement (FTA) negotiations between many countries (with the exception of North Korea) are proceeding apace. Regional economic and trade integration has continued to develop and there is little chance of disputes spinning out of control. However, North Korea, which shuns the outside world, is the greatest uncertainty.

(2) The US "Rebalancing" to Asia

Faced with mainland China's growing military and economic power, regional integration in the form of the Association of Southeast Asian Nations (ASEAN) plus 1 (mainland China) and ASEAN plus 3 (mainland China, Japan, and the ROK), and the gradual withdrawal of US troops from Iraq and Afghanistan, the United States has adopted a "rebalancing" policy with regard to its military strategy and economic deployment. While strengthening its ties with military allies, the US is also pushing for the Trans-Pacific Partnership (TPP) in an effort to maintain a balance.

Following his November 6, 2012 reelection, US President Barack Obama dispatched Secretary of Defense Leon Panetta and Secretary of State Hillary Clinton on trips to Asia, while he himself visited Thailand, Burma, and Cambodia, and attended the East Asia Summit (EAS). These moves have been interpreted as a reflection of President Obama's determination to underscore the US strategic pivot to the Asia-Pacific region, to which he attaches great importance.

(3) Impact of a US-EU Free Trade Zone on the Global Economy

In his 2013 State of the Union Address on Capitol Hill, President Obama announced that the US and the EU were planning to establish the world's largest free trade zone within the next two years. Negotiations will begin in June of this year with hopes of reinvigorating the long-sluggish economy. This will have a far-reaching impact on the whole world economy, especially mainland China, India, Brazil, and other emerging markets.

(4) Upturn in Global Economy Beneficial to the ROC's Economic and Trade Diplomacy

A preliminary solution has been found to the US fiscal cliff but the EU is still dealing with its debt issue. Financial markets' confidence is gradually being restored in affected countries. The Japanese Cabinet led by Prime Minister Shinzo Abe has announced a 20 trillion yen economic stimulus package and further relaxed Japan's currency policy—moves that are expected to benefit its domestic economy. Mainland China saw an upturn in its GDP in the fourth quarter of last year. These developments indicate that uncertainty in the global economy is gradually being removed and our businesses are now more optimistic about the future. According to the latest survey by the Taiwan Institute of Economic Research, the business climate in the manufacturing and service sectors improved in November and December 2012, a fact benefitingcial to our continued efforts at liberalization.

(5) The Internet as a New Political and Economic Arena

The Internet has many attributes—speed, volume, universal access, anonymity, equality, non-discrimination, low cost, and lack of effective controls. As in the initial stage of development of international relations, the Internet shows infinite growth potential and its penetration beyond boundaries especially favors the transmission of political messages and the conduct of commercial activities. It has brought fundamental change to government administration, entrepreneurial management, and political and diplomatic operations. MOFA is will closely monitoring its future developments in preparation for making an appropriate response.

2 *Administrative Measures Being Taken in Response to the Latest International Developments*

(1) An "Iron Triangle" Strategy for National Security Strengthens Viable Diplomacy and Expands International Space

Under the principle of "putting Taiwan first for the benefit of the people," continued efforts will be made to promote viable diplomacy, safeguard sovereignty, elevate our international status and dignity, gain global support, and expand our international room for survival and development.

(2) Strengthening Economic and Trade Diplomacy to Liberalize Economy and Trade

We have adopted the macroscopic strategy of "building up Taiwan while linking with the Asia-Pacific region and creating a global presence" in FTA negotiations with our major trading partners. We are promoting accession to the TPP and ASEAN plus 6 (i.e., the Regional Comprehensive Economic Partnership)., for which began negotiations for the latter began in January of this year, and which is expected to start operations in 2015, the organization will encompass a population of three billion, to be established in 2015. We have also taken a building block approach in seeking to sign bilateral investment agreements (BIA) and technical barriers to trade (TBT) agreements with other countries.

(3) Use of Mutual Reliance and Reciprocity in the Global Economy to Maintain Balanced Relations among East Asian Powers and Create a Global Environment Conducive to Peace and Prosperity

In an effort to establish a model for resolving regional disputes, we are committed to promoting the East China Sea Peace Initiative. This will safeguard sovereignty and protect regional peace, while reinforcing the stance via international platforms and the media that, whether from the perspectives of history, geography, practical use, or international law, the islands of Diaoyutai, Nansha (Spratly), Xisha (Paracel), Zhongsha (Macclesfield Bank), and Dongsha (Pratas) and their surrounding waters are an inherent part of the Republic of China. All parties should seek to resolve disputes through dialogue, negotiation, and joint development of resources for the advancement of regional peace, stability, and development.

(4) Employing Democracy and Culture as "Soft Power" to Raise our Profile in Keeping with our Diplomatic Objectives

We will introduce to the global community the ROC's achievements in democracy, freedom, and equitable prosperity to enhance our national image. We will also enrich the content of "viable diplomacy" through soft power and cultural diplomacy as we seek international recognition and support.

(5) Vitalization of Public Diplomacy to Complement Traditional Diplomacy and Increase of Policy Briefings

In addition to expanding international information services to help the global community better understand President Ma's efforts to achieve reconciliation across the Taiwan Strait and with other parts of the world as well as to advance regional peace and collective prosperity, the government has publicized our accomplishments as a peacemaker, a provider of humanitarian aid, a promoter of cultural exchange, a creator of new technologies and business opportunities, and a standard-bearer of Chinese culture. We have also formulated an "e-diplomacy policy" and are monitoring e-diplomacy developments in other countries vis-à-vis their successes, challenges they face, how they grow future prospects, and their impact on global governance—in order to harness opportunities for expanding our international space.

III Current Status and Substantive Achievements of the Viable Diplomacy Policy

1 *Consolidating Relations and Cooperation with Diplomatic Allies*

(1) Strengthening Mutual Visits by High-Ranking Officials and Deepening Friendships

Last December, I led a delegation to Guatemala and the Dominican Republic, where I met with President Otto Pérez Molina and President Danilo Medina, respectively. In addition, I led a delegation to Palau, Haiti, Saint Lucia, Saint Vincent and the Grenadines, and Saint Christopher and Nevis in January and February this year. During these visits, I subsequently met with (the incumbent yet outgoing) President Johnson Toribiong and President-elect Tommy E. Remengesau Jr. of Palau; President Michel Joseph Martelly of Haiti; Governor General Dame Pearlette Louisy and Prime Minister Kenny Anthony of Saint Lucia; Governor General Sir Frederick Ballantyne and Prime Minister Dr. Ralph E. Gonsalves of St. Vincent and the Grenadines; and Governor General Sir Edmund Lawrence and Prime Minister Denzil L. Douglas of St. Christopher and Nevis. These visits were a resounding success.

Moreover, since last September, a number of heads of state and other high-level officials of our diplomatic allies have led delegations to Taiwan, including President Christopher J. Loeak and Mrs. Loeak of the Marshall Islands; King Mswati III and Queen Inkhosikati La Ngangaza of the Kingdom of Swaziland; Vice President Roxana Baldetti of Guatemala; First Lady Cándida Montilla de Medina of the Dominican Republic; First Lady and Secretary of Social Inclusion

Vanda Pignato of El Salvador; Minister of Foreign Affairs and Attorney General Wilfred Peter Elrington and Mrs. Elrington of Belize; Minister of Foreign Affairs Samuel Santos López and Mrs. Santos of Nicaragua; Nitijela (lower house of parliament) Speaker Donald F. Capelle and Mrs. Capelle of Marshall Islands; Speaker of the Parliament Ludwig Scotty of Nauru; Senate President Claudius James Francis and House of Assembly Speaker Peter I. Foster of St. Lucia; Senate President Simon Dieuseul Desras of Haiti; National Assembly Speaker Evaristo do Espírito Santo Carvalho of Sao Tome and Principe; and Chamber of Duties President Victor Alcides Bogado González of Paraguay. These visits have helped further deepen mutual understanding and boost bilateral relations.

(2) Institutionalizing Foreign Aid to Improve the Well-being of the People of Diplomatic Allies

a. Carrying out our foreign aid policy in accordance with three principles of seeking proper goals, acting lawfully, exercising effective administration: MOFA adheres to these three principles when helping our diplomatic allies improve their infrastructure, healthcare, and people's quality of life. As of this January, Taiwan had dispatched 30 aid and service missions of all sorts, comprising in total 175 experts, technicians, and projects managers, to 29 countries for 84 joint projects. These have benefited the peoples of our partner countries allies and have further strengthened our bilateral relations with them.

b. Establishing a professional, legal, and transparent mechanism for foreign aid: To this aim, six relevant regulations, including the Regulations Governing the Planning, Appraisal, Implementation, Supervision and Performance Evaluation of International Cooperation and Development Affairs, were promulgated and enforced, thereby strengthening the legal framework for our foreign aid. In addition, MOFA has created an Official Development Assistance database to collect statistics on foreign aid provided by the whole country. The information gathered is included in the Taiwan Statistical Data Book published by the Council for Economic Planning and Development, and then a notification thereof is submitted to the OECD. In addition, MOFA drafts an annual report on international cooperation and development for review by the Legislative Yuan.

c. Transforming areas of foreign aid based on Taiwan's industrial advantages: In addition to providing diplomatic allies aid in traditional foreign aid areas, such as agriculture, husbandry, horticulture, and vocational training, Taiwan provides aid in fields where our industries have demonstrated great strengths, including information and communication technology (ICT), health and medical care, and technology. For example, we launched joint projects using geographic information systems in Central America for such countries as Guatemala, Honduras, and El Salvador. By using satellite and remote sensing technology, we help our diplomatic allies in a variety of areas, including land monitoring and natural disaster preparedness.

2 *Deepening Substantive Relations with Non-Diplomatic Allies*

(1) Relations with the United States: Comprehensive Development

Taiwan-US relations have been moving forward based on the "low key, surprise free" principle proposed by President Ma Ying-jeou more than four years ago. The two sides rebuilt mutual trust and engaged in frequent interaction, paving the way for substantive progress on important issues, including arms sales, Taiwan's inclusion in the US Visa Waiver Program (VWP), and US beef imports. In the last 30 years, Taiwan-US relations have never been better.

a. Visa Waiver Program
Taiwan has been included in the US VWP since November 1, 2012.

b. Pacific Islands Leadership Program (PILP)
Taiwan and the US agreed to co-organize the PILP through the signing of a Memorandum of Understanding on December 13, 2012. The program will provide intensive leadership courses to 125 mid- or high-level officials with potential and youth leaders who are senior staff of NGOs from Pacific island countries over the next five years.

c. New Agreement on Privileges, Exemptions and Immunities
The Agreement on Privileges, Exemptions and Immunities between Taiwan and the US was signed on February 4, 2013, in Washington, DC.

d. Official high-level interaction
Former Vice President Lien Chan, the representative for Taiwan's the ROC leader, conducted bilateral meetings with former Secretary of State Hillary Clinton, the US President's representative, at the 20th APEC Economic Leaders Meeting (AELM) on September 9, 2012 in Vladivostok, Russia.

e. Trade and Investment Framework Agreement (TIFA)
Our two countries publicly announced the resumption of consultations on the Trade and Investment Framework Agreement (TIFA) on February 1, 2013. Our Ministry of Economic Affairs initiated the talks with its US counterpart, which were led by Demetrios Marantis, the US Deputy Trade Representative, in Taipei on March 10, 2013.

f. Support of Taiwan by US Secretary of State

At his confirmation hearing, John Kerry, the newly appointed Secretary of State, indicated that he would continue to support US policy toward Taiwan and assist Taiwan in maintaining sufficient self-defense capabilities.

g. Support of Taiwan by US Congress

The US House of Representatives passed the Senate Concurrent Resolution No. 17 by voice vote on September 11, 2012, supporting Taiwan's participation in the International Civil Aviation Organization (ICAO).

h. Visits by senior US officials

The US continued to dispatch senior officials to Taiwan, including Demetrios Marantis, Deputy Trade Representative; Francisco J. Sánchez, Under Secretary of International Trade; Jose W. Fernandez, Assistant Secretary of State for Economic, Energy and Business Affairs; Joseph Krol, Associate Administrator of the National Nuclear Security Administration; Dawn L. McCall, Coordinator of the Bureau of International Information Programs; Mark Koumans, Deputy Assistant Secretary for International Affairs; and Atul Keshap, the US Senior Official for APEC.

i. Other visitors

The US continues to send delegations to Taiwan. Since the end of last August, 21 US delegations comprising 183 VIP guests have visited Taiwan.

(2) Relations with Europe/the EU: Stable Advancement

Since the Schengen visa waiver entered into effect in January 2011, MOFA has taken a multi-faceted, multi-layered and multi-channel approach to deepening its relations with Europe/the EU. As a result, the two sides have been able to engage in closer cooperation in the areas of trade and investment, culture, education, science and technology. The agenda of the 24th Annual Taiwan-EU Consultation last November showed the willingness of both sides to cooperate on various international issues and the broadening of Taiwan's relations with Europe/the EU.

a. Resolutions supporting Taiwan by the European Parliament

To promote Taiwan-EU economic and trade relations, last year on December 3 the International Trade Committee of the European Parliament established a Monitoring Group (MG) in charge of Taiwan-EU economic relations. This year on January 30, the Group initiated its first meeting, which is expected to pave the way for the signing of an EU-Taiwan Economic Cooperation Agreement (ECA).

b. Bilateral cooperation
Since last October, Taiwan has signed a total of six bilateral agreements with Germany, Poland, Ireland, Italy, Belgium, and the European Molecular Biology Conference (EMBO) / European Molecular Biology Organization (EMBO).

c. Visitors from Europe
From last August to this January, MOFA received 40 European delegations for a total of 157 visitors.

(3) Relations with Japan: Continued Deepening Partnership Despite Disagreements

a. Maintaining consultations with Japan based on the East China Sea Peace Initiative
Under the principle of "not relinquishing an inch of land", the government of the Republic of China (Taiwan) has reiterated its sovereignty over the Diaoyutai Islands and has proposed the East China Sea Peace Initiative. Under the initiative, the government has urged Japan to maintain regional peace, provide serious consideration to our bilateral relations, and hold pragmatic negotiations with us.

b. Heightening economic and trade cooperation based on our bilateral investment agreement
The signing of the Taiwan-Japan Bilateral Investment Agreement (BIA) last year on September 22 laid the foundation for expanded economic and trade cooperation. Since then, the two sides have signed a Mutual Recognition Agreement for certification on electrical and electronic products and an MOU on fostering industrial cooperation. We will continue to engage in consultations with Japan on a variety of items, such as tariffs, trade in services, and the flow of people and goods. By so doing, we can pave the road for the future signing of a bilateral economic cooperation agreement or a free trade agreement.

c. Visitors from Japan
Representative Hiroshi Nakai led a delegation to attend our National Day Celebration last year.

3 *Pragmatically Broadening Taiwan's Participation in International Organizations*

(1) World Trade Organization (WTO)

a. ROC Permanent Representative to the WTO Lai Shin-yuan has been serving as a coordinator for Recently Acceded Members (RAMs).

b. Taiwan has donated to the WTO Trade Facilitation Needs Assessment Trust and the Advisory Centre on WTO Law (ACWL). WTO Director-General Pascal Lamy welcomed Taiwan's contributions, stating that this demonstrated Taiwan's commitment to helping developing countries integrate into global economic and trade mechanisms.

c. Taiwan and the WTO jointly held a workshop on the Agreement on the Application of Sanitary and Phytosanitary Measures (SPS Agreement) for the Asia-Pacific region.

(2) World Health Organization (WHO)

Last year, Taiwan once again attended the World Health Assembly (WHA) as an observer and continued to seek to further expand its substantive participation in the WHO. In total, last year our officials and experts attended 12 WHO technical meetings in the name of Chinese Taipei.

(3) International Civil Aviation Organization (ICAO)

Luis Fernando Carrera Castro, Minister of Foreign Affairs of Guatemala and Council Member of the ICAO, signed a joint communiqué with me in December 2012, expressing support for the inclusion of Taiwan as an observer to the ICAO. In addition, the European Parliament passed last September its third resolution in support of Taiwan's bid in this regard. Likewise, PARLACEN (the Central American Parliament) also approved a resolution in December 2012 supporting Taiwan's bid to become an observer to the ICAO.

(4) Asia-Pacific Economic Cooperation (APEC)

a. MOFA will continue to promote economic and trade liberalization, and open up market access through the APEC platform so as to create conditions conducive to Taiwan's participation in the Trans-Pacific Partnership and the Regional Comprehensive Economic Partnership.

b. Indonesia will serve as host to the APEC forum in 2013. MOFA has already gained a full understanding of the main topics to be promoted this year as well as the arrangement for this year's ministerial and high-level meetings. We will seek to engage the other ministries and agencies of our government and coordinate their participation in these events. By taking part in APEC meetings and bilateral talks with other participants on joint cooperation, Taiwan can further strengthen its bonds with the other member economies.

(5) United Nations Framework Convention on Climate Change (UNFCCC)

Taiwan took part in the COP 18 of the UNFCCC at the end of 2012. In total, 18 countries spoke up for Taiwan or wrote to the UNFCCC Secretariat in support of our bid to join the organization.

(6) Other International Organizations and Activities

On September 23, 2012, Taiwan joined the South Pacific Regional Fisheries Management Organisation (SPRFMO).

4 *Engaging in Economic and Trade Diplomacy to Increase the Efficiency of Taiwan's International Economic and Trade Environment*

(1) Promoting the Signing of Bilateral Economic Cooperation Agreements (ECA)

Our talks with Singapore over the ASTEP and with New Zealand on an ECA have both entered the final stages of consultations. Meanwhile, Taiwan is working with think tanks from Indonesia, the Philippines, and India on the feasibility of signing a bilateral ECA with each of these countries in the future. Vietnam is also seriously considering to establish a research group with the aim to study such a possibility.

(2) Establishing a Task Force on ASEAN Affairs at the Taipei Economic and Trade Office in Jakarta, Indonesia: to Promote Taiwan's Participation in Regional Economic Integration.

(3) Boosting Taiwan's ICT Industry

Taiwan hosted the 2012 Workshop on ICT at the end of last year, with 13 mid- or high-level officials from 11 countries in West Asia, and Central and Eastern Europe taking part in the program. This event explored potential business opportunities and future joint ventures between the participating countries and Taiwanese enterprises.

5 *Assisting Young People to Participate in International Affairs, Thereby Further Spurring International Exchanges*

To broaden the international perspectives of Taiwan's youths and better leverage the country's soft power, MOFA continued to carry out a number of projects for youths, including Youth Ambassadors, High-School Student Diplomats, youth working holiday agreements, Taiwan Fellowships and Scholarships, overseas internship programs, Public Diplomacy Seminars for the general public and youths, National Development Courses, TaiwanICDF Overseas Volunteers and the Overseas Substitute Service, the International Youth Culture and Study Camp, and receiving delegations comprising youth scholars, as well as political and party leaders.

6 *Stepping Up Campaigns for Taiwan's Policies and Image*

MOFA arranged a number of interviews with the President by key international media outlets so as to introduce our major policies and positions. It also invited the media to cover overseas visits made by high-level officials from Taiwan. In addition, MOFA conducted media campaigns in order to elaborate on Taiwan's sovereignty claims over the Diaoyutai Islands and the South China Sea, as well as the East China Sea Peace Initiative and our attempts to join international organizations, such as the WHA, APEC, and the UNFCCC.

7 *Introducing Measures Aimed at Providing Greater Convenience for the Public and Foreigners Visiting Taiwan*

MOFA has worked hard to spur the inclusion of Taiwan into the visa-waiver and landing visa programs of other countries and territories, and to make it easier for foreigners to obtain better visa treatment when visiting Taiwan. Currently, 132 countries and territories grant ROC passport holders visa waivers or landing visas. Likewise, since September 2012, Taiwan has included Croatia and Brunei into its list of visa-free and landing visa treatment countries. In addition, to further improve passport services for the people of southern Taiwan, MOFA set up a Yunlin-Chiayi-Tainan office in Chiayi on December 28, 2012.

8 *Helping Restructure the Government and Boosting its Efficiency*

(1) Completing Relevant Supporting Regulations on Restructuring the Government and Boosting its Efficiency

In accordance with the Organization Act of Diplomatic Missions of the Republic of China (Taiwan), MOFA has completed relevant supporting regulations on the government's restructuring as well as relevant codes on streamlining authority and sharing resources when engaging in foreign affairs. To this end, MOFA intends to strengthen the coordination capabilities of its agencies, improve the overall performance of its overseas missions, and boost the Ministry's overall efficiency.

(2) Reviewing Human Resources and Adjusting Talent Development in Response to Government Restructuring so as to Further Boost Efficiency

In response to government restructuring, MOFA reviewed the human resources of its domestic and overseas news divisions in accordance with their workloads and made personnel adjustments accordingly. In total, MOFA added 7 overseas news divisions, and increased the staff of 15 missions and reduced that of 14 missions.

9 *Other Major Achievements*

(1) Promoting Chinese Culture and Setting up Taiwan Academies Abroad

MOFA actively assisted the Ministry of Culture in setting up Taiwan Academies and contact points worldwide. Thus far, Taiwan Academies have been established in 64 countries with 204 contact points, forming a global network for cooperation and partnership.

In addition, MOFA has actively introduced Chinese culture with Taiwan characteristics to the international community by assisting our art and cultural groups travel abroad to hold exhibitions and performances. It not only has helped the Taiwan Chefs Association introduce Taiwan's gourmet, but also has highlighted other aspects of Taiwan's multifaceted and fine culture. For example, MOFA helped the indigenous pop singer Suming with his band's tour to Fiji and two other South Pacific allies last November.

(2) Fostering Academic Diplomacy and Encouraging Scholars at Home and Abroad to Study Major Issues Related with our Foreign Policy

MOFA continues to encourage Taiwanese scholars to visit well-known universities, academic institutions, and think tanks for research and exchanges. In addition, this year the Taiwan Fellowship will offer grants to 75 outstanding scholars to come to Taiwan for research and study, thereby helping to consolidate our relations with academic communities worldwide.

(3) Carrying out Humanitarian Aid to Contribute to the International Community

a. MOFA purchased 200 tons of white rice in December 2012 for the Taiwan Root Medical Peace Corps and the Sun Lun Charitable Foundation, which was founded by Taiwanese businesspeople in Indonesia to help the poor in Indonesia.
b. At the end of December last year, MOFA helped the Eden Social Welfare Foundation donate 200 wheelchairs to physically and mentally challenged and orphans in Ho Chi Minh City in Vietnam, and another 100 wheelchairs to Nepal's anti-landmine organizations.

IV MOFA's Current Priorities and Outlook

1 *Creating a Friendly, Convenient, and Beneficial Environment to Expand Taiwan's International Participation*

With a virtuous cycle having been established in cross-strait relations thanks to viable diplomacy, MOFA will continue to strengthen the bonds between the Republic of China (Taiwan) and our diplomatic allies, and to deepen the mutually beneficial relations we enjoy with non-diplomatic allies. We will continue to seek meaningful and substantial participation in the UN system and functional inter-governmental organizations as we adhere to the principles of dignity, self-reliance, pragmatism, and versatility. This will allow for us to give back to the international community and to expand our room for development.

2 *Promoting the East China Sea Peace Initiative and Safeguarding Territorial Sovereignty*

Adhering to the principles of safeguarding sovereignty, shelving disputes, pursuing peace and reciprocity, and promoting joint exploration and development, we urge all parties concerned to resolve disputes in a peaceful manner based on the UN Charter and international law. We will promote the East China Sea Peace Initiative in two stages. In the first, we will focus on peaceful dialogue and mutually beneficial consultations; in the second, we will focus on the sharing and joint exploration of resources. Three concurrent sets of bilateral talks (between Taiwan and Japan, Taiwan and mainland China, and mainland China and Japan) will, we hope, gradually progress toward trilateral consultations on fisheries, mining, marine research and protecting the maritime environment, and maritime security and unconventional security. Our aim is to shelve disputes, create a win-win situation, and promote joint exploration and sharing of resources.

3 *Finding New Channels that Allow for Distribution, Marketing, and Talented Individuals to Bolster the Economy and Trade*

A task force has been established by MOFA to promote the economy and trade, and to assist MOFA staff in capacity-building related to economic and trade diplomacy. It aims to win procurement opportunities from foreign governments, to assist Taiwan's SMEs to expand into new emerging markets, to explore international business opportunities and marketing channels, and to promote the signing of FTA-level ECAs with major trading partners, so as to gain momentum for a dynamic that may be leveraged into our accession to the RCEP and TPP. Moreover, how well they have promoted the economy and trade will be a major factor in the annual performance assessments of missions abroad.

4 *Implementing Strategies to Assist Taiwan's Young People in International Exchanges so as to Foster People-to-people Diplomacy*

A task force has been established to promote young people's participation in international affairs. It will integrate various MOFA projects that help young people participate in international affairs. Employing a variety of marketing strategies while leveraging the power of the Internet and social networks, the task force will effectively help Taiwan's young people engage the world and young people from around the world better understand Taiwan. This will, in turn, promote Taiwan's soft power.

5 *Improving Policy Briefings and Exerting Soft Power through Cultural Exchanges*

MOFA will post its publications on its website to allow for easier global access; cooperate with major international TV channels to expand the global penetration of our message; improve policy briefings and explain our position concerning sovereignty over the Diaoyutai Islands and the South China Sea as well as the East China Sea Peace Initiative; and declare our readiness to participate in international organizations and regional economic integration. These efforts will craft a positive image of Taiwan that resonates around the world. MOFA will marshal its resources to improve Taiwan's image through publications, public diplomacy, and artists and arts groups. We will continue to monitor closely the coverage of Taiwan in the international media, and provide clarifications and rebuttals to inappropriate or incorrect reports in a timely fashion.

6 *Reinforcing Customer-Oriented Service and Enhancing Citizen Convenience in Living and Traveling*

As per government policy, MOFA will continue to review the requirements and measures that non-citizens must follow in applying for an ROC visa. We will continue in our effort to go paperless by introducing on-line applications for document authentication. This will improve service and build credibility. We will continue to improve MOFA emergency contact mechanisms the better to provide emergency assistance to ROC citizens traveling abroad, and will promote this service in the media so as to better ensure ROC citizens' safety. In addition, we will introduce convenient mobile consular services for overseas compatriots.

V Conclusion

The ROC's foreign policy aims to ensure sovereignty and security as well as to create an international environment supportive of national development. Due to Taiwan's unique international situation, we must take a pragmatic approach to diplomacy. As we move forward, we will adhere to the viable diplomacy policy while safeguarding sovereignty, promoting soft power; creating a friendly, convenient, and beneficial international environment for our country; giving back to the international community; improving service; and increasing administrative efficiency. We will further cooperate with such government agencies as the Ministry of Economic Affairs to promote economic and trade diplomacy, so as to lay a solid foundation for consolidating our sovereignty and our people's well-being.

Thank you for your time and attention.

Foreign Policy Report, 8th Congress of the Legislative Yuan, 4th Session (September 25, 2013)

On September 25, 2013, the Minister of Foreign Affairs, Mr. David Y. L. Lin was invited by the Foreign and National Defense Committee of the Legislative Yuan to report on the foreign policy of the Republic of China. The report is as follows:[2]

I Foreword

It is an honor for me to have been invited today to come and give a briefing to the Foreign and National Defense Committee on the diplomatic work that the Ministry of Foreign Affairs (MOFA) has performed recently. On behalf of MOFA, I would like to extend my appreciation to President Wang Jin-pyng, Vice President Hung Hsiu-chu, and all other members of the Legislative Yuan over the concern shown for foreign affairs and their active participation in parliamentary diplomacy.

The foreign policy of the Republic of China is aimed at safeguarding sovereignty and national security, and creating an international environment conducive to the nation's sustainable development. For this purpose, and to seek the balanced development of cross-strait and international relations, the government has promoted the policies of "cross-strait reconciliation" and "viable diplomacy." We have also integrated our strengths in a flexible and pragmatic manner in an effort to bolster substantive relations with countries

2 MOFA, Foreign Policy Report, 8th Congress of the Legislative Yuan, 4th Session (September 25, 2013), *available at* http://www.mofa.gov.tw/en/News_Content3.aspx?n=4BAF9BD5400A05D9&s=AD2C0693F4D93654.

around the world. One of the concrete results of these policies is that the number of countries and territories that grant ROC passport holders visa-waiver or landing-visa treatment has grown from 54 to 133 over the past five years, with the current figure accounting for 98 percent of countries ROC citizens visit most frequently. This has afforded greater convenience and respect for our citizens traveling abroad. Furthermore, 17 long years of negotiations with Japan culminated in the signing of the Taiwan-Japan Fisheries Agreement in April this year. In July, a Taiwan-New Zealand economic cooperation agreement (ANZTEC) was signed, laying the groundwork for the ROC's participation in regional economic integration. We have also made considerable progress in our bid to participate in the International Civil Aviation Organization (ICAO). All these achievements have come about as a result of concerted efforts by both the governing and opposition parties, and also bear testimony to the fact that our viable diplomacy policy has created more space on the international stage for the ROC.

Today, I will be discussing the current international climate, the viable diplomacy policy and its success, as well as future prospects for and the direction of our foreign diplomacy. Your comments and suggestions will be very much appreciated.

II The Current International Landscape

1 *The Emergence of a New Type of "Great Power" Relations Between the US and Mainland China*

The United States has reiterated several times its pledge to push forward with its "rebalancing toward Asia" policy, while mainland China is seeking to build a new type of "great power" relations with the US. Despite differences on several issues, both sides want to improve their relations and strengthen cooperation. During the fifth US-China Strategic and Economic Dialogue this past July, the two parties expressed their respective positions, but little was achieved in terms of a consensus. At a meeting in August, the US Secretary of Defense and mainland China's Minister of National Defense emphasized a new type of military cooperation in humanitarian assistance and anti-terrorism action. Overall, the United States and mainland China have maintained their strategic cooperative competition. However, the two sides need for there to be a peaceful external environment if they are to avoid their economic growth being affected.

MOFA will continue to closely monitor the development of these new great power relations and model of cooperation between the United States and mainland China. We are committed to seeking a strategic balance in hope of achieving a triple-win scenario for the United States, mainland China, and Taiwan.

2 *East Asian Security a Cause for Continued Concern*

Although tensions in the Korean Peninsula have eased, North Korea's nuclear threat continues to elicit a high degree of concern from countries around the world. Growing tension in the East China Sea has made the area another flashpoint in the Asia Pacific region. Since Japan announced on September 11, 2012, that it had nationalized the Diaoyutai Islands, mainland Chinese government vessels have entered waters surrounding the islands (which Japan claims to be part of its "territorial waters") at least 65 times, ratcheting up tensions. Disputes in the South China Sea have continued, as all parties concerned have increased their naval deployments and maritime law enforcement. Standoffs are reported frequently and military drills are held regularly. Should any of the parties concerned engage in zero-sum competition, it could cause a security dilemma.

The government is closely monitoring related developments and has continued to promote the East China Sea Peace Initiative, urging all parties concerned to remain calm and exercise restraint so that disputes can be peacefully resolved, and regional stability and prosperity can be jointly pursued.

3 *Continuing Integration of the Regional Economy*

Globalization and regional integration have been accompanied by the rising trend of regional free trade. Countries around the world are actively promoting regional economic integration and negotiating free trade agreements (FTAs). Integration processes have accelerated, including the Transatlantic Trade and Investment Partnership (TTIP) between the United States and the European Union, the Trans-Pacific Partnership (TPP), and the Regional Comprehensive Economic Partnership (RCEP).

Faced with the trend of regional economic integration, the ROC, in addition to signing follow-up pacts to the Cross-Straits Economic Cooperation Framework Agreement (ECFA), concluded an economic cooperation agreement (ECA) with New Zealand this July. We have also continued to negotiate ECAs with Singapore and other trade partners in order to create favorable conditions for our accession to such regional economic blocs as the TPP and the RCEP.

4 *Turmoil in the Middle East*

Tension in the Middle East, with continuing turmoil in Syria and Egypt, has affected global energy markets and strategic security. In particular, the Syrian civil war, which began two and a half years ago and has seen chemical weapons used, has caused mass civilian casualties. At the G20 summit in September, the leaders of the United States, France, and nine other nations issued a joint statement condemning the Syrian action. On September 16, UN Secretary General Ban Ki-moon reported investigation findings to the Security Council confirming that sarin gas had been used in the Syrian civil war. The ROC government stands with civilized nations that uphold the universal values of humanitarianism, human rights, and democracy.

The ROC has provided humanitarian assistance to Syrian refugees and will continue to monitor developments closely, assess their impact on the ROC, and take timely, necessary countermeasures.

5 *Growing Importance of Non-Conventional Security Issues*

Globalization has led to growing interdependence among countries. At the current stage, cross-border and non-conventional security issues are posing increasingly big challenges now that diverse powers in the international arena have become mutually dependent. Issues such as the European debt crisis, climate change, terrorism, cybersecurity, environmental protection, and energy have taken on greater significance, and developments in these areas could affect the development or very existence of countries worldwide.

MOFA will strengthen research and analysis on the aforementioned non-conventional security issues, and integrate resources with the relevant agencies so as to be able to respond to the newly emerging challenges.

III The Viable Diplomacy Policy and Related Accomplishments

The viable diplomacy policy, which the government began implementing in 2008, has not only created a positive environment for the development of cross-strait relations, but also laid a solid foundation for safeguarding sovereignty, expanding international space, and maintaining sustainable national development. In the past five years, we have maintained steadfast friendships with our diplomatic allies, enhanced our relations with non-diplomatic partners, and expanded our international space, signaling that viable diplomacy is, in fact, the right way to go.

1 *Consolidating Relations with Diplomatic Allies*

(1) Enhancing Mutual Visits by High-Ranking Officials and Deepening Friendships

i. President Ma Ying-jeou and the First Lady led a congratulatory delegation to the Holy See in March this year to attend the inauguration of Pope Francis, marking the first time that an ROC president had attended the installation of a new pontiff in the 71 years of our diplomatic relations. In August, President Ma headed another delegation to Paraguay for the inauguration of President Horacio Cartes, as well as to four other diplomatic allies—Haiti, Saint Christopher and Nevis, Saint Lucia, and Saint Vincent and the Grenadines. This head-of-state diplomacy was a resounding success.

ii. In July, I led a delegation to Solomon Islands to participate in the 35th Independence Day celebrations of this South Pacific ally.

iii. Since March of this year, a number of heads of state and other high-level officials of our diplomatic allies have led delegations to Taiwan. They include Prime Minister (and concurrently Minister of Natural Resources) of Tuvalu Willy Telavi; Minister for External Affairs, International Trade and Civil Aviation Alva Baptiste of Saint Lucia; President Christopher J. Loeak and the First Lady of the Marshall Islands; President Leonel Vásquez Búcaro of the Central American Parliament; Speaker Sabino Anastacio of Palau's House of Delegates; President Luis Federico Franco Gómez and the First Lady of Paraguay; King Mswati III of Swaziland; President Anote Tong and the First Lady of Kiribati; President Otto Pérez Molina and the First Lady of Guatemala; Governor-General Frank Kabui and the First Lady of Solomon Islands; and Minister of Foreign Affairs Samuel Santos López of Nicaragua. These visits have deepened mutual understanding and boosted bilateral relations.

(2) Institutionalizing Foreign Aid and Enhancing Cooperation in Various Fields

i. We are committed to carrying out our foreign aid policy in accordance with three principles—seeking proper goals, acting lawfully, and exercising effective administration—and assisting our diplomatic allies develop and improve their living conditions. As of August 2013, the ROC had dispatched 29 technical, medical, or other service missions—comprising a total of 161 experts, technicians, and projects managers—to 29 countries for 92 joint projects. These have benefited the people and won the affirmation and gratitude of our allies.

ii. A sound legal basis for our foreign aid missions and a professional, legal, and transparent foreign aid system have been established through the implementation of six related regulations, including the Regulations Governing the Planning, Appraisal, Implementation, Supervision and Performance Evaluation of International Cooperation and Development Affairs. In addition, MOFA compiles Taiwan's foreign aid statistics in its Official Development Assistance (ODA) database, and reports the statistics to the Organisation for Economic Co-operation and Development (OECD). Our efforts have won international approval.

iii. In addition to providing aid to diplomatic allies in such areas as agriculture, animal husbandry, horticulture, and vocational training, we will also restructure our foreign aid program by leveraging our industrial advantages in information and communications technology, medicine and healthcare, and science and technology. For example, we have promoted a satellite imaging and geographical information systems (GIS) technological cooperation program in Nicaragua, a clean energy project in six Pacific Island allies, as well as Papua New Guinea, and a program to train medical professionals in our diplomatic allies. All of these ventures have been warmly welcomed.

2 *Enhancing Substantive Relations with Non-Diplomatic Allies*

(1) Relations with the United States

Our government has promoted relations with the US in accordance with the "low key, surprise free" principle. The two sides have engaged in frequent interactions, rebuilding mutual trust and making considerable progress in security, economic, and trade cooperation.

i. Following the informal Obama-Xi summit in Sunnylands, California, on June 7 and 8 of this year, White House Deputy National Security Advisor Ben Rhodes said in a press interview that President Barack Obama had explicitly expressed his position on the Taiwan issue to mainland Chinese leader Xi Jinping. The US is clearly committed to Taiwan under the Taiwan Relations Act, which includes an obligation to provide Taiwan with defensive weapons. Moreover, the US strongly supports the improvements in cross-strait relations made over the past few years, which it hopes will continue in a manner acceptable to both sides.
ii. On August 1, 2013, the US House Committee on Foreign Affairs passed the Taiwan Policy Act of 2013, urging the US administration to enhance Taiwan-US relations by honoring its pledge to sell arms to Taiwan, loosening its rules on Taiwan-US engagement, negotiating a free trade agreement, and supporting Taiwan's participation in international organizations.
iii. During stopovers in New York and Los Angeles on August 11 and 19, respectively, President Ma spoke to US Deputy Secretary of State William Burns and Senate Foreign Relations Committee Chairman Robert Menendez (D-NJ) on the phone. He met with New York City Mayor Michael Bloomberg and Los Angeles City Mayor Eric Garcetti. This serves to show the solid foundation of mutual trust at the highest levels and close friendship between the two countries.

iv The Pacific Islands Leadership Partnership (PILP), jointly organized by Taiwan and the United States, aims to provide intensive training to 120 promising young leaders and mid- or high-level officials from Pacific Islands nations over a five-year period. This program highlights the close friendship between Taiwan and the US, and will significantly deepen our bilateral partnership.

v. Between March and August of this year, Taiwan received 89 US delegations comprising 715 guests. These included a delegation led by Deputy Trade Representative Demetrios Marantis to a meeting on the Taiwan-US Trade and Investment Framework Agreement (TIFA). Four senators and 16 representatives visited Taiwan, including Senate Foreign Relations Committee Chairman Robert Menendez; Chairman of the House Foreign Affairs Subcommittee on Asia and the Pacific Steve Chabot (R-OH); Representatives Gregg Harper (R-MS) and Kerry Bentivolio (R-MI); and Judy Chu (D-CA), Chair of the Congressional Asian Pacific American Caucus, and Vice Chair Madeleine Bordallo, (D-GU). Among the US state officials to visit Taiwan were Missouri Governor Jay Nixon, Idaho Governor C.L. "Butch" Otter, and Hawaii Governor Neil Abercrombie. The ROC and the US clearly share a close relationship.

(2) Relations with the European Union

The ROC has taken a multi-faceted, multi-layered, and multi-channel approach to deepening its relations with the European Union and its member countries. Closer cooperation in the areas of economy, trade, culture, education, science, and technology indicates a strengthening of relations between the ROC and the EU.

i. Open support from the European Parliament (EP) and countries in Europe: In March, the EP passed a report on EU-mainland China relations recognizing the positive developments in cross-strait relations, commending the close cross-strait economic and trade relations, supporting Taiwan's meaningful participation in international organizations, and calling for support for the East China Sea Peace Initiative.

ii. Bilateral cooperation and mutual visits:

   a. We signed a working holiday agreement with Belgium in March, a memorandum of cooperation on bilateral research and development, and innovation with the Czech Republic in June, and two memorandums of understanding with the United Kingdom, one on enhancing railway efficiency, and one on information exchange and cooperation.

b. As of August, MOFA had received 38 European delegations for a total of 189 visitors this year, including the EP's European Conservatives and Reformists Group Vice Chairman Ryszard Legutko.

(3) Relations with Japan

i. In an attempt to gain the right to discourse on the Diaoyutai Islands issue, the ROC government has promoted the East China Sea Peace Initiative. On August 5, we held the East China Sea Peace Forum in Taipei, which was well received both at home and abroad. On April 10 this year, the Taiwan-Japan Fisheries Agreement was signed as a direct result of the peace initiative. Indeed, after 17 years of bilateral negotiations, the two countries were finally able to make appropriate arrangements to resolve long-term fishery issues stemming from the overlapping of economic zones. The ROC reached the agreement with Japan under the principle of reciprocity, while upholding its sovereignty and position on related waters. This gained approval both at home and abroad, and received widespread coverage by international media. We made absolutely no concessions on the sovereignty issue, yet were able to make significant progress in the fishing rights issue. The Fisheries Agreement is applicable to a maritime zone of approximately 74,000 square kilometers, or twice the size of Taiwan. It expands our fishing area by approximately 1,400 square nautical miles (or 4,530 square kilometers). Furthermore, the ROC insisted on the incorporation of a "no-prejudice clause" in the pact to safeguard its sovereignty over the Diaoyutai Islands, a position it has firmly and consistently maintained.

ii. As of August, MOFA had received 11 Japanese delegations for a total of 128 visitors this year, including Akiko Santo, former Vice President of Japan's House of Councilors.

(4) Relations with New Zealand, Australia, India, and other Asia-Pacific Nations

i. On July 10, Taiwan signed an ECA with New Zealand. This high-standard, high-quality FTA fully demonstrates the ROC's determination to liberalize its economy and trade, and proclaims to the international community that the ROC is ready and willing to sign FTAs with its other trade partners. In May, we completed substantive talks with Singapore on an economic partnership agreement, for which we are now undertaking a legal scrubbing. Feasibility studies on FTAs with other trade partners such as India and Indonesia are also underway.

ii. In April, Taiwan and the Philippines signed an agreement on mutual legal assistance in criminal matters. On June 14, the first preparatory meeting on bilateral fisheries cooperation was held, and a consensus was reached to avoid the use of armed force and violence, and to establish mechanisms for law enforcement cooperation, emergency notification, and prompt release [of fishing vessels and fishermen]. Earlier in March, the Taiwan External Trade Development Council (TAITRA) signed a Carnet Protocol with the Federation of Indian Chambers of Commerce and Industry to facilitate the temporary duty-free admission of goods between Taiwan and India.

iii. MOFA received 14 delegations from Australia, New Zealand, India, and other Asia-Pacific countries in the first eight months of this year.

3 *Pragmatic Participation in International Organizations*

(1) World Trade Organization (WTO)

i. In 2012, the ROC proposed a trade in services agreement (TISA) with WTO members, such as the United States, Australia, and the EU. Formal talks began this June. TISA could be considered a multilateral FTA on trade in services with our major trade partners. This will help create more room for the ROC's foreign economic and trade development, as well as facilitate its integration into the regional economy.

ii. We are seeking to hold a national workshop on the WTO Agreement on Rules of Origin, which would pave the way for our participation in the activities of multilateral trade systems.

(2) Asia-Pacific Economic Cooperation (APEC)

i. Between March and August 2013, ministers and other senior officials from Taiwan attended five professional ministerial-level meetings at APEC, including the Trade Ministers' Meeting, as well as two Senior Officials' Meetings. Taiwan also held 13 APEC seminars during that period.

ii. In October, former Vice President Vincent Siew will lead a delegation to the Economic Leaders' Meeting (AELM) in Indonesia on behalf of the president. He will join with other economic leaders to discuss future prospects for the fair and sustainable growth of the Asia-Pacific region, as well as ways to strengthen APEC's role in multilateral trade systems.

(3) World Health Organization (WHO)

i. This year marked the fifth time that Taiwan was invited to attend the World Health Assembly (WHA). Minister of Health Chiu Wen-ta led a delegation to the event and shared the ROC's success in healthcare cooperation and development in his address. The ROC delegation held 21 bilateral talks on the sidelines, including with the US, Japan, and the EU.

ii. In April, the US Department of State submitted a report to the US Congress on helping Taiwan gain WHO participation, explicitly urging the WHO to adopt the WHA model and accept Taiwan. The ROC will build on this foundation to seek greater participation in other WHO meetings, activities, and mechanisms.

(4) International Civil Aviation Organization (ICAO)

i. The US administration and Congress have continued to support Taiwan's participation in international organizations. On July 12, President Obama signed into law House Resolution 1151 endorsing Taiwan's participation in ICAO. In September, 205 members of the EP sent a joint letter to the ICAO secretary general expressing support for Taiwan's bid. Earlier in June, UK Representative to the ROC Chris Wood said during an interview that the UK would be willing to support Taiwan's pragmatic participation in ICAO.

ii. At the invitation of the President of the ICAO Council, the Director-General of the Civil Aeronautics Administration (CAA) Shen Chi participated as a guest in the 38th ICAO Assembly, marking the first time that Taiwan has been invited to attend a meeting of a UN specialized agency since receiving the WHA invitation five years ago.

iii. A combination of three factors—support from the US, EU members, and other major countries and diplomatic allies; easing of cross-strait relations; and concerted effort by both the governing and opposition parties—have allowed us to move forward with our ICAO bid and achieve our preliminary objective of professional, pragmatic, dignified, and meaningful participation. Our government will put even more effort into finding appropriate avenues for participation in technical and regional ICAO meetings in order to enhance our civil aviation management capacity, and ensure the aviation rights and security of our citizens and other travelers.

(5) United Nations Framework Convention on Climate Change (UNFCCC) and other International Environmental Conventions

i. A number of countries and international organizations have recently passed resolutions supporting Taiwan's meaningful participation in the UNFCCC. These include the Central American Parliament, 18 US state legislatures, and the National Congress or Assembly of Palau, Paraguay, Nicaragua, and Haiti, as well as the 43rd General Assembly of the Asian-Pacific Parliamentarians' Union.

ii. As regards participation in international environmental conventions and organizations, the Environmental Protection Administration organized a delegation to the ordinary and extraordinary meetings of the conferences of the parties to the Basel, Rotterdam, and Stockholm conventions held in Geneva, Switzerland, in April.

(6) Other International Organizations and Activities

i. Taiwan has been elected to serve as vice chair of the Early Transition Countries Fund Assembly of the European Bank for Reconstruction and Development (EBRD) this year. We will continue to participate in the EBRD's cooperation projects, which will spur Taiwan's economic development and help its enterprises gain overseas business opportunities.

ii. In June, Taiwan and Saudi Arabia signed a memorandum of understanding on cooperation to combat money laundering under the framework of the Asia/Pacific Group on Money Laundering.

4 *Comprehensive Promotion of Diplomatic Work*

Given its special circumstances and many challenges in the global community, the ROC must employ a more viable, pragmatic, and flexible approach to using available resources to promote foreign diplomacy, as follows:

(1) Economic and trade diplomacy: MOFA's overseas offices are required to help Taiwanese companies explore new business opportunities. Their performance in this area will be taken into consideration in annual evaluations by MOFA (accounting for 25 percent of the total score). TAITRA will continue to be commissioned to hold business fairs in our diplomatic allies and other friendly nations to help create business opportunities for our small and medium enterprises, boost the ROC's national image, and raise the visibility of Made-in-Taiwan products. We will also send investment and trade delegations to our diplomatic partners and emerging economies to seek business opportunities.

(2) Public diplomacy: MOFA has achieved considerable success in its efforts to promote e-diplomacy. For example, its official website was ranked fifth in the 2013 government digital service survey by Business Next magazine. In order to foster global understanding and support, MOFA set up a single-window Foreign Press Liaison to provide timely information on the government's position on and response to important international issues. On April 15, MOFA arranged for the foreign press corps to interview President Ma. It also arranged a teleconference with Stanford University, and presidential interviews with the UK's Financial Times, Japan's Kyodo News, and the US's Bloomberg News.

The goal was to help the international community better understand ROC government policies and accomplishments.

(3) Cultural and academic diplomacy: MOFA has been active in introducing Chinese culture with Taiwan characteristics to the international community by assisting the Ministry of Culture (MOC) in setting up Taiwan Academies and contact points worldwide. Thus far, Taiwan Academies have opened in New York, Los Angeles, and Houston, while contact points have been set up in 64 countries. A global network for cooperation and partnership is being established this year in coordination with the MOC's Taiwan Academy cultural plan. Meanwhile, MOFA continues to offer Taiwan Scholarships and Taiwan Fellowships, with a total of 81 foreign scholars arriving in 2012 to engage in research in Taiwan. We plan to select 90 scholars to participate in next year's programs to maximize the effectiveness of our soft power diplomacy.

(4) Youth diplomacy: To broaden the international perspectives of Taiwan's youths, MOFA established a task force to promote young people's participation in international affairs and integrate the various international youth participation programs. In order to integrate the youth affairs handled by a variety of departments, in June MOFA set up a website called Taiwan's Youth Engage the World, which makes efficient use of the Internet and social networks to help Taiwan's youth engage the world and enable young people elsewhere to better understand Taiwan. Furthermore, MOFA has carried out a number of projects to develop young diplomats, including the International Youth Ambassador Exchange Program, High-School Student Diplomats, Public Diplomacy Seminars (for youths), Training Course on International Affairs for Future Talents in Taiwan's NGOs, and the 100-hour Camp for Young NGO Leaders.

5 *More Efficient Public Services*

To provide the public with a better service, MOFA has continued to improve and streamline its consular work and emergency disaster relief missions, as follows:

(1) In consular affairs, we have enhanced security with a passport design that prevents counterfeiting. We have also simplified regulations for visa applications by foreign nationals, sought better visa treatment for our citizens from a greater number of countries, and improved our document authentication service.

(2) Efforts have been made to provide timely and appropriate assistance to ROC overseas compatriots and citizens traveling abroad in the event of emergencies. For example, when Egypt violently suppressed protestors and descended into political turmoil, and when the international airport in Kenya's

capital of Nairobi was ravaged by fire, MOFA immediately set up an emergency bulletin board to allow citizens to leave messages that they were safe and to exchange information. Our overseas offices also provide necessary assistance to effectively ensure the safety of our citizens traveling abroad.

IV Future Outlook and Endeavors

With the rapidly changing international political and economic landscapes have come both challenges and opportunities. MOFA will continue to promote the viable diplomatic policy and, under the principles of flexibility and pragmatism, closely monitor global developments and create a friendly international environment.

1 *Moving Ahead with Viable Diplomacy and Cross-Strait Reconciliation to Create a Win-Win Scenario*

(1) The government's promotion of cross-strait reconciliation and the viable diplomacy policy has led to a significant improvement in cross-strait relations, and contributed to regional stability and development. We maintain solid relations with 23 diplomatic allies and have strengthened cooperation with the United States, Japan, the European Union, and other non-diplomatic partners in the areas of security, economy, trade, tourism, technology, culture, aviation, agriculture, and fisheries. This virtuous cycle is beneficial for expanding our international space.

(2) By strengthening dialogue and communication with other APEC members via the APEC platform, we have built up momentum for our accession to the TPP. We hope to build on our substantive relations with members of the Association for Southeast Asian Nations (ASEAN), as well as the ECFA we have signed with mainland China, so as to gradually become aligned with the RCEP.

2 *Integrating Soft and Hard Power to Create a New Dynamic for Diplomacy*

(1) The ROC is blessed with a wealth of soft power, such as democratic ideals, human rights, and culture, which, when combined with its economic and trade power, add up to smart power. This provides the most reliable basis for promoting diplomatic work.

(2) In order to strengthen and utilize the nation's hard power, MOFA and its overseas representative offices will continue to engage in economic and trade diplomacy to help revitalize the nation's economy and increase its competitiveness. Our main objectives are to promote the signing of ECAs with our main trading partners and pursue all available channels to participate in

the TPP, RCEP, and other regional economic integration efforts. This will lay a solid foundation for sustainable economic development. Our signing an ECA with New Zealand marks a good beginning to our economic and trade deployment in the Asia-Pacific region. We will build on this foundation to strengthen our economic and trade cooperation with other countries.

(3) In projecting soft power, MOFA will integrate the strengths of the public and private sectors in the areas of medicine, technology, education, and culture, so as to enable Taiwan to better connect and cooperate with the international community, as well as to upgrade our foreign aid and international humanitarian relief efforts. This will allow the world to better see and understand Taiwan. Indeed, integrating our soft and hard power will enhance the ROC's image and status in the international community.

V Conclusion

The ROC's foreign diplomacy aims to ensure sovereignty and security, as well as to create an international environment conducive to our national development. MOFA will adhere to the viable diplomacy policy while safeguarding sovereignty, integrating all types of power in a flexible and pragmatic way, strengthening substantive relations with other countries, creating a friendly and beneficial international environment for our country, and giving back to the global community.

We hope that both the governing and opposition parties will work together and, even more so, that legislators will remain committed to our diplomatic work, using our smart power to transform Taiwan into a facilitator of peace, a provider of humanitarian aid, a promoter of cultural exchange, a creator of new technologies and business opportunities, and a standard-bearer of Chinese culture. This will enhance our national image, and international status and influence, while enabling us to contribute substantively to the stability and prosperity of the Asia-Pacific region.

Thank you, and your advice and suggestions are much appreciated.

President Ma Ying-jeou's National Day Address

On October 10, 2013, President Ma delivered the National Day Address, titled "Stay the Course and Move Forward in Unity to Create a New Era for the Nation." The Address is as follows:[3]

3 Office of the President, President Ma Ying-jeou's National Day Address, Oct. 10, 2013, http://english.president.gov.tw/Default.aspx?tabid=491&itemid=30933&rmid=2355.

Legislative Yuan President Wang Jin-Pyng, President Tommy E. Remengesau, Jr. of the Republic of Palau; Prime Minister and Mrs. Gordon Darcy Lilo of Solomon Islands, Vice President Aja Dr. Isatou Njie-Saidy of the Republic of The Gambia; Delegations from abroad; Members of the diplomatic corps; Vice President Wu; Presidents of the Five Yuan of the ROC; Senior Advisors and National Policy Advisors; Heads of government agencies; Overseas compatriots; My fellow citizens: Good morning to you all!

Today is the 102nd National Day of our beloved Republic of China. On this day we happily celebrate the birthday of our nation and of course want to give thanks for the efforts of our predecessors. But more importantly, we want to stride toward the future. Our future will be of our own choosing. We need to ask ourselves a few questions: On the path of democratization, do we want to choose a civil society characterized by reason and tolerance? Or do we choose political infighting stemming from suspicion and confrontation? In cross-strait relations, do we want to choose mutually beneficial cross-strait rapprochement? Or do we choose a cross-strait standoff of tension and conflict? In the global economy, do we wish to be a bold nation that faces the challenges of free trade head on? Or do we choose to be a feeble people who hide beneath the umbrella of protectionism? These issues are all key to national development. These are crucial choices that the entire public must face together.

National Strategy: Remake the Nation, Identify our Niche, find a Viable Way Forward

In the face of these issues and choices, it is my duty as president to come up with a forward-looking and pragmatic national strategy. Domestically, this strategy must allow our country to remold its economy, politics, and society from the inside out. Externally, it must enable Taiwan to identify its niche amidst intense global economic competition, and to find a viable way forward within a complex international political environment. In short, this national strategy must allow our country to remold itself, find its proper place, and take a viable path forward.

Normalization of Peace; Institutionalization of Exchanges

In the past, Taiwan chose confrontation and isolationism, allowing the Taiwan Strait to rank alongside the Korean Peninsula as one of the two main East Asian flash points. Today, our strategy is to uphold the values of freedom and democracy while promoting rapprochement and cooperation with mainland China. After these five years of effort, the Taiwan Strait today has become one of the most peaceful waterways and most prosperous passageways in Asia.

My fellow citizens: The people of both sides of the Taiwan Strait are all Chinese by ethnicity. Cross-strait relations are not international relations. In the past five years or so, based on the 1992 Consensus whereby each side acknowledges the existence of "one China" but maintains its own interpretation of what that means, the two sides of the Strait have signed 19 agreements that have brought about direct sea and air transport links, visits to Taiwan by tourists from mainland China, mutual judicial assistance, economic cooperation, and other such breakthroughs. We've seen a lot of progress. For example, three years ago the two sides signed the Cross-Straits Economic Cooperation Framework Agreement (ECFA). This past June we further signed the Cross-Strait Trade in Services Agreement. And just four days ago, former Vice President Vincent C. Siew, who acted as my representative at the APEC summit this year in Indonesia, held talks while there with Mr. Xi Jinping, the leader of mainland China. In the meantime Wang Yu-Chi, the minister of our Mainland Affairs Council, also met during APEC with Zhang Zhijun, the minister of the mainland's Taiwan Affairs Office. It's noteworthy that the two ministers greeted each other by their official titles. The two sides have achieved these results by pursuing a basic policy of "facing reality, not denying each other's authority to govern, and together creating win-win solutions." The two sides should utilize frequent contacts and interaction to boost political trust, and should continue expanding and deepening exchanges in a variety of fields to further the people's welfare, while promoting the establishment of representative offices in each other's territory to better serve their people. By this approach we can take cross-strait cooperation to a new level, and revitalize Chinese society.

Global Access for our Citizens; Streamlined and Reformed National Defense

My fellow citizens, our strategy for peace has won unanimous international affirmation and secured substantive benefit and dignity for Taiwan. The ROC's relations with its diplomatic partners remain stable, while our relations with the US, Japan, ASEAN, New Zealand, Australia, the European Union, and other countries with which we currently do not have diplomatic relations, are continually improving. Also, the number of countries and areas from which our nation has obtained visa-waiver or landing-visa treatment has recently increased by one, to 134. This means that, for 98% of the jurisdictions to which the people of Taiwan travel most often, a visa is no longer needed.

Our policy of "viable diplomacy" has yielded huge rewards this year, with concrete accomplishments coming almost monthly. In February, the ROC and the US signed an "Agreement on Privileges, Exemptions and Immunities," which extends protections to each side's diplomats. In March, we resumed talks with the US under the Trade and Investment Framework Agreement after a hiatus of six years, and there has been considerable progress already. In April, we signed a fisheries agreement with Japan, resolving fishery disputes that had vexed our two nations for over 40 years. And we did this while attaining the goal of "achieving great progress on fishing rights without making any concessions on sovereignty." In May, we took part in the World Health Assembly for the fifth time, which generated many opportunities for bilateral meetings and dramatically boosted our international visibility. In July, our country signed an economic cooperation agreement with New Zealand. This is very significant because it is our first free-trade agreement with a non-diplomatic partner country. In August, we settled the dispute with the Philippines over the armed attack on our fishing vessel, the Guang Da Xing No. 28, securing justice for and upholding the rights and interests of our country's fishermen. In September, we participated as a special guest at the International Civil Aviation Organization Assembly for the first time in 42 years. And just this month we sent former Vice President Siew to take part in the APEC summit as the leader's representative. While there, he held bilateral talks with many leaders and leaders' representatives from around the Asia-Pacific region, including the US, mainland China, and Japan, further creating the necessary preconditions for us to participate in regional economic integration through, for example, membership in the Trans-Pacific Partnership. So, the Republic of China now is not only a peacemaker, but also a promoter of international cooperation.

Fellow countrymen, a peace strategy cannot ignore risks. When we have a peaceful environment, we are better able to vigorously pursue national defense reforms. A robust national defense capability is the foundation underpinning our "resolute defense, effective deterrence" strategy. The armed forces deserve affirmation and respect for the contributions and sacrifices they have made for Taiwan's security over the last six decades and more. Over the past few years, we have continued to purchase weapons of a defensive nature. We have begun putting a volunteer military service system in place, and have strengthened our technological capacity for warfare in order to further safeguard Taiwan's security.

After the tragic incident with army corporal Hong Zhongqiu in July, we promptly amended the law so that court martial cases are transferred to civilian courts, and began a comprehensive reform of military administration. While we must protect the human rights of soldiers and maintain discipline within the military, we must also improve the combat readiness of our military forces. We intend to ensure that our children can serve in the military with peace of mind, and that they can learn professional skills while they are there. And, more importantly, we want to boost morale among our troops and restore their sense of honor, so that they become respected by the public. These are my pledges to the nation.

Redefining Taiwan's Economy: A Free Economic Island and Key Value Chain

Fellow countrymen, Taiwan's economy is facing the twin challenges of globalization and regional integration. We must redefine ourselves. On the one hand, we must transform Taiwan into a global supplier of key components and precision equipment, as well as into a pioneer of innovative models for the service industry. On the other, we must actively engage in global competition and attract investment from around the world in order to develop export markets for our commodities and services. This will pave the way for Taiwan to truly become a "free economic island."

We are in the midst of integrating industrial and academic resources, and developing ten fundamental industrial technologies so that they take root in Taiwan and form the foundation for industrial innovation and upgrading in the future. We must actively help companies transform into "backbone enterprises" so they can develop key technologies and gradually establish themselves as "hidden champions" in the global supply chain.

In order to become a free economic island, Taiwan must comprehensively take part in regional economic integration and speed up the promotion of free economic pilot zones. There is nothing optional about our current situation; we have fallen well behind other countries, and the gap absolutely must be closed. According to 2012 statistics, as a result of obtaining free-trade agreements, Singapore received tariff exemptions or preferential rates on US$63 out of every US$100 worth of trade, and the corresponding figure for the Republic of Korea (ROK) was US$34. For Taiwan, this figure initially stood at just US$0.14. Now, three years after the ECFA came into effect, it has increased to US$4, which is still far behind Singapore and the ROK. Fellow citizens, how can we not be in a hurry to catch up?

We signed a Trade in Services Agreement with mainland China in June that could give a big boost to our service industry. Moreover, it could create the conditions for our participation in regional economic integration, and could potentially generate more job opportunities for our people. A good case in point is 31-year-old Ms. Mayuki Chou, who is the brand director of an online retailer based in Chiayi City called Tokyo Fashion. She told me that she firmly supports the signing of this agreement, since the preferential treatment for e-commerce businesses that the government has managed to secure is unprecedented. She feels it will allow many more excellent online stores like hers to set up official websites in mainland China and make inroads into the international market with their own brands.

Similarly, the chairman of Taipei-based online game developer XPEC Entertainment, Aaron Hsu, also told me that the review and approval process for bringing video game content to mainland China used to take at least six months, and sometimes dragged on seemingly forever. However, the Trade in Services Agreement will dramatically shorten the time to two months. This will be a big boost for Taiwan's video game companies eager to test the mainland market.

Another example is 85°C Café, which anyone in Taiwan will be familiar with. It began life as a corner coffee shop nine years ago in New Taipei City's Yonghe District, but today has made its way to Hong Kong, mainland China, the United States, and Australia after prospering in Taiwan. Of the 744 outlets it had around the world as of August 2013, 340 are in Taiwan, fully 395 are in mainland China, and nine are in the US and Australia. Its chairman, Wu Cheng-hsueh, shared with me his plan to set up an "85 Academy" in Taiwan to train 8,000 local recruits to meet the massive human resource requirements for opening outlets worldwide. He sees it as a way to give something back to his homeland.

Fellow countrymen, as president, I definitely want to help our young people realize their dreams. Like me, these courageous young people see limitless opportunities. Taiwan has many service sector entrepreneurs like this, so I say, why not let them try out their wings? Let's give them a chance to make their dreams come true!

In addition, the free economic pilot zones (FEPZs) have already entered the launch phase. The Executive Yuan has relaxed 12 regulations to dramatically streamline customs procedures applying to pilot zone firms when they outsource processing operations, so that new operating models based on smart logistics can be gradually established in these zones. The Shanghai Free Trade Zone officially opened recently, giving us yet another competitor. Therefore, we must step up efforts to open up our market. The Executive Yuan is actively deliberating on whether to allow other industrial activities in the FEPZs, such as the financial sector's wealth and asset management services. This is the right direction. We should expand the scope of liberalization for both domestic and international financial and economic activities. This will help Taiwan to advance more quickly toward the goal of becoming a "free economic island." We hope these liberalization measures, along with other industrial development plans, will generate NT$300 billion worth of investment and create 45,000 jobs in the next two years.

I would like to stress that only by opening up our market will Taiwan's young people have a grand stage for realizing their grand hopes. In this era of global competition, the use of labor has become more internationalized and flexible, so we have to put greater emphasis on investing in our youth than before. The government is stepping up efforts to develop a policy aimed at increasing employment opportunities for young people. The idea is to make them more employable and help them realize their dreams of starting businesses and finding jobs. In recent years, young students from Taiwan have won high marks in international invention and design competitions. This clearly demonstrates the effectiveness of our country's promotion of creativity education and cooperation between industry and academia. My fellow countrymen—"grand liberalization, grand skill sets, grand stage, and grand dreams"—these are the grand pledges we make to our young people!

My fellow countrymen, our hope is that Taiwan will become a "free economic island" characterized by what I like to call "the 3H's"—high productivity in its people, high added-value in its products, and most importantly, high incomes and well-being for its citizens as a result. This kind of Taiwan will become the top investment choice for businesses around the world. And for our people, it will be a happy home. However, unless we have the broadness of mind and courage to open up to the world, this will be beyond our reach.

Some are concerned that liberalization will have a negative impact on our country. However, economic competitiveness has always been Taiwan's strength. The flexibility and resilience of our enterprises, as well as our progress in many global competitiveness rankings, prove that our economy is strong and robust. The government has made thorough preparations for the possible adverse effects of liberalization. My fellow citizens, there is no need to sell ourselves short. Fear of competition will cause our economy to wither. Only if we have the courage to compete can we create economic prosperity. This is the only way forward for the structural transformation of Taiwan's economy.

Embracing a Civil Society; Showing Greater Concern for the Disadvantaged

My fellow countrymen, it is not just our economy that should be aligned with global trends. Our entire civilization must be aligned, as well. To my way of thinking, there are two indicators by which the degree of civilization in Taiwan's society can be measured: its civil society, and its concern for the disadvantaged.

Along the path to democratization, my responsibility as president is to continue reinforcing democratic beliefs and culture so as to build up civil society.

When we established democracy, we learned as we went; now we need to put civil society into practice in a nation that is already democratic. In concrete terms, a mature civil society demonstrates high-quality democracy. That is to say, under the principle of constitutionalism, human rights are protected, the rule of law is thoroughly implemented, and the judiciary is independent and impartial, so civil society is able to thrive. Under this philosophy, my foremost mission as president is to respect the Constitution and implement constitutional governance.

Fellow countrymen, I have full confidence in our society. We seek a civil society where diversity and tolerance are valued, governance is rational, citizens are friendly and caring, and government is actively responsive. Through dialogue, the citizenry and the government can jointly promote social progress, realize social reform, and foster rational competition among political parties. This may perhaps be a painful learning process that involves a lot of trial and error, but the fruits of this effort will allow us to savor the sweet reward of a happy Taiwan.

Anyone who comes to Taiwan discovers an abundance of volunteers and kind-hearted people. This is the most impressive thing about our country! Society has compassion, and the government has heart. We have amended the Public Assistance Act to raise the poverty line, thereby benefiting 660,000 disadvantaged people. Five-year-olds have been exempt from tuition since the 2011 school year, and subsidies have been made available to fund childcare allowances and parental leave allowances. These programs have benefited hundreds of thousands of people thus far. More importantly, the government has launched a National Pension scheme and a Labor Insurance Annuity scheme, thus providing pensions to 3.75 million people previously without social insurance, and to 9.62 million laborers.

In Taiwan, we care about the disadvantaged and gladly offer them assistance. We are building a vigorous civil society that cares for the disadvantaged. This is what makes Taiwan a benchmark for the Chinese-speaking world, and enables us to hold our heads high anywhere around the globe.

A Covenant with our Children

My fellow countrymen, now is the time to unite and move forward. The goal is clear, and our commitment firm: We must bequeath to our children a liberalized and prosperous economic environment, a rational and caring civil society, a peaceful cross-strait relationship, and a friendly and cooperative space for ourselves in the international community. This is our niche, and our way forward. This is the ROC's national strategy.

My fellow countrymen, we do not fear a long road, only a lack of direction. We do not fear difficulties, only faltering will. As long as we stay the course and have the courage to march forward, hope will be there before us.

Now, let us all join in proclaiming:

Long live freedom and democracy!

Long live the Republic of China!

Go Taiwan!

Thank you, everyone!

II Subjects of International Law

(No item reported under this section)

III International Organizations

General

Republic of China (Taiwan) and Intergovernmental Organizations

At the end of December 2013, the Republic of China (Taiwan) retains membership in 34 inter-governmental organizations listed in the following table:[4]

4 Wai Jiao Bu [MOFA], *Zhong Hua Min Guo Yi Bai Ling Er Nian Wai Jiao Tong Ji Nian Bao* [*2013 Ministry of Foreign Affairs Statistics Yearbook*] 19–20 (2014).

Name of Organization	Abbrev	R.O.C. Membership Established	Organization Establishment Date	Headquarters
Advisory Centre on WTO Law	ACWL	Mar. 8, 2004	July 2001	Geneva, Switzerland
Afro-Asian Rural Development Organization	AARDO	1968	Mar. 31, 1962	New Delhi, India
Agency for International Trade Information and Cooperation	AITIC	May 21, 2009	Feb. 23, 1998[5]	Geneva, Switzerland
Asian Development Bank[6]	ADB	Aug. 22, 1966	Aug. 22, 1966	Manila, Philippines
Asian Harmonization Working Party	AHWP	1999	1999	Hong Kong, SAR, China
Asian Productivity Organization	APO	May 11, 1961	May 11, 1961	Tokyo, Japan
Asian Vegetable Research and Development Center	AVRDC	May 22, 1971	May 22, 1971	Tainan, Taiwan
Asian/Pacific Group on Money Laundering	APG	Feb. 1977	Feb. 1997	Bangkok, Thailand

5 AITIC was established as an association and later transformed into an intergovernmental organization in 2004. AITIC, "About Us: AITIC in Short", http://www.acici.org/aitic/aboutus/index.html (last visited Mar. 13, 2012).

6 The Chinese Communist regime was admitted to the membership of the ADB in March 1986, the Republic of China still maintains its membership of the ADB though the latter decided to refer to it as "Taipei,China." The Republic of China protested this illegal change of its name and did not attend the annual meetings of 1986 and 1987. Since 1988, the Republic of China has attended the annual meetings under protest. The participation at meetings does not imply that the ROC has already accepted the name change to "Taipei,China."

(cont.)

Name of Organization	Abbrev	R.O.C. Membership Established	Organization Establishment Date	Headquarters
Asia-Pacific Association of Agricultural Research Institutions	APAARI	Apr. 7, 1999	Dec. 1990	Bangkok, Thailand
Asia-Pacific Economic Cooperation[7]	APEC	Nov. 1991	Nov. 26, 1989	Singapore
Asia-Pacific Legal Metrology Forum	APLMF	Nov. 1994	Nov. 1994	Ibaraki, Japan
Association for Science Cooperation in Asia	ASCA	1994	1970	Manila, Philippines
Association of Asian Election Authorities	AAEA	Feb. 1998	Jan. 1997	Manila, Philippines

7 At the Second APEC Ministerial Meeting in Singapore on July 29–30, 1990, Ministers acknowledged "the particularly significant role in the Asia Pacific region of the three economies of the PRC, Taiwan and Hong Kong" and agreed that consultations should proceed with the three economies, with a view to reaching arrangements agreeable to those three for all three to participate in APEC at the same time.

Ambassador See-Young Lee of the Republic of Korea in his capacity as the Chairman of the Senior Officials Meeting for the Third APEC Ministerial Meeting conducted consultations with the three and reached an agreement and reported on the result of his consultations to the Senior Officials Meeting in Kyongju, Korea on August 27–29, 1991.

Senior Officials of APEC welcomed the report of the Chairman and made a recommendation and reported back to the Third Ministerial Meeting that the three be invited to participate in APEC at the Third Ministerial Meeting.

At the Third Ministerial Meeting in Seoul on November 12–14, 1991, Ministers approved the recommendation of Senior Officials that the three should participate in APEC and became members of APEC. Currently, there are 21 members and 3 observers.

Name of Organization	Abbrev	R.O.C. Membership Established	Organization Establishment Date	Headquarters
Central American Bank for Economic Integration	CABEI	Nov. 10, 1992	May 31, 1961	Tegucigalpa, Honduras
Egmont Group of Financial Intelligence Units	Egmont Group	July 1998	June 24, 1997	Madrid, Spain
Extended Commission for the Conservation of Southern Bluefin Tuna	CCSBT	2002	May 20, 1994	Canberra, Australia
Food and Fertilizer Technology Center for the Asian and Pacific Region[8]	FFTC	Apr. 4, 1970	Apr. 4, 1970	Taipei, Taiwan
Inter-American Tropical Tuna Commission	IATTC	2010	May 31, 1949	La Jolla, California, United States
International Scientific Committee for Tuna and Tuna-like Species in the North Pacific Ocean	ISC	Jan. 30, 2002	May, 1996	Tokyo, Japan

8 FFTC was originally a specialized agency of Asian and Pacific Council (ASPAC). Since the ROC's withdrawal from the United Nations in 1971, the ministerial meeting of ASPAC has not been convened. Therefore, there are no more activities in that organization. In spite of that, the function of FFTC is still and continuously maintained and the ROC remains very active in the organization.

(cont.)

Name of Organization	Abbrev	R.O.C. Membership Established	Organization Establishment Date	Headquarters
International Association of Insurance Supervisors	IAIS	1994	1994	Basel, Switzerland
International Competition Network	ICN	Jan. 2001	Oct. 2001	N/A
International Cotton Advisory Committee	ICAC	1963	Sept. 5, 1939	Washington, D.C., United States
International Council for Information Technology in Government Administration	ICA	2010	1968	N/A
International Organization of Securities Commissions	IOSCO	1987	Apr. 1983	Madrid, Spain
International Satellite System for Search and Rescue	Cospas-Sarsat	June 4, 1992	1979	Montreal, Canada
International Seed Testing Association	ISTA	1962	1924	Zurich, Switzerland
Office International des Epizooties	OIE	Oct. 1, 1954	Jan. 25, 1924	Paris, France
South-East Asia Central Banks	SEACEN	Jan. 24, 1992	1966	Kuala Lumpur, Malaysia
South Pacific Regional Fisheries Management Organization	SPRFMO	Sept. 23, 2012	Aug. 24, 2012	Wellington, New Zealand

Name of Organization	Abbrev	R.O.C. Membership Established	Organization Establishment Date	Headquarters
Study Group on Asian Tax Administration and Research	SGATAR	Feb. 1996	May 1970	Bangkok, Thailand
Western and Central Pacific Fisheries Commission	WCPFC	Dec. 2, 2004	June 19, 2004	Pohnpei, Federated States of Micronesia
World Customs Organization (Technical Committee on Customs Valuation)	WCO	Jan. 2002	1952	Brussels, Belgium
World Customs Organization (Technical Committee on Rules of Origin)	WCO	Jan. 2002	1952	Brussels, Belgium
World Trade Organization	WTO	Jan. 1, 2002	Jan. 1, 1995	Geneva, Switzerland

Republic of China (Taiwan) and International Non-Intergovernmental Organizations

At the end of December 2013, the Republic of China (Taiwan) retains membership in 2165 international non-governmental organizations as listed in the following table:[9]

9 MOFA, *supra* note 4, at 88.

Nature of Organizations	Number
Agriculture, Forestry, Fisheries & Animal Husbandry	256
Business & Finance	123
Conservation	121
Culture & Art	117
Education	173
Electrical Engineering	6
Electronic Machinery	55
Engineering	31
Industrial Relations	26
Journalism	87
Law	91
Leisure & Entertainment	38
Medical Care	354
Mining & Energy	0
Religion & Philosophy	159
Research & Development Management	68
Social Welfare	128
Sport	107
Technology	114
Transportation & Tourism	54
Women and Scouts	57
Total	2165

International Civil Aviation Organization

ICAO Invites the Republic of China (Taiwan) to Attend the 38th Session of the ICAO Assembly

On September 19, 2013, the Civil Aeronautics Administration of the Ministry of Transportation and Communications issued the following press release concerning the invitation by the International Civil Aviation Organization (ICAO) to participate in the 38th Session of the ICAO Assembly:[10]

10 Ministry of Transportation and Communications, ICAO Invites the Republic of China (Taiwan) to Attend the 38th Session of the ICAO Assembly, Sept. 14, 2013, http://

On September 11th 2013, Mr. Roberto Kobeh González, President of the Council of the International Civil Aviation Organization (ICAO), sent a letter to Ms. Shen Chi, Director General of the Civil Aeronautics Administration (CAA), inviting her to lead a delegation to the 38th Session of the Assembly of ICAO to be convened September 24 to October 4 in Montréal, Canada, as his guests under the name "Chinese Taipei." The government of the Republic of China (Taiwan) welcomes this invitation, and in her reply of accepting this invitation, Director General Shen has outlined plans for the Taiwan delegation's participation.

To attend this year's ICAO Assembly will be the first and concrete step forward for Taiwan in its ICAO campaign since 2009. In the Assembly, Taiwan will gain better knowledge of the development of international aviation standards, obtain first-hand information crucial to aviation safety, and be able to exchange views on the international civil aviation matter with other countries and members of international civil aviation community. Overall speaking, Taiwan's capability and efficiency in regulating and servicing civil aviation in the region may be further strengthened. Furthermore, the rights and benefits of passengers from Taiwan as well as the rest of the globe can be better protected. In the future, Taiwan will continue to strive to participate in related ICAO meetings, mechanisms, and activities, so as to advance its relations with the regional and global civil aviation communities.

Taiwan's attendance at the Assembly marks an important step forward in its bid for meaningful participation in ICAO. This attributes to Taiwan's long-term commitment to international aviation standards and safety, which has been widely recognized. Due to improvements in cross-strait relations over the past few years and frequent exchanges between the peoples of the two sides, direct flights between Taiwan and mainland China have increased considerably, creating conditions favorable to Taiwan's substantive participation in ICAO. In addition, the support and assistance given for Taiwan by its diplomatic allies and other members of the international community have also helped ICAO understand the necessity for Taiwan to be included in the international civil aviation community. The ROC government is very grateful for these support and assistance.

Taiwan's participation in the Assembly will help enhance its capacity in aviation safety, flights control services, and aviation standards. Taiwan will also take advantage of this opportunity at the ICAO Assembly to boost its cooperation

---

www.motc.gov.tw/en/home.jsp?id=151&parentpath=0&mcustomize=news_view.jsp&dataserno=201309140004.

with the international civil aviation community and contribute to aviation safety, so as to assist ICAO in realizing a seamless global aviation network.

Letter from the Director-General of the Civil Aeronautics Administration (CAA) to the President of the Council of the International Civil Aviation Organization (ICAO)

On September 24, 2013, the Director-General of the Civil Aeronautics Administration of the Ministry of Transportation and Communications sent the following letter to the President of the ICAO Council:[11]

Dear Mr. President,
Following my reply letter dated September 12, 2013, I would like to once again express my sincere gratitude for the invitation you extended to us to attend the 38th Session of the ICAO Assembly. Your efforts and those of some Member States have together made our presence possible.

I would also like to take this opportunity to share some thoughts with you. International civil aviation depends to a great extent on multilateral cooperation to achieve the goals of safety, order, and sustainable development. The Taipei Flight Information Region (FIR), being solely managed by the Civil Aeronautics Administration, plays an important role in both regional and global air transportation. In line with the universal application of international aviation safety standards and provision of air transportation services, it is extremely important to include Chinese Taipei in the meetings and activities of the ICAO. I wish to assure you that Chinese Taipei cherishes this opportunity of being invited to this year's Assembly, and will comply with ICAO standards and recommended practices, just as it may also share its own successful experiences.

In 2011, the Administration successfully completed its Communication, Navigation, Surveillance and Air Traffic Management (CNS/ATM) modernization program, which provides more advanced ATC services and enables better coordination with neighboring FIRs. In 2012, we embarked on the Performance Based Navigation (PBN) implementation program to enhance the efficient use of airspace in Taipei FIR. In the meantime, we are eager to share with you our progress and experience in airman training, ATS upgrade and transition, automated coordination among FIRs, Safety Management System (SMS)

11 MOFA, Letter from the Director-General of the Civil Aeronautics Administration (CAA) to the President of the Council of the International Civil Aviation Organization (ICAO), *available at* http://www.mofa.gov.tw/Upload/RelFile/1125/115458/586ca9b5-6a52-4c24-8475-a95eb2f18909.pdf.

implementation, and safety surveillance data acquisition, etc. We anticipate and are confident that we can make contribution to the programs and activities of international civil aviation.

Looking ahead, the Taipei FIR would hope to further engage with ICAP in advocating for the Aviation System Block Upgrades program, which would lead to greater aviation safety, more optimal airspace utilization, and reduced carbon emissions. Environmental protection and going "green" are also areas in which we are willing to cooperate with ICAO.

We are also committed to sharing our experiences in aviation training, air traffic control system upgrades and conversions, cooperation with neighboring FIRs, aviation safety management, and safety surveillance data acquisition. Mr. President, we are willing and stand ready to make contributions and strengthen our civil aviation capacity through meaningfully participating in other ICAO meetings, mechanisms and activities.

On behalf of the Civil Aeronautics Administration, I thank you again for the invitation. This decision is a concrete step towards helping reach the ICAO goal of a seamless sky. I wish the 38th ICAO Assembly great success.

Sincerely,

Shen, Chi
Director General

IV Individuals

President Ma Welcomes International Experts to Taiwan to Review the ROC's First National Human Rights Report

On February 24, 2013, the Office of the President issued the following press release on the President's remarks at a ceremony welcoming a group of international experts invited to review the ROC's first national human rights reports:[12]

President Ma Ying-jeou and Vice President Wu Den-yih on the afternoon of February 24 were accompanied by Minister of Justice Tseng Yung-Fu (曾勇夫) in attending a ceremony to welcome a group of international experts who were in Taiwan to review the ROC's first human rights report. In addition to stating that this review of Taiwan's human rights report marks a

12 Office of the President, President Ma Welcomes International Experts to Taiwan to Review the ROC's First National Human Rights Report, Feb. 24, 2013, http://english.president.gov.tw/Default.aspx?tabid=491&itemid=29316&rmid=2355.

milestone in the development of human rights in the ROC, the president also urged government agencies to continue to improve mechanisms for human rights protection, thereby enabling the ROC to become a nation that truly protects human rights.

In remarks, the president stated that the United Nations (UN) passed the International Covenant on Civil and Political Rights and the International Covenant on Economic, Social and Cultural Rights in 1966. As a charter member of the UN, the ROC signed the two human rights covenants back in 1967. However, as the ROC subsequently lost its representation in the UN, it was unable to continue with work to ratify the two covenants.

President Ma stated that in a bid to protect human rights, he formally announced on Human Rights Day on December 10, 2008 that the ROC would work as quickly as possible to ratify the two covenants, and he realized that pledge on May 14 of the following year. The president acknowledged that the UN refused to accept the instruments of ratification presented by the ROC since the nation has lost its representation in the body, but said that the government decided to turn instead to the passage of an enforcement act that incorporates the covenants into domestic law and makes them binding upon all government agencies and the courts. As a result, he noted, it really isn't important to the ROC whether the instruments of ratification are deposited with the UN, as this is not a necessary condition for the content of the documents to become legally binding here. What is important, the president remarked, is that the ROC has demonstrated a sincere intent to implement the two covenants in Taiwan.

President Ma emphasized that circumstances make it impossible for the ROC's first official human rights report to be reviewed under the UN system. However, the government has still invited a group of scholars and experts to come to Taiwan and review the report in accordance with procedures that are used in the UN, which shows that the ROC regards freedom, democracy, human rights, and rule of law as important objectives of the nation and is determined to put them into practice, the president said.

The president stated that the protection of human rights has become an international trend, yet it is governments that are most prone to infringing on human rights, since history shows that governments have abused their authority and thus violated human rights. The ROC, he mentioned, has been no exception. With this in mind, it is crucial that the government has the ability to reflect on its actions and to demand of itself that it conform to international human rights standards, the president stated.

President Ma introduced that while the ROC implemented a constitution in 1947, the nation then fell under martial law for 38 years due to communist rebellion. Consequently, the ROC is still considered a young democracy, which is why it has invited a group of international human rights experts to Taiwan to review the report. He said he hopes the suggestions, reminders, and inspiration that are provided by the experts will help to promote the nation's progress in this regard.

The president stated that given his academic background in international law, he is extremely pleased to see that the ROC has progressed to this stage. He said that establishing freedom, democracy, human rights, and rule of law is what our forefathers sought at the time of our nation's founding, and is also an important part of what inspired him to study law. That the human rights report is now being reviewed shows that his personal dream is starting to become realized, the president remarked.

Vice President Wu, who serves as the Convener of the Presidential Office Human Rights Consultative Committee, stated that the review of the ROC's first national human rights report will take place from February 25 to 27. Ten international human rights experts will engage in a constructive dialogue with representatives from government agencies, he noted, adding that they will also meet with representatives of non-governmental organizations to gather the views of social groups. On March 1, the group will release its concluding observations and provide suggestions based on the current state of human rights here, he said. The vice president remarked that the Ministry of Justice will establish a mechanism to improve, monitor, and examine the state of human rights protections here. In this process, the ministry will bear in mind the shortcomings and suggestions provided in the concluding observations to ensure that the ROC is in compliance with the two covenants, he commented.

The group of international human rights experts included the following 10 persons: Nisuke Ando (director, Human Rights Research Institute at Kyoto University), Jerome A. Cohen (co-director, US-Asia Law Institute at the New York University School of Law), Mary Shanthi Dairiam (member, UN Development Program's Gender Equality Task Force), Asma Jilani Jahangir (president, Supreme Court Bar Association of Pakistan), Manfred Nowak (professor of international law and human rights at the University of Vienna), Philip G. Alston (professor of law at New York University and co-chair of the NYU Center for Human Rights and Global Justice), Theodoor Cornelis van Boven (professor emeritus of international law at Maastricht University of The Netherlands), Virginia Bonoan-Dandan (United Nations independent expert on human rights and international solidarity), Eibe Riedel (former member, UN Committee on Economic, Social and Cultural Rights), and Heisoo Shin (member, UN Committee on Economic, Social and Cultural Rights). During their stay in Taiwan, the members of the group will exchange opinions with government agencies and private organizations to help improve human rights here and bring Taiwan's protection of human rights in step with that of advanced nations.

Supreme Administrative Court Judgment
July 18, 2013
102-Pan-Zi No. 453

Keywords:
Environmental Impact Assessment, International Covenant on Civil and Political Rights, Legal Interest, Rights to Adequate Living Standards

Relevant Provisions:
Article 2 of the Act to Implement the International Covenant on Civil and Political Rights and the International Covenant on Economic, Social and Cultural Rights
Article 11 of the International Covenant on Economic, Social and Cultural Rights

Summary:
The appellants claimed that the 10 individual appellants, including Lin Chi-Tung (林啟東) (collectively, "Individual Appellants"), have the standing to file the subject lawsuit as (1) their "rights to adequate living standards" are protected under Article 2 of the Act to Implement the International Covenant on Civil and Political Rights and the International Covenant on Economic, Social and Cultural Rights as well as Paragraph 1, Article 11 of the International Covenant on Economic, Social and Cultural Rights, and (2) they are local residents who may be affected by the construction of the Taipei Dome (大巨蛋), and should be deemed interested parties with respect to the findings of the subject environmental assessment, review of the subject urban development and the subject construction permit. The appellants further claimed that the Organization of Urban Re-s (中華民國專業者都市改革組織; "OURs") and the Society of Wilderness (財團法人中華民國荒野保護協會; "SOW") are both NGOs organized under the Taiwan Civil Associations Act, aiming to promote environmental protection and thus have an interest in promoting the public's environmental awareness by participating in environmental decision-making procedures related to the construction of the Taipei Dome pursuant to the Aarhus Convention; the OURs and the SOW should be entitled to file a lawsuit when such interest is infringed. However, the Taipei City Government countered that there is no "right to promote public interest" under Taiwan law, and thus the OURs and the SOW have no standing to file the subject lawsuit.

The original judgment revoked the administrative decisions made by each of the Taipei City Government and the Ministry of the Interior [in part] and disallowed the claims of the appellants in part. The court held that the Individual Appellants have the standing to file a lawsuit against the findings of the environmental assessment because the living environment of the Individual Appellants may be affected by the subject construction, and the rights to adequate living standards under Article 2 of the Act to Implement the International Covenant on Civil and Political Rights and the International Covenant on Economic, Social and Cultural Rights as well as Paragraph 1, Article 11 of the International Covenant on Economic, Social and Cultural Rights should encompass a right to judicial remedy whenever substantive environmental rights are infringed. On the other hand, according to the Judicial Interpretation No. 329, the Aarhus Convention is not implemented as an internal law in Taiwan as Taiwan is not a signatory to the Aarhus Convention, i.e., Taiwan did not sign the Aarhus Convention, and thus the Legislative Yuan is not required to review the Convention. Accordingly, the OURS and the SOW cannot argue they have the standing to file the subject lawsuit pursuant to the Aarhus Convention.

The Administrative Supreme Court held that whether a person has "legal interest" should be determined by the thesis of protective regulations (保護規範理論). If the law stipulates that certain individuals may enjoy the right or grants those individuals who meet the statutory qualifications the right to request the agency or authority to perform certain obligations, there is no doubt that the purpose of such law is to protect certain individuals' rights. Nonetheless, a person who is not subject to an administrative decision may still have the standing to file a lawsuit if such person's legal right is deemed infringed under the thesis of protective regulations. However, such person is not allowed to file an administrative appeal or lawsuit if only his/her/its reflective interest such as political, economic and/or emotional interest is infringed. In this regard, the Administrative Supreme Court held that the Individual Appellants are permitted to file the subject lawsuit as they have legal interest in the findings of the environmental assessment rendered by the environmental impact assessment committee, and the subject urban development approval and construction permit issued by the Taipei City Government. However, the OURS and the SOW are non-juridical groups that are comprised of members, rather than members themselves. Even if the members of such groups are residents of the neighborhood of the subject construction project, neither the environmental assessment by environmental impact assessment committee, nor the urban development approval or the construction permit issued by the Taipei City Government will cause any damage to the "natural surviving" environment of the OURS or the SOW. Given that the aforementioned administrative decisions did not cause any damage to the OURS' or the SOW's rights or interests, the OURS and the SOW have no standing to file such a lawsuit to revoke the said administrative decisions.

Police Agency, Ministry of the Interior
October 7, 2013
Jing-Shu-Bao- Zi-10201518811

Keywords:
Freedom of Assembly, International Covenant on Civil and Political Rights, Principle of Proportionality

Relevant Provisions:
Act to Implement the International Covenant on Civil and Political Rights and the International Covenant on Economic, Social and Cultural Rights
Article 21 of the International Covenant on Civil and Political Rights
Assembly and Parade Act

Summary:
Given the enforcement of the Act to Implement the International Covenant on Civil and Political Rights and the International Covenant on Economic, Social and Cultural Rights, the police authorities should comply with Article 21 of the International Covenant on Civil and Political Rights in handling assemblies and parades cases and applying the relevant provisions of the Assembly and Parade Act. When implementing the measures under the Assembly and Parade Act, including the order to stop or the order to dismiss, the police authorities should comply with the principle of proportionality and the International Covenant on Civil and Political Rights, to implement the protection of human rights and the right to peaceful assembly and parade.

Supreme Court Judgment
October 21, 2013
102-Tai-Shang-Zi-4289

Keywords:
Death Penalty, International Covenant on Civil and Political Rights, Mental or Intellectual Disabilities

Relevant Provisions:
Articles 2, 3, and 8 of the Act to Implement the International Covenant on Civil and Political Rights and the International Covenant on Economic, Social and Cultural Rights
Article 289 of the Code of Criminal Procedure
Article 6 of the International Covenant on Civil and Political Rights
Article 3 of the Safeguards Guaranteeing Protection of the Rights of Those Facing the Death Penalty

Summary:
On May 14, 2009, the ROC ratified the International Covenant on Civil and Political Rights and the International Covenant on Economic, Social and Cultural Rights (collectively as the "Two Covenants"). The Legislative Yuan promptly enacted the Act to Implement the Two Covenants, which became effective on December 10, 2009. Article 2 of the aforesaid Act provides that the provisions in connection with human rights protection under the Two Covenants shall have equal effect as domestic law. Article 3 of the same Act provides that the applications of the Two Covenants shall make reference to their legislative purposes and interpretations made by the Human Rights Committee. As such, Paragraph 1, Article 6 of the International Covenant on Civil and Political Rights provides: "Every human being has the inherent right to life. This right shall be protected by law. No one shall be arbitrarily deprived of his life." Paragraph 2 of the same Article provides: "In countries which have not abolished the death penalty, sentence of death may be imposed only for the most serious crimes in accordance with the law in force at the time of the commission of the crime and not contrary to the provisions of the present Covenant and to the Convention on the Prevention and Punishment of the Crime of Genocide." Article 3 of the Safeguards Guaranteeing Protection of the Rights of Those Facing the Death Penalty approved by the Economic and Social Council of the United Nations, in its resolution 1984/50 dated May 25, 1984, prohibits the death sentence to be carried out on persons who have become insane. Moreover, in 2005, Paragraph 7 of the Human Rights Resolution 2005/59 issued by the High Commissioner for Human Rights of the United Nations urges all States that still maintain the death penalty not to impose the death penalty on a person suffering from any mental or intellectual disabilities or to execute any such person. In 2013, the conclusive opinion and the 57th suggestion of the first report on ROC government's implementation of the international human rights covenants, rendered by the panel of international independent experts, urged that before the death penalty is abolished, the ROC government should strictly follow relevant procedures and adopt

protective measures, especially that a death sentence cannot be pronounced to or carried out against those who are mentally or intellectually incapacitated. The above-mentioned rules have clearly indicated that even though the death penalty is prescribed under the Criminal Code, a human being's right to life deserves to be protected by law considering the irreversible effect of depriving a person of his/her life. Hence, the death penalty shall not be imposed unless the utmost crime has been committed in a cruel and undisputed manner where any correction and reconciliation is no longer available. Persons who suffer from mental or intellectual disabilities lack the understanding of criminal penalty and should, in fact, be treated as minors. Therefore, the aforesaid resolutions of the United Nations deem mentally or intellectually incapacitated persons as minors and forbid all States to sentence or carry out the death penalty against them.

The lower court failed to consider in its sentence that: (i) Article 3 of the Safeguards Guaranteeing Protection of the Rights of Those Facing the Death Penalty approved by the Economic and Social Council of the United Nations, in its resolution 1984/50 dated May 25, 1984, which prohibits the death sentence to be carried out on persons who have become insane; (ii) Paragraph 7 of the Human Rights Resolution 2005/59 issued by the High Commissioner for Human Rights of the United Nations in 2005 which urges all States that still maintain the death penalty not to impose the death penalty on a person suffering from any mental or intellectual disabilities or to execute any such person; and (iii) the conclusive opinion and the 57th suggestion of the first report on ROC government's implementation of the international human rights covenants, rendered by international independent experts, urges the ROC government to refrain itself from pronouncing or executing a death sentence against those who are mentally or intellectually incapacitated before the death penalty is abolished. As such, it is questionable as to whether pronouncing a death sentence on the appellant will constitute failing to apply the applicable law. Insofar as the defendant's interests are concerned, Paragraph 3, Article 289 of the Code of Criminal Procedure provides that after the conclusion of the argument on the law and facts among the prosecutor, defendant and defense attorney, the presiding judge shall provide the parties with opportunities to state opinions regarding sentencing. The said opinion can only be presented by the parties relating to sentencing only, which does not include the opinion made by the defense attorney or the parties in respect of the penalty concerned. This fails to provide sufficient protection to the defendant's human rights. Article 8 of the Act to Implement the Two Covenants provides that all levels of government agencies should review laws and regulations within their functions according to the Two Covenants and propose amendments to the inconsistent provisions therein within two years after the Act to Implement the Two Covenants comes into force. In this regard, Paragraph 3, Article 289 of the Code of Criminal Procedure which reads "After the conclusion of the argument pursuant to the preceding two sections, the presiding judge shall provide the parties with opportunities to state opinions regarding sentencing" is proposed to be amended as "After the conclusion of the argument pursuant to the preceding section, the presiding judge shall provide [prosecutor, defendant and defense attorney], in sequence, with opportunities to argue the sentencing and provide the claimant, the victim and his/her family members with opportunities to state opinions regarding the sentencing." To carry out the purposes of the Two Covenants, before the said amendment passed by the Legislative Yuan, the presiding judge should exercise its discretion over the litigation proceedings to the cases where the prosecutor requests for a death penalty in order to reach a more subtle and suitable sentencing. This is because once the death penalty becomes final and is enforced, remedial measures can no longer be adopted. As such, the presiding judge should provide the prosecutor, defendant and defense attorney with the chance to debate matters relating to the sentencing on the defendant so that the tribunal may incorporate the findings of oral arguments and opinions provided by the victim's family members before pronouncing an appropriate penalty for the crime committed under the effective law before any amendment can be made. Considering that the lower courts pronounced a death penalty before providing the prosecutor and the accused with the opportunity to debate on the sentencing, the judgment so rendered may not necessarily be in violation of the law but can hardly be deemed as a justifiable judgment.

V Territory and Territorial Jurisdiction

The Republic of China (Taiwan) Protests Vietnam Law Claiming South China Sea Islands

On January 7, 2013, the Ministry of Foreign Affairs issued the following statement, protesting against Vienam's law claiming South China Sea Islands:[13]

The Ministry of Foreign Affairs (MOFA) expresses its serious concern and firm opposition over Vietnam's Law on the Sea, which erroneously places the Shisha (Paracel) Islands and Nansha (Spratly) Islands under Vietnam's

13 MOFA. The Republic of China (Taiwan) Protests Vietnam Law Claiming South China Sea Islands. Jan. 7, 2013, http://www.mofa.gov.tw/en/News_Content.aspx?n=1EADDCFD4C6EC567&s=B30A1972A146D532.

sovereignty and jurisdiction. MOFA hereby solemnly reiterates the government of the Republic of China's position as follows:

1. Whether looked at from the perspective of history, geography or international law, the Spratly Islands, Paracel Islands, Chungsha Islands (Macclesfield Bank) and Tungsha (Pratas) Islands, as well as their surrounding waters, are an inherent part of the territory of the Republic of China (Taiwan). These archipelagoes therefore fall under the sovereignty of the Republic of China (Taiwan). The government reasserts that it enjoys all rights over the islands and their surrounding waters, and that it denies all unlawful claims to sovereignty over, or occupation of, these areas by other countries.
2. The government of the Republic of China (Taiwan) upholds the basic principles of "safeguarding sovereignty, shelving disputes, promoting peace and reciprocity, and encouraging joint exploration" to resolve South China Sea disputes. It hereby again calls on all neighboring countries to respect the principles and spirit of international law, exercise self-restraint, maintain freedom of navigation, and refrain from adopting unilateral measures that threaten the peace and stability of the region. Taiwan urges these countries to engage in dialogue rather than confrontation, so that a peaceful resolution can be reached.

President Ma Attends 2013 (5th) International Conference on Diaoyutai Islands Issue

On April 17, 2013, President Ma delivered the following remarks at the Fifth International Conference on Diaoyutai Islands Issue:[14]

On the morning of April 17, President Ma Ying-jeou attended the opening ceremonies of the 2013 (5th) International Conference on the Diaoyutai Islands Issue, held by Fu Jen Catholic University. The recent signing of a fisheries agreement between Taiwan and Japan contributes to peaceful resolution of disputes, said the president, who expressed hope that the pact could be a first step toward a resolution of the Diaoyutais issue, thereby promoting peace and prosperity in the East China Sea.

In remarks, the president first noted that China suffered defeat in the First Sino-Japanese War (1894–1895) and on April 17, 1895 the Qing court was forced to sign the Treaty of Shimonoseki with Japan, under which China ceded

14 Office of the President, President Ma Attends 2013 (5th) International Conference on Diaoyutai Islands Issue, Apr. 17, 2013, http://english.president.gov.tw/Default.aspx?tabid=491&itemid=29690&rmid=2355.

Taiwan and its appurtenant islands (including the Diaoyutais), along with the Penghu Islands, to Japan. That is why Fu Jen Catholic University, the president explained, specially selected this day 118 years after that important event to hold an international symposium on issues related to the Diaoyutais, making this conference all the more meaningful.

President Ma told the participants at the event that the Diaoyutais were discovered early in the 15th century by China, which named the islands and used them. In 1683, he said, the Diaoyutais, together with Taiwan, were annexed by the Qing court. Later, in 1812, China established Kavalan Subprefecture under the Taiwan prefectural government in the area today known as Yilan County. Many historical documents indicate that the Diaoyutais were part of Chinese territory during the Qing dynasty (1644–1911), he said, but after Japan's decisive victory in the First Sino-Japanese War, Japan claimed that the Diaoyutais were terra nullius. In addition, the Japanese Cabinet secretly resolved to include the Diaoyutais as part of Japan's territory, but the Japanese emperor did not issue an Imperial Decree to this effect in accordance with precedent, and the outside world was thus not informed. From the standpoint of international law, the president commented, this was merely an internal statement of intent by Japan's government, and had no force internationally.

President Ma further stated that the Japanese government has claimed that the Diaoyutais have been inherent territory of Japan's throughout history and in accordance with international law. This, however, does not correspond with the facts, the president said. Documents dating to 1884, he noted, show that Japanese citizen Tatsushiro Koga filed an application to develop the Diaoyutais, and Minister of Home Affairs Aritomo Yamagata ordered Okinawa Governor Sutezo Nishimura to study the matter. Sutezo reported that the islets had already been named by the Qing court and that historical records also showed the Diaoyutais to be territory of the Qing court. Aritomo, the president said, then sent a letter to Minister of Foreign Affairs Kaoru Inoue, who in 1885 ordered postponement of the plan to establish a national landmark on the islands. It was thus recognized that the Diaoyutais belonged to China, the president mentioned, adding that Japan did not have sovereignty over them. It was not until May of 1969 that the Japanese government established a boundary marker on the Diaoyutais, which was after the dispute over the islets came to the fore, so Japan's claim to be the first occupant of the islets is untrue, and is void ab initio under international law.

Article 2 of the Treaty of Shimonoseki mandated that China cedes to Japan "the island of Formosa, together with all islands appertaining or belonging to the said island of Formosa," and since the Diaoyutais are appurtenant to Taiwan, President Ma said, they were of course covered by Article 2. The president furthermore remarked that after World War II, Taiwan, and thus the Diaoyutais as well, were to be returned to the Republic of China in accordance with the Cairo Declaration, the Potsdam Proclamation, the Japanese Instrument of Surrender, and the Treaty of Peace between the ROC and Japan and Note No. 1 in the accompanying Exchange of Notes. The Diaoyutais should thus have been returned to the ROC along with Taiwan, he said. In other words, the legal basis for Japanese rule over the Diaoyutais vanished after 1945, the president remarked. From 1945 to 1972, the Diaoyutais were under the trusteeship of the United States, and the Japanese government did not actually rule over the islets, he noted. In 1972, the president added, the United States handed over "administrative control" of the Diaoyutais to Japan, but Japan still did not have sovereignty.

With respect to the recent Taiwan-Japan fisheries agreement, President Ma stated, the inking of this pact marks the single biggest change since the Diaoyutais controversy arose. The ROC has not made any concession on sovereignty, yet has made significant progress on fishing rights. The agreement, he said, applies to waters covering 74,000 square kilometers, which is double the size of Taiwan. In the future, Taiwan fishing boats operating in that area will not face interference by the Japanese, so Taiwan fishing boats now have another 1,400 square nautical miles (about 4,530 square kilometers) of waters in which to operate. Under this agreement, he noted, the area is jointly managed by both countries. In the future, the ROC will, under an institutionalized negotiation platform—a Taiwan-Japan fisheries committee—continue to talk with Japan on issues pertaining to sovereignty and other topics related to fishing rights in specific waters, the president commented.

President Ma stated that on August 5 of last year, the 60th anniversary of the Treaty of Peace between the ROC and Japan, he unveiled his East China Sea Peace Initiative, calling for all parties involved to shelve disputes and instead share fisheries resources. The president then announced further concrete steps to implement the initiative, calling for separate sets of bilateral talks to be held among the three concerned parties, followed by a round of trilateral negotiations. President Ma said that this initiative has come to be taken seriously in the international community, with the English-language The Japan Times and the UK's The Guardian supporting the spirit of the initiative. Japanese author Kenzaburo Oe, winner of the Nobel Prize in Literature 1994, also has expressed support, the president remarked.

President Ma stressed that the Taiwan-Japan fisheries agreement signals successful implementation of the East China Sea Peace Initiative. Even though the dispute over the sovereignty of the Diaoyutais has yet to be resolved, the fisheries agreement is a step forward. The president thanked the Japanese government for responding positively to the call by the ROC to resolve the dispute in a peaceful manner, and said he hopes the agreement will be a first step toward settling the sovereignty dispute over the Diaoyutais. The sharing of resources serves as a starting point from which to gradually reduce tensions among nations in the area, he commented, and will help to promote peace and prosperity in the East China Sea.

Among those attending the event were National Security Council Secretary-General Jason C. Yuan (袁健生), National Security Council Deputy Secretary-General Philip Y. M. Yang (楊永明), Minister of Foreign Affairs David Y. L. Lin (林永樂), Coast Guard Administration Minister Wang Ginn-Wang (王進旺), and Fu Jen Catholic University President Vincent Han-Sun Chiang (江漢聲).

The Republic of China (Taiwan) Protests the Philippines' Dispatch of Naval Vessels to Renai Shoal

On May 25, 2013, the Ministry of Foreign Affairs issued the following press release protesting against the Philippines' dispatch of naval vessels to Remai Shoal in the Nansha (Spratly) Islands:[15]

The Ministry of Foreign Affairs (MOFA) expresses its serious concern and firm opposition over the Philippines' dispatch of naval vessels to Renai (Second Thomas) Shoal in the Nansha (Spratly) Islands, which are the sovereign territory of the Republic of China. MOFA hereby solemnly reiterates the government's position as follows:

1. Whether looked at from the perspective of history, geography, or international law, the Spratly Islands, Xisha (Paracel) Islands, Zhongsha Islands (Macclesfield Bank), and Dongsha (Pratas) Islands, as well as their surrounding waters, are unquestionably the sovereign territory of the Republic of China. The Republic of China reasserts that it enjoys all rights over these four island groups and their surrounding waters. Second Thomas Shoal is located within the Spratly Islands, and the government denies all unlawful claims to sovereignty over, or occupation of, these areas by other countries.
2. The government has held to the principles of safeguarding sovereignty, shelving disputes, pursuing peace and reciprocity, and promoting joint exploration and development in dealing with disputes in the South China

15 MOFA, The Republic of China (Taiwan) Protests the Philippines' Dispatch of Naval Vessels to Renai Shoal, May 25, 2013, http://www.mofa.gov.tw/en/News_Content.aspx?n=1EADDCFD4C6EC567&s=6D08971C3230D0A1.

Sea. The Republic of China again calls on nations neighboring islands in the South China Sea to abide by the principles and spirit of international law, temper their actions, and refrain from implementing unilateral measures that could affect peace and stability in the South China Sea. Dialogue should replace confrontation, and parties should work together to seek a peaceful resolution to disputes concerning the South China Sea.

MOFA's Position Paper on the Diaoyutai Islands and the East China Sea Peace Initiative

On September 5, 2013, the Ministry of Foreign Affairs issued the following position paper on the Diaoyutai Islands and the East China Sea Peace Initiative:[16]

I Foreword

The Diaoyutai Islands 釣魚臺列嶼 are an island group appertaining to Taiwan under the administrative jurisdiction of Daxi Village 大溪里 in Toucheng Township 頭城鎮, Yilan County 宜蘭縣, Taiwan Province. Whether looked at from the perspective of history, geography, geology, practical use or international law, they constitute an integral part of the sovereign territory of the Republic of China (Taiwan).

With respect to the international dispute over the Diaoyutai Islands, the Republic of China has consistently expressed willingness to resolve the issue in a peaceful manner under the principles of the UN Charter and international law. To this end, it has proposed the East China Sea Peace Initiative.

II Evidence

1 *Geography*

The Diaoyutai Islands consist of five uninhabited islands-Diaoyutai Island 釣魚臺, Huangwei Islet 黃尾嶼, Nan Islet 南小島, Bei Islet 北小島 and Chiwei Islet 赤尾嶼-and three rocky reefs. Located to the northeast of Taiwan in the East China Sea, they cover an area of 6.1636 square kilometers. Among them, Diaoyutai Island is the largest at 4.3838 square kilometers. These islands are scattered between 25°40' to 26° N and 123° to 124°34' E. They lie 102 nautical miles north of Keelung, the largest port city in northeastern Taiwan, and 230 nautical miles south ofNaha, the capital city of Japan's Okinawa Prefecture. The shortest distance from the rest of the ROC territory is 73 nautical miles (Pengjia Islet 彭佳嶼), and from Japan 76 nautical miles (Yonaguni Island).

16 MOFA, The Republic of China's Sovereignty Claims over the Diaoyutai Islands and the East China Sea Peace Initiative, http://www.mofa.gov.tw/en/cp.aspx?n=38CD1D3C91067AEC.

The Diaoyutai Islands are situated in the northbound path of the Kuroshio Current and share the same monsoon zone with Taiwan. Thus, the air and water currents are favorable for sailing from northern Taiwan to the Diaoyutai Islands, and not favorable for sailing from the RyukyuIslands to the Diaoyutais.

2 *Geology*

The Diaoyutai Islands are situated on the continental shelf in the East China Sea. Formed by volcanic activity during the Tertiary Period, these rocky outcroppings are undersea extensions of mountain ranges in northern Taiwan, including Datun Mountain 大屯山 and Guanyin Mountain 觀音山. They are geologically a part of the same island chain as Huaping Islet 花瓶嶼, Mianhua Islet 棉花嶼 and Pengjia Islet, all of which are also situated northeast of Taiwan.

The water surrounding the Diaoyutai Islands is less than 200 meters deep. In contrast, the Okinawa Trough, which lies east of the group's easternmost islet of Chiwei and south of the Nan Islet and separates the Diaoyutai Islands from the Ryukyus, ranges between 500 and 2,717 meters deep. Chinese historical records refer to this natural boundary between China and the Ryukyu Islands as Heishuigou 黑水溝 (Black Water Trough) due to its dark water. Geologically, the oceanic crust beneath the Okinawa Trough is different from the continental crust beneath the East China Sea. Therefore, judging from the depth of the surrounding waters and their geology, the Diaoyutai Islands and the Ryukyu Islands are clearly unrelated.

3 *History*

According to official documents from the Ming and Qing dynasties (1368–1911), the Diaoyutai Islands were first discovered, named and used by the Chinese. Although long uninhabited, they were neither terra nullius (ownerless land) nor part of the Ryukyu Islands prior to their secret annexation by Japan in 1895. Chinese ownership of the islands was recognized by both the governments and peoples of Japan and the Ryukyus before 1895.

(1) Discovered, named and recognized as islands appertaining to Taiwan

The Diaoyutai Islands first appeared in Chinese historical records as early as 1403 during the Ming dynasty in the monograph Seeing off with a Favorable Tailwind 順風相送, indicating that these islands were discovered, named and used by the Chinese. In the centuries that followed, the Ming and Qing courts sent several investiture missions to the tributary state of the Ryukyu Kingdom for the purpose of bestowing the formal title to a new Ryukyu ruler. Chinese imperial envoys (or their deputies) kept detailed mission records (collectively known as Records of the Imperial Mission to Ryukyu 使琉球錄) that clearly described the geographical location of the Diaoyutai Islands and their border with the Ryukyu Kingdom, making the islands an important landmark along the China-Ryukyu navigation route. Throughout the Qing dynasty, some of the envoy mission records further specified that the Black Water Trough-which separated China and the Ryukyu Kingdom and is known today as the Okinawa Trough-forms a boundary between China and the outside world. The earliest such reference to the Diaoyutai Islands dates back to the Records of the Imperial Mission to Ryukyu by Chen Kan 陳侃 in 1534. In 1556,Zheng Shungong 鄭舜功, a Ming envoy to Japan, also recorded in A Glimpse into Japan 日本一鑑 the following passage, "Diaoyutai Island is a small islet belonging to Xiaodong 小東 [ancient name of Taiwan]," with an illustrated map that also included the islands. Clearly the Diaoyutai Islands appertained to Taiwan by the mid-16th century.

(2) Incorporated into coastal defense zone during Ming dynasty and territory during Qing dynasty

During the Ming dynasty, Japanese pirates ravaged the southeast coast of China. In 1561, Zheng Ruozeng 鄭若曾 showed the Diaoyutai Islands in his Coastal Defense Map 萬里海防圖. The next year, Hu Zongxian 胡宗憲, then Minister of Defense and commander-in-chief, included the Diaoyutai Islands in the Coastal Territories Map 沿海山沙圖 as part of the Compilation of Maps on Managing the Sea 籌海圖編, thereby incorporating the islands into the defense system for China's southeast coast.

This practice was continued in the Qing dynasty. In 1683, Taiwan was officially incorporated into Chinese territory as a prefecture of Taixia Circuit 臺夏道 under Fujian Province. The Diaoyutai Islands, being an island group appertaining to Taiwan, also became a part of Qing territory. In 1812, they were placed under the jurisdiction of Kavalan Office, which was given its current designation of Yilan County in 1885. The reports of imperial censors in the Qing dynasty as well as official gazetteers of Fujian Province and Taiwan Prefecture serve as the most authoritative historical records supporting the claim that the Diaoyutai Islands belong to Taiwan. For example, during the inspection tour of Taiwan in 1722, the imperial censor HuangShujing 黃叔璥 wrote Record of Missions to Taiwan and Adjacent Waters 臺海使槎錄. In volume 2, Military Defense 武備, Huang listed the patrol routes of the naval forces of Taiwan Prefecture, stating "in the seas to the north beyond the mountains is a mountain named Diaoyutai where a dozen large ships may be anchored."

Subsequently, Fan Xian's 范咸 Revised Gazetteer of Taiwan Prefecture 重修臺灣府志 (1747) and Yu Wenyi's 余文儀 Continued Gazetteer of Taiwan

Prefecture 續修臺灣府志 (1764) included Huang's references. The Kavalan Office Gazetteer 噶瑪蘭廳志 (1852) by Chen Shujun 陳淑均 and Illustrations of Taiwan 全臺圖說 (1872) by Zhou Maoqi 周懋琦, Taiwan's magistrate and superintendent of military affairs, also contained similar citations stating that "in the seas beyond the mountains is an island named Diaoyutai where a dozen large boats may be anchored."

In 1871, Chen Shouqi's 陳壽祺 Recompiled General Gazetteer of Fujian 重纂福建通志 further listed Diaoyutai Island under Kavalan Office of Taiwan in Volume 86, Coastal Defense and Strategically Important Places in All Districts 海防・各縣衝要. Given that these local gazetteers served primarily "to record history, assist governance, and inform the populace," their documentation of Qing marine patrol ships anchoring at Diaoyutai serve as both historical records and evidence of the Qing government's continuous rule. These local documents prove that the Diaoyutai Islands indeed were islands appertaining to Taiwan and formed part of the inherent territory of Qing China.

Moreover, the official Map of Imperial China and Foreign Lands 皇朝中外一統輿圖, published in 1863, marked the Diaoyutai Islands as part of China, as did foreign maps around that time. One example was An Illustrated Description of the Three Countries: The Map of the Three Provinces and 36 Islands of Ryukyu 三國通覽圖說?琉球三省并三十六島之圖 published in 1785 by Shihei Hayashi 林子平, a renowned Japanese military scholar. In this map, Hayashi marked the Diaoyutai Islands and China in red, and the 36 Ryukyu Islands in light yellow, showing that the Diaoyutai Islands belonged to China and were neither a part of the Ryukyu Islands nor *terra nullius*.

(3) Ryukyu territory confirmed to not include Diaoyutai Islands by Chinese, Japanese and Ryukyu diplomatic documents

In 1879, just before Japan abolished the tributary kingdom of Ryukyu and renamed it Okinawa Prefecture, Kochi ueekata Chojo Sho Tokuko 紫金大夫向德宏 wrote an official letter in reply to Japanese Foreign Minister Munenori Terashima 寺島宗則, confirming that the Ryukyu Islands consisted of 36 islets and that the "long stretch of" islands between Kume Island and Fuzhoubelonged to China. In 1880, Japan's minister to China presented a proposal to China's Zongli Yamen 總理衙門 [foreign affairs office] that the Ryukyu Islands should be divided between the two countries, which provided further evidence that no terra nullius existed between China and the Ryukyu Islands.

4 *Chinese Civilian Use of the Diaoyutai Islands*

The names of the three major islets of the Diaoyutai Islands (Diaoyutai Island, Huangwei Islet and Chiwei Islet) are all related to "fish" in Mandarin, showing that the people of China long ago realized that this area abounds with aquatic fauna, especially skipjack tuna and mackerel. In addition, due to the region's favorable geographical and climate conditions, it has been a traditional fishing ground for people based in Taipei, Keelung and Suao in northeastern Taiwan. They have used the islands for hundreds of years. This was the case before and during Japanese colonial rule (1895–1945), and continued after Taiwan's restoration to the Republic of China (1945). In fact, this remained true until the early 1970s, when the United States "returned" administrative control of the Diaoyutai Islands and Ryukyu Islands to Japan, whose ships then started to interfere with the operations of Taiwanese fishermen in the Diaoyutai waters.

In fact, even after Japan occupied Taiwan in 1895 and placed the Diaoyutai Islands under the jurisdiction of Ryukyu (Okinawa Prefecture), renaming them the Senkaku Islands in 1900, the Japanese governor-general of Taiwan continued to designate the Diaoyutai Islands and their surrounding waters as major skipjack tuna fishing grounds for Taiwanese fishermen in 1920. The area was also listed among Taiwan's "important fishing grounds" in Taiwan's Marine Products 臺灣水產要覽 published by the governor-general's office in 1925.

5 *Evaluation under International Law*

The origin of modern international law extends back to 16th- and 17th-century Europe. When the Diaoyutai Islands were found, named and used by the Chinese in the 15th century, modern international law had yet to come into existence. Therefore, it would not be appropriate to apply the principles of modern international law to Asian countries of the past, as such legislation was non-existent at the time. Nevertheless, by the strict standards of modern international law, the ROC's sovereignty claim over the Diaoyutai Islands still stands.

(1) The Diaoyutai Islands were not terra nullius in 1885. As such, Japan's claim of sovereignty over the Diaoyutai Islands by virtue of "discovery-occupation" is invalid.

According to official historical records, the Diaoyutai Islands were found and named by the Chinese, who had used and incorporated them for hundreds of years before Japan secretly annexed them in 1895. Taiwanese fishermen have continued to use the islands and their surrounding waters. Moreover, both Chinese and foreign maps of the 18th and 19th centuries marked the Diaoyutai Islands as Chinese territory. These concrete facts cannot be denied.

As such, Japan's claim of sovereignty over the Diaoyutai Islands by virtue of "discovery-occupation" under international law was invalid ab initio (from the onset), as such claims can only be made with respect to terra nullius. Before

1895, the Diaoyutai Islands had appertained to Taiwan, not the Ryukyu Islands, for more than 300 years and had been included in Qing China's territory along with Taiwan for over 200 years, demonstrating clearly that they were not terra nullius at that point in history. In addition, this fact was recognized by experts and government officials from both Japan and the Ryukyu Islands at that time. Therefore, Japan's current claim of sovereignty over the Diaoyutai Islands was null and void ab initio under international law, and as a result, has never been binding.

(2) Japan's attempt to annex the islands in 1885 thwarted

Moreover, the issue of sovereignty over the Diaoyutai Islands is strongly linked to the cession of Taiwan after the First Sino-Japanese War. In 1879, Japan annexed the Ryukyu Islands and embarked on a path to further expand its territory. According to related documents stored at Japan's Ministry of Foreign Affairs, National Archives and National Institute for Defense Studies, the Japanese government's territorial ambitions regarding the Diaoyutai Islands began in 1885. That year, Japan's Home Minister Aritomo Yamagata 山縣有朋 ordered Okinawa GovernorSutezo Nishimura 西村捨三 to survey the Diaoyutai Islands with the aim to set up a national marker on the islands. However, Nishimura reported in his survey that, as these islands had been discovered long ago by China and named and recorded in its official documents, the plan was inappropriate at that time and should be postponed. Undeterred, Yamagata secretly consulted with Minister of Foreign Affairs Kaoru Inoue 井上馨. Inoue replied in a highly confidential document (No. 38) that "Chinese newspapers have recently reported that Japan is planning to seize Qing islands near Taiwan. It would therefore be appropriate to postpone erecting a national marker to avoid arousing the Qing state's suspicion." Inoue further instructed that the matter "must not be made public through official gazettes and newspapers." The Meiji government's plan to establish a national marker was thus thwarted.

(3) Japan secretly occupied the Diaoyutai Islands as it defeated Qing China in the First Sino-Japanese War.

In July 1894, the First Sino-Japanese War broke out. By October, Japan had gained decisive victories both on land and at sea. Recognizing the balance of power had shifted and believing that the time was right, its Cabinet secretly granted permission to Okinawa Prefecture on January 14, 1895, to establish a national marker on the Diaoyutai Islands.

The Cabinet's secret decision was not made public through the normal procedure of an imperial decree, and the outside world knew nothing about this so-called "discovery-occupation." Therefore, the decision was merely an internal matter expressing the government's intentions and, under international law, not legally binding on Qing China, let alone the Republic of China of today. In fact, the Japanese government did not follow up on its secret decision to occupy the Diaoyutai Islands with any concrete actions to support its claim, such as by setting up a national marker or stationing troops there. It was not until May 1969 that a national marker was erected by Okinawa Prefecture following the eruption of disputes over the islands. Three months after Japan secretly occupied the Diaoyutai Islands (on April 17, 1895), the Qing court signed the Treaty of Shimonoseki ceding Taiwan to Japan. The official handover took place on May 8, 1895, when Taiwan (including the Diaoyutai Islands) formally became Japanese territory. Therefore, under the principles of international law, Japan's claim to sovereignty over the Diaoyutai Islands by virtue of "discovery-occupation" was invalid abinitio, and its takeover should be considered "cession."

In 1971, the Japanese government claimed, "From 1885 on, surveys of the Senkaku Islands [the Diaoyutai Islands] had been repeatedly made by the Government of Japan through the agencies of Okinawa Prefecture and by way of other methods. Through these surveys, it was confirmed that the Senkaku Islands had been uninhabited and showed no trace of having been under the control of the Qing Dynasty of China." However, this statement is historically inaccurate and can be refuted based on official Meiji documents from 1885 to 1895. The first crucial piece of evidence is a letter dated January 27, 1892, written by Okinawa Governor KanjiMaruoka 丸岡莞爾 to Navy Minister Sukenori Kabayama 樺山資紀, requesting that the Navy Ministry dispatch the Kaimon 海門艦 to survey the Diaoyutai Islands given that these islands were "not sufficiently investigated." However, the Navy Ministry declined the request due to "perilous seasonal weather." The second crucial evidence was the letter Okinawa Governor Shigeru Narahara 奈良原繁 wrote to the Home Minister on May 12, 1894, which stated, "…as no field surveys have been conducted since the investigation by the police of this prefecture in the 18th year of the Meiji Period [1885], it is difficult to provide any specific reports on them."

These historical documents not only serve to refute the statement by Japan's current government that "surveys of the Senkaku Islands had been thoroughly made," but also demonstrate that the Japanese government annexed the Diaoyutai Islands during the First Sino-Japanese War of 1894–1895.

(4) The Diaoyutai Islands should have been restored to the Republic of China along with Taiwan after the Second World War.

When Qing China was on the verge of losing the First Sino-Japanese War, Japan seized the opportunity to annex the Diaoyutai Islands, which appertain to Taiwan. In accordance with the Treaty of Shimonoseki, Taiwan was ceded to Japan. Article 2 of this instrument stipulated that Taiwan included "the island of Formosa [Taiwan], together with all the islands appertaining or belonging to the said island of Formosa." The Diaoyutai Islands, as a part of "the islands appertaining or belonging to the said island of Formosa," were ceded to Japan along with Taiwan. Therefore, the Treaty of Shimonoseki provided the only legal basis for the 50 years of Japanese rule over Taiwan, including the Diaoyutai Islands, starting in 1895.

On December 9 [Taipei Time], 1941, the day after the Japanese attack on Pearl Harbor, the Republic of China declared war against Japan, stating that "all treaties, conventions, agreements and contracts regarding relations between China and Japan are and remain null and void." On December 1, 1943, the Republic of China, the United States and the United Kingdom jointly promulgated the Cairo Declaration, which stipulated that the purpose of convening the Cairo meeting was to ensure that "all the territories Japan has stolen from the Chinese, such as Manchuria, Formosa, and the Pescadores (Penghu), shall be restored to the Republic of China. Japan will also be expelled from all other territories which she has taken by violence and greed." On July 26, 1945, Allied countries, namely, the Republic of China, the United States, the United Kingdom and the Soviet Union, issued the Potsdam Proclamation, Article 8 of which stated that "the terms of the Cairo Declaration shall be carried out." In the Japanese Instrument of Surrender signed on September 2, 1945, after the Japanese Emperor announced the country's unconditional surrender, Japan clearly accepted the Potsdam Proclamation. That is, the Japanese Instrument of Surrender combined all three documents. In 1969, the US Department of State put the three documents in volume 3 of Treaties and Other International Agreements of the United States of America, 1776–1949. The Japanese Instrument of Surrender was also included in volume 59 of The United States Statutes at Large published in 1946, as well as volume 139 of The United Nations Treaties Series published in 1952. This document is, therefore, legally binding on Japan, the United States and the Republic of China. Moreover, both the 1951 San Francisco Peace Treaty and the 1952 Treaty of Peace between the Republic of China and Japan stipulate that "Japan has renounced all right, title and claim to Taiwan (Formosa) and Penghu (the Pescadores)." In addition, Article 4 of the 1952 Treaty of Peace between the Republic of China and Japan further indicates that "All treaties, conventions, and agreements concluded before 9 December 1941 between Japan and China have become null and void as a consequence of the war." Article 10 of the Treaty also confirms that all the inhabitants and former inhabitants of Taiwan (Formosa) and Penghu (the Pescadores) and their descendents are nationals of the Republic of China. The Treaty's Exchange of Notes No. 1 confirms that the Treaty is applicable to ROC territory. Therefore theDiaoyutai Islands should have been restored to the Republic of China.

(5) Japan cannot use the principle of prescription in international law to justify its occupation of the Diaoyutai Islands.
After disputes regarding sovereignty over the Diaoyutai Islands occurred in 1971, Japan claimed that "From the 28th year of the Meiji Period (1895) till now (1971), no objection from foreign powers had been made to Japan's use of these islands." Based on the historical circumstances, this claim is invalid. During the period between 1895 and 1945, not only the Diaoyutai Islands, but also the entire island of Taiwan, were subject to Japanese occupation, and were therefore part of Japan's territory. As such, no other country challenged Japan's use of either Taiwan or the Diaoyutai Islands.

Between 1945 and 1972, while under the trusteeship of the US government, the Diaoyutai Islands were not ruled by Japan nor controlled by any other country. Therefore, US trusteeship did not have any significance in terms of sovereignty. During this period, the people of Taiwan, particularly fishermen, continued to use these islands without interference. Moreover, as the US armed forces assisted in defending the Taiwan Strait in accordance with the 1954 Mutual Defense Treaty between the United States and the Republic of China, there was no need for the Republic of China to negotiate with the United States on this issue. From 1968, however, disputes over the Diaoyutai Islands arose. The ROC government has repeatedly claimed sovereignty and lodged numerous diplomatic protests with Japan. Therefore, Japan's argument involving the principle of prescription is groundless.

As for the transfer of administration rights over the Diaoyutai Islands and the Ryukyu Islands from the United States to Japan in 1972, the United States officially notified the Republic of China on May 26, 1971, stating that it would restore to Tokyo the administration rights it had acquired from Japan and that this would not jeopardize any of the ROC's sovereignty claims. The US Senate later clarified that the US stance on the sovereignty issue was neutral and that the transfer of the Diaoyutai Islands' administration rights would not affect the basic position of any of the claimants. Judging from related diplomatic documents, the United States adopted-and has since maintained-a neutral stance on the Diaoyutai Islands' sovereignty issue, which it believed should be resolved through bilateral negotiations between the Republic of China and

Japan. Moreover, according to the Potsdam Proclamation, "Japanese sovereignty shall be limited to the islands of Honshu, Hokkaido, Kyushu, Shikoku and such minor islands as we [the Allies] determine." The United States regards the Potsdam Proclamation as a treaty, which was incorporated into the Japanese Instrument of Surrender and has binding power on the United States. Therefore, the United States does not have the right to unilaterally decide who possesses sovereignty rights over the Diaoyutai Islands.

III Conclusion

The Diaoyutai Islands were discovered, named and used by the Chinese in the 15th century, and were integrated into the Chinese coastal defense system during the Ming dynasty in the middle of the 15th century. After the Qing dynasty came to power in the 17th century, the islands, along with Taiwan, were incorporated into Qing China, as they appertain to Taiwan, and placed under the jurisdiction of Taiwan Prefecture. Like Pengjia Islet, the Diaoyutai Islands are clearly an inherent part of the territory of the Republic of China.

In the late 19th century, driven by expansionism, Japan attempted to occupy the Diaoyutai Islands. Due to a lack of power, however, it initially did not attempt to do so. Following a period of 10 years, Japan took advantage of the First Sino-Japanese War to secretly occupy the Diaoyutai Islands. Today, Japan is not willing to return the islands to the Republic of China in accordance with the 1943 Cairo Declaration, the 1945 Potsdam Proclamation, Japan's Instrument of Surrender of 1945 and the 1952 Treaty of Peace between the Republic of China and Japan. Japan's actions have seriously affected the relations between the Republic of China and Japan, as well as regional security and stability.

Ever since disputes over the Diaoyutai Islands started to emerge in the late 1960s, the ROC government has staunchly upheld the policy of "safeguarding sovereignty, shelving disputes, pursuing peace and reciprocity, and promoting joint development." It has also expressed willingness to resolve disputes through peaceful means in line with the UN Charter and relevant international laws and to enter into negotiations with Japan so as to shelve controversies and jointly explore and develop resources, with the aim of maintaining sovereignty, defending the rights of our fishermen and resolving disputes.

In September 2012, the Japanese government's move to nationalize three of the Diaoyutai Islands raised tension in the East China Sea. The Republic of China immediately lodged a protest and, in the spirit of the East China Sea Peace Initiative proposed by President Ma Ying-jeou on August 5 of the same year, called upon all parties concerned to (1) exercise restraint and refrain from taking any antagonistic actions; (2) shelve controversies and not abandon dialogue; (3) observe international law and resolve disputes through peaceful means; (4) seek consensus on a Code of Conduct in the East China Sea; and (5) establish a mechanism for cooperation on exploring and developing resources in the East China Sea. Concrete steps include moving from "three sets of bilateral dialogue to one set of trilateral negotiation," by "replacing confrontation with dialogue" and "shelving controversies in favor of consultations," so as to discuss the possibility of jointly exploring and developing resources in the East China Sea.

Since its announcement, the East China Sea Peace Initiative has received international recognition and affirmation. On April 10, 2013, the Republic of China and Japan formally signed the Taiwan-Japan Fisheries Agreement following the 17th round of bilateral fishery negotiations. This agreement, which embodies the spirit of the East China Sea Peace Initiative with regard to resolving disputes through peaceful means, successfully protects the rights and interests of ROC fishermen operating in the East China Sea.

The government of the Republic of China will continue to uphold its sovereignty over the Diaoyutai Islands and, in the spirit of the East China Sea Peace Initiative, seek peaceful and pragmatic solutions to disputes and endeavor to safeguard regional security.

VI State Responsibility

(No item reported under this section)

VII The Law of the Sea, Environment, Health, and Aviation

Republic of China (Taiwan) Signs Fisheries Agreement with Japan

On April 15, 2013, the Ministry of Foreign Affairs issued the following press release on the signing of the fisheries agreement with Japan:[17]

The Association of East Asian Relations (AEAR), representing the Republic of China (Taiwan), and the Interchange Association, representing Japan, held their 17th round of bilateral fisheries consultations at the Taipei Guest House on April 10, 2013. The ROC delegation, led by AEAR Chairman Liao Liou-yi, comprised officials from the ROC's Ministry of Foreign Affairs, Coast Guard Administration, and Fisheries Agency under the Council of Agriculture. The

17 MOFA, Republic of China (Taiwan) Signs Fisheries Agreement with Japan, Apr. 15, 2013, http://www.mofa.gov.tw/en/News_Content.aspx?n=1EADDCFD4C6EC567&s=D879E042D13F9135.

Japanese delegation, led by the Interchange Association Chairman Mitsuo Ohashi, comprised officials from Japan's Ministry of Foreign Affairs, Fisheries Agency, and Coast Guard. The talks concluded with the signing of a Taiwan-Japan fisheries agreement.

While staunchly safeguarding its sovereignty and position on maritime territories, Taiwan reached consensus with Japan under the principles of parity and reciprocity. The agreement will protect the rights and interests of Taiwanese fishermen operating within a designated zone. It will extend their fishing area by an additional 1,400 square nautical miles (approximately 4,530 square kilometers). An institutionalized mechanism in the form of a Taiwan-Japan fisheries committee will be established to conduct consultations on other issues regarding fishing grounds, bilateral fishery cooperation and the like.

Taiwan and Japan launched their first fishery talks in 1996 and, over the past 17 years, have held 16 formal meetings as well as numerous preparatory meetings and consultations. By setting aside disputes and agreeing to share fishery resources in this latest round of talks, the two sides were able to make appropriate arrangements and achieve concrete results concerning fishery issues arising from the overlapping of their respective exclusive economic zones (EEZ).

During the talks, Chairman Liao reiterated that the Diaoyutai Islands are an inherent part of the territory of the Republic of China and an island group appertaining to Taiwan. The waters around the Diaoyutai Islands have long been traditional fishing grounds of Taiwanese fishermen, whose fishing rights should be accorded full protection under the law. In order to strengthen the cordial relations between Taiwan and Japan and to better ensure regional peace, stability, and sustainable development, President Ma Ying-jeou on August 5, 2012, proposed the East China Sea Peace Initiative in hopes that through concerted efforts the parties concerned could transform the East China Sea into a "sea of peace and cooperation."

The agreement reached in this latest round of talks covers the fishing operations in the two countries' overlapping EEZs, but did not touch upon the issues of sovereignty claimed by the respective parties. The ROC's sovereignty extends to the waters within 12 nautical miles surrounding the Diaoyutai Islands. These waters are not included in the agreed upon designated zone.

Although both the Republic of China and Japan claim sovereignty over the Diaoyutai Islands, the ROC has staunchly adhered to its policy of "safeguarding sovereignty, shelving disputes, pursuing peace and reciprocity, and promoting joint development." It will continue to stand by its claim and safeguard our sovereignty over the Diaoyutai Islands, yielding nary an inch. This government has consistently taken a firm stance on defending sovereignty and protecting fishery rights and will not compromise sovereignty over fishery rights; we shall continue to negotiate with Japan while setting aside disputes.

The ROC insisted that a disclaimer be included in the agreement so as to ensure that the provisions of the agreement do not undermine the ROC's position on and interpretation of international law regarding its sovereignty and maritime claims, etc.

The Taiwan-Japan fisheries agreement will be applicable to a large maritime zone south of 27 degrees north latitude and north of Japan's Yaeyama Islands and Miyako Islands, thus protecting the operation rights of ROC fishing vessels. The operational zone extends beyond the so-called "temporary enforcement line," translating into a larger operating area for ROC fishing boats. As for the ROC's concerns pertaining to other operational waters and issues, consultations will be conducted through the future Taiwan-Japan fisheries committee, which in principle should meet once a year.

ROC fishing vessels will be able to operate within the agreement-designated zone without interference by Japanese government agency vessels. The ROC government will continue to protect the legal rights of its fishermen by maintaining the existing environment within the areas delineated by the temporary enforcement line north of 27 degrees north latitude and south of Japan's Yaeyama Islands and Miyako Islands.

Sovereignty cannot be divided or conceded, but resources can be shared. This concept embedded in President Ma Ying-jeou's East China Sea Peace Initiative served as the groundwork for this round of Taiwan-Japan fisheries consultations. Through engagement under this fundamental principle, the two countries were able to reach consensus on the provisions of the fisheries agreement. The agreement resolved fishery issues that have endured for 17 years, thereby marking a new milestone in their friendship. It is expected that this achievement will further strengthen the special friendship and overall cooperation between Taiwan and Japan.

ROC Statement on Beijing's Announcement of the East China Sea Air Defense Identification Zone

On November 24, 2013, the National Security Council issued the following press release concerning the statement on Beijing's announcement of the East China Sea Air Defense Identification Zone:[18]

The ROC National Security Council convened a meeting at 3 PM on November 23, 2013, with the heads of the ministries of the Interior, Foreign Affairs, National Defense, and the Mainland Affairs Council to discuss mainland China's announcement at 10 AM of the same day regarding the

18 MOFA, Press Release (Source: National Security Council Republic of China), Nov. 24, 2013, http://www.mofa.gov.tw/en/News_Content.aspx?n=1EADDCFD4C6EC567&s=C588063F9AE56208.

establishment of an "air defense identification zone" in the East China Sea. In response, the ROC government hereby states its position as follows:

1. The ROC maintains sovereignty over the Diaoyutai Islands, a fact which is not affected in any way by mainland China's announcement concerning an air defense identification zone. The ROC government will continue to defend its sovereignty over the Diaoyutai Islands, protect the interests of its fishermen, and engage in actions aimed at safeguarding the ROC's fishing rights.
2. With regard to the situation in the East China Sea, ROC President Ma Ying-jeou announced the East China Sea Peace Initiative on August 5, 2012, urging all parties concerned to exercise restraint, avoid actions that could escalate confrontation in the region, shelve disputes, not abandon dialogue, and observe international law, so as to resolve disputes in a peaceful manner. The ROC government calls on all parties concerned to continue to resolve disputes through peaceful dialogue, in order to prevent tensions in the region from rising.
3. With regard to the fact that the air defense identification zone announced by mainland China in the East China Sea overlaps to some extent with the ROC air defense identification zone, the ROC Armed Forces will adhere to the principles set forth in the East China Sea Peace Initiative, with the aim of resolving disputes peacefully. In addition, the ROC Armed Forces will take appropriate measures to ensure the safety of ROC airspace.
4. The ROC government is deeply concerned about developments in the region following mainland China's announcement of its air defense identification zone. It will keep in close contact with all parties concerned to safeguard regional peace and stability.

National Security Council of the ROC Responds to Beijing's Announcement of East China Sea Air Defense Identification Zone

On November 24, 2012, the Ministry of Foreign Affairs issued the following press release on the National Security Council's response to Beijing's Announcement of East China Sea Air Defense Identification Zone:[19]

The National Security Council of the ROC, in response to mainland China's Nov. 23 announcement that it has established an "East China Sea air

19 MOFA, ROC Responds to Beijing's Announcement of East China Sea Air Defense Identification Zone, Nov. 24, 2013, http://www.mofa.gov.tw/en/News_Content.aspx?n=1EADDCFD4C6EC567&s=25A4CC2F8DA32E10.

defense identification zone," has issued a statement reiterating the following principles:

The Diaoyutai Islands are an integral part of ROC territory, a fact which is unaffected by mainland China's declaration. The ROC government will continue to defend its sovereignty over the archipelago, protect the rights of Taiwan fishermen in surrounding waters, and maintain patrols to safeguard fishing activities. It is deeply concerned about developments in the region and will maintain close contact with all parties concerned to preserve regional peace and stability.

The NSC statement came following a meeting with heads of the ministries of the Interior, Foreign Affairs, National Defense and the Mainland Affairs Council at 3 p.m. the same day.

Regarding overlap between the air defense identification zones of the ROC and mainland China, the NSC said the ROC Armed Forces will adhere to the principles set forth in the East China Sea Peace Initiative, with the aim of resolving disputes peacefully, while taking appropriate measures to ensure the safety of ROC airspace.

President Ma Ying-jeou proposed the five-point peace initiative Aug. 5 last year, urging all parties to refrain from antagonistic actions; not abandon dialogue; observe international law; resolve disputes through peaceful means; and form a mechanism for exploring and developing resources on a cooperative basis.

The landmark Taiwan-Japan fisheries agreement which was signed April 10, resolving 40 years of disputes between the two countries, demonstrates the viability of the East China Sea Peace Initiative and serves as an empirical model for peaceful resolution of international disputes. It allows ROC fishermen to operate in areas twice the size of Taiwan with no concession on ROC sovereignty.

Located roughly 102 nautical miles northeast of Taiwan proper, the Diaoyutais are an uninhabited archipelago historically attached to the ROC.

Executive Yuan Reaffirms ROC Stance on Mainland China's Announcement of ADIZ

On November 30, 2013, the Ministry of Foreign Affairs issued the following press release on the Executive Yuan's position reaffirming the ROC stance on Mainland China's announcement of ADIZ:[20]

---

20 MOFA, Executive Yuan Reaffirms ROC Stance on Mainland China's Announcement of ADIZ, Nov. 30, 2013, http://www.mofa.gov.tw/en/News_Content.aspx?n=1EADDCFD4C6EC567&s=63D65B1C726D91A2.

The Executive Yuan released the following statement in Taipei on the evening of Nov. 29, 2013, reaffirming the Republic of China government position in the wake of mainland China's announcement of an "East China Sea air defense identification zone":

1. The National Security Council issued a four-point statement on Nov. 23, 2013, emphasizing that the government of the Republic of China will staunchly defend its sovereignty over the Diaoyutai Islands. It also reiterated the East China Sea Peace Initiative put forth by President Ma Ying-jeou, urging all parties concerned to exercise restraint and refrain from antagonistic actions; shelve disputes and not abandon dialogue; and observe international law, resolving disputes through peaceful means. The ROC government maintains an unquestionably clear and rock-solid stance on this matter.
2. Mainland China did not consult Taiwan prior to its announcement of its East China Sea air defense identification zone (ADIZ). This has resulted in overlap between Taiwan's and mainland China's air defense identification zones and flight information regions (FIR). The ROC government believes that this action is not conducive to the positive development of cross-strait relations. Taiwan will express its serious concerns regarding this matter to mainland China through appropriate channels.
3. The ROC Ministry of National Defense (MND), to safeguard national security and public welfare, has instructed the armed forces to carry out naval and air security missions in accordance with the existing ADIZ; standard military practices will not be changed due to the establishment of mainland China's East China Sea ADIZ. The MND will continue to strengthen information collection, monitoring and reconnaissance within Taiwan's ADIZ to keep track of all air and sea activity, provide early warning and ensure maritime and air security.
4. The Civil Aeronautics Administration of the Ministry of Transportation and Communications will relay the filing of flight plans for civil aircraft in accordance with relevant regulations and practices of the International Civil Aviation Organization (ICAO) regarding FIR notification, based on requests from airline companies in Taiwan and abroad, to ensure the safety of passengers.
5. The ROC government is deeply concerned about developments in the region and has unequivocally urged all parties concerned to resolve related regional disputes through peaceful bilateral or multilateral negotiations so as to jointly maintain regional peace and stability.

Guang Da Xing No. 28 Incident (May 9, 2013)

President Ma Holds National Security Council Meeting, Issues Demands Regarding Incident Involving Guang Da Xing No. 28 Fishing Vessel

On May 11, 2013, the Office of the President issued the following press release on the National Security Council Meeting on the Guang Da Xing No. 28 Incident:[21]

President Ma Ying-jeou convened a National Security Council meeting on the evening of May 11 to discuss an incident on May 9 in which a Philippine government vessel fired shots at a Taiwan fishing boat, the Guang Da Xing No. 28, resulting in the death of one ROC fisherman and serious damage to the fishing vessel. The president discussed the issue with senior government officials and during the meeting issued the following demands:

1. The ROC government demands that the government of the Philippines: issue a formal apology; provide compensation for the losses; promptly and thoroughly investigate the incident and severely punish those responsible for the killing; and initiate fishery agreement negotiations between the two countries as soon as possible.
2. The ROC government demands that the government of the Philippines provide a positive response within 72 hours of 12:01 a.m. on May 12. Otherwise, the ROC government will register its protest by: freezing the applications of Filipino laborers seeking to work in Taiwan; recalling the ROC's representative stationed in the Philippines; and requesting that the representative of the Philippines stationed in Taiwan return to the Philippines to help with the proper resolution of this incident.

Officials in attendance at the evening National Security Council meeting included Vice President Wu Den-yih, Secretary-General to the President Timothy Chin-Tien Yang (楊進添), National Security Council Secretary-General Jason C. Yuan (袁健生), Premier Jiang Yi-huah (江宜樺), Minister of Foreign Affairs David Y. L. Lin (林永樂), Minister of National Defense Kao Hua-chu (高華柱), Minister of Transportation and Communications Yeh Kuang-Shih (葉匡時), Minister of Justice Tseng Yung-Fu (曾勇夫), Minister of Economic Affairs Chia-Juch Chang (張家祝), Minister of the Coast Guard

21 Office of the President, President Ma Holds National Security Council Meeting, Issues Demands Regarding Incident Involving Guang Da Xing No. 28 Fishing Vessel, May 11, 2013, http://english.president.gov.tw/Default.aspx?tabid=491&itemid=29856&rmid=2355.

Wang Ginn-Wang (王進旺), Minister of Labor Affairs Pan Shih-Wei (潘世偉), and Minister of Agriculture Bao-ji Chen (陳保基).

MAC Position on Mainland China's Concern over Fatal Shooting of Taiwanese Fisherman by the Philippines

On May 16, 2013, the Mainland Affairs Council issued the following press release on regarding Mainland China's concern over the fatal shooting of Taiwanese fisherman by the Philippines:[22]

1. The killing of a Taiwanese fisherman by the Philippines is an act of atrocity in violation of international law. The ROC government has taken proactive and vigorous measures in making stern representations to the Philippines and demanding the Philippines to seriously respond to Taiwan's requests.
2. The MAC stated that, actions that are irrational, non-peaceful and in violation of international law should be condemned by all parties. Taiwan has also expressed gratitude towards parties such as the United States and the Mainland for expressing their concern over the incident. However, the "one China principle" advocated by mainland China is completely irrelevant to this case. Our interpretation of the "one China" is the Republic of China. It is hoped that this point is fully acknowledged by all parties so as to avoid hurting our people's feelings in dealing with this incident.
3. The MAC further stated that, it would be unacceptable to Taiwan if the Philippines conveyed proposals for follow-up negotiations or handling of the matter through mainland China. The MAC also stated that it trusted the Mainland to empathize, maintain mutual respect, and not intervene in Taiwan's disputes with third parties.

Official Statement of the Republic of China (Taiwan) on the Intentional Shooting Conducted by the Philippine Law Enforcement Vessel against the Guang Da Xsin 28

On May 18, 2013, the Ministry of Justice issued the Official Statement of the Republic of China (Taiwan) on the Intentional Shooting Conducted by

---

22 Mainland Affairs Council, MAC Position on Mainland China's Concern over Fatal Shooting of Taiwanese Fisherman by the Philippines, May 16, 2013, http://www.mac.gov.tw/public/Attachment/352815185029.pdf.

the Philippine Law Enforcement Vessel against the Guang Da Xsin 28. The Statement is as follows:[23]

The government of the Republic of China (Taiwan) formally issued two letters to request legal assistance from the Philippine government through the Taipei Economic and Cultural Office in the Philippines (TECO) before the departure of Taiwan's investigation team.

In the said letters, Taiwan government requests the Philippine government to provide assistance in the collection and inspection of evidence; in interrogating the perpetrators; and in providing the investigation reports. With the said assistances provided by the Philippine side, Taiwan government will be able to obtain the evidence collected by the Philippine authorities in the soonest possible time so that the liability of all the perpetrators could be clarified and determined afterwards.

It should also be noted that Resident Representative Antonio Basilio of the Manila Economic and Cultural Office (MECO) has stated publicly and clearly that the Philippine side will conduct joint investigation with its Taiwan counterpart in his letter to Taiwan's government and in his statement given in the previous press conference.

The results of Taiwan's investigation are as follows:

1. As stated in the report coded No.1021101517 made by the Institute of Forensic Medicine, Ministry of Justice, the Taiwanese victim died from a single perforating gunshot wound in the bottom left section of the neck, which perforated the left common carotid artery, trachea, esophagus, transverse thoracic burst fractures from L2 to L6, aorta, and upper lobe of the left lung, rupture of upper and lower lobes of the right lung causing massive bleeding and pneumothorax, hemothorax, hypovolemic shock, and respiratory failure. The forensic report further states that the severe transverse thoracic burst fractures from L2 to L6 of the victim suggested that the gunshot wounds were caused by high speed or powerful guns such as machine guns or rifled. Therefore, based on these medical evidences, the manner of death is "homicide".
2. Based on the bullets collected from Guang Da Xsin 28, the criminal investigators concluded that the ammunitions used were 7.62mm caliber shots, most likely coming from M14 rifle, M240 or M60 machine guns.

23 Ministry of Justice, Official Statement of the Republic of China (Taiwan) on the Intentional Shooting Conducted by the Philippine Law Enforcement Vessel against the Guang Da Xsin 28, May 18, 2013, https://www.moj.gov.tw/public/Attachment/351918563819.pdf.

However, there is still possibility that the wound was caused by other armaments which are also 7.62mm caliber.

3. After the 2nd check-up on the Guang Da Xsin 28, it was found out that the vessel has been shot by a total of 45 bullets. In addition, bullet remnants were not found on the surface of Guang Ta Hsin 28, thus omitting the possibility that Guang Ta Hsin 28 was trying to ram the Philippine law enforcement vessel, specifically the Maritime Control Surveillance 3001 (MCS-3001) which resulted to the defensive measure taken by the latter.
4. According to the relevant regulations of the international maritime law, even if the Philippine law enforcers on MCS-3001 were conducting an official duty, they should follow the procedures of warning, dispelling, boarding and detaining the illegal vessel, then proceed to the legal procedure. However, MCS 3001 failed to do the aforementioned measures which clearly showed that the personnel on board the ship totally ignored and violated the customs of the international law. Moreover, after double checking the Guang Da Xsin 28, it was found out that it has been shot with 45 bullets, not counting the missed shots since both sea vessels were in continuous motion. Most of those 45 bullets were shot at the cockpit, in which the four crew members were hiding. In addition, the wound was a result of a high speed rupturing gun shot. By combining the abovementioned evidences, it clearly shows that the Philippine law enforcers were intentionally shooting the Guang Da Xsin 28 crew members, which indicates their intent of murder. This kind of behavior should not be conducted by a civilized country. We believe that the Philippine government would never allow for this kind of act to be done to its people.
5. As shown in the VDR recorded by Guang Da Xsin 28, the exact location where the incident occurred is within the EEZ of the Republic of China and not in the Philippine territorial water.

Based on anonymous reports, the Philippine media has mentioned that the Philippine government is already in possession of a videotape of the incident and other relevant evidence; however, the said evidence from the Philippine side indicate different results from the preliminary reports yielded by Taiwan's investigation. Given the discrepancy of the two sides' reports, it is necessary for Taiwan and the Philippines to jointly form an investigation team to uncover the truth behind the incident. Following the Agreement on Mutual Legal Assistance (AMLA) signed by the two sides, the Taiwan government welcomes the Philippine government to send a team to Taiwan to join the investigation provided that they also follow appropriate procedure.

From the beginning, all the statements made by the Taiwan government have always been in accordance to the results of our investigation. However, the Philippine government has continuously accused and labeled the victim as the villain in the incident, without disclosing sufficient evidence to back up their claims. Therefore, we strongly urge the Philippine government to follow the same standard that Taiwan has done faithfully. They should first present their evidence before directing meaningless claims and accusations against the victim. If they are unable to produce sufficient evidence that will deem their claims as legitimate, it can be said that the Philippine government is purposely concealing the offense of their officials.

The Taiwan investigation team arrived in Manila on May 16 in hopes that they will be able to jointly conduct an immediate investigation with their Philippine counterparts in order to further shed light on what truly transpired during the May 9 incident. Their initiative to come to the Philippines is based on the sincerity and consent expressed by the Philippine government in conducting a joint probe prior to the investigation team's arrival. However, the Philippine government has tried to prolong and delay our requests for a joint investigation. Although we made some progress yesterday, we still feel discontent on the lack of sincerity and credibility exhibited by the Philippine side in cooperating with our team. For this very reason, all the members of the Taiwan investigation team has decided to go back to Taiwan immediately. We hope that the Philippine government understands that there is only one truth; and that the way to show sincerity is by proposing concrete and feasible proposals for bilateral cooperation which will pave the way for the clarification of truth. In this way, we will be able to determine the proper compensation to the victim's family and carry out the appropriate punishments to the perpetrators.

The ROC Government Takes a Pragmatic Approach toward Taiwan-Philippines Cooperation in the Investigation of the Guang Da Xing No. 28 Incident

On May 19, 2013, MOFA issued the following press release on the ROC's approach towards cooperation in the investigation of the Guang Da Xing No. 28 Incident:[24]

President Ma Ying-jeou of the Republic of China (Taiwan) instructed that the investigation into the shooting attack by a Philippine government vessel

24 MOFA, The ROC Government Takes a Pragmatic Approach toward Taiwan-Philippines Cooperation in the Investigation of the Guang Da Xing No. 28 Incident, May 19, 2013, http://www.mofa.gov.tw/en/News_Content.aspx?n=1EADDCFD4C6EC567&s=8AC3DA871C2BA430.

on the Taiwan fishing boat Guang Da Xing No. 28 should be dealt with on the basis of "parity and reciprocity," and that a "consensus should be reached so as to quickly resolve the issue." Subsequently, on May 16 the ROC government sent an investigation team to the Philippines to show that it takes the incident very seriously and reiterate its solemn position. Taiwan has aimed to convey to the Philippines its strong determination to unveil the truth behind the incident, and urge the Philippines to fulfill the latter's promises to conduct a thorough, transparent and fair judicial investigation at an early date, so as to punish the perpetrators and provide just compensation. In addition, the team was to establish a communication channel with its Philippine counterparts. The Taiwan investigation team achieved a number of concrete results during its stay in the Philippines. It convened an international press conference in order to increase awareness of the incident and receive a positive response in the mainstream media and public opinion of the Philippines. It was able to gradually rectify the biased stance of the Philippines and promote Taiwan's position in the international media. At the same time, the Philippines expressed willingness to cooperate with Taiwan on this issue through parallel investigations, discuss a date for the next meeting between the investigation teams of the two sides, and establish communication channels for mutual judicial assistance so as to pave the way for future negotiations.

The significance of the Taiwan investigation team's visit to the Philippines is due to the following accomplishments:

1. Showing the Philippines and the international community that the ROC takes the incident very seriously and adding pressure to the Philippine government for it to conduct a fair and thorough judicial investigation

Prior to the investigation team's departure for Manila, the ROC had already imposed countermeasures against the Philippines on May 15. It had anticipated then that the Philippines might change its attitude and create difficulties for the Taiwan investigation team. Nevertheless, in order to show the Philippines and the international community that the ROC takes the incident very seriously and to exert pressure on the Philippine government, the Taiwan investigation team decided to travel to the Philippines as planned on May 16. The Philippines, after the Taiwan investigation team's arrival, delayed the provision of judicial assistance, claiming technicalities as their reason. Following further negotiations, the Philippines finally agreed to carry on with the bilateral judicial assistance and cooperation as well as to a meeting and exchange of investigation materials between the Taiwan investigation team and the Philippines' National Bureau of Investigation on May 20.

2. Holding international press conference in the Philippines to present the ROC's investigation findings to the people of the Philippines and the international community

Before returning to Taiwan on May 18, the Taiwan investigation team held an international press conference at the Taipei Economic and Cultural Office (TECO) in the Philippines. It issued a solemn statement in both Chinese and English, provided some of its findings, and presented evidence showing that the Philippine patrol personnel had violated international law, adopted illegal use of force, and killed an ROC fisherman. The team conveyed the details of the incident to the people of the Philippines and the rest of the world through the local and international media present at the press conference. Taiwan's investigation findings were reported by major Philippine news media on May 19, thus updating the people of the Philippines, rebutting the biased stance of the Philippine government, and promoting Taiwan's position in the international media.

3. Establishing communication channels for mutual judicial assistance and cooperation to pave the way for future negotiations

Philippine Secretary of Justice Leila de Lima stated publicly on May 17 that Taiwan's investigation team could not engage in a joint investigation with their counterparts in the Philippines. However, the two sides could conduct parallel investigations and adopt a cooperation mechanism for the two sides' teams to travel to each other's country to question witnesses and gather evidence, thereby promoting substantive legal mutual cooperation. The Philippines stated that it would also send an investigation team to Taiwan.

On May 17 afternoon, Antonio I. Basilio, the Philippine representative to Taiwan, and Amadeo R. Perez, Jr., Chairman of the Manila Economic and Cultural Office (MECO) paid a visit to TECO in the Philippines. They notified Taiwan's investigation team that the Philippine Department of Justice had accepted Taiwan's request for judicial assistance, and would arrange for Taiwan's investigation team to meet with the Philippine National Bureau of Investigation to exchange materials related to the investigation. In addition, they expressed that the Philippines has submitted a request to Taiwan for mutual judicial assistance. Taiwan's investigation team to the Philippines was therefore able to establish a mechanism for mutual judicial assistance that will allow the investigation to proceed in a pragmatic manner. In the future, the investigation can continue as instructed by President Ma Ying-jeou so that the principles of "parity and reciprocity" can be upheld and that "consensus can be reached so as to quickly resolve the issue." Taiwan will continue negotiating with the Philippines in order to complete the investigation and bring the Filipino perpetrators to justice.

Details on the Taiwan investigation team's visit to the Philippines regarding the Shooting Attack of Taiwan fishing boat Guang Da Xing No. 28 by a Philippine government vessel

Before the Taiwan investigation team departed for the Philippines, the Taipei Economic and Cultural Office (TECO) in the Philippines had already conferred with Philippine investigators on May 13 regarding relevant details of the two sides' investigation. TECO also sent an official letter to the Manila Economic and Cultural Office (MECO) on May 14 to request their assistance in urging the Philippine Department of Justice to meet with Taiwan's investigation team following its arrival in the Philippines. On May 15, the Philippine National Bureau of Investigation agreed to set up a meeting between investigators of the two sides at 3 PM on May 16 at the National Bureau of Investigation, so as to discuss the progress of the investigation and jointly review relevant evidence.

In a letter provided by the Philippine Representative to the ROC Antonio I. Basilio on May 14, as well as in his comments at a press conference in the early hours of May 15, it was clearly indicated that the Philippines and the ROC would jointly conduct an investigation in order to determine responsibility for the incident. When applying for visas with MECO on May 15 before its departure for the Philippines, the Taiwan investigation team clearly stated that the purpose of its visit was to investigate this case. The team departed for the Philippines at 7:30 AM on May 16.

Because the Philippines did not provide a positive and sufficient response to the ROC's four demands, the ROC on May 15 refused to meet with MECO Chairman Amadeo R. Perez, Jr.—the personal envoy of Philippine President Benigno S. Aquino III—and implemented two waves of countermeasures. Subsequently, when the Taiwan investigation team arrived in Manila on May 16, the Philippines indicated that it could not cooperate with Taiwan's investigation at that time, stating that the ROC request should have been made through MECO and that its Department of Justice had not received notification from MECO. The Philippines canceled its May 16 meeting with the Taiwan team, causing a delay in the investigation.

In the afternoon of May 17, TECO received a letter from MECO and the Department of Justice expressing the Philippines' willingness to meet with the Taiwan investigation team the following week. The Department of Justice stated in its letter that owing to the Philippines' legal and policy constraints, it could not agree to a joint investigation with the ROC, but it could offer assistance and provide its investigation report to the Taiwan investigation team. Meanwhile, the Philippine Secretary of Justice said in an interview that the two parties could conduct "parallel investigations."

Philippines Violated International Law in the Guang Da Xing No. 28 Incident

On May 28, 2013, the Ministry of Foreign Affairs issued the following press release on the Philippines' violation of international law in the Guang Da Xing Incident:[25]

On May 9, 2013, the Republic of China (Taiwan) fishing boat Guang Da Xing No. 28 (GDX 28) was hotly pursued and violently attacked by a Philippine government vessel in the overlapping exclusive economic zones between Taiwan and the Philippines, causing the death of one Taiwan fisherman and severe damage to the boat, including engine failure. As the Philippine government vessel involved was on official duty, the Philippine government should be held accountable for these wrongful actions and assume responsibility for the incident. Important international precedents that show similarities include the 1935 case of the Canadian registry ship I'm Alone v. the United States, the 1961 case of the Red Crusader incident between the UK and Denmark, and the 1999 case of the M/V Saiga No. 2 at the International Tribunal for the Law of the Sea.

The Philippines has violated international law in the following ways:

(1) The principle of avoiding the use of force and basic procedures for the use of force

In accordance with principles of hot pursuit as stipulated in international law, the use of force should be avoided. Acts including giving visual or auditory signals to stop, firing water cannons or firing shots across the bow should be conducted according to universally accepted international standards for boarding and inspection, and should not go beyond what is reasonable and necessary. Firing indiscriminately at the unarmed fishing boat GDX 28 is far removed from the Philippine claim of self-defense.

(2) The principle of proportionality in the use of force

25 MOFA, Philippines Violated International Law in Guang Da Xing No. 28 Incident, May 28, 2013, http://www.mofa.gov.tw/en/News_Content.aspx?n=1EADDCFD4C6EC567&s=1919FFE461CB8DF2.

The GDX 28 is a small fiberglass fishing boat measuring 14.7 meters in length and weighing 15.15 tons. This unarmed boat was attacked by an armed Philippine government vessel measuring 30 meters in length, weighing 115.45 tons, and with a tonnage more than six times larger. Initial investigations found at least 45 bullet entry holes in the hull of the fishing boat, mostly concentrated in the cockpit where the crewmembers hid. This indicates that the intention was to kill, which is not in keeping with the principle of proportionality.

(3) The principle of humanity in international law

The principle of humanity in international law is universally accepted by the global community. International maritime law attaches great importance to this principle, which is embodied in the United Nations Convention on the Law of the Sea and related international legal precedents. That the Philippine government vessel fired repeatedly on an unarmed fishing boat without any concern for the safety of those onboard shows a complete lack of humanitarian consideration. Paragraph 3 of Article 73 of the UN Convention on the Law of the Sea, which is based on the principle of humanity, clearly applies to this case. The paragraph stipulates that penalties for violations of fisheries laws "may not include imprisonment . . . or any other form of corporal punishment."

(4) The duty to provide assistance in international maritime law

A basic principle in international maritime law is the obligation to provide assistance to vessels in distress at sea. This principle is embodied in Article 98 of the UN Convention on the Law of the Sea, which mandates that it is an international obligation to render assistance to vessels in distress. The Philippine government vessel, which the Philippines claimed was engaged in a law-enforcement operation, fired at the GDX 28, disabling the boat and making it unseaworthy. It showed no concern as to whether any of the crewmembers might have been injured or killed. Furthermore, it sailed away without taking such measures as boarding, inspection, or arrest as would be required if it were, as claimed, a law-enforcement operation. By failing to provide assistance to the drifting GDX 28, the Philippine government vessel did not fulfill its duty to offer assistance in accordance with international maritime law. It also clearly evidences the fact that it carried out the malicious attack and indiscriminate firing under the pretext of conducting an official assignment.

MOFA's Announcement regarding the Restoration of Cooperative and Friendly Relations between the ROC and the Philippines

Following the constructive response of the Philippine government to the shooting incident involving the Taiwan fishing boat Guang Da Xing No. 28, the Ministry of Foreign Affairs issued the following press release on the restoration of cooperative and friendly relations between the two countries:[26]

On August 8, 2013, ROC Minister of Foreign Affairs David Y. L. Lin received Chairman of the Manila Economic and Cultural Office (MECO) Amadeo R. Perez, Jr., and the Philippine Representative to Taiwan Antonio I. Basilio. With respect to the Philippine government's formal written response over the shooting of the Taiwan fishing boat Guang Da Xing No. 28 by a Philippine government vessel, Chairman Perez gave the following explanation:

1. The President of the Philippines, Benigno S. Aquino III, authorized MECO Chairman Amadeo R. Perez, Jr., to travel to Taiwan as his personal representative to express the deep regret and apology of the president and people of the Philippines to the family of crew member Hong Shi-cheng, the victim of the fatal shooting incident involving a Philippine government vessel, as well as to the people of Taiwan.
2. Under arrangements made by the Taipei Economic and Cultural Office (TECO) in the Philippines and MECO, the Philippine National Bureau of Investigation (NBI) and the Pingtung District Prosecutors Office coordinated their respective investigations on this tragic incident. Based on the evidence collected, the Philippine Coast Guard personnel appear to have broken the law. The NBI thus recommended that the perpetrators be charged with homicide and obstruction of justice and have appropriate administrative and disciplinary actions taken against them. Accordingly, the Philippine National Prosecution Service (NPS) will initiate necessary proceedings in accordance with the law. The Philippine Department of Justice has promised to promptly start the prosecution process in accordance with the NPS investigation results.
3. In order to prevent such unfortunate incidents from recurring, TECO and MECO held the first preparatory meeting on fisheries cooperation on June 14. The two sides agreed that they would refrain from using force or

26 MOFA, Following the Constructive Response of the Philippine Government to the Shooting Incident Involving the Taiwan Fishing Boat Guang Da Xing No. 28, the Government of the Republic of China Announces that Cooperative and Friendly Relations between the Two Countries Are Being Restored, Effective Immediately, Aug. 9, 2013, http://www.mofa.gov.tw/en/News_Content.aspx?n=1EADDCFD4C6EC567&s=AA4F0D91DF247AE5.

violence when enforcing fisheries laws and regulations. They also agreed to inform each other of their respective maritime law enforcement procedures and establish a mechanism for prompt notification of the other party when undertaking a law enforcement operation against any fishing vessel or crew members of the other party. Moreover, they agreed to set up a mechanism for the prompt release of detained fishing vessels and their crews.

4. Attorneys appointed by MECO and Mr. Hong Shi-cheng's family have reached an agreement to settle the matter.

Since the Guang Da Xing No. 28 shooting incident on May 9, the ROC government has taken a positive, firm, and rational approach to negotiations with the Philippines. The ultimate goal is to seek justice for the victim's family, protect the rights of its fishermen, and safeguard the nation's position and dignity, in the hope that the incident can be resolved properly and peacefully.

The Philippine government has responded positively to the four demands proposed by the ROC government as follows:

1. With regard to an official apology, MECO Chairman Amadeo R. Perez, Jr. was fully authorized to express the deep regret and apology of the president and people of the Philippines to the family of Hong Shi-cheng and the people of Taiwan, and traveled to Xiaoliuqiu on August 8 to publicly apologize to the victim's family.
2. Attorneys for the victim's family and for the Philippine side have reached an agreement on compensation.
3. In terms of promptly and thoroughly investigating the incident and severely punishing those responsible for the killing, the Philippine NBI formally unveiled its investigation report August 7, and recommended that eight coast guard personnel be prosecuted for homicide and four for obstruction of justice. The Philippine Department of Justice has promised to file charges against them as soon as possible.
4. With respect to initiating fishery agreement negotiations between the two countries as soon as possible, the first preparatory meeting held between the two sides on June 14 produced some concrete results. A conclusion was signed after the meeting in which the two sides guaranteed that to prevent incidents such as the Guang Da Xing No. 28 shooting incident from recurring they would refrain from using force. After an exchange of letters between relevant authorities on each side, they agreed to review maritime law and enforcement procedures to put into practice the consensus reached during the meeting. Both sides also

agreed to continue negotiating on issues such as conserving fishery resources and managing fishing operations.

Given that the Philippines has expressed its good will and apology both in writing and in deed, the ROC government hereby declares that all sanctions imposed against the Philippines are lifted as of August 8. It also calls on the Philippines to:

(1) promptly prosecute the perpetrators;
(2) hold the next round of fishery talks so as to strengthen fishery cooperation;
(3) continue to enhance the mechanism for maritime law enforcement without the use of force, and prevent similar tragedies from recurring; and
(4) promptly mend the bilateral relationship, especially in trade and economy, and promote the signing of an economic cooperation agreement.

Furthermore, to ensure the fishing operation rights and safety of its fishermen, the ROC government will continue routine patrols of its EEZ to the south.

On May 9, the day of the incident, the ROC government immediately lodged a strong protest with the Philippine government. It also requested an official apology, the arrest of the perpetrators, and compensation. On May 11, the ROC issued four demands for (1) a formal apology; (2) compensation for losses; (3) a prompt and thorough investigation, as well as fitting punishment of those responsible; and (4) initiation of fishery agreement negotiations between the two countries. Later, the ROC government imposed 11 sanctions on the Philippines, making its stance explicit and pressing the Philippines to promptly provide a positive and concrete response to its four demands.

A mutual judicial assistance process was initiated based on the Agreement on Mutual Legal Assistance in Criminal Matters signed by the ROC and the Philippines. The ROC and the Philippines dispatched their respective investigation teams to each other's countries on May 27. The two sides jointly compared and verified their findings on June 6 and 7. Both sides released their investigation reports on August 7. The conclusions of the Philippine investigation and its recommendation to prosecute the offenders are generally consistent with the findings and recommendations of the ROC report.

The ROC government and its 118 overseas missions have provided relevant information to allow the international community to better understand what actually happened in this incident. Consequently, it garnered support in political and academic circles, as well as from the public, in many countries. To date, nearly a thousand reports worldwide have objectively portrayed the case.

In addition, the ROC government instructed relevant authorities such as the Coast Guard Administration to step up patrols in its EEZ to safeguard the safety and rights of Taiwan's fishermen. The ROC continued to negotiate with the Philippines through diplomatic channels to prevent similar tragedies in the future. On June 14, officials from the Ministry of Foreign Affairs, Fisheries Agency under the Council of Agriculture, and Coast Guard Administration traveled to the Philippines to meet with officials from the Philippine Department of Foreign Affairs, Bureau of Fisheries and Aquatic Resources under the Department of Agriculture, and Coast Guard under the Department of Transportation and Communications for the first preparatory meeting on fisheries talks. This meeting produced some concrete results.

ROC President Ma Ying-jeou, Premier Jiang Yi-huah, and Minister of Foreign Affairs David Y. L. Lin have, on more than one occasion, called on the Philippines to shoulder its responsibility in this tragedy. To avoid conflicts between the two peoples, they also urged people in Taiwan to be rational and treat Filipinos working and living here with kindness. In addition, the ROC Coast Guard Administration vessel Wei Hsing recently rescued three Filipino fishermen adrift in waters south of Taiwan and arranged their safe and speedy return to the Philippines, demonstrating the country's spirit of humanitarian assistance.

The Republic of China is a peace-loving country. After the incident occurred, the appeals and actions of the ROC government have been consistent with the UN Charter and international law, the aim being to resolve the dispute through peaceful means.

The ROC government is grateful for the support of its people, regardless of their political affiliation, in its handling of this case. Given the traditional friendship between the two countries, the ROC is prepared to take concrete actions to strengthen its cordial and cooperative relations with the Philippines in such fields as trade and economy, science and technology, and culture.

VIII The Law of Treaties

(No item reported under this section)

IX Diplomatic, Consular, and Similar Relations

Statement by the Republic of China on Its Relations with the Republic of The Gambia

On November 15, 2013, the Ministry of Foreign Affairs issued the following statement on the ROC's relations with the Republic of The Gambia:[27]

The President of the Republic of The Gambia, Sheikh Professor Alhaji Dr. Yahya A. J. J. Jammeh, stated in a letter to the Embassy of the Republic of China in The Gambia on November 14, 2013, that The Gambia has decided to terminate diplomatic relations with the Republic of China, effective immediately. The Republic of China expresses surprise and regret over The Gambia's decision.

In his letter to the ROC government, President Jammeh pointed out that The Gambia and the Republic of China have for many years enjoyed close and mutually beneficial cooperation in various fields, producing remarkable results. President Jammeh extended his gratitude for the Republic of China's friendship and cooperation, as well as his appreciation for the significant achievements the two countries have attained since diplomatic relations were established 18 years ago.

The ROC government reiterates that, since diplomatic ties with The Gambia were restored, the Republic of China has put forward and undertaken a variety of programs in The Gambia that have enhanced the livelihood of the Gambian people and have been well received by all sectors of society. At the same time, The Gambia has long been a staunch supporter of the Republic of China in the international arena. The Republic of China and The Gambia have also held frequent, high-level exchanges. This year, for example, the Vice President of The Gambia, Aja Dr. Isatou Njie-Saidy, led a delegation to attend celebrations marking the ROC National Day. Indeed, the diplomatic relations between the Republic of China and The Gambia have always been cordial.

The ROC government attaches great importance to the longstanding and friendly relations between the two countries, and has already conveyed its solemn position on President Jammeh's decision through appropriate channels.

27 MOFA, Statement by the Republic of China on Its Relations with the Republic of The Gambia, Nov. 15, 2013, http://www.mofa.gov.tw/en/News_Content.aspx?n=1EADDCFD4C6EC567&s=91214A9C199231A3.

The Government of the Republic of China Terminates Diplomatic Relations with the Republic of The Gambia to Uphold National Dignity and Principles of Viable Diplomacy

On November 18, 2013, the Ministry of Foreign Affairs issued the following statement on the termination of diplomatic relations with the Republic of The Gambia:[28]

The government of the Republic of China decided, on November 18, 2013, to terminate diplomatic relations with the Republic of The Gambia in order to uphold the dignity of the nation and the principles of viable diplomacy. It will close its embassy in The Gambia, recall its technical missions, and end all bilateral cooperation projects. This is the ROC government's response to the November 14 announcement by Gambian President Yahya A. J. J. Jammeh that The Gambia was terminating diplomatic relations with the ROC on the grounds of "strategic national interest."

Since diplomatic relations with The Gambia were restored in July 1995, the ROC had actively provided the country with assistance through cooperation projects beneficial to its development and the livelihood of the people in the areas of education, agriculture, medical care, military affairs, and basic infrastructure. The contributions that these programs made to The Gambia's economic development and the people's welfare were widely recognized and well received by all sectors of society there. In addition, officials from the two countries held frequent exchange visits and their people enjoyed close contacts. Based on the principles of sincerity, honesty, and justice, the ROC has always treated The Gambia as a friend and brother, and regrets its abrupt decision.

The ROC government will not allow this event to affect its efforts to expand its space on the international stage and promote viable diplomacy. With a resolute and pragmatic approach, it will maintain relations with countries that stand firm on justice and treat the ROC with equality, and will work jointly with them to gain the international status that the ROC deserves. It will also continue to fulfill its international obligations and remains committed to enhancing the welfare of its people.

28 MOFA. The Government of the Republic of China Terminates Diplomatic Relations with the Republic of The Gambia to Uphold National Dignity and Principles of Viable Diplomacy. Aug. 18, 2013, http://www.mofa.gov.tw/en/News_Content.aspx?n=1EADDCFD4C6EC567&s=0F614E6987FC91A2.

X Peaceful Settlement of International Disputes

East China Sea Peace Initiative Viable Model for Regional Peace

On November 25, 2013, the Ministry of Foreign Affairs issued the following background information on the East China Sea Initiative:[29]

The East China Sea Peace Initiative, proposed on Aug. 5, 2012, by President Ma Ying-jeou of the Republic of China (ROC), provides a viable empirical model for peaceful resolution of regional disputes, especially following Beijing's Nov. 23, 2013, announcement that it has established an "East China Sea air defense identification zone."

The day after the announcement, the ROC National Security Council issued a press release reaffirming ROC sovereignty over the Diaoyutai Islands, outlining the East China Sea Peace Initiative and measures to ensure the safety of ROC airspace, and stressing that the government is deeply concerned about regional developments and will maintain close contact with all parties.

The disputed ADIZ includes the Diaoyutais, claimed by the ROC, Japan and mainland China. Beijing's declaration has drawn strong responses from Washington and Tokyo, warning of escalating tensions and potential for conflict in the region.

With the risk of an incident rapidly increasing, the ROC calls on all parties to adhere to the pragmatic approach of the East China Sea Peace Initiative, which has proven its viability in the Taiwan-Japan fisheries agreement that was signed April 10, 2013.

The initiative, in line with the government's commitment to acting as a peacemaker, urges all parties to replace confrontation with dialogue, shelve territorial disputes through negotiations, formulate a code of conduct in the East China Sea and engage in joint development of resources.

By emphasizing cooperation over conflict and refocusing attention on the sharing of economic resources, the initiative can help parties rise above nationalism and territorial claims, and see beyond their own interests in order to safeguard regional peace and stability.

---

29 MOFA, East China Sea Peace Initiative Viable Model for Regional Peace, Nov. 25, 2013, http://www.mofa.gov.tw/en/News_Content.aspx?n=1EADDCFD4C6EC567&s=1D3413716D7C2A8D.

East China Sea Peace Initiative and the Use of Dialogue to Resolve Disputes

On December 6, 2013, the Office of the President issued the following press release on President Ma's interview with Japan's *Mainichi Newspapers*:[30]

With respect to mainland China's announcement of an East China Sea ADIZ, President Ma acknowledged that the move has triggered strong concerns, including in the ROC. He remarked that the mainland's ADIZ includes the Diaoyutai Islets, which is part of ROC territory. He said that on the same day that mainland China announced its ADIZ, the ROC issued a statement reiterating its sovereignty over the Diaoyutais. The ROC, he noted, will vigorously defend its sovereignty over the islets and will also protect the rights of its fishermen to operate in that region.

President Ma stated that the Diaoyutais have been the subject of heightened tensions in the East China Sea since the spring of last year, which has caused instability in the region. It was with this in mind that he unveiled his East China Sea Peace Initiative on August 5 last year, urging all sides to avoid action that would escalate the conflict. The initiative, he said, also called on all parties to resolve the dispute through peaceful dialogue.

President Ma pointed out that the third point of the statement issued by the ROC indicates that the mainland's ADIZ partially overlaps with the ROC's in an area of about 23,000 square kilometers, but training exercises involving the ROC's military aircraft will continue as normal in the area. The president said that Taiwan has used various avenues to express its serious concern to mainland Chinese authorities, adding that the ADIZ announcement by the other side is not conducive to positive cross-strait relations.

President Ma further explained that the Taipei Flight Information Region (TFIR) is administered by the ROC's Civil Aeronautics Administration. At present, he said, 14 international aviation routes pass through the skies over Taiwan. He noted that if an airline whose flights pass through the TFIR requests Taiwan to forward its flight plans to mainland China, Taiwan will provide this service. He added that in fact when civilian aircraft from Taiwan are to pass through Japan's Flight Information Region, Taiwan provides flight plans to the Japanese authorities, as the ADIZs of the two countries overlap by one degree of longitude, or about 60 nautical miles. When aircraft from Taiwan head to Dalian or Qingdao in mainland China, they pass through this overlapping area, he

30 Office of the President, East China Sea Peace Initiative and the Use of Dialogue to Resolve Disputes, Dec. 6, 2013, http://english.president.gov.tw/Default.aspx?tabid=1124&itemid=31481&rmid=3048.

commented. The reporting of flight plans to another nation has long been practiced, so Taiwan is willing to forward flight plans to mainland China if any airline flying through the TFIR requests it. President Ma stated that the foremost priority of Taiwan is to ensure the safety of civil aircraft. The United States, he said, has similarly suggested that its own airlines provide flight plans to mainland Chinese authorities for the sake of aviation safety.

The last point of the statement urged all parties with overlapping ADIZs in the East China Sea to resolve the issue through bilateral negotiations. Taiwan, the president remarked, has adopted this same stance vis-à-vis mainland China. In the future, Taiwan will inform mainland China of its position that the latter should not further establish an ADIZ in the South China Sea.

After he unveiled the East China Sea Peace Initiative on August 5 of last year, the president remarked, Taiwan and Japan held fishing negotiations in late November, and on April 10 of this year signed a fisheries agreement covering roughly 70,000 square kilometers of seas around the Diaoyutai Islets. As a result, the operations of fishermen in the area will not be restricted by either country, he noted, adding that this was an important breakthrough that resolved a 40-year fishing dispute in the Diaoyutais. The ROC government and Japan had previously held 16 rounds of negotiations without any result, the president said. He noted that the signing of the fisheries agreement between the two was an extremely important step that is helping to minimize the dispute. This is proving to be one of the most effective means of promoting peace, he said.

As for the bilateral economic relationship, President Ma stated, economic, trade, and investment ties between the ROC and Japan date back 60 years, and enormous strides have been seen in recent years. Two years ago, for example, Taiwan and Japan signed the Taiwan-Japan Bilateral Investment Arrangement, which has done much to promote two-way investments. Then, on November 5 of this year, the two sides signed a series of financial and economic agreements covering such matters as speedy review of patent applications and cooperation in the exchange of electronic documents. Noting the enormous volume of trade between the two sides—Japan is Taiwan's second largest trading partner and Taiwan is Japan's fifth largest—the president expressed hope for progress toward an economic cooperation agreement or an economic partnership accord.

President Ma described the "building block" approach that Taiwan has adopted in pursuing economic cooperation agreements with other nations. Noting that Japan has already decided to enter the Trans-Pacific Partnership (TPP) and in the future will play an important role in the Regional Comprehensive Economic Partnership, which links it with ASEAN, the president said the ROC also would be pleased to participate in the two regional economic integration initiatives, and therefore an economic cooperation agreement between Taiwan and Japan would be in the interests of both sides.

Asked about his stance on the military balance of power between the two sides of the Taiwan Strait and measures that the ROC is taking, President Ma stated that since he took office in 2008 his administration has worked actively to improve relations with mainland China, the United States, and Japan. Taiwan and mainland China have signed 19 agreements, and mutual trust is gradually being built up between the two sides, he said.

The ROC government has consistently sought, under the framework of the ROC Constitution, to maintain the status quo of "no unification, no independence, and no use of force" in the Taiwan Strait, and to promote peaceful cross-strait ties under the "1992 Consensus," whereby each side acknowledges the existence of "one China" but maintains its own interpretation of what that means, he said. In addition, the president pointed out, the priority of issues for the two sides to address would be "pressing matters before less pressing ones, easy matters before difficult ones, and economic matters before political ones."

As for political topics, President Ma mentioned, Taiwan and mainland China have not gone out of their way to avoid such issues in negotiating the 19 agreements over the past five years. For instance, he noted, the Cross-Strait Joint Crime-Fighting and Judicial Mutual Assistance Agreement signed in 2009 touches on the issue of judicial jurisdiction, which is quite politically sensitive. However, Taiwan did not avoid discussing this topic, he remarked.

The president said Taiwan and mainland China are presently negotiating an agreement that would pave the way for the establishment of cross-strait representative offices. Again, he commented, this is a politically sensitive issue, but Taiwan is not avoiding it. The main principle in such negotiations, the president said, is whether such agreements would help to promote cross-strait relations and involve an urgent need to protect the wellbeing of the people on both sides of the Taiwan Strait. Where there is urgency, Taiwan will advance the timetable based on the principle of "pressing matters before less pressing ones, easy matters before difficult ones, and economic matters before political ones."

As for the US strategy of "rebalancing toward Asia" and the importance of ensuring security in the Asia-Pacific region, President Ma stated, the ROC has always been a peace-loving nation, and the US "rebalancing" policy, is intended to maintain regional peace and stability, so the ROC in principle supports the rebalancing. He commented that Taiwan and the United States have maintained close contact on matters of importance, and the United States has welcomed the stances adopted by Taiwan. Examples include the unveiling of the ROC's East China Sea Peace Initiative last year, he said, and the recent announcement by mainland China of its ADIZ in the East China Sea.

Asked about his view of Japanese Prime Minister Shinzo Abe's active push for a change in the interpretation of the Japanese constitution so as to ease restrictions on Japan's participation in collective self-defense, President Ma commented that since the end of World War II, the United States and Japan have established a relationship that emphasizes security assurance. Their Treaty of Mutual Cooperation and Security, he said, has made an important contribution to stability and peace throughout Asia. The ROC, the president remarked, has also consistently expressed support for this. With respect to Prime Minister Abe's position on Japan's constitution and other possible steps, President Ma called on Japan, as a mature democracy, to consider the reactions and feelings of its neighbors and adopt the wisest course of action.

MOFA's Position on the Republic of Korea's Announcement of Its Air Defense Identification Zone

On December 9, 2013, the Ministry of Foreign Affairs issued the following press release in response to the Republic Korea's announcement of its Air Defense Identification Zone:[31]

The Ministry of Defense of the Republic of Korea formally announced at 1 PM (Taipei time) on December 8, 2013, an expansion of its Air Defense Identification Zone (KADIZ). The expanded zone overlaps the air defense identification zones of other countries, which could trigger disputes and heighten tensions. The Ministry of Foreign Affairs (MOFA) of the Republic of China (Taiwan) urges all parties concerned to work together to resolve regional disputes through peaceful dialogue, so as to prevent tensions from escalating, and maintain regional peace and stability.

MOFA emphasizes that President Ma Ying-jeou proposed the East China Sea Peace Initiative on August 5, 2012, in response to developments in the region. It encourages the parties concerned to resolve disputes peacefully by exercising restraint and refraining from taking antagonistic actions, by shelving controversies and not abandoning dialogue, and by observing international law. The initiative has been well received throughout the international community, and its spirit and principles merit the serious consideration of the parties concerned.

31 MOFA, Ministry of Foreign Affairs of the Republic of China Urges All Parties Concerned to Resolve East China Sea Disputes through Peaceful Dialogue, Dec. 9, 2013, http://www.mofa.gov.tw/en/News_Content.aspx?n=1EADDCFD4C6EC567&s=83C053F18BC1F4A2.

President Ma Attends Academic Conference on Contemporary International and Transnational Law

On December 14, 2013, the Office of the President issued the following press release on the President's remarks at the Annual Conference of the Chinese (Taiwan) Society of International Law:[32]

In remarks, the president noted that the CSIL was established in 1958, and is the oldest academic association focusing on international law in Taiwan. In 1961, the organization became a chapter of the London-based International Law Association (ILA), he said. President Ma mentioned that he joined the organization over 30 years ago and served as its president from 2000 to 2003.

The president stated that the CSIL has distinguished itself through its publications, academic research, extension programs, and international law moot court competitions. The organization has also been an active participant in the work of the ILA, he said, pointing out that it hosted the ILA Asia-Pacific Regional Conference in 1995 and the 68th Conference of the ILA in 1998, thus making significant contributions to exchanges and interaction in the field of international law. In addition, the CSIL won high praise in 2004 for its Chinese (Taiwan) Yearbook of International Law and Affairs, which the Executive Yuan's National Science Council ranked second in a list of the best specialized publications in Taiwan. Furthermore, the quality of the English version of this publication has been recognized by the renowned British publisher Cameron May, which together with the CSIL now acts as joint publisher of the yearbook.

In discussing concrete steps the ROC has taken to put international law (including the law of the sea and aviation law) into practice, President Ma mentioned as examples the signing by Taiwan and Japan in April of this year of a fisheries agreement, the ROC's handling of the Guang Da Xing No. 28 fishing boat incident that took place in May, and its handling of mainland China's November announcement of an Air Defense Identification Zone (ADIZ) in the East China Sea.

The president said the ROC has consistently maintained the position that the Diaoyutai Islets are inherent territory of the ROC and are appurtenant to Taiwan. With respect to the sovereignty dispute over these islands, he pointed out, on August 5 of last year he unveiled the East China Sea Peace Initiative, which stresses that "although sovereignty over national territory cannot be compromised, natural resources can be shared." He said he put forward the

32 Office of the President, Upholding Territorial Dignity and Resolving Disputes via Peaceful Means, Dec. 14, 2013, http://english.president.gov.tw/Default.aspx?tabid=1124&itemid=31506&rmid=3048.

peace initiative in hopes that all parties would adopt peaceful measures to resolve the dispute, thereby reducing tensions in the region. Subsequently, Taiwan and Japan on April 10 of this year signed a fisheries agreement, which designates an area of over 74,000 square kilometers, south of 27 degrees latitude and north of the Yaeyama Islands and Miyako Islands, as a legal fishing zone for fishermen from both nations, said the president. He added that this agreement is not affected by the laws of either nation and that the Diaoyutais and the seas in the neighboring 12 nautical miles are not included.

As for the Guang Da Xing No. 28 shooting incident of this past May, in which a Philippine government vessel fired upon a Taiwanese fishing boat, damaging the boat and killing a Taiwanese fisherman, the government issued a four-point statement following the incident and then adopted economic sanctions. Ultimately, the Philippines made a formal apology for the incident and agreed to provide compensation, he said. The president stated that while Taiwan and the Philippines have yet to sign a fisheries agreement, the two have held two rounds of negotiations and have reached a consensus on "refraining from the use of force or violence in law enforcement actions," "sharing their basic maritime law enforcement procedures," "establishing a mechanism for one side notifying the other side," and "setting up a mechanism for the prompt release of detained fishing vessels and their crews following arrests."

President Ma stressed that the ROC is a reasonable nation with a "humanitarian spirit." Despite the fishing boat incident, Taiwan still transported material donations to aid in the rescue and relief effort after parts of the Philippines suffered devastation from Typhoon Haiyan. To date, he said, Taiwan's monetary donations and disaster relief goods have come to over US$10 million.

Regarding the East China Sea ADIZ recently announced by mainland China, the president pointed out, ADIZs are established to provide early warning and identification. But this concept is not expressly addressed in international law and differs from the concepts of territorial airspace, territorial waters, and territory. He added that the ROC government immediately issued a four-point statement, as follows: 1) the ROC reiterates its sovereignty over the Diaoyutai Islets; 2) the ROC urges other nations to refer to its East China Sea Peace Initiative that was unveiled last year, and to use peaceful means to resolve disputes; and calls upon all parties involved to carry out bilateral dialogues on overlapping areas in the ADIZ so as to prevent accidents; 3) the ROC's Air Force will continue to carry out exercises and training activities as normal in the ROC's ADIZ, but because mainland China did not consult Taiwan before announcing its ADIZ in the East China Sea, the ROC will continue to express its serious concern; in particular, mainland China's behavior is not conducive to positive cross-strait relations; 4) for many years now, when an aircraft from

Taiwan had intended to pass through another country's ADIZ, Taiwan has provided flight plans to that nation's civil aviation authorities. Therefore, when an aircraft from another country intends to fly through the area where the ADIZs of Taiwan and mainland China overlap, Taiwan is willing to receive the flight plans from the airlines and forward them to the mainland authorities.

Lastly, the president stressed that the ROC will continue to act as a peacemaker in the international community and use peaceful means to resolve disputes. It will also turn to bilateral dialogue and international law to resolve issues. President Ma said that this is not just an outmoded way of thinking, but rather the correct attitude in handling international affairs.

XI Arms Control, Use of Force, and International Criminal Law

ROC's Condemnation of North Korea's Provocative Nuclear Test

On February 20, 2013, the Ministry of Foreign Affairs issued the following statement on the ROC's condemnation of North Korea's provocative nuclear test:[33]

The Democratic People's Republic of Korea (North Korea) conducted a third nuclear test at 11:57 A.M. local time (10:57 A.M. Taipei time) on February 12, 2013. This nuclear test and a recent satellite launch are grave violations of United Nations Security Council Resolutions 1718, 1874, and 2087. The Republic of China (ROC) solemnly condemns North Korea for provocative actions taken in defiance of UN resolutions and in contempt of the repeatedly stated concern and admonition of the international community.

The ROC supports the denuclearization of East Asia and reiterates its support for the resolution of issues involving the Korean Peninsula through peaceful negotiation. The ROC Ministry of Foreign Affairs therefore calls on the North Korean authorities to abide by Security Council resolutions and refrain from actions that may endanger regional security so as to maintain peace, stability, and prosperity, both on the Korean Peninsula and in East Asia.

33 MOFA, The Republic of China Condemns North Korea's Provocative Nuclear Test and Calls for Rational Resolution of Disputes, Feb. 20. 2013. http://www.mofa.gov.tw/en/News_Content.aspx?n=1EADDCFD4C6EC567&s=21EB130B845D5447.

ROC Government Concerned about use of Chemical Weapons in the Syrian Civil War

On August 31, 2013, the Ministry of Foreign Affairs issued the following statement on the use of chemical weapons in the Syrian Civil War:[34]

Recent developments in the Syrian civil war have elicited worldwide attention. Information from multiple sources indicates that chemical weapons have been used on civilians during recent clashes in Syria, resulting in severe injuries and loss of life. The Republic of China (Taiwan), based on respect for human rights and the universal values of democracy, calls upon the Syrian government and opposition groups to resolve domestic political disputes through peaceful means, and condemns any acts involving the use of violence or inhumane methods that harm civilians.

For the Syrian refugees who have fled to Jordan, based on humanitarian considerations, the ROC government has provided 50 pre-fabricated housing units and five brand-new fully equipped rescue vehicles for use in providing aid to the refugees.

XII International Economic Relations

Supreme Court Decision
January 30, 2013
102-Tai-Shang-Zi-193

Keywords:
Bankruptcy Order, Hong Kong, Territorialism, Universalism

Relevant Provisions:
Articles 1 and 4 of the Bankruptcy Act
Article 174 of the Code of Civil Procedure
Article 1 of the Law Governing the Choice of Law in Civil Cases Involving Foreign Elements
Article 38 of the Laws and Regulations Regarding Hong Kong & Macao Affairs

34 MOFA. ROC Government Concerned about Use of Chemical Weapons in Syrian Civil War, Aug. 31, 2013, http://www.mofa.gov.tw/en/News_Content.aspx?n=1EADDCFD4C6EC567&s=806EA1B3981AAAB3.

Summary:

Both parties disputed the effectiveness of the order made by a Hong Kong court approving the compulsory winding-up of the appellee from the perspective of Taiwan law. The appellant claimed that the Court of First Instance of the High Court of the Hong Kong Special Administrative Region ("High Court of Hong Kong") ruled on September 19, 2008 in favor of the compulsory winding-up of the appellee in accordance with the Companies Ordinance of Hong Kong due to the appellee's inability to pay its debts; the compulsory winding-up procedure is equivalent to the bankruptcy procedure of the ROC. The High Court of Hong Kong selected Paul Jeremy Brough, Edward Simon Middleton and Patrick Cowley as the liquidator of the appellee (Paul Jeremy Brough has been discharged of his duty as the liquidator by the High Court of Hong Kong due to his retirement; the other two persons are collectively referred to as: "Edward and Patrick"). However, according to Article 4 of Taiwan Bankruptcy Act, the abovementioned order of the High Court of Hong Kong should be invalid in the ROC. The appellee lacks the standing to bring the subject suit to court.

The Supreme Court held as follows: with respect to the extraterritorial effect of a bankruptcy order, there are universalism, territorialism and eclecticism to be considered. In the past, foreign legislative models adopted territorialism, which means that a bankruptcy order is only effective in the country where the bankruptcy is declared and does not affect the property of the bankrupt in foreign countries. Taiwan Bankruptcy Act adopts territorialism and thus Article 4 of the same Act provides that the settlement or bankruptcy order made in a foreign country is not effective on the property of the debtor/bankrupt in the ROC. However, with the development of international business and trade, if territorialism is still adopted, it will prevent the development of international commerce. It is therefore necessary to amend territorialism to implement the principles of equality since territorialism is no longer appropriate given the internationalization of economic activities. Furthermore, the United Nations or many of the developed countries have amended territorialism and the amendment adopts principles of universalism. For example, the Model Law on Cross-Border Insolvency promulgated by the United Nations Commission on International Trade Law (UNCITRAL), the European Council Regulation (EC) No. 1346/2000 of May 29, 2000 on insolvency proceedings of European Union and Law Relating to Recognition and Assistance for Foreign Insolvency Proceedings of Japan.

The draft amendment of Taiwan Bankruptcy Act reads, "A foreigner, foreign juridical person or unincorporated association has the same position as a ROC person, juridical person or unincorporated association in a settlement or bankruptcy proceeding." And the draft amendment contains the provisions regarding the recognition of foreign debt clearance proceedings. However, before the amendment of the Bankruptcy Act becomes effective, Article 4 of the current Bankruptcy Act adopts territorialism. It is not possible to apply a logical interpretation or expand the scope of such article to foreign debt clearance proceedings which are different from the settlement or bankruptcy under the Bankruptcy Act in nature. Accordingly, by literal interpretation, the applicable scope of such article should be restricted to foreign debt clearance proceedings which are equivalent to the settlement or bankruptcy under the Bankruptcy Act.

According to the Companies Ordinance of Hong Kong, a company's inability to pay its debts is not a prerequisite for the High Court of Hong Kong to order the compulsory winding-up of such company. It is only one of the reasons for the High Court of Hong Kong to order the compulsory winding-up. After a company is ordered to be compulsorily wound-up by the High Court of Hong Kong, the right to dispose of the company's property will not necessarily be transferred to the liquidator. If such right is transferred to the liquidator by a court order, the liquidator may file a suit for the property of the company in his/her name. Otherwise, the liquidator will need to obtain the approval from the court or a committee of inspection to file a suit or defense in the name of the company or as the representative of the company. The provisions above are different from Taiwan Bankruptcy Act, which provides that the prerequisite of bankruptcy procedure is the debtor's inability to pay his/her/its debts (Article 1 of Taiwan Bankruptcy Act). The term "inability to pay debts" refers to the fact that the debtor's assets and funds/credit are insufficient to satisfy his/her/its debts. After the bankruptcy of the debtor is declared, the debtor loses the right to manage and dispose of the property which belongs to the bankruptcy estate, and the proceedings of all actions concerning the bankruptcy estate shall be stayed automatically until a qualified person assumes the action pursuant to the Bankruptcy Act or the bankruptcy proceeding is concluded (Paragraph 1, Article 174 of the Code of Civil Procedure). The receiver, after assuming the action, will be acting on behalf of the debtor/bankrupt based on certain qualifications in the receiver's name, rather than in the name of the debtor/bankrupt or his/her/its representative.

Based on the reasons above, the Taiwan High Court held that the compulsory winding-up under the Companies Ordinance of Hong Kong is not subject to Article 4 of the Bankruptcy Act. Edward and Patrick have obtained the authorization of the committee of inspection to act as the agent at litem of the appellee and file the subject suit. They have been duly authorized and the appellee has the standing to bring the subject suit to court. Furthermore, the suit arising from the contract between the parties involves foreign elements.

By Article 38 of the Laws and Regulations Regarding Hong Kong & Macao Affairs, Article 1 of the Law Governing the Choice of Law in Civil Cases Involving Foreign Elements shall apply mutatis mutandis to this case; the provisions of the Code of Civil Procedure regarding jurisdiction apply as well. The Taiwan Taipei District Court should have international jurisdiction over the suit filed by the appellee.

Intellectual Property Office, Ministry of Economic Affairs
June 21, 2013
Ref. No.: Tian-Tzu-Yu-Chien-Zi-1020621b

Keywords:
Copyright Notice, Principle of Protection upon Creation

Relevant Provisions:
Article 13 of the Copyright Act
Article 401 of the Copyright Law of the United States
Article III of the Universal Copyright Convention

Summary:
Whether the customary way in which a copyright notice is issued internationally or in other countries satisfies the term "in a normal way" under Article 13 of the Copyright Act should be subject to the applicable laws of the country. Under the principle of protection upon creation, any work will be provided copyright protection as soon as it is created, even if no notice of copyright has been given.

Taiwan Copyright Act adopts the principle of protection upon creation, which means that any work will enjoy copyright protection as soon as it is created, without requiring any specific symbol or words. With respect to adding notice on the work, according to Paragraph 2, Article III of the Universal Copyright Convention and Article 401 of the U.S. Copyright Law, the copies of the work should bear the symbol ©, the name of the owner of copyright and the year of first publication at an appropriate location as to give reasonable notice of the claim of copyright. In addition, if the work will be updated continuously, a period of copyright may be indicated on the copies of the first publication.

Whether the way in which a copyright notice is provided internationally or in other countries above satisfies the term "in a normal way" under Article 13 of the Copyright Act, so that the person whose name appears on the copyright notice will be presumed to be the author of the work, should be subject to the applicable laws of the country. However, even if no notice of copyright has been placed, in accordance with Taiwan Copyright Act, the copyright protection provided upon the completion of the work will not be affected.

Republic of China Signs Economic Cooperation Agreement with New Zealand

On July 10, 2013, the Ministry of Foreign Affairs issued the following press release on the signing of an economic cooperation agreement with New Zealand:[35]

The Republic of China (Taiwan, ROC) and New Zealand signed an economic cooperation agreement (ECA) in Wellington, capital of the South Pacific nation, on July 10, 2013, at 13:30 Taipei time. New Zealand is the first member country of the Organisation for Economic Cooperation and Development to ink an ECA with the ROC, which carries special significance for the ROC's future efforts to pursue similar agreements with other countries. The signing of the ECA opens a new chapter in ROC-New Zealand economic and trade cooperation. The Ministry of Foreign Affairs (MOFA) recognizes and is pleased that the pact will create greater economic and trade benefits for both nations.

The signing of the ROC-New Zealand ECA underscores the ROC's commitment to trade liberalization. It also represents a declaration to the international community that it is prepared to seek similar deals with its other trade partners.

New Zealand is a founding member of the Trans-Pacific Partnership (TPP) and a member of the Regional Comprehensive Economic Partnership (RCEP). Signing an ECA with New Zealand further opens up the Taiwan market, fully demonstrating the ROC's determination and commitment to play a role in regional economic integration while creating favorable conditions for its accession to the TPP and the RCEP. This will strengthen the ROC's cooperative relations with relevant countries.

The economic cooperation agreement contains 25 chapters and, in parts, WTO-plus provisions that are more favorable than standard WTO obligations. In addition to providing general market access, the ECA covers new issues including e-commerce, competition policy, the environment, and cooperation between indigenous peoples. It is a high-quality, high-standard, and comprehensive ECA that aims to eliminate tariffs altogether.

In 2012, two-way trade between Taiwan and New Zealand totaled US$1.207 billion. Taiwan ranks No. 10 and No. 13 among New Zealand's export markets

35 MOFA, Republic of China Signs Economic Cooperation Agreement with New Zealand, July 20, 2013. http://www.mofa.gov.tw/en/News_Content.aspx?n=1EADDCFD4C6EC567&s=671D5A31B877631F.

and import suppliers, respectively. Taiwan's major imports from New Zealand are primary farm, livestock, and forestry products, while principal exports from Taiwan to its South Pacific partner are electronic, electrical, refined petroleum products, and metals. This indicates that the trade and industrial structures of the two countries strongly complement each other, and that the ECA will have a significant complementary effect on their economic development. Given the absence of highly competitive industrial items manufactured in New Zealand, the agreement stands to be a positive for almost all of the ROC's industrial products, particularly petrochemicals, semiconductors, stainless steel, electronic components, plastic products, and precision machinery. On the other hand, Taiwan will open up to the high-quality fruit, milk products, red wine, and mutton produced in New Zealand. Greater reciprocal market access is expected to create more business opportunities for both sides.

As members of the World Trade Organization (WTO), the ROC and New Zealand enjoy the right to sign trade agreements under the WTO framework. Negotiated and signed in accordance with WTO rules, the pact is formally named the Agreement between New Zealand and the Separate Customs Territory of Taiwan, Penghu, Kinmen and Matsu on Economic Cooperation (ANZTEC).

The Republic of China's Ministry of Foreign Affairs will build on this foundation and continue to work with other ministries to negotiate bilateral agreements with other nations under the principle of making multiple contacts and concluding ECAs one by one. This will help remove market barriers for Taiwan's companies and facilitate the ROC's accession to the TPP and the RCEP. This, in turn, will integrate Taiwan into the regional economy and expand its international trade.

The Republic of China (Taiwan) and the Republic of Singapore Sign an Economic Partnership Agreement

On November 7, 2013, the Ministry of Foreign Affairs issued the following press release on the signing of an economic partnership agreement with Singapore:[36]

The Republic of China (Taiwan) and the Republic of Singapore signed an economic partnership agreement in Singapore at 9:30 am on November 7, 2013. This agreement is highly significant as Singapore is Taiwan's 5th largest trade partner and the 1st Southeast Asian country to enter such an agreement with Taiwan. Singapore, a founding member of the Trans-Pacific Partnership

36 MOFA, The Republic of China (Taiwan) and the Republic of Singapore Sign an Economic Partnership Agreement, Nov. 7, 2013, http://www.mofa.gov.tw/en/News_Content.aspx?n=1EADDCFD4C6EC567&s=9757CEE1F5C097C2.

(TPP), is also a member of the Regional Comprehensive Economic Partnership (RCEP). Taiwan's signing of an economic cooperation agreement with New Zealand and Singapore should help pave the way for Taiwan to join the TPP and the RCEP, two regional economic and trade agreements.

Taiwan and Singapore enjoy close economic relations, with bilateral trade reaching US$28.2 billion in 2012, making the latter Taiwan's 5th largest trade partner, 4th largest export market, 8th largest source of imports, and 9th largest source of foreign direct investment. Likewise, Taiwan is Singapore's 8th largest trade partner, 10th largest export market, and 5th largest source of imports.

The two sides, being members of the World Trade Organization (WTO), have the right to conclude trade agreements under the framework of the WTO. The bilateral partnership agreement was signed following WTO standards and formally named the Agreement between Singapore and the Separate Customs Territory of Taiwan, Penghu, Kinmen and Matsu on Economic Partnership (ASTEP).

Consisting of 17 chapters, ASTEP is a high-quality, high-standard, and comprehensive economic partnership agreement that covers a wide range of areas, with chapters on trade in goods, rules of origin, customs procedures, sanitary and phytosanitary measures, technical barriers to trade, e-commerce, trade in services, investment, competition policy, government procurement, intellectual property, resolution of disputes, and systemic regime. Taiwan and Singapore formally launched consultations on ASTEP in May 2011 and concluded them in May 2013, with the two sides carefully reviewing the legal text before signing the agreement.

Singaporehas signed 20 regional or bilateral free trade agreements with 31 trade partners, and its trade system adheres closely to international standards. Indeed, ASTEP will help bring Taiwan in line with international practices. In his National Day address on October 10 this year, President Ma Ying-jeou highlighted the ROC government's forward-looking and pragmatic national strategy. One of the goals of this strategy is to transform Taiwan into a "free economic island," an important aspect of which is to push for Taiwan's comprehensive participation in regional economic integration. The signing of ASTEP will strengthen Taiwan's development toward an open trade regime, overall competitiveness, and ability to respond to competitors. It also demonstrates to the international community Taiwan's commitment to trade and investment liberalization, and will serve as an example for Taiwan's negotiations with other countries with regard to economic cooperation agreements. Furthermore, ASTEP will boost momentum for Taiwan's efforts to join the TPP and RCEP and participate in regional economic integration, and will move Taiwan closer to reaching its goal of becoming a "free economic island."

The Ministry of Foreign Affairs will continue to work closely together with other relevant government agencies, so as to actively promote Taiwan's participation in regional economic integration. By adhering to the principle of "making multiple contacts and concluding agreements one by one," Taiwan aims to sign free trade agreements or economic cooperation agreements with its main trade partners. The ultimate goal is to play a meaningful role in regional economic integration, so as to boost Taiwan's economic and trade development, strengthen its industries, and enhance the people's welfare.

Taiwan-New Zealand Economic Cooperation Agreement to Formally Enter into Force December 1, 2013

On November 22, 2013, the Ministry of Foreign Affairs issued the following press release on the entry into force of the Taiwan-New Zealand Economic Cooperation Agreement:[37]

The Republic of China's Representative to New Zealand Charng Yii-lih and Director Stephen Payton of the New Zealand Commerce and Industry Office exchanged letters on behalf of their respective countries November 20, 2013, confirming that the Taiwan-New Zealand economic cooperation agreement will enter into force December 1. The pact will accord businesses in the two countries Year 1 reduced tariff rates starting January 1, 2014, and allow greater mutual market access, as economic and trade cooperation relations between Taiwan and New Zealand enter a new phase.

The Taiwan-New Zealand economic cooperation agreement was signed July 10 and ratified by the Legislative Yuan October 29. New Zealand is the first member of the Organisation for Economic Co-operation and Development to conclude an economic cooperation pact with the ROC. This carries special significance for future efforts to sign similar agreements with other trade partners. The Ministry of Foreign Affairs strongly affirms this move while the government of New Zealand has highly commended and thanked the ROC government for efficiently and speedily wrapping up legislative ratification of the agreement. The pact is expected to create greater economic and trade benefits for both sides, and to enhance the closeness and stability of the bilateral relationship.

---

37 MOFA. Taiwan-New Zealand Economic Cooperation Agreement to Formally Enter into Force December 1, 2013. Nov. 22, 2013, http://www.mofa.gov.tw/en/News_Content.aspx?n=1EADDCFD4C6EC567&s=B118591B89438459.

New Zealand is a founding member of what is to become the Trans-Pacific Partnership (TPP) and a member of what is slated to become the Regional Comprehensive Economic Partnership (RCEP). The Taiwan-New Zealand economic cooperation agreement signifies a trend toward further opening up Taiwan's markets and amply demonstrates the ROC's determination and diligent efforts to achieve Taiwan's active integration into the overall regional economy. It also creates conditions conducive to Taiwan's accession to the TPP and the RCEP, and strengthens its cooperative relations with pertinent countries.

XIII Private International Law

Supreme Court Decision
July 18, 2013
102-Tai-Shan-Zi-1367

Keywords:
Civil Procedure, Mutual Recognition, Singapore

Relevant Provisions:
Article 402 of the Code of Civil Procedure

Summary:
The determination of "appearing before the court" prescribed under Subparagraph 2, Paragraph 1, Article 402 of the Taiwan Code of Civil Procedure should rely upon the fact as to whether the defendant was entitled to fully exercise the defense rights substantially. In the event that a party to the foreign litigation proceedings has been informed of the commencement of the trial, may adequately prepare his/her/its responses and exercise the defense rights substantially, regardless of whether such party had personally received the notice of the commencement of the trial or participated in the oral arguments, the judgment so rendered should meet with the requirement of "appearing before the court". "Contrary to the public order" provided in Subparagraph 3, Paragraph 1, Article 402 of the same Code means that the legal effect of the foreign judgment rendered by a foreign court or the basis of rendering such a foreign judgment will violate the fundamental legislative intent, legal principles, value and guidelines commonly shared by the society. "Mutual recognition" prescribed under Subparagraph 4, Paragraph 1, Article 402 of the same Code

does not mean that a foreign country and the Republic of China (hereinafter the "ROC") shall mutually recognize the sovereignty or government authority of each other under International law. Instead, "mutual recognition" shall refer to the reciprocity in recognizing the judgments rendered by each other. If a foreign court has not explicitly rejected the enforcement of the judgments issued by ROC courts, ROC courts should take the initiative to uphold the enforceability of such foreign courts' judgments for the sake of reciprocity. The criteria for a foreign court to recognize the judgments issued by the ROC courts should not significantly deviate from the major principles stipulated under the Taiwan Code of Civil Procedure. The law does not require the former to be entirely consistent with the provisions under the Taiwan Code of Civil Procedure. If another jurisdiction had not explicitly denied the final and binding judgment rendered by an ROC court and the foreign judgment rendered at issue does not contravene with Subparagraphs 1 to 3, Paragraph 1, Article 402 of the Taiwan Code of Civil Procedure, the ROC court hearing the case should recognize the enforcement of such a foreign judgment, which will better suit the actual needs of the ROC in light of ROC's diplomatic predicament. The lower court in this case held that the contents of the Singapore court's judgment involve contractual claims only, both parties appeared at the court hearing and no procedural error can be found in any procedural aspect. The said foreign judgment should not be deemed as violating the public order or good morals of the ROC since it does not contradict the public interest of the ROC and the society or the morals shared by the nationals. Moreover, an ROC judgment can be used as a cause of action for a separate claim to be enforced in Singapore in accordance with the common law thereof. Given that Singapore courts had not explicitly denied the judgments rendered by ROC courts and ROC courts can reasonably expect their judgments to be enforced under the common law of Singapore, the requirement of "mutual recognition" of Subparagraph 4, Paragraph 1, Article 402 of the Taiwan Code of Civil Procedure should be deemed satisfied. Hence, the appellee's claim for recognizing and enforcing the judgment rendered by the Singapore court on the breach of contract claim between the parties hereof, as annexed to the lower court's judgment, in the ROC should be granted.

XIV Others

Supreme Administrative Court Judgment
March 28, 2013
102-Pan-Zi No. 137

Keywords:
Peking University, Regulations Governing the Accreditation of Schools in Mainland China

Relevant Provisions:
Article 22 of the Act Governing Relations between the People of the Taiwan Area and the Mainland Area
Article 96 of the Administrative Procedure Act

Summary:
The appellant is a Taiwan national who obtained a Ph.D. degree from Peking University Law School after having completed the doctoral courses at said law school from September 2003 to July 2007; his thesis and oral defense of the thesis meet the relevant requirements to pass. The appellant, in August 2011, took exams on the Constitution and the Administrative Law (for attaining academic credential from a higher education institution in China) held by National Chung Hsing University which was engaged by the appellee. After passing the written exams, the appellant applied for a review of his thesis in October 2011. The thesis was delivered to three experts and scholars in the fields that the appellant chose when he took the exams. Two of the three experts and scholars determined that the thesis did not meet the requirements to pass. Such result of the review was then submitted to the commission in charge of recognizing academic credentials from China, to which the appellee is subordinate, for resolution. After the resolution, the appellee notified the appellant that his thesis did not meet the requirements to pass. The appellant challenged such result and filed an administrative appeal, which was dismissed. The appellant further filed an administrative lawsuit, which was also dismissed by the court. The appellant thus filed this appeal.

Given the differences between Taiwan's educational systems and courses and China's, as well as to prevent the degradation of Taiwanese students' right to education, and to protect Taiwanese nationals' health and safety, Paragraph 1, Article 22 of the Act Governing Relations between the People of the Taiwan Area and the Mainland Area ("Act") stipulates that the eligibility of an applicant, guidelines for diploma recognition, applicable procedures and other matters for compliance with respect to the recognition of the academic credentials issued for educational programs in China shall be drafted by the Ministry of Education and then submitted to the Executive Yuan for approval. This court holds that the foregoing purposes are reasonable and justifiable. In addition, given that the subject case involves political, economic and social considerations and determinations with respect to cross-strait affairs, the authority responsible for the scrutiny of the constitutionality of law will respect such determination (or delegation of power) with respect to the recognition of the academic credentials that was made by the legislative body, which represents various voices of the people and commands sufficient information. Therefore, if the regulations governing the recognition of academic credential from China stipulated by the competent authority do not contain obvious, significant defect, the judicial body should respect such regulations, and allow the administrative body to have the autonomy to make decisions. Accordingly, the Rules on the Recognition of Academic Credentials ("Rules") and the Major Points of the Procedures for Attaining Academic Credentials ("Major Points") stipulate the standards for the recognition of master or doctorate degrees obtained from higher educational institutions in China from September 18, 1992 to September 3, 2000. Under the Rules and the Major Points, in addition to taking written exams on the specialized subjects, an applicant should submit the thesis completed during his/her education in China after passing the written exams. Such thesis will be categorized according to the fields it relates to, and be delivered to the experts and scholars of such fields for a substantive review. Unless such thesis passes the review, the applicant will not be able to obtain the certificate of equivalent diploma issued by the appellee. Such certificate is recognition that the diploma of the applicant is equivalent to those from the same kinds and levels of schools in Taiwan. The Rules and the Major Points were stipulated in accordance with the Act and do not exceed the scope authorized by the Act. Furthermore, considering (1) the change of relationship between Taiwan and China, (2) the government's policy to allow the recognition of academic credentials from China as well as to recruit Chinese students to study in Taiwan, and (3) the fairness and coherence of the recognition of academic credentials from China and those from Taiwan, Article 11 of the Rules and Paragraph 2, Point 8 of the Major Points stipulate different procedures for the recognition of academic credentials, depending on whether the applicants studied in China before or after the amendment to the Act took effect. Given that such differentiation was made on the basis of the government's policy on the recognition of academic credentials from China, the differentiation standard has a reasonable relevance to the goal of the policy. Moreover, to prevent false academic credentials and eliminate the public's concerns regarding the impact of the recognition of academic credentials from China, Item 5(2), Paragraph 2, Point 8 of the Major Points stipulates in detail the procedures and standards for the recognition of Chinese academic credentials. Under said Item 5(2), a thesis should be substantively reviewed so as to (1) establish complete and sound credential review measures and mechanism for preventing frauds, and (2) ensure the credibility and quality of the recognition of academic credentials from higher institutions in China. The differentiation made under the Rules and the Major Points should be adequate.

On the other hand, although Subparagraph 2, Paragraph 1, Article 96 of the Administrative Procedure Act requires an administrative decision to include a statement of reasons, such requirement is to (1) have the administrative agency review the relevant facts and/or issues carefully, (2) reduce the incorrectness or defect of the administrative decision, and (3) enable the exercise of judicial review when the person subject to the administrative decision resorts to an administrative remedy so as to adhere to the principle of clarity and definiteness of law. However, to prevent administrative efficiency from being affected, for (1) those administrative decisions of a special nature whereby it would be difficult to include a statement of reasons, and (2) those requiring professional determination which should be respected, Subparagraph 5, Article 97 of the Administrative Procedure Act stipulates an exception to the requirement of having to include a statement of reasons if "the administrative decision relates to examination, assessment and verification procedure in respect of specialized knowledge, skills or qualification." The exams of academic credentials held by the appellee according to the Act, the Rules and the Major Points are to verify whether an applicant has the "qualifications" equivalent to those obtained from the same kinds and levels of schools in Taiwan; thus the administrative decision without a statement of reasons does not constitute a violation of the Administrative Procedure Act.

President Ma Attends the Opening Ceremony of the 2013 ILA-ASIL Asia-Pacific Research Forum

On May 16, 2013, the Office of the President issued the following press release on the President's remarks at the opening ceremony of the 2013 ILA-ASIL Asia-Pacific Research Forum:[38]

On the morning of May 16, President Ma Ying-jeou attended the opening ceremonies of the 2013 International Law Association (ILA)-American Society of International Law (ASIL) Asia-Pacific Research Forum. The president stated

38 Office of the President, President Ma Attends Opening Ceremonies of 2013 ILA-ASIL Asia-Pacific Research Forum, May 16. 2013, http://english.president.gov.tw/Default.aspx?tabid=491&itemid=29930&rmid=2355.

that Taiwan uses peaceful means to resolve controversies, citing as examples its handling of cross-strait relations and the Diaoyutai Islets sovereignty dispute. In addition, the president reiterated his calls for the government of the Philippines to take responsibility for the Guang Da Xing No. 28 incident and respond positively to the four demands of the ROC.

With respect to the May 9 incident in which a Philippine government vessel fired upon the Taiwanese fishing vessel Guang Da Xing No. 28, killing a fisherman and causing serious damage to the boat, President Ma emphasized that the indiscriminate use of force by the crew of the Philippine government vessel in overlapping exclusive economic zones of the Philippines and Taiwan was unjustified and illegal under the principles of general international law as well as the provisions of the United Nations Convention on the Law of the Sea of 1982. Such outrageous behavior, he stated, cannot be tolerated by the international community, thus the ROC government has demanded that the government of the Philippines offer a formal apology, provide compensation for the losses, promptly and thoroughly investigate the incident and severely punish those responsible for the killing, and initiate fishery agreement negotiations between the two countries as soon as possible. These four demands, he added, are entirely in accordance with the standards and practices of international law. The Philippine government should own up to its responsibility for the incident and deal with the aftermath, he stressed, but the Philippine government did not respond to the demands within the 72-hour time limit, therefore the ROC has adopted 11 sanctions against the Philippines, including the recall of its representative stationed in the Philippines, imposition of a temporary freeze on all applications by Filipino laborers seeking to work in Taiwan, issuance of a "code red" alert as a warning to tourists from Taiwan considering visiting the Philippines, and suspension of bilateral agricultural, technology, and economic interaction.

President Ma stated that the killing of an unarmed, innocent civilian on the high seas is an act that no civilized nation can tolerate. He said that the ROC is a peace-loving nation that has consistently advocated the adoption of peaceful means to resolve disputes, adding that it has realized this principle on multiple occasions. The president called on the Philippine government to embrace this same attitude and act as a responsible stakeholder.

Because the theme of this year's forum is "International Law and Dispute Resolution: Challenges in the Asia Pacific," the president spoke about how he has used peaceful means since taking office to handle cross-strait relations and the sovereignty dispute over the Diaoyutai Islets.

In discussing cross-strait relations, President Ma stated that after the Chinese Civil War (1927–1937; 1945–1949) ended in 1949, the Communist Party controlled the Chinese mainland while the ROC government retreated to

Taiwan. Over the 64 years since then, he said, the mainland and Taiwan have been administered by separate authorities, and though the Communist Party maintains that it overthrew the ROC government and established the "Central People's government of the People's Republic of China," in fact the ROC government has not vanished, the president noted, pointing out that the ROC government still exercises effective rule over Taiwan, Penghu, Kinmen, and Matsu. President Ma noted that the Constitution of the ROC was enacted in 1947, when China was still unified, and was therefore, ipso facto, a "one China" constitution. The ROC Constitution, he said, still indicates that mainland China is "the territory of the Republic of China according to its existing national boundaries." The Chinese mainland still falls within our "existing national boundaries" as referred to in the ROC Constitution, said the president, adding that even with the two sides of the Taiwan Strait under divided rule, the ROC government still could not possibly recognize the existence of another state in our mainland China territory.

President Ma said that cross-strait relations are not state-to-state relations but special relations, which means that the international law issue regarding recognition of states does not even exist in cross-strait relations. However, he said, it is an objective fact that the Communist Party has ruled mainland China for 64 years. We cannot and need not deny that the Communist Party is the actual governing authority of mainland China, he stated. If the two sides denied each other's authority to govern, he asked, how could they possibly interact? The president said that this is why he advocates a policy of "mutual non-recognition of sovereignty, and mutual non-denial of governing authority."

The president further explained that he got the inspiration for the abovementioned policy from the Basis of Relations Treaty signed between East Germany and West Germany in 1972. This article makes no mention of sovereignty ("Souveränität" in German). Instead, it uses the term "Hoheitsgewalt," which means "supreme power" or, in other words, "authority to govern." President Ma said that the principle of "mutual non-recognition of sovereignty, and mutual non-denial of governing authority" is in accordance with the ROC Constitution and is also completely consistent with our mainland policy of maintaining the cross-strait status quo of no unification, no independence, and no use of force under the framework of the ROC Constitution. Moreover, it is also in line with the "1992 Consensus, whereby each side acknowledges the existence of "one China" but maintains its own interpretation of what "one China" means. This is the most pragmatic way to describe and interpret the cross-strait status quo, he said, adding that it is also the best way to reduce mutual hostility, shelve our sovereignty dispute, and foster cross-strait peace.

President Ma further stated that since he took office the two sides of the Taiwan Strait have held eight formal rounds of negotiations and signed 18 agreements that cover such issues as: direct cross-strait postal, transportation, and trade links; visits to Taiwan by mainland Chinese tourists; food safety; the employment of mainland fishing crews; animal and plant quarantine; law enforcement cooperation and mutual judicial assistance; financial supervision of banks and other financial services providers; economic cooperation; and IPR protection. The president said that currently 616 scheduled direct flights operate weekly between cities on the two sides of the Taiwan Strait, compared with only weekend and holiday charters in the past. In addition, the number of annual visits made by mainland Chinese to Taiwan has grown from 270,000 to about 2.5 million, he added. Furthermore, over 17,000 mainland Chinese students were studying in Taiwan as of last year, compared with some 800 when he took office. The president also indicated that joint efforts to combat crime have yielded impressive results. The number of scam cases in Taiwan has dropped by half, he mentioned, and losses caused by scams have been shaved by 75% (NT$14 billion).

The president emphasized that the ROC has adopted pragmatic policies, establishing institutionalized negotiations to gradually establish mutual trust and usher in an unprecedented era of peace between the two sides. In the future, he said, the government will continue to work to expand and deepen cross-strait interaction through means including the mutual establishment of representative offices on each side and a comprehensive review of the Act Governing Relations between the People of the Taiwan Area and the Mainland Area. The objective, the president stated, is to achieve peace and prosperity on both sides of the Taiwan Strait.

The president then turned his remarks to the sovereignty dispute over the Diaoyutai Islets. President Ma explained to the experts and scholars in attendance that prior to the Japanese government's move to nationalize the Diaoyutais in September 2012, he had already unveiled his East China Sea Peace Initiative in the preceding month of August, calling on all parties involved to be prudent, shelve controversies, and resolve disputes peacefully, because "sovereignty over national territory cannot be compromised, but natural resources can be shared," he stated.

President Ma remarked that he had taken part in the Defend the Diaoyutais Movement 40 years ago as a university student, and to this day he still firmly believes that the Diaoyutais belong to the Republic of China, but if this controversy is to be resolved, it will have to be done peacefully. The first step in this process, he said, is for the parties involved to cooperate in the use of living and non-living resources. That is why the ROC and Japan resumed fishing negotiations in September 2012, which ultimately led to the signing of a bilateral fisheries agreement between the two on April 10 of this year. The agreement establishes a joint conservation and management zone where fishermen from both sides can operate. With respect to the sovereignty dispute, the president commented, the agreement includes a "no prejudice" clause which stipulates that there is nothing in the fisheries agreement that could prejudice other legal claims by either side. President Ma said that the signing of this agreement for the first time points to a possible way to deal with the 40-year sovereignty dispute over the Diaoyutais, and establishes a good model for the handling of similar territorial disputes of national territory.

The president stated that the experience of history tells us that if international controversies are to be resolved peacefully, the disputing parties must acknowledge reality, shelve controversies, and respect international law. President Ma remarked that the ROC government, in the course of its efforts to improve cross-strait relations and resolve its fishing disputes with Japan, has clearly shown itself to be a peacemaker, thus proving both in theory and in practice that we are in fact capable of playing this role.

Among those attending the opening ceremonies of the conference were ILA Treasurer and German Branch President Torsten Stein, Co-Chair Edmund Sim of the ASIL's Pacific Rim Interest Group, National Chengchi University Vice President Bih-jaw Lin (林碧炤), and Chinese (Taiwan) Society of International Law President Chun-I Chen (陳純一), and Deputy Minister of Foreign Affairs Simon Shen-Yeaw Ko (柯森耀).

President Ma Attends International Conference on 70th Anniversary of Cairo Declaration

On December 1, 2013, the Office of the President issued the following press release on the President's remarks at the International Conference on the 70th Anniversary of the Cairo Declaration:[39]

On the morning of December 1, President Ma Ying-jeou went to the Academia Historica to attend an exhibit on the Cairo Declaration and the International Conference on the 70th Anniversary of the Cairo Declaration, which is being held by the Ministry of Foreign Affairs and National Chengchi University. In addition to elaborating on the process that led to the signing of the Cairo Declaration and its important historical significance, the presi-

39 Office of the President, President Ma Attends International Conference on 70th Anniversary of Cairo Declaration, Dec. 1, 2013, http://english.president.gov.tw/Default.aspx?tabid=491&itemid=31367&rmid=2355.

dent also reiterated a four-point statement by the ROC government on mainland China's recent announcement of a new East China Sea Air Defense Identification Zone. President Ma called on all parties involved to engage in dialogue as soon as possible in order to reduce tension in the East China Sea.

After arriving at the Academia Historica, the president first toured the facility and viewed the items in the special exhibition, including a documentary film about the Cairo Conference, an original copy of the Cairo Declaration, and a log of the signatories at the ceremony for accepting Japan's surrender in Taiwan Province of the China War Theater, along with news reports on the Cairo Conference. In remarks, the president noted that December 1 marks the 70th anniversary of the Cairo Declaration, and is also the 70th anniversary of the ROC government's demand that after World War II Japan must return to the Republic of China all the territories it had stolen from the Chinese, such as Taiwan and the Penghu Islands. President Ma said that he is deeply honored to have been invited to appear at this event.

The president stated that the eight-year War of Resistance against Japan was the most important period in modern Chinese history. Victory in the war was a brilliant feat for the Chinese people, he said, adding that it was due not just to the joint efforts of the ROC army and the general public, but also to critical international assistance. President Ma remarked that the United States provided the most important assistance, while at the same time the ROC's diplomatic efforts also played a crucial role.

The president mentioned that the Cairo Conference was convened in November 1943 and was one of 14 summits held during World War II. It was also the only international summit in which Generalissimo Chiang Kai-shek (蔣中正), the chairman of the ROC's Nationalist Government, took part. He pointed out that the participants at the Cairo Conference discussed the strategy of the Allied forces in Europe and Asia. Also, the heads of state of the Republic of China, the United States, and the United Kingdom exchanged opinions on the re-establishment of a post-war international order in East Asia, and issued the Cairo Declaration. The declaration included the following very important provision relating to the ROC: "All the territories Japan has stolen from the Chinese, such as Manchuria, Formosa (Taiwan), and the Pescadores (Penghu) shall be restored to the Republic of China." This established the basis for the return of Taiwan and the Penghu Islands to the ROC, he said. At the same time, Generalissimo Chiang during the conference supported the independence of Korea and Vietnam after the conclusion of the war, and opposed abolishing Japan's imperial system, thus demonstrating the far-sighted vision befitting the leader of a major East-Asian nation and one of the world's four major powers, the president remarked.

President Ma emphasized that the Cairo Conference was the first time that the ROC had participated in an international conference as one of four major powers, and that Generalissimo Chiang showed a willingness to "help the weak and small, forgive enemies, and do what is right rather than grab for spoils." The president said that Generalissimo Chiang together with the United States and Great Britain settled the post-war blueprint for East Asia, whereby the ROC would recover Manchuria, Taiwan, and the Penghu Islands, and would help Korea and Vietnam pursue independence. At the same time, Japan's territory would be restricted to its four major islands. "This was an epochal event at that time, and it also had a decisive impact on the subsequent state of East Asia," President Ma commented.

The president also praised the efforts of Wang Chung-hui (王寵惠), the secretary general of the ROC's Supreme National Defense Council, who during World War II represented the government in non-military negotiations with the Allied forces.

In response to some who have described the Cairo Declaration as a simple press release and not a treaty, the president stated that the declaration was always treated during the war as part of the body of wartime documents. Pointing to the Potsdam Proclamation of July 1945 as an example, President Ma noted that Article 8 of that document clearly states: "The terms of the Cairo Declaration shall be carried out and Japanese sovereignty shall be limited to the islands of Honshu, Hokkaido, Kyushu, Shikoku and such minor islands as we determine." In addition, the Imperial Rescript of the Termination of the War issued by the Japanese emperor on August 14, 1945 and the Japanese Instrument of Surrender signed in September 1945 both indicated that Japan was willing to accept the Potsdam Proclamation issued by the ROC, the United Kingdom, the United States, and the Soviet Union, he said. Moreover, the United States and Japan both include in their official treaty collections the Cairo Declaration, the Potsdam Proclamation, and the Japanese Instrument of Surrender. For instance, he noted, they are included in "Treaties and Other International Agreements of the United States of America 1776–1949" and "United States Statutes At Large," as well as a collection of treaties by Japan's Ministry of Foreign Affairs, and the "United Nations Treaty Series," which indicates that the Cairo Declaration has the binding force of international law. In accordance with international law, therefore, any substantive pledge made by a head of state while in office and within his or her authority is legally binding, said the president.

President Ma also mentioned that according to international precedent, after the conclusion of a war, the parties involved typically sign a treaty that serves as a basis for the cessation of hostilities. The ROC was not present at the signing of the San Francisco Peace Treaty, he said, but both the San Francisco Peace Treaty and the Sino-Japanese Peace Treaty provide that "Japan has renounced all right, title, and claim to Taiwan (Formosa) and Penghu (the Pescadores)," and that "all treaties, conventions, and agreements concluded before 9 December 1941 between Japan and China have become null and void as a consequence of the war." Article 10 of the Sino-Japanese Peace Treaty states: "nationals of the Republic of China shall be deemed to include all the inhabitants and former inhabitants of Taiwan (Formosa) and Penghu (the Pescadores) and their descendants." At the same time, he pointed out, in the Exchange of Notes accompanying the treaty, Note No. 1 confirmed the understanding that the treaty would be applicable to all the territories which were then, or which might thereafter be, under the control of the ROC. This, he said, proves that Taiwan is a part of the Republic of China.

Turning his remarks to mainland China's announcement on November 23 of an East China Sea Air Defense Identification Zone (ADIZ), the president stated that this action has triggered deep concern in the United States, Japan, Korea, and Taiwan, and that regional tensions have begun to rise. In response, he said, the ROC government on that day and again on November 29 issued the following four-point statement: 1) the ROC reiterates its sovereignty over the Diaoyutai Islets; 2) the ROC's Air Force will continue to carry out exercises and training activities as normal in the ROC's air defense identification zone, but the ROC will go through channels to express to mainland Chinese authorities its serious concern about this situation, which stems mainly from the fact that mainland China did not consult Taiwan before announcing its ADIZ in the East China Sea; 3) Taiwan urges other nations to refer to the ROC's East China Sea Peace Initiative that was unveiled last year, and to use peaceful means to resolve disputes; and 4) the ROC Civil Aeronautics Administration of the Ministry of Transportation and Communications will relay the filing of flight plans for civil aircraft in accordance with relevant regulations and practices of the International Civil Aviation Organization (ICAO) regarding FIR notification, based on requests from airline companies in Taiwan and abroad, to ensure the safety of passengers.

In the interest of maintaining peace in the East China Sea and reducing tensions in the region, the president called once again upon all parties involved to avoid any action that would exacerbate tensions. He also expressed hope that Taiwan and mainland China will engage in a bilateral dialogue and at the same time carry out negotiations on overlapping areas in the ADIZ so as to restore the East China Sea to a state of peace and cooperation.

Cross-Strait Relations

President Ma Attends Reception to Mark 20th Anniversary of Koo-Wang Talks

On April 29, 2013, the Office of the President issued the following press release on the President's remarks at a reception marking the 20th anniversary of the Koo-Wang Talks:[40]

On the morning of April 29, President Ma Ying-jeou visited the Straits Exchange Foundation (SEF) to attend a reception marking the 20th anniversary of the Koo-Wang talks, a series of discussions between then-SEF Chairman Koo Chen-fu (辜振甫) and then-Chairman Wang Daohan (汪道涵) of the Association for Relations Across the Taiwan Straits (ARATS) that began in Singapore in 1993. In addition to praising Mr. Koo and Mr. Wang for their contributions to peace in the Taiwan Strait, the president stressed that our government policy on mainland China and cross-strait relations must be carried out under the framework of the ROC Constitution and the principle of "putting Taiwan first for the benefit of the people." At the same time, he called for expansion and deepening of cross-strait relations in a wide variety of fields, including economic and trade ties, to forge greater mutual understanding and more wide-ranging cooperation.

In remarks, the president stated that on the same day 20 years earlier, SEF Chairman Koo and ARATS Chairman Wang met in a spirit of "negotiating as equals, maintaining reciprocity, and creating a win-win situation." The two signed four agreements in Singapore: the Agreement on the Use and Verification of Certificates of Authentication Across the Taiwan Straits; the Agreement on Matters Concerning Inquiry and Compensation for [Lost] Registered Mail Across the Taiwan Straits; the Agreement on the System for Contacts and Meetings between SEF and ARATS; and the Joint Agreement of the Koo-Wang Talks. While the focus of these agreements was limited to technical matters, the president remarked, the talks nevertheless marked the first time that the two governments had authorized formal negotiations since the two sides of the Taiwan Strait came under the rule of separate governments in 1949. The significance of these talks attracted the attention of the world, and marked an important milestone by setting the foundation for peace between the two sides, he added.

---

40 Office of the President, President Ma Attends Reception to Mark 20th Anniversary of Koo-Wang Talks, Apr. 29, 2013, http://english.president.gov.tw/Default.aspx?tabid=491&itemid=29765&rmid=2355.

The fall of the Berlin Wall in 1989, President Ma stated, set in motion the collapse of communism in the Soviet Union and Eastern Europe. In 1990, he said, the two Germanys reunified and the Cold War came to an end. In 1989 in mainland China, however, some 10 years after authorities there began instituting reform and opening up, the Tiananmen Incident took place. But the impetus toward reform could not be stopped. In Taiwan, under the leadership of then-ROC President Chiang Ching-kuo (蔣經國), martial law had already been lifted in 1986, following which democratic reforms were instituted, including lifting of the ban on establishing political parties, newspapers, and magazines. President Ma pointed out that in 1987 Taiwan began allowing the public to go back to mainland China to visit relatives, which marked an end to the "three nos" policy on cross-strait ties, namely "no contact, no negotiation, and no compromise." Cross-strait relations that had been frozen for 40 years began to thaw, he commented.

The president mentioned that in August 1988 the Executive Yuan established the Mainland Affairs Task Force to coordinate the handling of mainland affairs. This body was formally upgraded into the Mainland Affairs Council (MAC) in 1991, he said. At that time, the newly elected Second National Assembly had begun to amend the Constitution. Then-President Lee Teng-hui (李登輝) announced the termination of the Period of National Mobilization for Suppression of the Communist Rebellion, which meant that the Chinese communists would no longer be referred to as a "rebel group." The National Assembly then abolished the Temporary Provisions Effective During the Period of National Mobilization for Suppression of the Communist Rebellion, thus returning Taiwan to constitutional normalcy, and adopted a set of Additional Articles of the Constitution "to meet the requisites of the nation prior to national unification." The Additional Articles set forth a "free area" and a "mainland area" as the bases for interaction between the two sides, and authorize the government to enact special laws to govern the cross-strait relationship. On the basis of the Additional Articles, said the president, the MAC drafted the Act Governing Relations between the People of the Taiwan Area and the Mainland Area to govern cross-strait relations prior to national unification. In 1991, he mentioned, Taiwan established the SEF and mainland China founded the ARATS, thus completing a major change in ties between the two sides.

President Ma mentioned that in November 1992 the two sides reached the so-called "1992 Consensus," whereby each side acknowledges the existence of "one China" but maintains its own interpretation of what that means. This set the stage for a subsequent round of Koo-Wang talks in April 1993 that marked the commencement of a new era in which the two sides would "use negotiation to alleviate confrontation, and replace conflict with reconciliation." The president stated that he first became involved in cross-strait affairs in 1987. In May 2006, 13 years after the Koo-Wang talks, he visited Singapore in his capacity as Kuomintang chairman and Taipei City mayor. While he was there, special arrangements were made for him to visit the NOL Building, the site of the first round of Koo-Wang talks. President Ma remarked that at that time the atmosphere between the two sides was quite tense, in contrast to the harmony during the first Koo-Wang talks, which made quite a deep impression on him. The president mentioned that the most valuable asset left to us by the Koo-Wang talks is the approach of "engaging in technical negotiations and seeking common ground while respecting differences."

President Ma furthermore explained that despite achievement of the "1992 Consensus" and the holding of talks between Mr. Koo and Mr. Wang in 1993, friction began to arise between the leaders of the two sides of the Taiwan Strait following the Thousand Island Lake Incident in 1994. In 1995, he said, mainland China unilaterally declared a halt to negotiations between the SEF and the ARATS, saying that Taiwan had violated the consensus. Then during the 1996 presidential election campaign here, mainland China resorted to verbal threats and military scare tactics, launching missiles into the seas around Taiwan. At that time, the United States even dispatched two aircraft carrier battle groups to cruise in the waters off Taiwan, he said. Clouds of war hung over the Taiwan Strait, and the situation was extremely explosive. It was not until 1998, after the two sides expressed their intention to ease the tense relations, that Mr. Koo and Mr. Wang held discussions in Shanghai. Mr. Wang at that time pledged to visit Taiwan the following year, the president said. Unfortunately, on the eve of his visit, high-ranking officials here suddenly announced the so-called "two-state theory." Mr. Wang subsequently cancelled his trip and never did realize his desire to visit Taiwan, he commented.

President Ma also mentioned that when the Democratic Progressive Party came to power in 2000, it denied the existence of the "1992 Consensus" and instead adopted the "one country on each side" stance while calling for Taiwan to rejoin the United Nations. These policies, the president noted, once again caused cross-strait tensions to rise. Mainland China, he commented, even adopted the Anti-Separation Law. The two sides had once again come to the brink of conflict, the president said, adding that it was not until 2008 when governing power changed hands again that there was a chance to change the situation.

President Ma reiterated that after he took office in 2008, he immediately declared that the government would, under the framework of the ROC Constitution, maintain the status quo of "no unification, no independence, and no use of force" in the Taiwan Strait, and promote the resumption of cross-strait relations under the "1992 Consensus." Over the past five years, he said, former SEF Chairman Chiang Pin-kung (江丙坤) and former ARATS Chairman Chen Yunlin (陳雲林) have held eight rounds of negotiations, which have yielded 18 cross-strait agreements covering such matters as: direct transportation, postal, and trade links; tourism; food safety; health and medicine; fishermen; quarantine; joint combating of crime; economic cooperation; intellectual property protection; financial supervision; currency settlement; reporting of nuclear incidents; and investment protection. The president mentioned that the number of scheduled weekly flights between the two sides has increased from zero to 616, with airlines serving nearly 50 airports on either side of the Taiwan Strait, which has created unprecedented conveniences for travelers. Meanwhile, the number of mainland Chinese tourists to Taiwan has already surpassed 7 million, which has played an important role in bolstering Taiwan's tourism industry. President Ma also said that cross-strait cooperation in combating crime has helped to net over 4,700 criminals engaged in scam operations, thereby reducing the number of scam crimes by 20,000 and alleviating some three-quarters of the losses that could have been inflicted (which comes to roughly NT$14 billion). Most recently, the president stated, two suspects who had placed bombs on one of Taiwan's high-speed trains were apprehended in mainland China and speedily returned to Taiwan thanks to cooperation in this respect. The president also pointed out that people have been infected by the H7N9 strain of avian flu in mainland China and that authorities here have been kept updated by their mainland counterparts on the situation there. He said that mainland China recently has even provided samples of the virus so that a vaccine can be manufactured here. Cooperation between the two sides has become extremely close in this area, he commented.

President Ma remarked that the improvement in cross-strait relations has been well received by other nations, and has improved Taiwan's relations with the international community. For instance, he said, Taiwan and Japan have signed a Taiwan-Japan Bilateral Investment Arrangement and a fisheries agreement, whereas nothing of the sort had previously been achieved in the 40 years since diplomatic ties were severed. As for relations between Taiwan and the United States, he noted, former US Secretary of State Hillary Clinton has described Taiwan as an important security and economic partner of the United States. Furthermore, Taiwan on November 1 last year formally became the 37th member of the US Visa Waiver Program and the only one with which the United States does not maintain formal diplomatic relations. President Ma also pointed out that the European Union has not only supported participation for Taiwan in the World Health Assembly and other international organizations, but also was one of the first areas to provide visa-free courtesies to ROC nationals, which sparked a move by other countries to follow suit. The president noted that 132 jurisdictions now provide visa-free courtesies or landing visas to ROC nationals, which is a milestone in the diplomatic history of the ROC.

With respect to cross-strait economic, trade, and cultural ties, President Ma noted, negotiations on a cross-strait agreement on trade in services are nearing completion and a pact on trade in goods is also in the works. Both of these agreements will be extensions of the Cross-Straits Economic Cooperation Framework Agreement signed three years ago, he said, commenting that this shows the two sides are moving toward their objective of realizing free trade. The president mentioned that three years ago the two sides signed the Cross-Strait Agreement on Intellectual Property Rights Protection and Cooperation, which has enabled cross-strait cultural ties to flourish. He expressed confidence that there will be further strengthening in such ties once the agreement on trade in services is finalized.

President Ma then discussed mainland Chinese students and tourists coming to Taiwan. He mentioned that over 17,000 mainland Chinese students are studying here, and the government here now recognizes diplomas from 111 mainland Chinese academic institutions, compared with 41 in the past. This coming autumn, he noted, Taiwan will begin allowing graduates from mainland technical colleges to come here to continue their studies at two-year technical institutes. The most important significance of mainland students coming to study here is that young people on both sides will forge friendships at an early age, which will help lay a lasting foundation for the development of cross-strait peace. In addition, he pointed out, since over 7 million visits are made between the two sides each year, Taiwan hopes that each side will establish representative offices in the other jurisdiction as soon as possible to provide timely and efficient assistance to cross-strait travelers. Furthermore, so long as national security is not compromised, the government here intends to carry out a comprehensive review and subsequent amendment of the Act Governing Relations between the People of the Taiwan Area and the Mainland Area with an eye to better safeguarding human rights and boosting efficiency. This effort will enable cross-strait relations to move forward in a steadier manner, he said.

President Ma emphasized that the government is efforts to promote its mainland policy and cross-strait relations must be carried out under the framework of the ROC Constitution and in line with the principle of "putting Taiwan first for the benefit of the people." In addition, the priority of issues for the two sides to address would be "pressing matters before less pressing ones, easy matters before difficult ones, and economic matters before political ones," he said. Both at home and abroad, Taiwan will not promote "two Chinas," "one China, one Taiwan," or "Taiwan independence," the president emphasized. The peaceful and mutually beneficial interaction between the two sides over the past five years has created a positive model for East Asia and the world in the use of peaceful means to resolve differences, he noted. These results have not come easy, the president added, saying that we should cherish them and of course work to continue them.

Looking to the future, the president expressed hope that peace and prosperity between the two sides can continue to be promoted on the basis of the "1992 Consensus," whereby each side acknowledges the existence of "one China" but maintains its own interpretation of what that means. At the same time, he said, in working to expand and deepen the relationship in such areas as economic and trade ties, culture, technology, environmental protection, society, rule of law, and human rights, he intends to stick to a policy of "mutual non-recognition of sovereignty, and mutual non-denial of governing authority," the president said. This, he remarked, will promote greater understanding and cooperation among the people of the two sides of the Taiwan Strait.

Among those attending the activity were Presidential Senior Advisors Cecilia Y. Koo (辜嚴倬雲) and Chiang Pin-kung, Secretary-General to the President Timothy Chin-Tien Yang (楊進添), National Security Council Secretary-General Jason C. Yuan (袁健生), Mainland Affairs Council Minister Wang Yu-Chi (王郁琦), SEF Chairman Lin Join-sane (林中森), and Mr. Wang Zhizhong (汪致重), son of former ARATS Chairman Wang Daohan.

MAC's Statement on Establishing Reciprocal Institutions between the Straits Exchange Foundation (SEF) and the Association for Relations Across the Taiwan Straits (ARATS)

On June 12, 2013, the Mainland Affairs Council issued the following statement on the reciprocal institutions to be established by the Straits Exchange Foundation (SEF) and the Association for Relations Across the Taiwan Straits (ARATS):[41]

1. The government promotes peaceful development of cross-strait relations in accordance to the Constitution of the Republic of China (ROC) and the Act Governing Relations between the People of the Taiwan Area and

41 Mainland Affairs Council, MAC: The Republic of China is a Sovereign, Independent State; Cross-Strait Relations Positioned in Accordance to Constitution and Does Not Parrot the Mainland's "One China Principle", June 12, 2013, http://www.mac.gov.tw/public/Attachment/37111474374.pdf.

the Mainland Area, which pragmatically positions the relationship across the Strait as "one Republic of China with two areas." According to the Constitution, the ROC is a sovereign, independent country with territorial claim covering both Taiwan and the Mainland, thereby the government naturally cannot recognize the existence of another country on ROC Mainland territory, and thus, we cannot recognize the other side as a country. As such, the relationship across the Strait is certainly not a "state to state" relationship. In terms of national identity, the government governs the country in accordance to the ROC Constitution; there are no such issues such as self-belittlement or parroting of the Mainland's "one China" principle.

2. Cross-strait relations have smoothly developed over the past five years with substantive and pragmatic realization by the two sides on the "mutual non-recognition of sovereignty and mutual non-denial of authority to govern" concept. Furthermore, throughout the process of negotiations on the reciprocal establishment of the SEF and ARATS institutions, the government has stood firm to the established position and made no concessions on national sovereignty or the public's well-being. There is no possibility whatsoever of conducting political negotiations with the other side on cross-strait positioning before consensus has been formed domestically.
3. The MAC stressed that the purpose of establishing reciprocal institutions between the SEF and ARATS is to serve the people on both sides and to protect their rights and interests. Many issues of concern included into the negotiation agenda are of political sensitivity, such as that of travel document application, humanitarian visits to citizens whose personal freedom have been restricted, codes of conduct for personnel dispatched by the two sides, and other matters related to rights guarantees and constraints. The government has not merely treated the above said issues as general issues, but rather has taken a pragmatic approach in the negotiation process and actively sought out Taiwan's best interests. The government has also adhered to the consistent principle of transparency in the negotiation process and related legal procedures; it has conducted ample communications with all sectors, and has also accepted legislative oversight.
4. The MAC reiterated that the government has always abided by relevant legal procedures in authorizing the SEF to conduct cross-strait negotiations, voices raising concern over negotiations becoming "KMT-CPC negotiations" do not exist. It is the government's responsibility to defend national interests and safeguard the people's well-being, therefore the

government attaches great importance to the concerns of all sides on the issue of establishing SEF-ARATS reciprocal institutions, and will continue in the future to take all suggestions under advisement and fully communicate with the public to dispel unnecessary doubts. The MAC also appealed to all sides to regard the issue of reciprocal SEF-ARATS institutions establishment in a rationalized manner, and work together to carry out this important national policy.

Conclusion of the Ninth Round of Cross-Strait High-Level Talks

On June 22, 2013, the Mainland Affairs Council issued the following press release on the conclusion of the Ninth Round of Cross-Strait High-Level Talks:[42]

The Ninth Round of Cross-Strait High-Level Talks between the Straits Exchange Foundation (SEF) and the Association for Relations Across the Taiwan Straits (ARATS) successfully concluded today (June 22). Accompanied by Chairman Lin Join-sane of the SEF and the negotiation delegation, Minister Wang Yu-chi of the Mainland Affairs Council (MAC) delivered an achievement report to Premier Jiang Yi-huah at the Executive Yuan, submitted the text of the Cross-Strait Trade in Services Agreement, and later attended the press conference held at the Executive Yuan.

The MAC stated that, the Trade in Services Agreement is only a part of the comprehensive Economic Cooperation Framework Agreement (ECFA). The signing of the Agreement will create development niches for Taiwanese businesses in the Mainland and effectively enhance and expand the specific benefits of the ECFA. On this basis, the government will further promote progress of ECFA follow-up negotiations on trade in goods and dispute settlement issues. The signing of the Cross-Strait Trade in Services Agreement is also beneficial to Taiwan's active participation in regional economic integration as it conveys to the international community the message of further trade liberalization in Taiwan. The MAC stated that it will promptly promote the implementation of related market opening measures after enforcement procedures have been completed so as to substantively realize results of the Trade In Services Agreement.

The MAC stated that the government promotes negotiations between the SEF and ARATS with the interests and well-being of the people in mind. Public opinion surveys conducted by the MAC indicate that nearly 70% of the public support the handling of issues related to cross-strait exchanges through

42 Mainland Affairs Council, MAC: Ninth Round of Cross-Strait High-Level Talks Successfully Concluded; Two Sides to Jointly Work on Agreement Enforcement and Implementation, June 22, 2013, http://www.mac.gov.tw/public/Attachment/37111419757.pdf.

institutionalized negotiations between the two sides; and 74% of the people approve of the government's negotiations with mainland China on cross-strait trade in services issues. This shows that the government's policy position and course in promoting institutionalized cross-strait negotiations is consistent with the expectations of mainstream public opinion in Taiwan. In the future, the government will continue to formulate related supporting measures to reduce the impact on related industries, while at the same time, it will also strengthen communication with all sectors to dispel people's doubts, thereby gain public support for cross-strait negotiations.

Regarding the negotiation issues for the tenth round of talks, the MAC stated that the two sides have laid a foundation and achieved phased results in negotiations on the ECFA follow-up issues of trade in goods and dispute settlement, avoidance of double taxation across the Strait, and the reciprocal establishment of institutions by the SEF and ARATS. The MAC will also coordinate with relevant competent authorities and carefully deliberate and promote negotiation work on meteorological, earthquake and other issues. As to the signed agreements, the MAC will continue to coordinate with related ministries, review the implementation status, and encourage cooperation and improvements by the Mainland side in order to maximize effects and results of the agreements' implementation.

During the briefing on the results of the talks, Premier Jiang expressed grateful approbation to all personnel involved in the negotiations, and also acknowledged the smooth and successful conclusion of agreement signed in this round of high-level talks. Premier Jiang also pointed out that the signing of the Trade in Services Agreement is beneficial to mutual market opening across the Strait. However, the Premiere said, it is hoped that competent authorities, in conjunction with relevant ministries and departments, will fully coordinate to formulate supporting measures to respond to likely impacts of the service trade agreement, while at the same time increase communication and explanation to the public on views recently voiced by certain businesses and media.

The MAC stressed that institutionalized negotiations between the SEF and ARATS are now operating in a normalized manner. The government will adhere to the principles of "national demand, public support, and legislative oversight" and the negotiation position of dealing with "urgent matters before non-urgent ones, easy matters before difficult ones, and economic matters before political ones," while at the same time uphold established policy objectives and promote them in a gradual and steady approach. The MAC called on the two sides to jointly establish a peaceful environment for cross-strait development on the current negotiation basis, and to set the improvement of the people's well-being as the core objective in further cross strait development.

President Ma's Remarks on the Benefits of the Cross-Strait Trade in Services Agreement

On July 27, 2013, the Office of the President issued the following press release on the President's remarks on the benefits of the Cross-Strait Trade in Services Agreement:[43]

On the evening of July 27, President Ma Ying-jeou visited Jenn Lann Temple in Dajia District, Taichung City to address a crowd assembled in the square in front of the temple on the benefits of the Cross-Strait Trade in Services Agreement. In addition to dispelling false claims about the agreement, the president also explained how it will benefit Taiwan.

In remarks, President Ma explained that Taiwan relies on exports for 70% of its economic growth, so the government has always sought to minimize barriers to exports while maximizing facilitative measures. He stated that Taiwan's main competitors in Asia, including Korea, Japan, and Singapore, have all signed more free trade agreements than Taiwan has. In addition, the agreements signed by these nations account for 35%, 18.7%, and 64% of their overall trade, respectively, and these figures could rise to 82%, 72.2%, and 88%. The president then compared these figures with those on Taiwan's free trade agreements, which presently cover 4.18% of Taiwan's total trade volume, with the possibility that this percentage could rise to 36.9%. Taiwan thus lags far behind the three nations mentioned above, he stated.

President Ma mentioned that in an effort to avoid being at a competitive disadvantage, three years ago Taiwan signed the Cross-Straits Economic Cooperation Framework Agreement (ECFA) with mainland China. The Cross-Strait Trade in Services Agreement is part of the broader ECFA agreement, he said, and hopefully by the end of this year the two sides will also sign the Cross-Strait Trade in Goods Agreement, as this would encourage other nations to sign economic cooperation agreements with Taiwan and effectively reduce tariffs on Taiwan's exports. For instance, the president stated, Taiwan and New Zealand in May of last year began negotiations on the Agreement between New Zealand and the Separate Customs Territory of Taiwan, Penghu, Kinmen and Matsu on Economic Cooperation (ANZTEC). This pact was signed on July 10 of this year, he pointed out, noting that the negotiation process went very quickly.

President Ma also acknowledged that the signing of the Cross-Strait Trade in Services Agreement has sparked considerable debate. He said that the

43 Office of the President, President Ma Attends Event in Central Taiwan to Speak on Benefits of Cross-Strait Trade in Services Agreement, July 27, 2013, http://english.president.gov.tw/Default.aspx?tabid=491&itemid=30484&rmid=2355.

government's efforts to publicize the content of the agreement have been insufficient, while inaccurate information has been repeatedly aired by the media. For instance, the president commented, some have said the agreement opens Taiwan's doors to some four million to five million laborers from mainland China in the service sector, but this is absolutely not true. In fact, he said, the government has allowed mainland Chinese enterprises to invest in Taiwan for over three years and 398 firms have been set up here so far. In this period, however, only 216 mainland Chinese managers and professionals have come to Taiwan, while these investments have created 6,771 job opportunities here. Moreover, the ROC government each year carefully checks the Taiwan entry permits of mainlanders working here, and does not issue them alien permanent resident certificates, so fears about a big wave of "investment immigrants" from the mainland are unfounded, he commented. In addition, the president stated, Taiwan liberalized laundry services in 1991, but only two foreign laundry companies do business here. This compares with 6,000 local laundry shops, which is the accurate number and not only 3,000 as some have claimed, he said.

President Ma stated that service-sector companies from Taiwan have done quite well in the mainland. For instance, the coffee shop 85°C, Wang Steak restaurants, RT-Mart, Les Enphants children's clothing stores, and Formosa Optical do business throughout mainland China. In addition, in the wake of the signing of the ECFA, mainland China each year screens roughly 10 films from Taiwan, while no limit is placed on the number of Taiwanese films screened in mainland China, he said. Mainland Chinese films screened in Taiwan over the past two years have generated box office receipts of roughly NT$67 million, while the box office receipts of Taiwanese films screened in the mainland have reached NT$3 billion, which shows that Taiwanese films are very competitive. The president also pointed out that the Cross-Strait Trade in Services Agreement will allow the 800 films produced in mainland China each year to have post-production work done on them in Taiwan, which is a potential boon for firms here.

President Ma stressed that an important constant throughout Taiwan's history is that "engagement brings prosperity, while isolation brings atrophy." Taiwan has no choice but to open its doors, otherwise the size of its market will become smaller and smaller. The president stated that the signing of the Cross-Strait Trade in Services Agreement will bring significantly more benefits to Taiwan than harm. Furthermore, the president commented, the Ministry of Economic Affairs three years ago budgeted NT$95 billion over a period of 10 years to assist industries that are impacted by the agreement.

After completing his initial remarks, the president hosted a prize quiz on the Cross-Strait Trade in Services Agreement. Members of the audience participated enthusiastically in the quiz, which helped them better understand the content of the pact.

Realization of "Mutual Non-Denial" and the Normalization of Cross-Strait Official Interactions

On October 6, 2013, the Mainland Affairs Council issued the following press release concerning "mutual non-denial" and the normalization of cross-strait official interactions.[44]

The Mainland Affairs Council (MAC) stated today (October 6) that Minister Wang Yu-chi exchanged brief pleasantries with Taiwan Affairs Office (TAO) Director Zhang Zhijun during a spontaneous exchange after the "Siew-Xi Meeting" outside the meeting venue, where the two sides addressed each other by their official titles. This indicates a substantive realization of "addressing realities and mutual non-denial" spirit between the two sides and also represents a good start in normalizing official cross-strait interactions, highlighting the important implications for regular interactions between the MAC and TAO in the future.

The MAC said that, Minister Wang pointed out to Director Zhang during the brief exchange that regular exchange visits by competent persons in charge of cross-strait affairs on both sides is needed so that they may further build mutual understanding and strengthen communication on issues of mutual concern. Director Zhang responded positively to Minister Wang's suggestion and invited Minister Wang to visit the Mainland when time is appropriate.

Minister Wang also emphasized to Director Zhang that they had acted out the role of consultants to the "Siew-Xi Meeting", conducted smooth communications, and carried out all arrangements. Competent authorities for cross-strait affairs should also establish regular contact mechanisms so as to facilitate communication between the two sides. Such a channel would help the two sides understand each other better and facilitate promotion of respective operational tasks.

The MAC stressed that Minister Wang and Director Zhang addressed each other by their official titles during the exchange, demonstrating mutual respect

44 Mainland Affairs Council, MAC Minister Wang and TAO Director Zhang Address Each Other by Official Titles, Substantively Realizing "Mutual Non-Denial" and Setting a Good Start for the Normalization of Official Interactions across the Strait, Oct. 6, 2013, http://www.mac.gov.tw/public/Attachment/3102411342782.pdf.

and pragmatism between the two sides, which has also major significance for deepening cross-strait mutual trust and enhancing benign interactions. The MAC stated that the meeting between Minister Wang and Director Zhang marks an important milestone in the institutionalization of cross-strait relations and expressed strong affirmation towards the pragmatic attitude taken by the Mainland.

Treaties/Agreements and Official, Semi-Official or Unofficial Agreements Concluded by the Republic of China (Taiwan) with other Countries in 2013

Chronological List

Country/ Organization	Name of Treaty/Agreement	Signing Date
Czech Republic	Memorandum of Understanding on Nuclear Cooperation between the Atomic Energy Council of the Republic of China (Taiwan) and State Office for Nuclear Safety of the Czech Republic	2012/12/27 2013/01/18
Indonesia	Agreement on Agricultural Technical Cooperation between the Taipei Economic and Trade Office, Jakarta, Indonesia and the Indonesian Economic and Trade Office to Taipei	2013/01/31
United States	Agreement on Privileges, Exemptions and Immunities between the Taipei Economic and Cultural Representative Office in the United States and the American Institute in Taiwan	2013/02/04
Guatemala	Canje de Notas sobre la Prórrpga del Convenio de Cooperación Técnico-Agropecuaria entre la República de China (Taiwán) y la República de Guatamala	2013/02/21
Belgium	Agreement between the Taipei Representative Office in the EU and Belgium and the Belgian Office, Taipei on a Working Holiday Program	2013/02/27 2013/03/05

 | DOI 10.1163/9789004306509_010

(cont.)

Country/ Organization	Name of Treaty/Agreement	Signing Date
Japan	亞東關係協會與公益財團法人交流協會漁業協議公益財団法人交流協会と亜東関係協会との間の漁業秩序の構築に関する取決め [Fisheries Agreement between the Association of East Asian Relations and the Interchange Association, Japan]	2013/04/10
South Africa	Arrangement between the Taipei Liaison Office in the Republic of South Africa and the South African Liaison Office in Taipei on Cooperation in the Fields of Agriculture, Forestry and Fisheries	2013/04/14
Philippines	Agreement on Mutual Legal Assistance in Criminal Matters between the Taipei Economic and Cultural Office in the Philippines and the Manila Economic and Cultural Office in Taiwan	2013/04/19
Honduras	Memorandum of Understanding between the National Immigration Agency of the Ministry of the Interior of the Republic of China (Taiwan) and the Directorate General of Immigration and Aliens under the Ministry of Interior and Population of the Republic of Honduras Concerning Cooperation in Immigration Affairs and Human Trafficking Prevention	2013/04/23

Country/ Organization	Name of Treaty/Agreement	Signing Date
Solomon Islands	Agreement on Technical Cooperation between the Government of the Republic of China (Taiwan) and the Government of Solomon Islands	2013/04/25
United States	Modification #1, #2 to Agreement between the Taipei Economic and Cultural Representative Office in the United States and the American Institute in Taiwan for Implementing Arrangement #3 Provisions of Operation, Maintenance, and Reconditioning Support for the WSR-88D System to the Agreement between the American Institute in Taiwan and the Taipei Economic and Cultural Representative Office in the United States for Technical Cooperation in Scientific and Weather Technology Systems Support	2013/04/26
United States	Implementing Arrangement No. 1 to the Agreement between the Taipei Economic and Cultural Representative Office in the United States and the American Institute in Taiwan for Technical Cooperation Associated with Development, Launch and Operation of a Constellation Observing System for Meteorology, Ionosphere and Climate Follow-On Mission (FormosaT-7/Cosmic-2)	2013/04/26 2013/05/29

(cont.)

Country/ Organization	Name of Treaty/Agreement	Signing Date
Republic of Korea	Memorandum of Understanding between the National Communications Commission the Republic of China (Taiwan) and the Korea Communications Standards Commission the Republic of Korea on Cooperation in the Field of Broadcasting and Communications	2013/05/07
United States	Implementing Arrangement #25 Development of a Hazardous Weather Monitoring and Forecast System Pursuant to Agreement between the Taipei Economic and Cultural Representative Office in the United States and the American Institute in Taiwan for Technical Cooperation in Meteorology and Forecast Systems Development	2013/05/07 2013/07/26
Saudi Arabia	Memorandum of Understanding between the Investigation Bureau, Ministry of Justice, Republic of China (Taiwan) and the Ministry of Interior in the Kingdom of Saudi Arabia Concerning Cooperation in the Exchange of Financial Intelligence Related to Money Laundering and Financing of Terrorism	2013/06/04
United States	Memorandum of Understanding between the Taipei Economic and Cultural Representative Office in the United States and the American Institute in Taiwan Concerning Cooperation in Fisheries and Aquaculture	2013/06/06 2013/06/18

Country/ Organization	Name of Treaty/Agreement	Signing Date
Austria	Memorandum of Understanding between the Taiwan Food and Drug Administration and the Federal Office for Safety in Health Care / Austrian Agency for Health and Food Safety on Cooperation Concerning Safety Information of Medical Products	2013/06/19 2013/07/09
Paraguay	Memorandum of Understanding between the National Immigration Agency of the Ministry of the Interior of the Republic of China (Taiwan) and the National Migration Administration of the Ministry of the Interior of the Republic of Paraguay Concerning Cooperation on Immigration Affairs and Human Trafficking Prevention	2013/06/24 2013/07/11
United States	Implementing Arrangement Number 10 Consultancy Services for the Enhancement of the CWB Regional NWP System and Operational Implementation of Autonowcaster for CWB to the Agreement between the Taipei Economic and Cultural Representative Office in the United States and the American Institute in Taiwan for Technical Cooperation Associated with Establishment of Advanced Data Assimilation and Modeling Systems	2013/06/27 2013/09/10
New Zealand	Agreement between the Separate Customs Territory of Taiwan, Penghu, Kinmen, and Matsu and New Zealand of Economic Cooperation	2013/07/10

(cont.)

Country/ Organization	Name of Treaty/Agreement	Signing Date
Vietnam	Agreement between the Taipei Economic and Cultural Office in Vietnam and the Vietnam Economic and Cultural Office in Taipei on the Cooperation in Immigration Affairs	2013/07/10
United States	Extension of Agreement for Technical Cooperation in the Field of Environmental Protection between the Taipei Economic and Cultural Representative Office in the United States and the American Institute in Taiwan	2013/07/16
United States	Agreement between the Taipei Economic and Cultural Representative Office in the United States and the American Institute in Taiwan for Technical Cooperation in Atmospheric Monitoring, Clean Energy, and Environmental Science	2013/07/16
United States	Implementing Arrangement #10 to the Agreement between the Taipei Economic and Cultural Representative Office in the United States and the American Institute in Taiwan for Technical Cooperation in the Field of Environmental Protection	2013/07/16
Saint Christopher and Nevis	Agreement between the Government of the Republic of China (Taiwan) and the Government of the Federation of Saint Christopher and Nevis on the Renewable Energy Policy Consultant-Dispatching Project	2013/07/19

Country/ Organization	Name of Treaty/Agreement	Signing Date
South Africa	Arrangement between the Taipei Liaison Office in the Republic of South Africa and the South African Liaison Office in Taipei on Cooperation in the Fields of Arts and Culture	2013/07/24
South Africa	Arrangement between the Taipei Liaison Office in the Republic of South Africa and the South African Liaison Office in Taipei on Mutual Legal Assistance in Criminal Matters	2013/07/24
Guatemala	Canje de Notas sobre la Prórroga del Convenio sobre el Establecimiento de la Misión de Servicio a la Inversión y al Comercio en Centroamérica entre el Gobierno de la República de China (Taiwán) y el Gobierno de la República de Guatamala	2013/07/30
United States	Memorandum of Understanding between the American Institute in Taiwan and the Taipei Economic and Cultural Representative Office in the United States Regarding Scientific Exchange Activities	2013/09/03
United States	Agreement between the Taipei Economic and Cultural Representative Office in the United States and the American Institute in Taiwan for Cooperation in the Global Learning and Observations to Benefit the Environment Program	2013/09/06

(cont.)

Country/ Organization	Name of Treaty/Agreement	Signing Date
Hungary	Memorandum of Understanding between the Taipei Representative Office in Hungary and the Hungarian Trade Office in Taipei on the Development of Economic Cooperation	2013/09/10
United States	Exchange of Letters between the Coordination Council for North American Affairs and the American Institute in Taiwan Concerning the Agreement on Mutual Granting of Rent-Free Use of Property	2013/09/11 2013/10/16
Thailand	Agreement on Educational Cooperation between the Taipei Economic and Cultural Office in Thailand and the Thailand Trade and Economic Office in Taipei	2013/09/11
United Kingdom	Memorandum of Understanding between the Taipei Representative Office in the UK and the British Trade and Cultural Office, Taipei on Cooperation in Intellectual Property Rights	2013/09/13 2013/09/17
Spain	Memorandum of Understanding on the Patent Prosecution Highway (PPH) Mottainai between the Taiwan Intellectual Property Office (TIPO) and the Spanish Patent and Trademark Office (SPTO)	2013/09/20
Honduras	Canje de Notas sobre la Prórroga del Convenio de Asistencia Técnica y Cooperación Agropecuaria entre la República China (Taiwán) y la República de Honduras	2013/09/24

Country/ Organization	Name of Treaty/Agreement	Signing Date
United States	Agreement between the Taipei Economic and Cultural Representative Office in the United States and the American Institute in Taiwan for Technical Cooperation Associated with Establishing Satellite-Based Marine Oil Monitoring Collaborative Activity	2013/10/09 2013/10/17
Belgium	Memorandum of Understanding between Taiwan Food and Drug Administration and Belgian Federal Agency for the Safety of the Food Chain on Cooperation Concerning Food Safety	2013/10/18
Germany	Arrangement between the Taipei Representative Office in the Federal Republic of Germany and the German Institute in Taipei on the Transfer of Sentenced Persons and Cooperation in the Enforcement of Penal Sentences	2013/10/23
Belize	Agreement between the Government of the Republic of China (Taiwan) and the Government of Belize on Cooperation in Information and Communication Technology (ICT) (2014–2019)	2013/10/29
Japan	Memorandum of Understanding between the Association of East Asian Relations and the Interchange Association for the Mutual Cooperation in the Field of Priority Document Exchange	2013/11/05

(cont.)

Country/ Organization	Name of Treaty/Agreement	Signing Date
Japan	Arrangement between the Association of East Asian Relations and the Interchange Association for the Establishment of the Framework of the Cooperation on the Medical Products Regulation	2013/11/05
Japan	亞東關係協會與公益財團法人交流協會間關於海上航機搜 索救難合作之協議書 亜東関係協会と公益財団法人交流協会との間の海上における航空機の捜索救難の協力に関する取決め [Arrangement between the Association of East Asian Relations and the Interchange Association for the Cooperation of Maritime Aircraft Search and Rescue]	2013/11/05
Japan	Arrangement between the Association of East Asian Relations and the Interchange Association for the Mutual Cooperation on Electronic Commerce	2013/11/05
Japan	亞東關係協會與公益財團法人交流協會間加強鐵路業務交流及合作瞭解備忘錄亜東関係協会と公益財団法人交流協会との間の鉄道分野における交流と協力の強化に関する了解覚書 [Memorandum of Understanding between the Association of East Asian Relations and the Interchange Association for the Enhancement of Exchange and Cooperation of Railway Affairs]	2013/11/05

Country/ Organization	Name of Treaty/Agreement	Signing Date
Singapore	Agreement between Singapore and the Separate Customs Territory of Taiwan, Penghu, Kinmen and Matsu on Economic Partnership	2013/11/07
Saint Christopher and Nevis	Agreement between the Government of the Republic of China (Taiwan) and the Government of St. Christopher (St. Kitts) and Nevis on Cooperation in Information and Communication Technology (ICT) (2013–2018)	2013/11/08
World Trade Organization	政府採購協定修正議定書之接受書 [Instrument of Acceptance of the Protocol Amending the Agreement on Government Procurement]	2013/11/08
Israel	Arrangement between the Taipei Economic and Cultural Office in Tel Aviv and the Israel Economic and Cultural Office in Taipei on Gainful Occupation for Family Members of a Member of a Representative Office or Consular Post	2013/12/10
Israel	Memorandum of Understanding in the Field of Environmental Protection between the Taipei Economic and Cultural Office in Tel Aviv and the Israel Economic and Cultural Office in Taipei	2013/12/10
Saint Christopher and Nevis	Agreement on Agricultural Technical Cooperation between the Government of the Republic of China (Taiwan) and the Government of Saint Christopher and Nevis	2013/12/11

Selected Texts

In the interest of conserving space for the materials published in this Yearbook, only selected treaties and agreements concluded by the Republic of China with other countries listed in the Yearbook will be included in the following section. The full text of the treaties may be viewed in "Treaties between the Republic of China and Foreign States," a volume compiled by the Ministry of Foreign Affairs of the Republic of China. It is also available on the website of the Ministry of Foreign Affairs, the Republic of China at http://n006.mofa.gov.tw/mofatreatys/IndexE.aspx.

Japan

*Fisheries Agreement between the Association of East Asian Relations and the Interchange Association, Japan**

The Association of East Asian Relations and the Interchange Association, Japan (hereafter referred to as "the two Associations"), in accordance with Point 3 of the Arrangement between the Association of East Asian Relations and the Interchange Association for the Establishment of the Respective Overseas Offices, signed on December 26, 1972, agree to cooperate in obtaining the approval of their respective competent authorities on the following items:

Article 1

This Agreement aims to ensure peace and stability in the East China Sea, promote friendly and reciprocal cooperation, sustain and make reasonable use of marine biological resources in exclusive economic zones, and maintain order in fishing operations.

Article 2

(1) In order to sustain and make reasonable use of marine biological resources and maintain order in fishing operations, and based on the consensus that concrete measures need to be established post haste

* This is a non-official translation. The original, authentic Chinese text of this Agreement is available at http://www.mofa.gov.tw/Upload/WebArchive/1024/dedce49b-d2ab-4183-a500-00c330d8be9a.PDF (last visited Mar. 6, 2015).

regarding waters in the East China Sea south of 27 degrees north latitude, this Agreement applies to the exclusive economic zone enclosed by line segments connecting, in order, the coordinates listed below (hereafter referred to as "the agreement-designated zone").

(a) 27 degrees north latitude, 126 degrees 20 minutes east longitude
(b) 27 degrees north latitude, 122 degrees 30 minutes east longitude
(c) 24 degrees 46 minutes north latitude, 122 degrees 30 minutes east longitude
(d) 24 degrees 49 minutes 37 seconds north latitude, 122 degrees 44 minutes east longitude
(e) 24 degrees 50 minutes north latitude, 124 degrees east longitude
(f) 25 degrees 19 minutes north latitude, 124 degrees 40 minutes east longitude
(g) 25 degrees 29 minutes 45 seconds north latitude, 125 degrees 20 minutes east longitude
(h) 25 degrees 30 minutes north latitude, 125 degrees 30 minutes east longitude
(i) 25 degrees 32 minutes 17 seconds north latitude, 125 degrees 30 minutes east longitude
(j) 25 degrees 40 minutes north latitude, 126 degrees east longitude
(k) 26 degrees 30 minutes north latitude, 126 degrees east longitude
(l) 27 degrees north latitude, 126 degrees 20 minutes east longitude

(2) Given the current complexity of the fishing situation, and to meet the special need to sustain and make reasonable use of marine biological resources and maintain order in fishing operations, waters in the agreement-designated zone that are enclosed by line segments connecting, in order, the coordinates listed below are defined as a "special cooperation zone."

(a) 26 degrees 30 minutes north latitude, 126 degrees east longitude
(b) 26 degrees 20 minutes north latitude, 125 degrees 30 minutes east longitude
(c) 25 degrees 32 minutes 17 seconds north latitude, 125 degrees 30 minutes east longitude
(d) 25 degrees 40 minutes north latitude, 126 degrees east longitude
(e) 26 degrees 30 minutes north latitude, 126 degrees east longitude

(3) The two Associations will request their respective competent authorities to provide maximum assistance in ensuring that marine biological resources in the special cooperation zone are sustained and used reasonably and that order in fishing operations is maintained, based on the following principles:

(a) Fishery workers from Taiwan and Japan (hereafter referred to as "the two Parties") shall be accorded the greatest possible respect on the basis of friendly and reciprocal cooperation.
(b) The greatest possible effort shall be made to create a fishing environment that will prevent disputes arising between fishery workers from the two Parties.
(c) Consultations on concrete matters related to operations in the special cooperation zone will be conducted by the Taiwan-Japan Fishery Committee established in accordance with Article 3 of this Agreement.

(4) Under the premise of cooperation to prevent over-exploitation that may jeopardize the sustainability of marine biological resources, the two Associations shall request their respective competent authorities to complete related legal measures within 30 days of this Agreement's signing such that their respective fishery laws and regulations will not apply to fishery workers from the other Party operating in waters in the agreement-designated zone that are enclosed by line segments connecting, in order, the coordinates listed below.

(a) 27 degrees north latitude, 126 degrees 20 minutes east longitude
(b) 27 degrees north latitude, 122 degrees 30 minutes east longitude
(c) 24 degrees 46 minutes north latitude, 122 degrees 30 minutes east longitude
(d) 24 degrees 49 minutes 37 seconds north latitude, 122 degrees 44 minutes east longitude
(e) 24 degrees 50 minutes north latitude, 124 degrees east longitude
(f) 25 degrees 19 minutes north latitude, 124 degrees 40 minutes east longitude
(g) 25 degrees 29 minutes 45 seconds north latitude, 125 degrees 20 minutes east longitude
(h) 25 degrees 30 minutes north latitude, 125 degrees 30 minutes east longitude

(i) 26 degrees 20 minutes north latitude, 125 degrees 30 minutes east longitude
(j) 26 degrees 30 minutes north latitude, 126 degrees east longitude
(k) 27 degrees north latitude, 126 degrees 20 minutes east longitude

(5) Aiming to sustain and make reasonable use of marine biological resources and to maintain order in fishing operations, the two Associations shall, on the basis of friendly and reciprocal cooperation, continue to conduct consultations on waters of concern to the two Parties.

Article 3

(1) In order to achieve the aims of this Agreement, the two Associations shall establish a Taiwan-Japan Fishery Committee (hereafter referred to as "the Committee").
(2) The Committee shall be composed of two members representing, or serving as proxies of, each of the two Associations.
(3) The Committee shall discuss the items listed below and record the results of its discussions in its minutes. The two Associations shall submit the Committee's minutes to their respective competent authorities and request that necessary measures be taken so that their content may be implemented.

(a) Items of cooperation to ensure that the agreement-designated zone is not over-exploited in such a way that the sustainability of marine biological resources is jeopardized;
(b) Items of cooperation to ensure safe navigation and operation of fishing vessels in the agreement-designated zone; and
(c) Other items of fishery cooperation.

(4) Representatives or proxies of either of the two Associations may convene meetings and invite representatives of relevant authorities or organizations having professional expertise to serve as special members of the Committee.
(5) The Committee shall in principle meet once a year, alternating between Taipei and Tokyo. The two Associations may call for an extraordinary meeting if one such is deemed necessary.
(6) The Committee may hold a joint meeting with private-sector fishery groups if it deems this necessary.

(7) All decisions made by the Committee shall require the unanimous approval of all members present at the meeting.

Article 4

Nothing in this Agreement or measures adopted to implement this Agreement by the competent authorities shall prejudice the respective position of the two parties on the law of the sea law issues.

Article 5

This Agreement shall enter into effect on the day of its signing. This Agreement may be terminated by either of the two Associations with six months' advance written notification to the other party of its intention to terminate this Agreement.

This Agreement is signed by representatives of the two Associations in Taipei on April 10, 2013, in duplicate in Chinese and Japanese, both texts being equally authentic.

For the Association of East Asian Relations	For the Interchange Association, Japan
Liao Liou-yi	Mitsuo Ohashi

New Zealand

Agreement between the Separate Customs Territory of Taiwan, Penghu, Kinmen, and Matsu and New Zealand on Economic Cooperation*

***

Preamble

The Separate Customs Territory of Taiwan, Penghu, Kinmen, and Matsu (hereinafter referred to as "Chinese Taipei") and New Zealand, collectively referred to as "the Parties" and individually as "a Party":

* ANZTEC includes 25 Chapters and 8 Annexes, as well as the Implementing Arrangement on Rules of Origin Operational Procedures, the Implementing Arrangement on Film and Television Co-Production, and the bilateral Airport Transport Agreement and its Annex. The full text of the agreement is available at http://fta.trade.gov.tw/ftapage.asp?k=1&p=9&n=457&a=358 (last visited Mar. 2, 2015).

BUILDING on their rights and obligations under the World Trade Organisation ("WTO");

MINDFUL of their commitment to the Asia-Pacific Economic Cooperation ("APEC") goals and principles, and in particular the efforts of all APEC economies to meet the APEC Bogor Goals of free and open trade;

BELIEVING that open, transparent and competitive markets are the key drivers of economic efficiency, innovation, wealth creation, employment and consumer welfare;

RECOGNISING that the strengthening of their economic partnership through an Economic Cooperation Agreement, which removes barriers on the trade of goods and services and investment flows, will produce mutual benefits for the Parties;

CONFIRMING their shared commitment to trade facilitation through removing non-tariff barriers and reducing costs to the movement of goods between Chinese Taipei and New Zealand;

RECOGNISING the significance of good governance and good regulatory practice in creating a predictable, transparent and consistent business environment to enable businesses to conduct transactions freely, and use resources efficiently and take investment and planning decisions with certainty;

DESIRING to enhance the competitiveness of their firms in global markets including through protecting and promoting the competitive process and the design of regulation that minimises distortions to competition;

CONSIDERING the benefits of enhancing communication and cooperation on labour and environment;

MINDFUL that fostering innovation and the promotion and protection of intellectual property rights will encourage further trade, investment and cooperation between the Parties;

RECOGNISING their right to regulate, and to introduce new regulations on the supply of goods, services and investment in order to meet government policy objectives;

DESIRING to strengthen the cooperative framework for cultural and people-to-people contacts between indigenous peoples in the Separate Customs Territory of Taiwan, Penghu, Kinmen and Matsu and New Zealand's Māori and expand and facilitate trade and economic relations between them;

Have agreed as follows:

CHAPTER 1 INITIAL PROVISIONS

Article 1 Establishment of Economic Cooperation Agreement

The Parties, as members of the WTO and consistent with the provisions of the WTO Agreement, hereby agree to liberalise trade in services, duties and other regulations of commerce in this Economic Cooperation Agreement.

Article 2 Objectives

The objectives of this Agreement, as elaborated more specifically through its principles and rules, are to:

(i) encourage expansion and diversification of trade between the Parties;
(ii) eliminate barriers to trade in, and facilitate the movement of, goods and services between the Parties;
(iii) substantially increase investment opportunities between the Parties;
(iv) promote conditions of fair competition in and between the Parties;
(v) ensure effective protection and enforcement of intellectual property rights in the Parties;
(vi) encourage the use of good regulatory practices (as set out in Annex D ("Strengthening Implementation of Good Regulatory Practices") of the 2011 APEC Leaders' Declaration)[1] for the planning, design, implementation and review of regulation; and
(vii) provide an effective mechanism to prevent and resolve trade disputes.

---

1 In interpreting the third paragraph of Annex D:
- the term "draft measures" is to be read as a reference not only to the draft text of regulations, but also to proposals for regulations as set out in documents such as policy proposals, discussion documents,or summaries of proposed regulations; and
- the commitments referenced are each to be read as subject to the qualifier "to the extent possible".

Article 3 General Definitions

For the purposes of this Agreement, unless otherwise specified:

Agreement means this *Agreement between the Separate Customs Territory of Taiwan, Penghu, Kinmen and Matsu and New Zealand on Economic Cooperation.*

customs administration means:

(a) in respect to New Zealand, the New Zealand Customs Service; and
(b) in respect to Chinese Taipei, the Taiwan Customs Administration.

customs duty includes any duty or charges of any kind imposed in connection with the importation of a good, and any surtaxes or surcharges imposed in connection with such importation, but does not include:

(a) charges equivalent to an internal tax imposed consistently with GATT 1994, including excise duties and goods and services tax;
(b) any anti-dumping or countervailing duty applied consistently with Article VI of GATT 1994, the WTO *Agreement on Implementation of Article VI of the General Agreement on Tariffs* and Trade 1994, and the WTO *Agreement on Subsidies and Countervailing Measures*; and
(c) fees or other charges that:

    (i) are limited in amount to the approximate cost of services rendered; and
    (ii) do not represent a direct or indirect protection for domestic goods or a taxation of imports for fiscal purposes;

Customs Valuation Agreement means the *Agreement on Implementation of Article VII of the General Agreement on Tariffs and Trade 1994*, which is part of the WTO Agreement;

days means calendar days;

enterprise means any entity constituted or organised under applicable law, whether or not for profit, and whether privately-owned or governmentally-owned, including any corporation, trust, partnership, sole proprietorship, joint venture, association, or similar organisation and a branch of an enterprise;

enterprise of a Party means an enterprise which is organised or constituted under the laws of that Party, and a branch located in a Party and carrying out business activities there;

GATS means the *General Agreement on Trade in Services*, which is part of the WTO Agreement;

GATT 1994 means the *General Agreement on Tariffs and Trade 1994*, which is part of the WTO Agreement;

Harmonised System or HS means the Harmonized Commodity Description and Coding System of the World Customs Organization;

measure means any measure by a Party, whether in the form of a law, regulation, rule, procedure, decision, administrative action or any other form;

natural person of a Party means a citizen or a permanent resident of a Party under its laws;

person means a natural person or an enterprise; and

WTO Agreement means the *Marrakesh Agreement Establishing the World Trade Organization*, done on April 15, 1994.

Article 4 Interpretations

In this Agreement, unless the context otherwise requires:

(a) This Agreement shall be interpreted in accordance with the rules of interpretation applicable to the WTO Agreement, and as informed by its jurisprudence mutatis mutandis.
(b) Where anything under this Agreement is to be done within a number of days after, before or of a specified date or event, the specified date or the date on which the specified event occurs shall not be included in calculating that number of days.

*** [The following chapters include Chapter 2: Trade in Goods; Chapter 3: Rules of Origin; Chapter 4: Customs Procedures and Cooperation; Chapter 5: Trade Remedies; Chapter 6: Sanitary and Phytosanitary Measures; Chapter 7: Technical Barriers to Trade; Chapter 8: Competition; Chapter 9: Electronic

Commerce; Chapter 10: Intellectual Property; Chapter 11: Government Procurement; Chapter 12: Investment; Chapter 13: Cross-Border Trade in Services; Chapter 14: Temporary Entry of Business Persons; Chapter 15: Air Transport Services; Chapter 16: Trade and Labour; Chapter 17: Trade and Environment; Chapter 18: Film and Television Co-Production; Chapter 19: Cooperation on Indigenous Issues; Chapter 20: Transparency; Chapter 21: Dispute Settlement; Chapter 22: Institutional Provisions; Chapter 23: General Provisions; and Chapter 24: General Exceptions]

CHAPTER 25 FINAL PROVISIONS

Article 1 Annexes and Footnotes

The Annexes and footnotes to this Agreement shall constitute an integral part of this Agreement.

Article 2 Amendments

This Agreement may be amended by agreement in writing by the Parties and such amendments shall come into force on such date or dates as may be agreed between them.

Article 3 Entry into Force, Duration and Termination

1. Entry into force of this Agreement shall be subject to the completion of the necessary domestic procedures of both Parties. The Parties shall notify each other in writing upon the completion of such procedures. This Agreement shall enter into force on the date specified in such written notification.
2. This Agreement shall remain in force until one Party gives written notice of its intention to terminate it, in which case this Agreement shall terminate 180 days after the date of the notice of termination.

IN WITNESS WHEREOF the undersigned, being duly authorised thereto, have signed this Agreement.

DONE in duplicate in the English language, on 10 July 2013, at Wellington.

For the Separate Customs Territory Of Taiwan, Penghu, Kinmen And Matsu	For New Zealand

Singapore

*Agreement between Singapore and the Separate Cusstoms Territory of Taiwan, Penghu, Kinmen and Matsu on Economic Partnership**

Singapore and the Separate Customs Territory of Taiwan, Penghu, Kinmen and Matsu (hereinafter referred to as "Chinese Taipei"), hereinafter collectively referred to as "the Parties" and individually as "a Party";

Conscious of their bonds of longstanding friendship and strong trade and investment relationship;

Reaffirming their commitment to securing trade liberalisation and an outward-looking approach to trade and investment;

Convinced that their economic integration would generate larger economies of scale, provide greater work opportunities, and enhance transparency for economic activities for their businesses as well as for other businesses in the Asia-Pacific region;

Sharing the belief that an Economic Partnership Agreement between the Parties would improve their attractiveness to capital and human resources, and create larger and new markets, to expand trade and investment not only between them but also in the region;

Affirming their commitment to fostering the development of open market economy in the Asia-Pacific region, and to encouraging economic integration of Asian economies in order to further the liberalisation of trade and investment in the region;

Reaffirming that this Agreement shall contribute to the expansion and development of world trade under the multilateral trading system embodied in the *Marrakesh Agreement Establishing the World Trade Organization* (hereinafter referred to as the "WTO Agreement");

Building on their respective rights and obligations under the WTO Agreement and other multilateral, regional and bilateral instruments of cooperation; and

Resolved to promote reciprocal trade and investment, and to avoid circumvention of benefits of regional trade integration, through the establishment of clear and mutually advantageous trade rules, and industry as well as regulatory cooperation;

HAVE AGREED as follows:

---

* ASTEP includes 17 Chapters and 17 Annexes. The full text of the agreement is available at http://fta.trade.gov.tw/ftapage.asp?k=2&p=9&n=456&a=329 (last visited Mar. 2, 2015).

CHAPTER 1 GENERAL PROVISIONS

Article 1.1 Establishment of Free Trade Area

The Parties to this Agreement, consistent with Article XXIV of GATT 1994 and Article V of GATS, hereby establish a free trade area in accordance with the provisions of this Agreement.

Article 1.2 Enforcement

1. Each Party is fully responsible for the observance of all the provisions of this Agreement.
2. In fulfilling its obligations and commitments under this Agreement, each Party shall ensure their observance by all levels of its government and by non-governmental bodies in the exercise of governmental powers delegated by the government or authorities within its territory.

Article 1.3 Objectives

The objectives of this Agreement as elaborated more specifically through its principles and rules are to:

(a) liberalise and facilitate trade in goods and services and expand investment between the Parties;
(b) establish a cooperative framework for strengthening the economic relations between the Parties;
(c) establish a framework conducive for a more favourable environment for their businesses and promote conditions of fair competition in the free trade area;
(d) establish a framework of transparent rules to govern trade and investment between the Parties; and
(e) create effective procedures for the implementation and application of this Agreement.

Article 1.4 Relation To Other Agreements

2. The Parties reaffirm their existing rights and obligations with respect to each other under existing bilateral and multilateral agreements to which the Parties are party, including the WTO Agreement.

3. In the event of any inconsistency between this Agreement and other agreements to which the Parties are party, the Parties shall immediately consult with each other with a view to finding a mutually satisfactory solution, taking into consideration customary rules of public international law.
4. Notwithstanding paragraph 2, if this Agreement explicitly contains provisions regarding such inconsistency as indicated in paragraph 2, those provisions shall apply.

Article 1.5 Reference To Other Agreements

1. For the purposes of this Agreement, any reference to articles in GATT 1994 or GATS includes the interpretative notes, where applicable.
2. Any reference in this Agreement to any other treaty or international agreement shall be made in the same terms to its successor treaty or international agreement to which the Parties are party.

CHAPTER 2 GENERAL DEFINITIONS

For the purposes of this Agreement, unless otherwise specified:

Agreement means the *Agreement between Singapore and the Separate Customs Territory of Taiwan, Penghu, Kinmen and Matsu on Economic Partnership*;

APEC means the Asia-Pacific Economic Cooperation;

citizen means:

(a) with respect to Singapore, any natural person who is a citizen of Singapore within the meaning of its Constitution and its domestic laws; and
(b) with respect to Chinese Taipei, any natural person who has the citizenship of Chinese Taipei with personal identification registration with the authorities of Chinese Taipei in accordance with its domestic laws;

Customs Valuation Agreement means the *Agreement on Implementation of Article VII of the General Agreement on Tariff and Trade 1994*, which is part of the WTO Agreement;

days means calendar days including weekends and holidays;

enterprise means any corporation, company, association, partnership, trust, joint venture, sole-proprietorship or other legally recognised entity that is duly incorporated, constituted, set up, or otherwise duly organised under the law of a Party, including branches, regardless of whether or not the entity is organised for pecuniary gain, privately or otherwise owned, or organised with limited or unlimited liability;

existing means in effect at the time of entry into force of this Agreement;

GATS means the *General Agreement on Trade in Services*, which is a part of the WTO Agreement;

GATT 1994 means the *General Agreement on Tariffs and Trade 1994*, which is a part of the WTO Agreement;

generally accepted accounting principles means the recognised consensus or substantial authoritative support in the territory of a Party with respect to the recording of revenues, expenses, costs, assets and liabilities, the disclosure of information and the preparation of financial statements. These standards may encompass broad guidelines of general application as well as detailed standards, practices and procedures;

Harmonized System (HS) means the Harmonized Commodity Description and Coding System, including its General Rules of Interpretation, Section Notes and Chapter Notes and amendments thereto;

measure means any law, regulation, procedure or administrative action, requirement or practice;

natural person of a Party means a citizen or permanent resident of a Party;

permanent resident means any person who has the right of permanent residence in the territory of a Party;

person means a natural person or an enterprise;

person of a Party means a citizen, permanent resident or an enterprise of a Party;

territory means:

(a) with respect to Singapore, its land territory, internal waters and territorial sea, as well as any maritime area situated beyond the territorial sea which has been or might in the future be designated under its national law, in accordance with international law, as an area within which Singapore may exercise sovereign rights or jurisdiction with regards to the sea, the sea-bed, the subsoil and the natural resources; and
(b) with respect to Chinese Taipei, in the context of this Agreement and consistent with Article XXIV of GATT 1994 and Article V of GATS the land and sea constituting the Separate Customs Territory of Taiwan, Penghu, Kinmen and Matsu as applied in the WTO;

central level of government means:

(a) for Singapore, the national level of government; and
(b) for Chinese Taipei, the central level of government;

local level of government means:

(a) for Singapore, entities with sub-national legislative or executive powers under domestic law, including Town Councils and Community Development Councils; and
(b) for Chinese Taipei, a special municipality, county or city, and any other local governments in accordance with the provisions of its Local Government Act; and

WTO Agreement means the *Marrakesh Agreement Establishing the World Trade Organization*, done on 15 April 1994.

*** [The following chapters include Chapter 3: Trade in Goods; Chapter 4: Rules of Origin; Chapter 5: Customs Procedures; Chapter 6: Sanitary and Phytosanitary Measures; Chapter 7: Technical Barriers to Trade; Chapter 8: Cross-Border Trade in Services; Chapter 9: Investment; Chapter 10: Competition; Chapter 11: Electronic Commerce; Chapter 12: Government Procurement; Chapter 13: Intellectual Property Cooperation; Chapter 14: Transparency; Chapter 15: Dispute Settlement; and Chapter 16: Exceptions]

CHAPTER 17 ADMINISTRATION AND FINAL PROVISIONS

Article 17.1 Review on the Implementation of the Agreement

1. In addition to the provisions for consultations elsewhere in this Agreement, the Parties shall meet within a year of the date of entry into force of this Agreement to review the implementation of this Agreement; thereafter, subject to mutual agreement, the Parties may meet biennially or otherwise as appropriate.
2. Pursuant to paragraph 1, the Parties may:

   (a) review the implementation and application of the provisions of this Agreement including the work of any committees and working groups established under this Agreement;
   (b) establish and delegate responsibilities to any ad hoc or standing committees, working groups or expert groups to:
      (i) assign them with tasks on specific matters;
      (ii) study and recommend to the Parties any appropriate measures to resolve any issues arising from the implementation or application of any part of this Agreement; or
      (iii) to consider, upon either Party's request, new issues not already dealt with by this Agreement; and
   (c) consider any other matter that may affect the operation of this Agreement.

Article 17.2 Contact Points

1. Each Party shall designate a lead agency as specified in Annex 17 to serve as the contact point to facilitate communications between the Parties on any matter covered by this Agreement.
2. For the purposes of this Agreement, all communications or notifications to or by a Party shall be made through its contact point.

Article 17.3 Annexes and Appendices

The Annexes and Appendices to this Agreement shall constitute integral parts of this Agreement.

Article 17.4 Amendments

1. The Parties may agree on any amendment to this Agreement.
2. When so agreed, such an amendment under paragraph 1 shall enter into force and constitute an integral part of this Agreement after the Parties have exchanged written notification certifying that they have completed necessary internal legal procedures and on such date or dates as may be agreed between the Parties.

Article 17.5 Entry into Force

This Agreement shall enter into force thirty (30) days after an exchange of written notifications, certifying the completion of the necessary legal procedures of each Party.

Article 17.6 Termination

Either Party may terminate this Agreement by written notification to the other Party and such termination shall take effect six (6) months after the date of the notification.

IN WITNESS WHEREOF the undersigned, being duly authorised thereto, have signed this Agreement

DONE in duplicate in the English language, on 7 November 2013, at Singapore.

FOR THE SEPARATE CUSTOMS TERRITORY OF TAIWAN, PENGHU, KINMEN AND MATSU	FOR SINGAPORE
Mr. Fa-Dah Hsieh Representative Taipei Representative Office Singapore	Mr. Calvin Eu Trade Representative Trade Office in Singapore in Taipei

United States

Agreement on Privileges, Exemptions and Immunities between the American Institute in Taiwan and the Taipei Economic and Cultural Representative Office in the United States

Whereas the American Institute in Taiwan and the Taipei Economic and Cultural Representative Office in the United States:

Are charged with responsibility on behalf of their respective authorities for conducting and facilitating commercial, cultural and other relations between the people of the United States and the people on Taiwan;

Have, since 1980, consistent with domestic law and customary international law as applicable to the authorities they represent, performed consular functions and provided consular assistance, including the visitation of detained persons, on behalf of their respective authorities;

Have operated pursuant to the agreement on privileges, exemptions and immunities between the American Institute in Taiwan and the Coordination Council for North American Affairs, signed at Washington, DC, October 2, 1980;

Have reviewed the laws of their respective authorities, including, in the case of AIT, the Taiwan Relations Act of 1979; and

Have gained practical experience with the operation of the 1980 agreement and are mindful of the value in making reciprocal and appropriate modifications to ensure that they enjoy such privileges and immunities as may be necessary for the effective performance of their functions;

Have therefore reached the following agreement:

Article 1

For the purposes of this agreement, the following expressions shall have the meanings hereunder assigned to them:

(a) "AIT" or "the Institute" shall refer to the American Institute in Taiwan;
(b) "TECRO" shall refer to Taipei Economic and Cultural Representative Office in the United States;
(c) "Counterpart organizations" shall refer, collectively, to AIT and TECRO;
(d) "Primary office" shall refer, respectively, to the TECRO Office(s) located in the metropolitan area of the District of Columbia and to the AIT Office(s) (including a Chinese language school) located in Taipei;
(e) "Subsidiary offices" shall refer, in the case of TECRO, to the branch offices known as "Taipei Economic and Cultural Offices" located outside of the metropolitan area of the District of Columbia as described in article 2 below and, in the case of AIT, to its branch office(s) in Kaohsiung or in other locations as provided in accordance with article 2;
(f) "Designated employee of a primary office" means any person, including the head of such primary office, who is duly notified to and accepted by the receiving counterpart organization as a designated employee of the sending counterpart organization at its primary office and who exercises functions related to conducting and facilitating commercial, cultural and other relations between the people of the United States and the people on Taiwan, as well as any person employed in the administrative or technical service of such primary office. It shall not apply with respect to any person who is a national or is permanently resident in the jurisdiction in which the receiving counterpart organization is headquartered;
(g) "Designated employee of a subsidiary office" means any person, including the head of such subsidiary office, who is duly notified to and accepted by the receiving counterpart organization as a designated employee of the sending counterpart organization at one of its subsidiary offices and who exercises functions related to conducting and facilitating commercial, cultural and other relations between the people of the United States and the people on Taiwan, as well as any person employed in the administrative or technical service of such subsidiary office. It shall not apply with respect to any person, who is a national of or is permanently resident in the jurisdiction in which the receiving counterpart organization is headquartered;
(h) "Designated employees" of a counterpart organization shall comprise the persons described in paragraphs (f) and (g) of this article;
(i) "Jurisdiction in which the receiving counterpart organization is headquartered" refers, in the case of AIT, to the United States, and in the case of TECRO, to Taiwan. "Central authorities" refers to the U.S. federal government or its equivalent on Taiwan, and "local authorities" refers to

state, provincial, county, city, and other forms of municipal government within the United States or their equivalents on Taiwan.

Article 2

TECRO may operate a primary office in the metropolitan area of the District of Columbia and may also operate subsidiary offices in twelve cities within the United States and in such other additional locations as may be agreed upon between the counterpart organizations. AIT may operate a primary office in Taipei and may also operate a subsidiary office in Kaohsiung and in such other additional locations as may be agreed upon between the counterpart organizations.

Article 3

(a) Each counterpart organization shall possess the capacity: (i) to contract; (ii) to acquire and dispose of real and personal property; and (iii) to institute legal proceedings.

(b) In order that it may effectively perform its functions, each sending counterpart organization shall enjoy in the territory in which the receiving counterpart organization is headquartered, immunity from suit and legal processes equivalent to those enjoyed by public international organizations in the United States, which for purposes of this agreement means the restrictive theory of immunity as reflected, for example, in 28 U.S.C. sections 1602 et seq.

Article 4

(a) Each counterpart organization shall undertake to ensure that the other counterpart organization and its personnel will receive all privileges, exemptions and immunities as set forth in this agreement and to take all possible measures, as appropriate, to secure adequate protection of the other counterpart organization's premises and personnel, so as to facilitate proper execution of that organization's functions.

(b) The receiving counterpart organization shall facilitate issuance of identification cards to persons who enjoy benefits under this agreement.

(c) The sending counterpart organization shall notify the receiving counterpart organization of the termination of services or of the departure of any person enjoying the benefits of this agreement.

(d) Should the receiving counterpart organization determine that the continued presence of any person enjoying the benefits of this agreement is not desirable, it shall so inform the sending counterpart organization. After such person shall have had a reasonable length of time to depart, to be determined by the receiving counterpart organization, he or she shall cease to enjoy such benefits.

(e) No person shall, by reason of the provisions of this agreement, be considered as receiving any privileges or immunities other than such as are specifically set forth herein.

Article 5

Each counterpart organization shall facilitate the issuance of appropriate visas for designated employees of the other organization, as well as members of their immediate family forming part of their households.

Article 6

(a) The sending counterpart organization shall be free to communicate for all purposes related to the performance of its functions and shall enjoy inviolability for all correspondence related to its functions.

(b) The bag carrying the correspondence referred to in the preceding paragraph and other articles related to the performance of the counterpart organization's functions shall neither be opened nor detained.

(c) The packages constituting such a bag must bear visible external marks of their character and may contain only documents or articles intended for the performance of the organization's designated functions. There are no limits on the permissible size, weight, or quantity of properly designated bags. The packages constituting such a bag may be comprised of crates, lift vans, boxes, and envelopes or other types of containers. The designated carriers of such bags, who shall be provided with a document indicating their status and the number of packages constituting such bags, shall be protected in the performance of their functions. The designated carrier shall enjoy personal inviolability and shall not be liable to any form of arrest or detention.

(d) The sending counterpart organization may designate such carriers *ad hoc*. In such cases, the provisions of paragraph (c) of this article shall apply, except that the privileges and immunities of an *ad hoc* carrier shall cease when the bag in his charge shall have been delivered to the consignee.

(e) Bags carrying such correspondence and articles may be entrusted to the captain of a commercial aircraft scheduled to land at an authorized port-of-entry. The captain shall be provided with a document indicating the number of packages constituting the bag, but the captain shall not be considered to be a designated carrier of such bags. The sending counterpart organization may send one of its members to take possession of such a bag directly and freely from the captain of the aircraft.

Article 7

(a) The wages, fees or salaries of any designated employee of a sending counterpart organization to the extent such wages, fees or salaries are received in connection with the performance of authorized functions, shall be exempt from taxation imposed by the central or local authorities of the jurisdiction in which the receiving counterpart organization is headquartered.

(b) Wages, salaries and fees paid by the sending counterpart organization to its designated employees shall not be subject to withholding for purposes of taxation by the central or local authorities of the jurisdiction in which the receiving counterpart organization is headquartered. The sending counterpart organization and its designated employees, shall be exempt from making contributions for unemployment or similar insurance, social security, or other programs adopted by the central or local authorities of the jurisdiction in which the receiving counterpart organization is headquartered.

(c) Unless such immunity be expressly waived, the primary and subsidiary offices of the sending counterpart organization shall be immune from forced entry and search and, if owned by such organization, shall also be immune from attachment, execution, requisition, expropriation or any other form of seizure or confiscation. Physical movable property (including means of transport) used for the purposes of the primary office shall be immune from forced entry and search and, if owned by such organization, shall also be immune from attachment, execution, requisition, expropriation or any other form of seizure or confiscation. Financial assets and bank accounts used for the purposes of the primary and subsidiary offices shall be immune from attachment, execution, requisition, or any other form of seizure or confiscation. The archives and documents of the sending counterpart organization shall be inviolable at all times and wherever they may be.

(d) Real property used for the performance of the sending counterpart organization's authorized functions and for which the counterpart organization would be liable for payment of taxes shall be exempt from central and local taxation of the jurisdiction in which the receiving counterpart organization is headquartered. The property, income, operations, and other transactions of the sending counterpart organization shall be exempt from taxation by the central and local authorities of the jurisdiction in which the receiving counterpart organization is headquartered. The exemptions provided in this article, however, shall not apply to any property which is not used for the purposes of the sending counterpart organization or successor organizations.

(e) Designated employees of each sending counterpart organization shall be immune from suit and all legal processes relating to acts performed by them within the scope of their authorized functions, unless such immunity is specifically waived by the sending counterpart organization in accordance with article 9.

(f) The receiving counterpart organization shall undertake to ensure that the primary and subsidiary offices of the sending counterpart organization and the designated employees of the sending counterpart organization shall be exempt from payment of central and local sales, value added, or other similarly imposed consumption taxes, except those normally included in the price of goods and services. This exemption shall not, however, extend to charges for specific services rendered.

(g) The receiving counterpart organization shall undertake to ensure that the primary and subsidiary offices of the sending counterpart organization and the designated employees of the primary office of a sending counterpart organization shall be exempt from all taxes and dues imposed by central or local authorities of the jurisdiction in which the receiving counterpart organization is headquartered in connection with the ownership or operation of a motor vehicle. The receiving counterpart organization shall undertake to ensure that the primary and subsidiary offices of the sending counterpart organization and designated employees of such offices shall also be exempt from payment of central excise taxes on gasoline, diesel fuel and lubricating oil.

(h) A sending counterpart organization and its designated employees and their immediate families forming part of their households, except nationals or permanent residents of the jurisdiction in which the receiving counterpart organization is headquartered, shall be entitled, insofar as customs duties, customs clearance, and internal revenue taxes imposed by reason of importation of baggage and effects, as well as laws regulating entry into and departure from the jurisdiction in which the receiving counterpart organization is headquartered, alien registration and fingerprinting, and registration of foreign agents are concerned, to the privileges, exemptions and immunities equivalent to those accorded under similar circumstances in the United States to public international organizations, their officers and employees as well as members of their families.

(i) With respect to the treatment of authorized communications and imposition of taxes for authorized communications, a sending counterpart organization shall be entitled to privileges, exemptions and immunities equivalent to those accorded a public international organization in the United States.

Article 8

In addition to the privileges, exemptions and immunities described in paragraph (e) of article 7 of this agreement:

(a) Designated employees of a primary office shall enjoy immunity from the criminal jurisdiction of the central and local authorities in the jurisdiction in which the receiving counterpart organization is headquartered.

(b) Designated employees of a primary office shall not be liable to any form of arrest or detention. Central and local authorities in the jurisdiction in which the receiving counterpart organization is headquartered shall treat all designated employees of a primary office with due respect and shall take all appropriate steps to prevent any attack on their person, freedom or dignity.

(c) Designated employees of a primary office shall not be obliged to give evidence as a witness in criminal, civil, administrative, or other proceedings.

(d) The private residence of designated employees of a primary office shall be immune from forced entry and search, and if such residence is owned by the sending counterpart organization, shall also be immune from attachment, execution, requisition, expropriation or any other form of seizure or confiscation.

(e) The papers, correspondence, and property of a designated employee of a primary office shall not be subject to forced entry, search, attachment, execution or any other form of seizure or confiscation by the central or local authorities of the jurisdiction in which the receiving counterpart organization is headquartered: (1) in matters involving the exercise of criminal jurisdiction; and (2) in matters involving the exercise of civil or administrative jurisdiction if related to acts performed within the scope of such individual's authorized functions. The baggage and household goods of a designated employee shall not be exempt from inspection upon entry and exit from the jurisdiction in which the receiving counterpart organization is headquartered.

(f) The immediate family members of a designated employee of a primary office forming part of his or her household, except nationals or permanent residents of the jurisdiction in which the receiving counterpart organization is headquartered, shall enjoy the same immunity from criminal jurisdiction and arrest and detention as the designated employee.

(g) The head of a subsidiary office and one designated deputy head of such office shall not be liable to arrest or detention pending trial, except in the case of a criminal offense punishable by one year or more in prison and pursuant to a decision by the competent judicial authority.

(h) Central and local authorities in the jurisdiction in which the receiving counterpart organization is headquartered shall treat all designated employees of a subsidiary office with due respect and shall take all appropriate steps to prevent any attack on their person, freedom or dignity.

(i) Designated employees of a subsidiary office may be called upon to attend as witnesses in the course of judicial or administrative proceedings.

  i. Such employees shall not, except with respect to matters falling within the scope of paragraph (e) of article 7, decline to give evidence.
  ii. Such employees are under no obligation to give evidence concerning matters connected with the exercise of their functions or to produce official correspondence and documents relating thereto.
  iii. Such employees are also entitled to decline to give evidence as expert witnesses with regard to the law of the jurisdiction in which they are headquartered.
  iv. If an employee described above should decline to provide evidence, no coercive measure or penalty may be applied to such person.

Article 9

(a) With respect to privileges and immunities set forth in articles 7 and 8 of this agreement enjoyed by designated employees of a primary office, the head or acting head of that primary office or of that organization's headquarters office may waive such privileges and immunities.

(b) With respect to privileges and immunities set forth in articles 7 and 8 enjoyed by designated employees of a subsidiary office, the head or acting head of that subsidiary office or primary or headquarters offices may waive such privileges and immunities.

(c) With the exception of paragraph (d), below, a waiver of any of the privileges, exemptions and immunities provided in this agreement shall in all cases be express.

(d) The initiation of proceedings by designated employees of a counterpart organization in a matter in which he or she might enjoy immunity from civil jurisdiction under this agreement shall preclude his or her invoking immunity from such jurisdiction in respect of any counterclaim directly connected with the principal claim.

(e) The waiver of immunity from jurisdiction for purposes of civil or administrative proceedings shall not be deemed to imply a waiver of immunity from the measures of execution resulting from the judicial decision; in respect of such measures, a separate waiver shall be necessary.

Article 10

This agreement shall replace the Agreement on privileges, exemptions and immunities between the American Institute in Taiwan and the Coordination Council for North American Affairs, signed at Washington, DC, October 2, 1980.

Article 11

This agreement may be modified at any time by mutual consent.

Article 12

This agreement is effective on the date of signature and will remain in effect indefinitely. It may, however, be terminated by either party upon one year's prior written notice to the other party or, otherwise, by mutual agreement.

IN WITNESS WHEREOF the undersigned duly authorized for this purpose have signed this agreement.

DONE at Washington, DC, on this 11th day of February, 2013, in the English and Chinese languages, each text being equally authentic.

For the American Institute in Taiwan:	For the Taipei Economic and Cultural Representative Office in the United States:
______________________________	______________________________

Table of Cases

 | DOI 10.1163/9789004306509_011

Index

Guidelines for Submissions to the Chinese (Taiwan) Yearbook of International Law and Affairs

BRILL
NIJHOFF

The *Chinese (Taiwan) Yearbook of International Law and Affairs* commenced publication in 1981 under the auspices of the Chinese (Taiwan) Society of International Law. The Yearbook publishes on multi-disciplinary topics with a focus on international and comparative law issues regarding Taiwan, Mainland China and the Asia-Pacific. The Yearbook invites submissions of unsolicited articles, comments, case analyses and book reviews.

Submission of Manuscripts

Please send an electronic version of your manuscript by e-mail to the Editorial Board, at: yearbook@nccu.edu.tw. The attachment should contain the manuscript, a cover letter and a resume. While electronic submissions are strongly preferred, submissions may be made by post alternatively. In such cases, please send one hard copy of your manuscript along with a disk or CD copy to: Chinese (Taiwan) Society of International Law, P.O. Box 1–171, Mucha, Taipei 116, Taiwan, ROC.

Layout of Manuscripts

Submissions should be typewritten in Microsoft Word format. The maximum length of manuscripts is not limited. The Yearbook encourages submissions of manuscripts under 25,000 words, the equivalent of 50 journal pages, texts and footnotes included. We prefer manuscripts with double-spaced text and footnotes in 12-point Times New Roman font. The *Pinyin* system of translation should be used in reference to publications in Chinese.

Copyright

Copyright in the work shall remain the property of the publisher. The authors will have the right to reproduce their article in other publishing works. On

Disclaimer

Statements of fact and opinion in the Yearbook are those of the respective author(s). The Yearbook makes no representation, express or implied, concerning the accuracy of the articles and does not accept legal responsibility, including but not limiting to copyright infringement issues, arising therefrom. Opinions expressed and terms used, such as Taiwan, the Republic of China (ROC), Mainland China, the People's Republic of China (PRC), and so forth in the Yearbook are the authors'. They do not necessarily reflect those of the Chinese (Taiwan) Society of International Law and the Editorial Board of the Yearbook.

www.ingramcontent.com/pod-product-compliance
Lightning Source LLC
LaVergne TN
LVHW010541300926
849162LV00002B/201